Command at Sea

FIFTH EDITION

Command at Sea

Capt. James Stavridis, USN
and Vice Adm. William P. Mack, USN (Ret.)

Naval Institute Press   **Annapolis, Maryland**

Library of Congress Cataloging-in-Publication Data
Stavridis, James.
    Command at sea / James Stavridis and William P. Mack. — 5th ed.
      p.   cm.
    Includes bibliographical references and index
    ISBN 1-55750-841-0 (alk. paper)
    1. Leadership.   2. United States. Navy—Officers' handbooks.
  I. Mack, William P., 1915–   . II. Title.
  VB203.S73   1998
  359.3'3041—dc21   98-38781

Printed in the United States of America on acid-free paper ∞
06 05 04 03   9 8 7 6 5 4 3

All photographs are from official U.S. Navy sources.

Contents

Preface to the Fifth Edition

If you can find an original first edition of *Command at Sea,* written by Captain Harley F. Cope in 1943—perhaps in a used bookstore—buy it, read it, and cherish it. The book is a true classic of the seagoing community, written at the height of World War II by an experienced and combat-tested commanding officer. Terse and compact, it begins with the words, "Every young officer who is worth his salt looks forward eagerly to his first command, whether it be a destroyer, a minesweeper, a submarine, a PT, or an auxiliary. There is a tremendous thrill in taking over your first ship." These words ring as true today—as we enter the twenty-first century—as they did in the twentieth-century Navy of Captain Harley Cope; and indeed in the nineteenth-century Navy of Captain John Paul Jones and Commodore John Barry.

Given the timeless quality of command at sea, the question then arises, why are new editions of this classic required?

The reason is the relentless tide of change in much of the mechanics of how command at sea is executed. Since the very fine fourth edition of *Command at Sea* by Vice Adm. William P. Mack and Cdr. Albert H. Konetzni Jr. was published in 1982, some of the key changes include:

- Lessons learned from operations in the Persian Gulf, Bosnia, and Haiti, which have reshaped many aspects of seagoing command practice and maritime operations.
- Changes to the Unified Command Plan and command relationships have altered the commanding officer's chain of command, geographic and functional responsibilities of the Unified Combatant Commanders, and the principles of OPCON (Operational Control), TACON (Tactical Control), and COCOM (Combatant Command).

- The Goldwater-Nichols Act of 1986 has placed an increased premium on joint and combined operations.
- The fleet itself has changed dramatically in every way imaginable. Many new ships and squadrons have been commissioned (DDG-51, PC-1, AOE-1, SH-60F/B, SSN-688-I, *Seawolf,* F/A-18 E/F), and many more ships and squadrons have been decommissioned (BB, CG-26, CG-16, DDG-2, FF-1078, A-7, *Permit-Sturgeon* SSNs). The fleet has shrunk in ships and submarines from a high of around 580 in the late 1980s to only about 340 today.
- Women serve in virtually all Navy ships.
- Maintenance, automatic data processing, logistics both afloat and ashore, and communications/information/intelligence functions have all changed dramatically.

The world moves on, and so there is much to revise in this edition. But the continuing thread throughout all five editions of *Command at Sea* is simply this: command remains the absolute heart of the Navy. And whether you are involved in command of a ship, submarine, or aircraft squadron, there are special challenges and rewards associated with every aspect of that command.

My hope is simply to continue the work begun by Captain Cope over a half-century ago, bringing to this task the collected lessons of the many superb officers who have worked on *Command at Sea* in the intervening years, particularly Vice Admiral William P. Mack, USN (Ret.), who was the lead author of several previous editions. In addition to the wisdom already contained in *Command at Sea,* I have tried to add contemporary lessons from today's Navy operating at sea. Like anyone else who has served at sea, I have been particularly influenced by and must acknowledge several exceptional commanding officers under whom I was privileged to serve for extended periods, including Captain Fritz Gaylord, USN (Ret.), my CO in *Hewitt* (DD-966); Rear Admiral Ted Lockhart, USN (Ret.), my captain in *Valley Forge* (CG-50), and Captain Larry Eddingfield, USN (Ret.), my CO in *Antietam* (CG-54). Among many others, they stand out in their sharing of ideas and the setting of a fine example in command at sea. I would also like to thank several serving flag and commanding officers for their thoughts on the subject of command at sea, including Vice Admiral Al Krekich, Vice Admiral Hank Giffin, Vice Admiral Bob Natter, Vice Admiral Dan Murphy, Rear Admiral Cutler Dawson, Rear Admiral Bill Putnam, Rear Admiral Kevin Green, Rear Admiral Scott Fry, Rear Admiral Tim LaFleur, Rear Admiral Mike Mullen, Rear Admiral Jim Metzger, Commander Mike Abrashoff, Commander Gerry Roncolato, Commander Charlie Martoglio, and Lieutenant Commander Steve Davis. It goes without saying that any errors of fact or judgment are mine alone.

An editorial note: much of this fifth edition is still true to the earlier editions, and thus the reader will often find the use of strictly masculine pronouns. Where these appear, it should be understood that they refer to both the men and women serving so well today in virtually all the warships of the U.S. Navy. In all the new and revised sections of the work, an effort has been made to refer to both genders, which is clearly appropriate in today's virtually fully integrated Navy.

Lastly, I would like to acknowledge the help and support of my family in this project, particularly two fine officers who have both served as naval commanding officers during their distinguished careers: my father, Colonel P. G. Stavridis, USMC (Ret.), and my father-in-law, Captain R. A. Hall, USN (Ret.). To them, and to their generation of outstanding naval officers, I dedicate this volume.

In the end, we all know that command at sea is an art; and that it is not fully learned by reading books like this. But it is an art built on knowledge, study, and the practice of a great and important profession. So I close with the hope that this small volume may continue to be of help to all who accept the responsibility and accountability of command at sea in the ships, submarines, and aircraft squadrons of the twenty-first-century U.S. Navy.

—Capt. James Stavridis, USN

First published in 1943, this book has served as an important aid in the preparation for and execution of what should be any officer's foremost professional ambition: *command*. Since that first edition, ably written by Captain Harley F. Cope, USN, the Navy has expanded and contracted in size, experienced a dramatic increase in its technical sophistication, and undergone major—some might say drastic—social changes. Yet, although the ships, the aircraft, and the sailors of the Navy of 1943 and that of 1998 differ drastically in so many ways, the need for strong, principled leadership has been a constant and, therefore, the basic philosophy of command outlined by Captain Cope has remained at the core of every edition. The case is no different with this, the fifth edition of *Command at Sea*.

Like his distinguished predecessors, this edition's lead writer, Captain James Stavridis, USN, has performed a magnificent job of changing the book to reflect recent social, political, and technological developments, while preserving that which is timeless. He is exceptionally well qualified to do so. Captain Stavridis's career includes a very successful tour as captain of the USS *Barry* (DDG-52) and, as this edition goes to press, he is in command of Destroyer Squadron 21. Jim also has written numerous professional books and articles, and he is recognized throughout the Navy as a superb author. As I end my involvement with this important book, I am certain I leave it in extremely capable hands.

—Vice Adm. William P. Mack, USN (Ret.)

Preface to the First Edition

Every young officer who is worth his salt looks forward eagerly to his first command, whether it be a destroyer, a minesweeper, a submarine, a PT, or an auxiliary. There is a tremendous thrill in taking over your first ship. She is your ship—all yours—but the way to success is dotted with pitfalls for the unwary, the careless, and the diffident. From the moment you, as the new skipper, step aboard you are on trial before your officers and men. Responsibility for the ship as well as for the crew is yours.

Particularly in time of war, when promotion is rapid and officers with comparatively little experience must frequently assume command, it is important that the officer have as complete an understanding as possible of the special duties and tasks with which he will be faced—the duties of both task force and independent naval operations, and the responsibility of maintaining a happy and efficient ship.

The officer with many years of sea experience has been afforded the opportunity to observe various commanding officers. Perhaps unconsciously he has thought to himself, "If I were skipper I would do it this way," and when command comes to him he has already made definite plans regarding the course he intends to follow. The inexperienced junior officer getting his first command often wishes that such opportunities had been afforded him.

There is no sure formula for success as a commanding officer. Some officers are natural leaders; others are not. Some have had the benefit of a long and good background of experience under competent commanding officers that others have not enjoyed. Some make mistakes, but it must be remembered that mistakes are greatly magnified if committed a second or third time, for one is expected to profit by mistakes.

In these pages, I have drawn from my experience and from the experience of others to present as fully and as specifically as possible the situation that will confront you as a commanding officer of your ship, and to suggest solutions to the problems which you will inevitably face.

—Capt. Harley F. Cope, USN

Command at Sea

1

Taking Command

The Captain carried them all
For him, there was no fixed watch, no time set aside when he was free
*   to relax and, if he could, to sleep.*
He was strong, calm, uncomplaining, and wonderfully dependable.
That was the sort of captain to have.

—Nicholas Monsaratt, "The Cruel Sea"

Command at Sea

The experience of command of a ship at sea is unforgettable; it is without parallel or equal. The responsibility is heavy, but the rewards—which become embedded in the very fabric of your life—are priceless. The captain of the U.S. Navy warship stands as part of a long, unbroken line that stretches from the very founders of the Continental Navy through the great captains of America's wars at sea, and on to the next generation of twenty-first-century leaders.

U.S. Navy Regulations, fully updated last in 1990, states that "the responsibility of the commanding officer for his or her command is absolute," and that "the authority of the commanding officer is commensurate with his or her responsibility." These are simple, clear, binding statements. No amount of explanation can alter their placement of ultimate responsibility—whether for success or failure—squarely on the shoulders of the captain in command.

In this respect, though the size of a ship may be important as a measure of her capability or durability, the smallest minesweeper is

Taking command is a great moment for any officer.

equal to the largest aircraft carrier in terms of responsibility and reward. The commanding officers of both are "captains," regardless of the number of stripes they wear on their sleeves. Each must ensure the safety of the ship and crew, as well as the accomplishment of all assigned missions. Likewise, the skipper of an aircraft squadron assumes full and complete responsibility for the performance of a command at sea.

To achieve success in command, the captain must work through those whom he or she leads; little can be accomplished alone, no matter how brilliant one's individual talents. Admiral Chester Nimitz, on the occasion of a call by several of his captains, said, "Commanding a ship is the simplest task in the world, even if at times it seems complicated. A captain has only to pick good courses of action and to stick to them no matter what. If he is good and generally makes good decisions, his crew will cover for him if he fails occasionally. If he is bad, this fact will soon be known, and he must removed with the speed of light."

The successful commanding officer, then, must learn to become as one with his or her wardroom and crew; yet, at the same time, he or she must remain above and apart. This unique relationship has been the subject of study and story for centuries. It changes, yet it is timeless. It is a skill to be mastered in turn by each commander.

Two days prior to the Battle of Java Sea, in which HMS *Exeter* would be sunk in the dark early days of World War II in the Pacific, her commanding officer, Captain O. L. Gordon, Royal Navy, was having a late-evening drink at a Surabaya hotel with a group of young British and American junior officers. One of the American officers asked him how he felt about going to sea the next morning to meet the approaching Japanese naval force. Gordon knew that his ship would have little chance of surviving, but he smiled anyway as he said, "I would not trade all the Queen's jewels for the privilege of commanding *Exeter* tomorrow. I have the finest group of men ever to man a ship of war. They will not fail me, and they know I will not fail my Sovereign. We may not survive, but we will leave our mark." When the battle began, the gigantic battle ensign flown by the ship was an inspiration to the Allied ships that accompanied her. They knew she would be commanded well, and therefore would fight well.

Even the realm of literature is full of allusion to the art of command. Perhaps the best-known and most frequently quoted commentary on command at sea was written by Joseph Conrad, a writer who had himself commanded at sea as a merchant sailor:

The Prestige, Privilege and the Burden of Command

Only a seaman realizes to what extent an entire ship reflects the personality and ability of one individual, her Commanding Officer. To a landsman this is not understandable, and sometimes it is even difficult for us to comprehend,—but it is so.

A ship at sea is a distant world in herself and in consideration of the protracted and distant operations of the fleet units the Navy must place great power, responsibility and trust in the hands of those leaders chosen for command.

In each ship there is one man who, in the hour of emergency or peril at sea, can turn to no other man. There is one who alone is ultimately responsible for the safe navigation, engineering performance, accurate gunfiring and morale of his ship. He is the Commanding Officer. He is the ship.

This is the most difficult and demanding assignment in the Navy. There is not an instant during his tour of duty as Commanding Officer that he can escape the grasp of command responsibility. His privileges in view of his obligations are most ludicrously small; nevertheless command is the spur which has given the Navy its great leaders.

It is a duty which most richly deserves the highest, time-honored title of the seafaring world—"CAPTAIN."

Conrad's thoughts on command are echoed by one of fiction's great captains, Jack Aubrey of Patrick O'Brian's superb series of sea novels about the nineteenth-century Royal Navy. Captain Aubrey's command philosophy is stated in a few sentences that are worth bearing in mind: "His idea of a crack ship was one with a strong, highly-skilled crew that could out-maneuver and then outshoot the opponent, a taut but happy ship, an efficient man-of-war—in short a ship that was likely to win at any reasonable odds."

A great deal has been written about command at sea over the years, but perhaps the thought that best sums up this most fulfilling assignment come from another classic of sea literature, *The Caine Mutiny*. In it, Herman Wouk's immortal character Lieutenant Keefer expressed it well: "You can't understand command till you've had it." And once you have had command, you are changed forever, marked as one who has stood in the long line of captains at sea.

The Accountability of Command

In navies in general, and in the U.S. Navy in particular, strict accountability is an integral part of command. Not even the profession of medicine embraces the absolute accountability found at sea. A doctor may lose a patient under trying circumstances and continue to practice, but a naval officer seldom has the opportunity to hazard a second ship.

There have been, at times, those who question the strict and undeviating application of accountability in the Navy; but those who have been to sea have always closed ranks against the doubters. In 1952, for example, the destroyer *Hobson* collided with the aircraft carrier *Melbourne* during night flight operations. Damage was extensive, and the loss of life was heavy. There were extenuating circumstances, but the *Wall Street Journal* of May 1952, in a frequently quoted discussion of the disaster, concluded:

> On the sea, there is a tradition older than the traditions of the country itself—it is the tradition that with responsibility goes authority and with them both goes accountability.
>
> It is cruel, this accountability of good and well intentioned men. But the choice is that or an end to responsibility and finally, as the cruel sea has taught, an end to the confidence and trust in the men who lead. For men will not long trust leaders who feel themselves beyond accountability for what they do.

The enormous burden of this responsibility and accountability for the lives and careers of others—and often the outcome of great issues

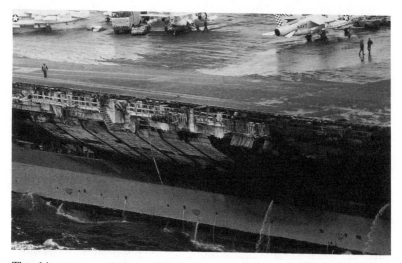

The ultimate arena of responsibility, collision at sea. The USS *John F. Kennedy,* shown here shortly after her collision with the USS *Belknap,* suffered relatively little damage.

as well—is the reason for the liberality of orders to officers commanding ships of the U.S. Navy. The inexperienced officer may erroneously take this liberality to reflect vagueness or indecision on the part of superiors. Nothing could be further from the truth. It is provided to give the commander the flexibility necessary to carry out his or her orders.

One incident in the 1970s led ultimately to a reinforcement of the doctrine of the absolute accountability of command. The incident began with the collision of the USS *Belknap* and the USS *John F. Kennedy,* in which the *Belknap* lost eight men and suffered $100 million in damages. The tragic results of the collision are shown in the accompanying photographs.

The court-martial that followed caused many naval officers to reconsider the issues surrounding accountability of commanding officers. The Chief of Naval Operations, Admiral J. L. Holloway III, is-

The *Belknap* in her collision with the *John F. Kennedy* suffered heavy damage and many casualties. Responsibility was found to rest with her commanding officer.

sued a memorandum dated 2 October 1976 discussing the entire issue. This document, which sets forth the circumstances of the collision and of the consequent administrative and judicial processes, is presented in Appendix 5.

In subsequent years, several additional cases of groundings, collisions, and fires at sea have further emphasized the complete accountability of the commanding officer for the actions of the ship. Of note in this regard, and worth reviewing with the wardroom on occasion, are the grounding of USS *Spruance* in the Caribbean in 1989, the collision of the USS *Kinkaid* with a merchant tanker in the Straits of Malaga in 1991, and the collision of the aircraft carrier USS *Theodore Roosevelt* with the cruiser *Leyte Gulf* in 1997. In each case—as well as in other instances of the mishandling of ships at sea—the doctrine of full accountability has been strongly enforced in the U.S. Navy, and will continue to be at the very heart of command at sea.

The Independence of the Commander

Traditionally, American commanding officers have been directed to accomplish missions without being told specifically *how* to do so. Occasionally they may be referred to doctrine or example about how their tasks might be performed, or how they have been carried out in the past. The choice of action, however, remains theirs to make; it is required only that their methods support intelligently the objectives of command.

In recent years, however, this traditional independence has been modified in practice. The issue today is not too much liberality, but rather a growing tendency of high command to exercise control in too great detail. There are several factors contributing to this trend. First, command in the present-day atmosphere of worldwide political unrest requires extraordinary sensitivity to an extremely complex web of global relationships. The post–Cold War world has complicated the missions undertaken by individual ships, submarines, and aircraft squadrons. Second, the ability of global media organizations to place the spotlight on naval operations has increased exponentially over the past few years. With CNN flying overhead and the wire services constantly requesting and obtaining permission to visit U.S. Navy warships at sea, the latitude of the CO to act independently has been proscribed simply due to the unrelenting glare of publicity. Third, and most significantly, technological advances have given the entire chain of command the ability to track and direct virtually every aspect of naval operations at sea.

Notwithstanding all the "help" from outside sources, there is still an extraordinary level of responsibility on the shoulders of the captain. The CO will make the decision whether or not to fire in an individual engagement; when and how to execute boardings at sea; when and how to undertake a medical evacuation—indeed, the time, method, and ultimate execution of a thousand discrete decisions remains the responsibility of the captain. In most cases, higher authority will respect the judgment of the captain at the scene, and there is little likelihood of that changing in the near future.

Orders to Command

The day you receive orders to take command of a U.S. Navy warship or squadron will be a memorable one. You will probably sit back in your chair and reflect on the challenges and rewards that lie ahead. Normally, there will be a considerable "pipeline" of training that will precede your assumption of command, including a leadership course, training in your community (surface or submarine prospective commanding officer's course, refresher flight training), and tactical study on the appropriate coast at either Tactical Training Group Atlantic or Pacific.

Once you have orders in hand, you should contact your relief to arrange your schedule and work out a turnover plan. Your initial contact is normally a letter or phone call, and should include your personal plans: when you will move your family, your housing plans in the homeport, the date you would like to report, and so forth. The officer you are relieving will work with you to decide on an appropriate plan for the turnover and a change of command date.

Bear in mind that the preparations for the turnover, the change of command, and the details associated with each are almost entirely under the direction of the incumbent commanding officer. Unless there is an overriding reason you cannot comply with the incumbent's wishes, you should accept them.

Once these matters have been settled, both officers can then begin preparations for the change of command. Appendix 1 includes material you will find helpful.

Preparations for Change of Command

Prior to reporting to your new command, it is appropriate to ask the current CO to send you a "care package" with basic information about the ship, submarine, or squadron. The key here is not to generate new work for the command, but rather to obtain "on the shelf" publications and products that will prepare you to hit the deckplates running. The following are some of the items you might find useful to review before stepping aboard to begin turnover:

- A ship's social roster of both officers and chiefs. Try to learn their names before you report, and have a solid understanding of responsibilities and the chain of command. Some commands will put together a book with photos and biographies of the key leaders in the ship—this is very helpful, but should be something voluntarily provided.
- A damage control handbook for the command.
- A copy of the operating schedule, both short and long range.

This will be classified, so it should be sent to your current command or a pipeline school for your review.

- Copies of recent issues of the ship's newsletter and ombudsman helpline.
- An engineering handbook.
- CO's battle orders, standing orders, typical set of night orders, engineering orders, and any standard tactical maneuvering doctrine. This applies to squadrons as well as ships and submarines.
- Anything else the incumbent thinks might be useful.

Navy Regulations and appropriate type commanders' instructions provide guidance for the change of command process. *Navy Regulations* requires that both officers inspect the ship, exercise the crew at general quarters and general drills, discuss any defects that may be present, and transfer all unexecuted orders, official correspondence, and information concerning the command and its personnel. Specific requirements include a current audit of the post office, turnover of magazine and other keys, and an inventory and audit of registered publications. The officer being relieved must complete and sign fitness reports, logs, books, journals, and other required documents.

Each type commander requires some augmentation or variation in these basic procedures.

Generally, all of these requirements can be met on a conventionally powered vessel in about five days, regardless of the ship's employment. A relatively standard procedure in the fleet today is to have the prospective CO arrive on a Monday and take command with appropriate ceremony on Friday.

The turnover period should be long enough to permit the new commander to determine the combat readiness of the ship, primarily by observing appropriate general drills. Of particular importance is the damage control readiness of the organization, and this is best ascertained by observing the efforts of the Damage Control Training Team (DCTT), which should be well led by the executive officer and capable of conducting realistic, stressful drills "within the lifelines." Another key indicator of an efficient ship is the readiness and performance of the navigation team. Focus specifically on the ability to navigate and the damage control readiness, and almost everything else can be quickly brought up to the mark if necessary.

As the relieving officer, you should review carefully with the previous CO the handling characteristics of the ship. Ask how she accelerates and handles in various sea states. If you are not familiar with the ship type from previous assignments, you will have to take much of this information on faith until you gain experience. It will be helpful to review some of the literature on your class, both in recent *Proceedings* articles and in the appropriate sections of the classic *Naval Shiphandling*.

Assuming you have a full five days for the turnover, you can augment the basics of shiphandling, navigation, and damage control. The next issue for the new commanding officer is the state of the combat system and the engineering plant. Both are critical components of your command's ability to fight and win at sea. Next in priority is a careful review of the supply status of the command. Spend half a day with each of your department heads—whether you are taking command of a ship, submarine, or squadron—and try to gauge the readiness, morale, cleanliness, and general state of their department. Each department head will probably give you a binder full of turnover information, from the biographies of the officers and chiefs to the inventory of critical bulkhead-mounted spares. Read the binder in the evening or after you assume command, and spend your turnover week walking through the hangers or on the deckplates getting to know your people.

The following are some additional items to concern yourself with *after* you have ascertained the navigation, damage control, supply, engineering, and combat systems status of your command:

- Read the fleet, type, and unit commanders' instructions.
- Start the process for updating your security clearance, if this has not already been done.
- Forward a photograph and a short biography to the Chief of Naval Information. This is in addition to the photo and biography required for the Naval Military Personnel Command.
- Review the last administrative inspection checklist, the last ma-

terial, supply, and medical inspection checklists, the last Operational Propulsion Plant Examination (OPPE) checklists, the naval technical proficiency inspection results, and—for nuclear-powered ships—the recent Operational Reactor Safeguards Examination results. For a squadron, review the similarly key material and corrosion inspection results. Focus on trends.

- Study the ship's organization, the ship's orders, and the type commanders' orders and manuals. Hopefully, you've already done this with your "read ahead" package and during the pipeline training.
- Review financial areas, such as the wardroom mess and any small accounts. Trouble can often lurk here.
- Review the ship's classified files and methods of handling such items. A thorough review of all these areas is required by regulations—ensure that it is complete and accurate by spot-checking a few areas.
- Review the status of the 3-M (Maintenance and Materials Management) and PQS (Personnel Qualification Standards) programs. Accompany your predecessor or the XO on several spot checks of both programs. You will make an instant statement about your standards with your comments during your first few spot checks—which should wait until *after* you take command.
- Review in detail the procedures associated with weapons release authority, and the location and use of all firing keys in your combat system.

The key throughout all of the relieving process is that you are being shown the ship by your predecessor. This is not the time or place to begin putting your own ideas, philosophies, or standards in place. There will be plenty of opportunity for that—after the change of command.

During the relieving process you should be alert, interested, and noncommittal. The crew will be observing you intently for the least reaction, and word will fly through the command about "the new skipper." Stay on a very even keel throughout the turnover process, and politely take everything in.

Report of Transfer of Command

Navy Regulations requires that a letter report of the routine change of command be prepared and signed by the officer relieved and endorsed by the individual relieving. This letter should be addressed to your immediate superior, with copies to the CNO and others in the chain of command.

Give this letter report your careful attention. Be sure that all substantial deficiencies affecting the operational readiness and safety of the ship are listed. Key problems should be noted, but it is certainly not expected that all minor deficiencies will be listed. Use your professional judgment.

Bear in mind that the letter will immediately become a high-priority, high-visibility "to do" list for your entire chain of command. Be judicious in your comments, and recognize that you are not an inspector, but rather the new team captain—draft the letter accordingly.

The Change of Command Ceremony

Now that all examinations and inspections are complete, you are ready to take part in the traditional ceremony of the change of command. For your part, you should prepare a copy of your orders reduced to the most basic language, such as the following:

From: Chief of Naval Personnel
To: Commander John Paul Jones
Subject: Relief of Command

Proceed to the port in which USS *Barry* (DDG-52) is located and report as relief for the Commanding Officer.

You will also be expected to make *extremely brief* remarks upon assumption of command. The traditional formula is no more than two to three minutes in length, and includes an acknowledgment of key guests and family members, a word of thanks to the crew for their hard work in preparing and executing the change of command, a complimentary remark about your predecessor, and an enthusiastic comment about future operations with the command. Anything longer is simply not appropriate. This is the day for the outgoing CO to hold center stage. Your time will come all too soon.

Navy Regulations provides that at the time of turning over command, all hands should be mustered, that the officer about to be relieved shall read the orders of detachment and formally turn command to the successor, and that this officer should then read the orders in turn and assume command.

This is a simple and straightforward requirement. Prior to World War II it was usually carried out strictly as set forth with the simplest of ceremonies. Guests were seldom, if ever, invited, and usually the unit commander attended. Since the war, however, it has become customary to invite numerous civilian guests, family members, the chain of command, and the commanding officers of all ships present. The arrangements are entirely the prerogative of the incumbent CO, who schedules the ceremony, issues the invitations, and announces the time and place of the change of command. The oncoming CO merely sends an invitation list to the incumbent.

There is a growing trend in the fleet today to return to the simpler ceremonies of the past. This is particularly true when the ship's schedule is compressed and the effort of staging an elaborate change of command ceremony does not fit well with the ship's schedule. This is completely a matter to be decided by the outgoing CO. There is a wonderful simplicity and elegance that goes with an at-sea change of command, which involves simply the ship, captain, and crew. Many officers feel that there is no better place to take command than on the rolling deck of a ship at sea.

A good reference on the entire process of the change of command is *Naval Ceremonies, Customs, and Traditions* (published by Naval Institute Press). In general, a change of command will be a full-dress affair, held in a dignified and ceremonious fashion. It is very much an all-hands evolution; all members of the crew not actually on watch should attend. The officers and enlisted personnel should be stationed, if possible, so that they and the two commanding officers are facing each other. The ceremony was established so that the outgoing commander could bid farewell to all of the officers and sailors attached to the crew.

The basic change of command ceremony and the layout of the ceremonial area are presented in Appendix 2.

Courtesies Due a Relieved Commanding Officer

Remember that *Navy Regulations* provides that the officer relieved, although without official authority in the command from the moment of relief, is still entitled to all ceremonies and distinctions accorded while in command until actual departure from the ship, submarine, or squadron. When departing, the outgoing CO should be given side honors appropriate to a commanding officer, and should be offered the use of the gig. Some ships use officers and chiefs as side boys, a remnant of times past when officers rowed their old captain ashore.

The officer relieved should make every effort to depart promptly and completely. If possible, most or all of his or her baggage should be disembarked before the ceremony.

Upon Taking Command

When the relieved commanding officer and the guests have departed, your real work begins at last. The first requirement, once again—as it will always be—is to ensure that the ship and her crew are in safe condition and able to perform as required. There are also administrative matters to take care of, including the issuance of any new orders; new standing night orders or battle orders may be required.

The next item of business will be making of calls. An officer assuming command shall, at the first opportunity thereafter, make an official visit to the senior to whom he or she has reported for duty. The circumstances of this call will vary widely depending on the ship's schedule, location, and the relationship with the senior. For a ship or submarine commanding officer, this typically will involve a call on the squadron commander. For the skipper of an aviation squadron, this will mean a visit to the commander of the air group. Follow the traditions of your area, and don't hesitate to call the chief of staff for the squadron or the deputy commander of the air group to obtain guidance. In general, you should make an appointment to come by and pay a call the week following your assumption of command. Be prepared to give your new boss an assessment of your command, remembering that you were aboard not as an inspector, but as the new team captain. Don't ever portray the officer you have relieved in a bad light or complain about any aspect of your new command—but be honest in evaluating capabilities and readiness. If there are problems, state them and indicate your plan to improve them to standards. Your new senior will probably take the opportunity to give you a few words about squadron or air group philosophy, which will be very helpful.

You should also drop by the operations shop at the squadron or air group, as well as paying a courtesy call on the first flag officer in your chain of command; this will normally be the battle group commander.

It is a good idea to call on the senior officer present afloat (SOPA) as well. For example, if you are a destroyer captain tied up at a pier, the pier SOPA will normally be a cruiser skipper, and you should drop by for a cup of coffee and present your respects. In general, whenever your ship ties up at a pier in homeport you should see the pier SOPA; if at a naval station outside of homeport, it is customary to call on the CO of the station. If your ship ties up at a shipyard for repairs or alongside a tender, a call on the CO is also appropriate. Check local SOPA regulations for specifics.

Philosophy of Command

Throughout long years of preparation for command, every naval officer studies leadership techniques, observes senior officers in command, and gradually formulates certain thoughts and ideas concerning the proper way to lead. You should now be eager to put those ideas to the test of practice as a commanding officer. Your officers and sailors are waiting to find out what your policies are and how you will communicate your ideas to them.

This can be done in several ways. Some simply allow the passage of time and events to reveal their philosophies and expectations. They never openly define it. Many successful commanders have taken this path, particularly those not skilled in communications, either written or verbal. Most COs, however, have found it better to establish a quick rapport with their officers and sailors by addressing them directly and as soon as practicable. This initial address need not be long, formal, or all-inclusive; but it should be carefully prepared, and it should include the most important elements of command.

What are these elements? Our first source is Title 10 of the *U.S. Code*—the basic law governing the U.S. military. In it the basic elements of American command philosophy are clearly stated:

> Commanding officers and others in authority in the naval service are required to show in themselves a good example of virtue, honor, patriotism, and subordination. They will be vigilant in inspecting the conduct of all persons, they will guard against and suppress dissolute and immoral practices according to regulations. They will take all necessary and proper measures under the laws, regulations, and customs to promote and safeguard the morale, physical well being, and general welfare of the officers and enlisted personnel under their command.

These requirements are law. You must meet them all.

In addition, however, there are several keys to command philosophy that have stood the test of time quite well and should be considered as you assume your command. They are drawn from a wide range of leaders at sea, from Admiral Lord Nelson to Admiral Arleigh Burke. Not all may fit your command style, but you should think about each idea and consider how it might fit into your individual philosophy of command.

The first is the simplest. You must take care of your people. Every crew will very quickly sense the difference between a commanding officer who doesn't put the welfare of the crew at the top of the command's priorities and one who does. Mission accomplishment is the reason your command exists; but the best way of ensuring that you accomplish the mission—from a command perspective—is by taking care of the people. If you take care of the people, you will accomplish the mission. It really is that simple.

Taking care of your people involves a wide variety of actions on the part of a CO, including taking an active interest in every aspect of professional development, training, safety, advancements, messing, berthing, and recreation. Admiral Lord Nelson was the first and strongest proponent of this approach. His crews—in a time of brutality, squalor, and constant deprivation—were trained, advanced, well cared for, and properly fed. His concern for the sailors was famous throughout the fleet. And his ships, although tautly run, were happy and invariably triumphed in battle. Admiral Ernest King—one of the toughest and most demanding officers in U.S. naval history—was likewise well known for helping his officers and crew members in every way, even years after they had left his command. Take a similar and sincere approach to your crew, and your command will be similarly successful.

The second great key to command is likewise a simple one. You must know your command. This is an increasingly important requirement, reflecting the increased complexity inherent in command of a modern Aegis destroyer, a *Seawolf*-class submarine, or a squadron of F/A-18E/F aircraft. Fifty years ago, an entire warship was less complicated than today's propulsion plant, airborne radar, or sonar suite.

In order to most fully understand your command, you will build on the general principles of science and engineering you studied in school. Throughout the long Navy pipeline of schools leading to command, you will have had ample opportunity to learn about the details of your command—take full advantage. Even after you arrive on your ship, you should have a program in place that educates you (and other officers and chiefs) in the technical aspects of the command. Some COs ask to look at a technical manual each week; others arrange lectures in the wardroom; and some spend a week focusing on each department, learning week-by-week the complexities of their ship, submarine, or aircraft. If you are to be the best warfighter in your command, you must be the system expert as well. Whatever your leadership style, don't slight this requirement. Some of the Navy's greatest innovators have also been great leaders—Admiral Bradley Fiske, Assistant Secretary of the Navy Theodore Roosevelt—who understood the importance of knowledge in command. Roosevelt, in an address before the 1892 graduating class of the Naval Academy, reminded the new officers: "It cannot be too often repeated that in modern war, the chief factor in achieving triumph is what has been done in the way of thorough organization and training before the beginning of war."

Related to this is the importance of ensuring that others in the ship are also knowledgeable in the systems. If you have shown your own interest in a thorough knowledge of the command and have made it plain to your officers and sailors that you expect the same from them, you will find that they will respond eagerly. This means hard work: arranging classes, making time available, and providing paths of advancement and qualification for all officers and sailors. But the rewards will be great—both for them and for you.

A third key is embedded in your own character. You must be loyal, honest, and ethical in all your dealings—both private and public. Let it be known that you expect honesty at all times, both up and down the chain of command. Never tolerate the covering up of unsavory facts—of trying "fog one by," as one recent CNO used to say. Require that all reports be honest and thorough.

A good model to follow can be found in the words attributed to John Paul Jones and memorized by generations of midshipmen:

> It is by no means enough that an officer of the Navy be a capable mariner. He must be that, of course, but also a great deal more. He should be as well a gentleman of liberal education, refined manners, punctilious courtesy, and the nicest sense of personal honor.
>
> He should be the soul of tact, patience, justice, firmness, and charity. No meritorious act of a subordinate should escape his attention or be left to pass without its reward, even if the reward is only a word of approval. Conversely, he should not be blind to a single fault in any subordinate, though at the same time, he should be quick and unfailing to distinguish error from malice, thoughtlessness from incompetency, and well meant shortcoming from heedless or stupid blunder.
>
> In one word, every commander should keep constantly before him the great truth, that to be well obeyed, he must be perfectly esteemed.

All who observe you in command should draw the conclusion that you are a patient leader. Set the highest of standards, but recognize that not everyone will be able to attain perfection, especially on the first try. Virtually everyone in your crew will want to work hard and perform well; it is up to you and your chain of command to give them the opportunity and motive for doing so. Swearing and outbursts of temper are not acceptable methods of correcting behavior. Giving in to the temptation to throw a fit will simply add more confusion to a situation that is already unacceptable. Your job is to bring order out of chaos, not to create more disorder. Firm direction with continuous follow-up will solve virtually any problem.

A good commanding officer must understand human nature and the motivation of sailors. You must be able to reconcile the differences between subordinates of strong character so that they cooperate rather than collide. Your personal demeanor must radiate energy; you must appear to be strongly determined to achieve the goals you set for your command. You must electrify your subordinates, yet remain personally cool while doing so.

A fourth key to command philosophy is the tone of the command. Even the smallest ship or squadron, undergoing the most demanding employment, can maintain an excellent tone. The first thing contributing to a good tone is appearance. Let your crew know that you want a combat-ready command, clean at all times, and you will get it. Frequent and thorough sweep downs will do more to keep up everyday appearances than excessive painting and scrubbing, and will generate pride in those doing the work. Again, most sailors understand that you learn a great deal about a ship from the appearance of the ship's boats and their crews. Additionally, a ship or squadron's quarterdeck speaks volumes about attitude at a command. Finally, a ship is also known by the personal appearance of its officers and crew.

Admiral Raymond Spruance was a master at setting the tone of a ship. He produced quiet confidence in his officers by showing them he trusted them. When a potentially dangerous situation began to develop underway, Captain Spruance would quietly ask what the officer of the deck intended to do, rather than giving specific orders to solve the problem. His officers soon learned that he trusted them, that he would let them take the initiative when danger threatened, right up until the last minute, when he would take charge if necessary. The tone of this bridge and quarterdeck was one of assurance and professional ability. The attitude below decks was the same, for Spruance insisted that his officers foster the same relationships with their juniors that he had demonstrated to them. His ships were superbly commanded, and they had superb tone.

Communications with the crew is a fifth key element in your command philosophy that is well worth considering before you take command. Any sailor will do the job better knowing what is to be done and when it has to be finished. This can and will be communicated by your XO, and is primarily the job of the chain of command. What is important for you as commanding officer is to articulate to your crew *why* a given task must be accomplished. Your crew should know and understand how each challenge undertaken by your ship, squadron, or submarine fits into the larger picture of combat readiness and the U.S. Navy. You can do this in a wide variety of ways.

Some commanding officers have a brief "captain's corner" in the plan of the day. This gives them an opportunity to think about and write—in just a few short phrases—what is currently "on the plate" of the command and how it fits together. It is also a place where you as commanding officer can give a short burst of philosophy, comment on safety, pass along a compliment, make a general warning, or communicate anything you consider important to the crew on a daily basis. You should also—on a ship or submarine—use the general announcing system to communicate ideas. Don't overdo it, but jumping on the 1MC at least once a day—particularly while underway—is a great boost for the crew. Additionally, many ships and submarines today have internal TV systems. This is an ideal medium—if you're a good speaker, you come across well on camera, and you don't overuse it. Perhaps once a week, try to appear on TV for your crew members, preferably speaking without notes—honestly, naturally, and sincerely.

Boldness is another quality worth considering in forming your command philosophy. Many of the tactical evolutions routinely performed by small, fast warships or high-performance aircraft place them in what a merchant marine officer or an airline pilot would consider extremely dangerous circumstances. The considered yet bold acceptance of this continual hazard must be an integral part of a commanding officer. You must train yourself to make quick decisions with the conn, the engineering plant, the section of aircraft, and the weapons system; and your reactions must be based on knowledge so that they are sound and correct. Recklessness has no place at sea, but without boldness our ships and aircraft cannot realize their full potential for combat. Boldness is not the property of a ship or squadron as a whole; it is an attitude of the commanding officer and the officers serving in the command, and it must be fostered, tempered, and encouraged.

Two of the Navy's boldest leaders at sea in the twentieth century were Admirals William "Bull" Halsey and Arleigh Burke. Admiral Halsey once commented on his reputation as an aggressive warfighter by saying, "Most of the strategists think I was a poor strategist, and maybe they were right, but I had to execute a lot of their strategic plans that wouldn't have worked if I hadn't pushed them boldly and aggressively." And perhaps the best comment on boldness was made Admiral Burke, who, in the days after the World War II, said: "Decide how you want to make your attack, and be sure you have a sound and simple plan. Then you hit him with everything you have. Do it fast. If your ship can't make 31 knots, crank it up as fast as it will go. Then pound! Pound! Pound! You may think the enemy isn't yielding, but if you keep it up, he'll weaken, and suddenly you'll break through."

Lastly, in putting together your thoughts on a command philosophy, remember—don't take yourself too seriously. A sense of humor goes a long way in the demanding business of going to sea, and you could do a great deal worse than to remember the words of Satchel Paige: "Don't look back. Someone might be overtaking you."

Look ahead, don't take yourself too seriously, and resolve above all to enjoy every minute of your command tour. The day of your relief will come all too soon.

2

Commissioning a Ship or Submarine

And see! She stirs!
She starts—she moves—she seems to feel
The thrill of life along her keel,
And, spurning with her foot the ground,
With one exulting, joyous bound,
She leaps into the ocean's arms

— Longfellow, "The Building of the Ship"

Placing a new ship (or a recommissioned older one) in commission is one of the most challenging tasks a naval officer can undertake. As prospective commanding officer (PCO), you are the on-site representative for the type commander and shipbuilding program manager, and must coordinate the myriad issues associated with both building the ship and putting together a cohesive fighting team. The job is made more challenging by the way the precommissioning crew is assembled—generally only about one-third will have ever been to sea before, and many of your veterans will be returning to sea after years of disassociated shore duty. Additionally, every program, every policy, and every instruction has to be scripted from scratch and implemented for the first time. It is a fascinating and rewarding tour, but it will no doubt be one of the most difficult. At its essence, however, training the crew to operate safely at sea is the PCO's most important task.

Your Role in Ship Construction

Each major shipyard in the United States has a supervisor of ship-building, conversion, and repair (SUPSHIP) assigned to monitor the day-to-day progress of ship construction. The SUPSHIP normally reports to Naval Sea Systems Command and an overall program manager who is responsible for your ship from cradle to grave. The SUP-SHIP is an engineering duty officer who is well versed in the ins and outs of the process, and is the best source of information on how to interface with the shipbuilder. It is in your best interest to meet with the shipbuilder as quickly as possible after you are notified that you will be the PCO of one of the vessels under construction in the yard. For the most part, the SUPSHIP controls the funding and quality assurance process that is critical to getting your ship built correctly.

The SUPSHIP will assign a ship superintendent to serve as your single point of contact and spearhead the construction of your ship on the waterfront. The ship superintendent will also be an engineering duty officer or a government employee with years of shipbuilding experience, and will be the government's "go-to" person to get things done. Your relationship with your ship superintendent will be one of the most important factors in getting the ship built the way you want it. The shipbuilder will also assign a hull manager as the waterfront director for your ship. One of the most important things you can do is to establish a close, personal working relationship with your hull manager and his or her team of craftsmen.

The reality of the process is, however, that the shipbuilder is generally working from a fixed-price contract on a vessel similar to dozens of others the yard has already built. Your role is not to critique the substance of how your hull manager assembles the product—he or she knows how to build ships, and you are probably not in a position to offer much in the way of helpful advice. You *can,* however, help to set a positive tone between the shipbuilder, the SUPSHIP, and the precommissioning crew that encourages teamwork and emphasizes training, quality assurance, and ship cleanliness. Additionally, you play an important role by bringing an operator's perspective to the production and review process.

Navy Regulations and various type commander instructions address the role of the PCO, but none of them capture the inherent nature or challenges of the process. You are essentially on independent duty, and although the type commander will sign your fitness report, he or she will expect you to report regularly until the ship is nearly complete. Each type commander and program manager has different reporting requirements, but many of the traditional weekly progress reports have been canceled or assumed by the SUPSHIP.

It is important to quickly develop an understanding of the basic design and layout of the ship, and of the upcoming changes that will affect her later in life. The contract from which the vessel is built is years old and does not recognize the variety of ship alterations that will be installed within weeks of ship custody transfer. It is imperative to also develop a close working relationship with the program manager's representatives—they have the information on what the future holds and need your input to do their work correctly. Personal visits, frequent phone calls, and regular e-mails are important tools in continuing to build this relationship.

One of the most important things you provide to the shipbuilding process is feedback. The SUPSHIP is often too close to the problem to see what you see, and the program manager is too far away to know what sailors need to do their jobs better. Regular, quality, detailed correspondence can have a direct, positive influence on how your ship and others are built. It is important for you and your crew to have access to and understand the ship specifications that govern construction. You have a vested interest in the quality of the product that the SUPSHIP and his or her staff do not. An intimate knowledge of the specs will allow you to be a force for positive change and corrective action. Finally, and perhaps most significantly, you bring the operator's perspective to the process. You are the only one who does, and part of your job is to represent all the sailors who will sail in your ship.

The Precommissioning Unit

The precommissioning unit (PCU) is the organization that will eventually become your command. Each shipyard has a building to support the PCU, assemble the crew, and continue the training and integration process. The focus of effort during this phase should be to get the administrative requirements completed so that you can focus on training as the ship gets closer to completion. The personality and reputation of the crew are built first and foremost at the PCU; it is a critically important rung on the ladder.

While "prospective commanding officer" is the most commonly used title for your role, it is actually a misnomer. "PCO" is descriptive only; no legal consequences flow from being a PCO. (*Note:* Because of the requirements for monitoring the reactor plant as it installed, this is not true for nuclear vessels. PCOs in nuclear ships are actually designated commanding officers after they report.) After you report to the building yard and the Commander, Naval Sea Systems Command (or a designated representative), designates the PCU a "separate and detached command," you technically become the officer in charge (OIC) of the PCU. Your nonjudicial punishment authority is, therefore, that of an OIC, not a CO. The PCU begins the vessel's transition to a United States Ship at ship custody transfer, and the designation "USS" is officially given at the commissioning ceremony. It is interesting to note that a new ship is placed "in service—special" when custody for the vessel shifts to the government and the DD-250 form is signed by the SUPSHIP. It is placed "in commission without ceremony" weeks before the actual ceremony.

The PCU exists to assemble and provide a structure for the crew. Your emphasis in the first days of the PCU should be on setting up the administrative procedures that will govern the ship after you move aboard, and then, more importantly, to train the crew. The sailors generally arrive in phases—technical experts and leadership first, and the balance of the crew later. The manning process is cumbersome at best, and demands the dedicated effort of your XO and command master chief, and close liaison with the Bureau of Naval Personnel (BUPERS) to make it work.

In many cases, the building yard is a long way from the primary Navy training sites in Norfolk and San Diego. To accommodate the large influx of sailors destined for a new ship, the Fleet Training Centers have created precommissioning detachments (PCD) to support integration, administration, and training schedules. The PCD is an administrative creation only—everyone assigned to the PCD falls under the authority of the commanding officer of the Fleet Training Center. The structure does allow, however, for the precommissioning crew to be assembled in a common area, develop team dynamics, work together, train, and prepare to transition to the building yard. Management of individual training pipelines is the most important function for the PCD.

In most building yards, there will be either a Navy Fleet Introduction Team or a team of private contractors hired by the program manager to help with the integration and training process. These are usually very strong groups with vast experience with precommissioning crews. Heeding their advice on how to do it better can make the difference between a good precommissioning experience and a bad one.

The Precommissioning Crew

Building a warfighting team from the disparate group of individuals assigned to the PCU may be the biggest challenge you face as PCO. The crew will come from a wide variety of backgrounds, few of them with significant experience in your class of ship, and many with no seagoing experience at all. *Training the crew to operate safely at sea is your most important task.*

Although there is a nominal precommissioning screening process for sailors who receive orders to a PCU, there will still be those who arrive unprepared for the rigors of precommissioning duty. They may have significant personal or family problems, or not be physically qualified. There is no such thing as a "hand-picked precom crew," and the leadership challenges are in many cases greater than on a normal fleet ship because of the lack of structure that exists in the early days of the PCU.

BUPERS will assign a single point of contact for officer and enlisted detailing, and will look to you to do the same. The detailer will work two or three ships at a time, and is your best advocate in the bureau. He or she will write orders to route prospective crewmembers from their previous command, through the PCD, to the PCU, and, eventually, to the ship. Because this process is so complicated and so closely tied to the well-being of the crew, your point of contact must understand the subtleties of the detailing process and the associated issues related to household goods moves, family separation, and training requirements. Many sailors do not understand the accounting codes in their orders and make bad decisions for themselves and their families because they do not know the rules. Crewmembers are required to fulfill a two-year minimum activity tour after ship custody transfer.

It is important to have a well-run "welcome aboard" program in place for the new crew. Many will be coming from remote areas, and the information provided in a welcome aboard package will help ease the transition and stress associated with what may be three permanent change of station (PCS) moves in less than two years. Publish a newsletter, write letters home to the families, set up an aggressive family support group—each of these will provide you a vehicle to discuss the ship's schedule and the importance of long-range planning in the life of each family.

Launching

The launching ceremony has changed a great deal over the past few years. Rarely does a ship "slide down the ways"; more often today she is pushed into a drydock and floated out, or pushed in sideways off of the construction platform. The official ceremony is still notable for the designation and presence of a ship's sponsor who breaks the traditional bottle of champagne across the bow.

Launching is completely the responsibility of those who built the ship. It is *their* ceremony, and you and your crew will be invited to participate as much as your schedules and travel requirements support. You will have an opportunity to meet and socialize with the significant players in the building of your ship, but you will have little to do with the ceremonial aspects of this event.

In most cases, the PCO is not involved with the designation of the sponsor. Sponsor candidates are screened and eventually selected by the Secretary of the Navy. Sponsors will, whenever possible, have some association with the ship's namesake, but may be the wife of a senior political or military leader. Liaison with the sponsor at the christening is an important part of the process—you will have a lifelong association with her, and this is the first opportunity for the two of you to meet and discuss plans for the ship and commissioning ceremony.

Sea Trials

Sea trials (or builder's trials) are the best training opportunity your crew will have before moving aboard, but they are completely the responsibility of the shipbuilder, who will hire a civilian master who is responsible for the safety and navigation of the ship, and will use shipyard operating engineers to work the equipment and stand watches. You and your crew will have the opportunity to inspect the ship as she operates, participate in the quality assurance effort, and write trial cards on the discrepancies. You will be given a limited number of seats on each trial and will be able to bring some of the crew to sea. It is a training opportunity not to be missed.

The specifics of sea trials vary by ship class and program manager. For Aegis ships, the PCO will be temporarily assigned to the SUP-SHIP in order to be in a position to accept custody for and fire the missiles and guns. You will execute a demanding training regimen prior to going to sea for builder's trials, and will be the sole point of coordination for all evolutions that involve live ammunition.

The last trial, frequently called an acceptance trial, is customarily sponsored by the SUPSHIP, who presents the ship to the Board of Inspection and Survey (INSURV) for final acceptance. If INSURV accepts the vessel, they will authorize the SUPSHIP to accept the ship on behalf of the government and the ship is placed "in service—special."

Ship Custody Transfer to Sail Away

The period of time between ship custody transfer (SCT) and sail away may be the busiest of your entire life. The ship must be loaded with the consumables, repair parts, equipment, computers, and paperwork that will allow her to operate smoothly when the crew moves aboard. The load-out process itself is an arduous task that demands a well-polished plan and the commitment of senior leaders and crew alike. This period is made significantly more difficult by the arrival of the balance crew at the PCU just prior to move aboard; many of these sailors are new accessions, and are unsure of their roles and what to do, let alone how to take custody of a new ship. In just a few weeks, this group has to be indoctrinated to you, your XO, the organization, the shipyard, and the precom process.

After load out, the crew will move out of the PCU and aboard the ship. It is a difficult transition because you are now responsible for the safety and operation of the ship and crew, while no one is yet qualified to operate the equipment or stand the watches. The degree of pain suffered at move aboard is a direct reflection of the quality of the training program implemented during the earliest PCU days.

The months between move aboard and sail away are dedicated to learning the ship and preparing for operations at sea. The emphasis should necessarily be on fire fighting, damage control, safe steaming, and safe navigation. A comprehensive program of certifications and fast cruises will help this process along. Your ISIC will be involved in the light-off certification, crew certification, and final fast cruise.

Commissioning

Commissioning is the highlight of the ship construction process. It is a ceremony rich in tradition, and is an opportunity to reaffirm the role of the Navy, acknowledge its heritage, recognize the crew and their families, and thank the SUPSHIP and shipbuilder for their support and expertise. Commissioning ceremonies are high-interest media events and are often attended by thousands of people. You play the key role in the commissioning process; the success of your commissioning ceremony will be dependent on the amount of quality, personal attention you offer.

The location of the commissioning ceremony is largely your decision. Although it is generally easier to hold the ceremony in the builder's yard prior to sail away, most PCOs choose other sites for historical or political reasons. Pick a site as early in the process as is possible, and work with the program manager and the Secretary of the Navy's office to secure the official site designation. As soon as the site is chosen, it is imperative that you contact local political organizations, Navy League chapters, and other interested parties to designate a commissioning committee and assign its chairman. You should

A ship's commissioning day is her official "birthday" as a U.S. Navy warship and should always be attended by pomp and circumstance. Here, USS *Russell* is dressed for the occasion.

have a site and a committee formally designated at least a year prior to the commissioning ceremony.

Commissioning preparations will take up an inordinate amount of your time as the date of the ceremony approaches. The once bimonthly meetings will occur nearly every week, and you (and your XO and commissioning coordinator) will spend many hours on the phone arranging details. You will need to travel to the commissioning site frequently and be prepared to respond to emergent tasking and crises. An aggressive, creative public affairs program will ease the burden and help make your ceremony memorable.

It is your responsibility to liaison with the commissioning committee and keep them headed fair as they help plan the ceremony. Since the Navy will pick up the bill for only a portion of the festivities, the committee will by necessity be involved in large-scale fund-raising on your behalf. It is important for you to review the ethics regulations on what you can and cannot do, know, and be involved with as the committee raises funds. In most cases, there is a CO's reception this night before the commissioning, a VIP breakfast the morning of the ceremony, and a reception after the ceremony that are paid for directly and solely by the commissioning committee. The government will pay to set up the dais, chairs, public-address system, and decorative bunting. There will likely be experienced contractor support from the program manager.

You are responsible for nominating principal speaker candidates and forwarding the recommendations to the Secretary of the Navy for final selection. In some cases, the speaker may change only days prior to the actual ceremony, so it is important to be flexible. Likewise, the composition of your platform guests can—and usually does—change right up to the last minute. Your commissioning coordinator has to be prepared to implement changes as they occur.

Post-Commissioning

After commissioning, your ship will begin an extensive post-delivery test and trial period where you will run the new ship through the paces, fire missiles, shoot the guns, learn underway replenishment, and sail to the new homeport. Despite being primarily an engineering evaluation of your ship, the post-trial period provides the finest training opportunities available in the Navy today.

In most cases, the shipbuilder will assign a warranty engineer who will ride the ship and take care of emergent issues during the one-year warranty/guarantee period. Except in the cases of specific government-furnished equipment, the warranty engineer will be the shipbuilder's single point of contact for repairs and documentation of discrepancies for correction during Post Shakedown Availability (PSA). This individual, normally an experienced ship engineer, will be able to access the building yard for repair parts, technical information, and support of any kind. He or she should be treated as an integral member of your wardroom, with appropriate messing and berthing. In most cases, the warranty engineer will fit extremely well into a close-knit and productive wardroom, and will provide you with invaluable assistance through the first year of commissioned service while your ship is still under warranty.

During PSA, your ship will return to a shipyard for completion of items left unfinished during construction, correction of those items discovered during shakedown and covered by warranty, and installation of new items that were not ready while the ship was still in the builder's yard. PSAs run from one to four months, depending on ship class, and may or may not be executed in the parent builder's yard. The challenge during PSA is to maintain the sharp edge the crew will have developed while operating the ship at sea during shakedown.

Precommissioning Philosophy

Building a ship is a special experience, and from the moment you assemble your team you should strive to instill a sense of teamwork, loyalty to the ship, and dedication to the very challenging task at hand. Think about developing a philosophy for your precommissioning experience, perhaps including some of the ideas below from previously successful PCOs:

- Ensure that each new sailor receives, upon assignment to the ship, a letter from you explaining the precommissioning process, including its special rewards and challenges.

- Work closely and continuously with BUPERS to ensure that all assigned crewmembers are qualified—remember, you will have *everyone* as a team together for at least three years, which is remarkable in today's Navy. Assemble a team that you want to work with for a prolonged period.
- While you are involved in the construction side of the precommissioning process, your XO should focus on the training, manning, and personnel side. This will mean initial separation between you, with your XO in the prospective homeport and you in the building yard. Work hard to maintain connectivity and consistency between the two detachments.
- Spend plenty of time talking to other PCOs, especially those who are taking ships through the process just ahead of you. There is never a need to reinvent the wheel—don't place excessive burdens on your team simply because you want to be "different." Evaluate what those ahead of you have accomplished, and if it works—take it on board!
- Fuse your entire crew as quickly as possible and get them to the building yard. Next, work hard to get them into the ship at the very first opportunity.
- Take every opportunity to get them to sea on other ships of the class while your ship is being built. One day at sea on a similar ship is worth a month in a school or a week walking around the building yard.

Final Thoughts on New Construction

The construction of a new ship is a an ongoing leadership challenge, but one that comes with great rewards. Perhaps no commanding officer will have the impact that the first one does. Certainly no single crew will ever play as important a role in establishing the standards, reputation, and legacy that will follow the ship throughout her life. The first crew will forever be a group like Nelson's "band of brothers" because they are the plank owners, and they survived the crucible of precommissioning duty together.

Now that the commissioning ceremony is over, however, your time in command has really just begun. If you have trained your crew well, put in place an effective organization, and stayed abreast of the construction issues during the long process, your ship and crew will be ready to make the transition to a team of warfighters and join the fleet as an operational asset.

3

Organization and Administration of the Command

The Captain, in the first place, is lord paramount. He stands no watch, comes and goes when he pleases, is accountable to no one, and must be obeyed in everything, without a question even from his chief officers.

—Richard Henry Dana, *Two Years Before the Mast* (1840)

The wooden sailing vessels that comprised the great navies of Richard Henry Dana's nineteenth century were small, simple ships when compared with their modern counterparts. Most of the crew's efforts were put into manning the sails. Roughly half the men stood watch at all times when underway, ready to change or trim a huge area of canvas. Potential enemies came into sight slowly, giving the ship time to shift to its battle organization, which provided for manning the guns with approximately half the crew, while the remainder tended the wheel and sails. The ship either sailed, fought, or did both at once. The ship's organization could therefore be simple. There was essentially a single watch, quarter, and station bill, a simple battle organization, no administrative boards except for an occasional court-martial, and only a few other bills, such as fire, collision, and prize crew. The administrative needs of the crew were tended to by a select and small group of specialized workers: cook, sailmaker, carpenter, and so forth. A handful of officers stood watch and administered the ship, all under the eye of the captain.

Modern navies, of course, are quite different. A smaller percentage of the crew is directly involved in propulsion, and this number continues to decline as automation further reduces manning requirements in gas turbine main engineering spaces. Guns, missiles, torpedoes, electronics, and communications equipment are extremely complex, requiring a large complement of well-trained men and women. During wartime, instant attack can be expected from the air, from the surface, and from the depths of the sea. There are higher numbers of specialized administrators—mess specialists, yeoman, disbursing clerks—to tend to the needs of the crew. More officers are embarked to manage and oversee the complex system that is today's warship.

Reflecting these technological changes, the ship's organization has ballooned. The modern warship still has a watch, quarter, and station bill and a battle organization, but there are many other bills and boards as well, many of them quite complicated. Besides general quarters (condition I) and normal steaming (condition IV), there are at least two other principal watch conditions and several minor ones.

As ships become more complex, the trend throughout the twentieth century has been for their organizations to follow suit. Yet today, as we enter the twenty-first century, there are many new technologies emerging that may move us back toward the simpler manning arrangements of the nineteenth century. This unfolding revolution in military affairs, with its emphasis on high-technology systems, stealth, precision engagement, and network-centered warfare is permitting a reassessment of the ways in which we man, organize, and administer our modern warships. Over the next several decades, it seems likely that there will be a decline in the overall manning of warships, which will lead to changes in every aspect of administrative and battle bills. While this chapter will focus on "traditional" twentieth-century approaches to manning, it is important for every commanding officer to work toward streamlining and improving the overall efficiency of his or her command.

General Principles of Organization

The *Standard Organization and Regulations of the U.S. Navy, OP-NAVINST 3120.32C (SORN)*, describes some of the principles of organization in Chapters 3, 4, and 6. You should read these chapters carefully. We will cover most of those same basic principles here.

The dictionary definition of the word *organize* is "to bring into systematic relation the parts of a whole." The *SORN*, in Chapter 1, defines *organization* as the orderly arrangement of materials and personnel by functions.

The *SORN* goes on to state that sound organization is essential for good administration, that organization must be designed to carry out the objectives of command, and that it should be based on division of activities and on the assignment of responsibilities and authority to individuals within the organization. Further, to ensure optimum efficiency, all essential functions must be identified as specific responsibilities of a given unit or person. There must be a clear definition of individual duties, responsibilities, and authority.

Planning an Organization. To assist you in planning, the *SORN* defines several basic terms. We will list them here as well, since they will be used repeatedly throughout this chapter:

Accountability refers to the obligation of the individual to render an accounting of the proper discharge of his or her responsibilities.

Authority is the right to make a decision in order to fulfill a responsibility, the right to require action of others, or the right to discharge particular obligations placed upon the individual.

Delegation is the right of a person in authority to send another to act or transact business. Authority may be delegated, but accountability may never be.

There is nothing new about these definitions. They have been used and understood since the inception of the Navy.

Setting up an Organization. Chapter 1 of the *SORN* sets forth the steps in setting up an organization. Your ship, when you relieve, will already have an operating organization; or, if you commission a new

The captain sets the tone for the entire ship, and his touch is felt everywhere and by everybody on board.

unit, you will be required to develop one. You should occasionally review the validity of your organization by doing the following:

1. Prepare a statement of objectives or of missions and tasks.
2. Familiarize your key planners with the principles of organization.
3. Group the ship's functions logically so that they can be assigned to appropriate segments of the organization.
4. Prepare manuals, charts, and functional guides.
5. Establish policies and procedures.
6. Indoctrinate key personnel concerning their individual and group responsibilities.
7. Set up control measures to ensure the achievement of your objectives.

The *SORN,* in Article 131, also sets forth these four principles of organization to serve as guidelines:

1. *Unity of Command.* Each person should report only to one superior. One person should have control over each segment of the organization. Lines of authority should be simple, clear-cut, and understood by all.

2. *Homogeneity of Assignment.* Functions should be grouped homogeneously, with individuals assigned to groups in accordance with their abilities.

3. *Span of Control.* A senior should be responsible for from three to seven individuals. The span of control should be varied according to the type of work, its complexity, the responsibility involved, and the senior's capabilities.

4. *Delegation of Authority and Assignment of Responsibility.* Authority delegated to subordinates should be commensurate with their ability. Generally, authority should be delegated to the lowest level of competence in the command.

Organizational Authority. Chapter 3 describes in some detail the derivation of the authority of officers. Petty officers also derive that authority which comes from position in an organization. *Navy Regulations,* Articles 1021 and 1037, is the source of authority for both. The exact kinds and limits of authority exercised by each individual will be defined by ship, department, division, and other direction specific to the organization.

Organizational Directives. All ship organization is ultimately derived from *Navy Regulations.* Article 0804 provides that all commands will be organized and administered in accordance with law, *Navy Regulations,* and the orders of a competent authority, and that all orders and instructions issued by a commanding officer will be in accordance with these directives. Article 0874 goes on to state that the CO should never leave the ship without an organized force sufficient to meet emergencies and, consistent with requirements, capable of conducting operations.

Article 0843 sets forth relations with military units and personnel embarked for passage but not part of ship's company. Briefly, this article provides that such units will be subject to the orders of the ship's commanding officer, will comply with the CO's uniform and other regulations, and will perform their share of mess and other common duties, but that they will otherwise be administered through their own organization. When a unit is embarked for transportation only, its officer in command retains authority, subject only to the overriding authority of the CO.

After *Navy Regulations,* the next level of guidance is the *SORN.* We have already covered some of its matter relating to organizational philosophy. Most of the *SORN,* however, is devoted to covering shipboard organization in detail. Chapter 1 covers basic organization; Chapter 2, standard unit organization; Chapter 3, the organization of departments, divisions, boards, and committees; Chapter 4, watch organizations; and Chapter 6, standard bills. The development of each subject is so complete that many sections can be adopted almost verbatim by any ship.

The next input to your organizational efforts will be your type commander. Many type commanders promulgate a standard organization and regulations manual for each type under their command. Some use the *SORN* as their basic organization, with modifying addenda at the back of the book. Others have kept their old standard organizations, modifying them to correspond to the standard. Some few have written completely new standard organizations. In any event, each type organization directive must conform to the standard directive.

The final level of detail is your own ship's organization. You may make it as simple or as complicated as you desire, but bear in mind that it must still conform to the standard organization set forth in the *SORN.* Note again that the italicized sections of the standard cannot be modified. Other sections may be changed in detail as you see fit, but not in principle.

After reviewing these directives, you are now ready, if commanding a new ship, to promulgate your own organizational instructions and standing orders. These will include a battle bill (with a condition watch system); a watch, quarter, and station bill; administrative, operational, and emergency bills; a safety program; a training program; and the necessary boards and committees. The *SORN* includes fifty bills and twenty-eight boards and committees. We can all be thankful not all of them are necessary on most ships.

If you are taking command of a ship already in commission, you will be spared the time-consuming task of organizing your ship. You will, however, want to spend some time determining what changes you want to make, and this will cover much of the same ground, though at a faster pace.

We will now cover briefly the major components of the task of organizing a ship. Again, most of the required reference material is in the *SORN* and in your type commander's addenda or standard manual.

Organization for Battle

A warship is built to fight, and your ship's allowance of officers and sailors has been tailored to that task. Anyone without a battle station is not needed aboard. A sailor's place in the battle bill should be source of pride. Many a ship's cook or barber has fought as a gun or mount captain, or as a vital member of a missile or torpedo crew. This feeling of pride should be encouraged, particularly since the technical requirements of today's weapons have made such qualification by nontechnical personnel more difficult.

Battle Bill. The chief directive for the formulation of your battle bill is NWIP 3–20.31, *Surface Ship Survivability.* This confidential publication describes shipboard battle organization and conditions of readiness, and should be used as your guide. It will be supplemented by a type commander's standard battle bill. You will probably have to adapt both bills somewhat for your ship, since today's rapid changes in weaponry and equipment are resulting in a variety of subclasses within each class.

The battle bill assigns sailors to stations according to (a) their qualifications and (b) the requirements of the various weapons, equipment, and machinery of the ship. Where possible, divisions or parts of divisions should be assigned to related battle stations as a group; for example, MP division, to the engine and auxiliary spaces; first division, to mount 51. When this is impracticable, you should make every effort to assign sailors who work together administratively to battle stations where they can continue to work as a team.

Condition watch teams will be formed from the battle organization (condition I). They will man selected ship control, communications, weapons, and engineering stations. A few "idlers," or non-watchstanders, should be left over to man commissary stations, key administrative posts, and a few other billets.

If war should break out on your watch, you will initially be tempted to keep the crew at general quarters for long periods of time. As the newness of being at war wears off, however, you will have to deal with the fact that your officers and crew still need rest and food, that a minimum of personal and ship cleanliness is still required, and, in general, that the work of the ship must continue even under conditions of high readiness for combat. Theoretically, condition IE will allow the crew to take care of these necessities while still retaining all the offensive and defensive capabilities of condition I. You should anticipate the need, over long periods at GQ, for even further easements in certain aspects of readiness. Plan to have your cooks and mess personnel so distributed in the battle bill that they can be spared for food preparation and service even during GQ. While they are otherwise occupied, the ship should still be able to open fire, and they can quickly be summoned back to battle stations.

Another factor to plan for, either before the initiation of action or soon thereafter, is to make provision for the rotation of those personnel whose duties require close and continuous concentration. Examples of these are lookouts, radio watch personnel, radar operators, talkers, sonar operators, and throttlemen. The safety of the ship may depend on their alertness; ensure that they stay fresh by providing reliefs.

Condition Watch Organization

According to NWIP 3–20.31, the condition watches to consider when making up your condition watch bill are:

Condition I:	General quarters.
Condition II:	Halfway between general quarters and normal watch (for large ships only).
Condition III:	Wartime cruising. Approximately one-third of the crew will be on watch. Armament will be manned to match threat conditions. Some idlers.

Condition IV:	Normal peacetime cruising.
Condition V:	Peacetime watch in port. Enough personnel aboard to man emergency bills and to get underway.
Condition VI:	A variation of condition V permitting more relaxed readiness when ship is not able to get underway.
Condition IA:	Amphibious battle stations. Reduced armament readiness; boat launching and control stations fully manned.
Condition IAA:	Variation of condition I to meet AA threat.
Condition IAS:	Variation of condition I to meet ASW threat.
Condition IE:	Temporary relaxation of condition I to allow rest or messing of crew.
Condition IM:	Variation of condition I to meet mine threat.

In preparing bills for the above conditions, bear in mind that in wartime (and that is what we are preparing for), condition watches, continued for hours on end, will soon "get old." Even in peacetime, after eight hours of daily watch not much is left of a person's productive time. In wartime, you should find yourself able to modify condition watches to allow some men to sleep on station or to work in the vicinity of their stations. For example, a mount crew might keep a talker and a trainer awake and on station, while the remainder of the crew sleeps, rests, or works in the same general area.

Watch Organization

The *SORN,* Chapter 4, covers in detail the watch organization of ships in general, both in port and underway. In making up your own watch bills, remember that those portions of the *SORN* in italics must be included as they are. The other parts of the chapter may be modified as you desire.

Development of a Watch Organization. You should, in developing your watch organization, start with the requirements of the *SORN.* Figure 3–1 shows standard arrangements which should fit any type or size ship. Review them and the *SORN,* and deliberate on what you yourself will feel comfortable with. Delete those functions that do not

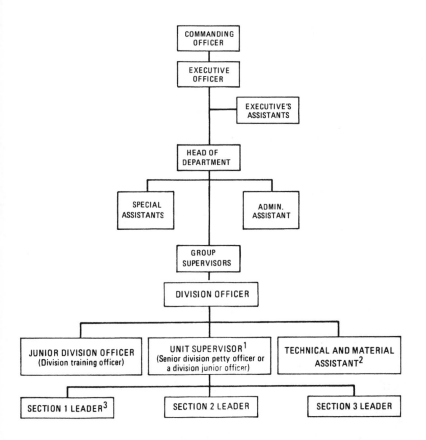

1. When a division has more than one function, such as deck and weapons responsibilities, it would have a supervisor for each of these functions.
2. Usually a warrant officer or limited duty officer assigned to supervise the maintenance and repair of certain material or equipment.
3. The number of sections in each division will depend on the number of watch sections in the individual unit

Figure 3–1. Department organization.

apply to your own ship, add your own ideas, and the result should constitute your watch bill in chart form. You should then refine this, using the ideas of your heads of departments, and modifying your draft as necessary to suit the qualifications of your personnel. The last step is the writing and printing of written directives for your organization book. These should fully delineate the responsibilities and duties of each watchstander.

This would be a good time, also, to set up a training system, to make sure the personnel who will stand these watches will be properly qualified, and will in turn pass on their skills to others.

Establishment of Watches. Once your watch organization is in print and a training system is in place, you are ready to implement the watch system. The *SORN* requires that watches of the officer of the deck and the engineering officer of the watch be continuous. Marine officers below the grade of major may stand OOD watches in port and JOOD watches at sea. Petty officers and noncommissioned officers may be used as OODs in port in addition to your officers. It is increasingly common today to see chiefs and first class petty officers qualify as underway OODs.

The general duties of watch officers are set forth in the *SORN,* Article 410. Subsequent articles cover orders to sentries, watchstanding principles, conditions for the firing of weapons, length of watches, performance of duty while on watch, setting and relieving the watch, and special watches. Your instructions, with the italicized portions of the *SORN* included, should be all your watchstanders need to read to stand a taut and knowledgeable watch. Additional information is available to them in the *Watch Officer's Guide,* published by Naval Institute Press.

Logs. The two main logs to be kept by your watches are the Deck Log and the Engineering Log. Other important records are the Magnetic Compass Record, the Bearing Book, the Engineer's Bell Book, and the CIC Log. Give your personal attention to the keeping of these documents. They are important historical records and also legal documents; there are a number of reasons they might be referred to in years to come.

Unit Bills

A unit bill sets forth the commanding officer's policy and directions for assigning personnel to duties or stations for specific purposes or functions. The *SORN* states that unit bills will include the following elements:

1. A preface, stating the purpose of the bill.
2. Assignment of responsibility for the bill's maintenance.
3. Information of a background, or guidance, nature.
4. Procedure, containing the information and policies necessary to interpret the material.
5. The special responsibilities of each person with regard to planning, organizing, directing, and controlling the functions and evolution of the bill.

Chapter 6 of the *SORN* contains sample bills for every conceivable type of ship for every possible contingency or evolution. They are intended as a guide for type commanders and commanding officers. Your type commander will probably have modified the bills in the *SORN* to suit his or her desires and the types of ships he or she commands. You, in turn, may modify further the bills that concern your particular ship.

Watch, Quarter, and Station Bill

The watch, quarter, and station bill is the division officer's summary of the personnel assignments for each of the other bills the ship uses. As its title states, it lists the watches, berthing assignments, and bill assignments for each officer and sailor. It is the working document for the division officer. It should reflect this importance by being kept up-to-date and neatly written, and should be posted for ready reference by all personnel. The supply system can furnish standard forms, replacements, and bulkhead-mounted holders, should these not be already available. Most ships maintain these bills on computers, but posting copies is still a good idea.

Command Organization

While the primary organization for a ship (and the reason for its existence) is the battle organization, it remains a fact that 95 percent of

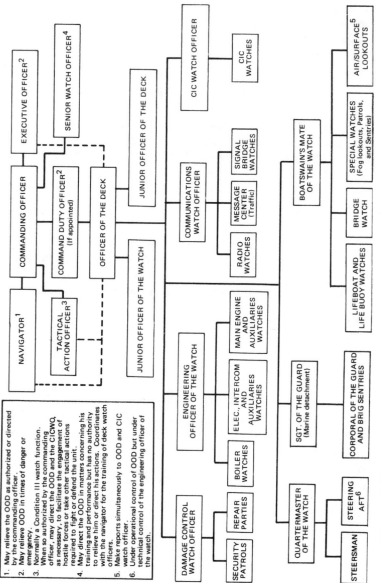

1. May relieve the OOD as authorized or directed by the commanding officer.
2. May relieve OOD in times of danger or emergency.
3. Normally a Condition III watch function. When so authorized by the commanding officer, may direct the OOD and the CIC/WQ, as necessary, to facilitate the engagement of hostile forces or take other tactical actions required to fight or defend the unit.
4. May direct the OOD in matters concerning his training and performance but has no authority to relieve him or direct his actions. Coordinates with the navigator for the training of deck watch officers.
5. Make reports simultaneously to OOD and CIC watch officer.
6. Under operational control of OOD but under technical control of the engineering officer of the watch.

Figure 3-2. Watch organization underway—Condition IV watch

ship's time even in war is spent on administration. This requires an organization of its own, the ship's organization plan. Figure 3–2 shows a typical administrative organization of a large ship; yours might be much smaller. The normal progression of organization is from the CO through the XO, heads of departments, division officers, and so down to the section leaders and nonrated sailors. Figure 3–3 shows the resulting lines of authority and responsibility. We will now proceed to discuss each level of organization in greater detail.

Heads of Department. In addition to the specific duties and responsibilities assigned to a department head (DH) by his or her billet, each one also has certain general duties. First of all, the DH is the representative of the CO in all matters pertaining to the department, and must conform to policies and orders. All persons in the department are subordinate. The DH may confer directly with the captain concerning matters relating to the department, bypassing the XO, whenever he or she believes such action necessary for the good of the department or the ship. (Of course, the DH should use this right sparingly, and should inform the XO as soon as possible.) The DH must keep the CO informed as to the general condition of machinery and equipment, particularly in cases that might affect safety or operational readiness, and must not disable machinery or equipment without permission.

The more specific responsibilities of each head of department are set forth in the *SORN*. You should read them carefully and insist that your heads of departments do likewise. Aside from normal duties, additional specific requirements are laid on a department head during the precommissioning period, during fitting out, and during the period prior to detachment. For example, before being relieved, the DH is required to inspect the department, submitting a joint report with the relieving officer to the commanding officer. You should read this portion of the *SORN* carefully, and insist that your department heads do likewise.

Division Officers. Officers are assigned to command major divisions of each department. Their position in the organization of the command is shown in Figure 3–1. They are assigned by junior division officers, enlisted section leaders, and other leading petty officers.

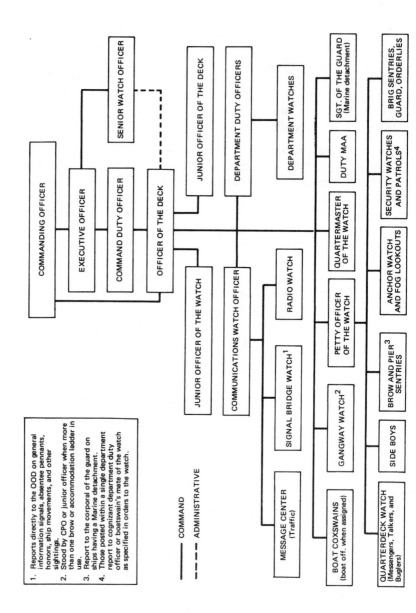

COMMANDING OFFICER

EXECUTIVE OFFICER

SENIOR WATCH OFFICER

COMMAND DUTY OFFICER

OFFICER OF THE DECK

JUNIOR OFFICER OF THE DECK

DEPARTMENT DUTY OFFICERS

DEPARTMENT WATCHES

JUNIOR OFFICER OF THE WATCH

COMMUNICATIONS WATCH OFFICER

MESSAGE CENTER (Traffic)

SIGNAL BRIDGE WATCH[1]

RADIO WATCH

QUARTERMASTER OF THE WATCH

SGT. OF THE GUARD (Marine detachment)

DUTY MAA

BOAT COXSWAINS (boat off. when assigned)

GANGWAY WATCH[2]

PETTY OFFICER OF THE WATCH

ANCHOR WATCH AND FOG LOOKOUTS

SECURITY WATCHES AND PATROLS[4]

BRIG SENTRIES, GUARD, ORDERLIES

QUARTERDECK WATCH (Messengers, Talkers, and Buglers)

SIDE BOYS

BROW AND PIER[3] SENTRIES

1. Reports directly to the OOD on general information signals, absentee pennants, honors, ship movements, and other sightings.
2. Stood by CPO or junior officer when more than one brow or accommodation ladder in use.
3. Report to the corporal of the guard on ships having a Marine detachment.
4. Those posted within a single department report to cognizant department duty officer or boatswain's mate of the watch as specified in orders to the watch.

——— COMMAND

- - - - ADMINISTRATIVE

The division officer (DO) occupies an essential place in the ship and is the final officer link between you and your crew. The DO's performance of duty is essential, since the enlisted sailors see the DO daily; they will react strongly to his or her leadership, good or bad. The *SORN* lists the DO's specific duties, but a more detailed reference is *The Division Officer's Guide,* published by Naval Institute Press.

Boards and Committees. A board, or committee, is a group of persons organized under a president, chairman, or senior member to evaluate problems in depth and to make recommendations to higher authorities for action. Many organizational functions in the Navy lend themselves to administration by these groups. Article 304 of the *SORN* describes the composition and purpose of the most common ones aboard ship. You will probably not need them all, but some will prove useful by undertaking long or detailed analysis of matters that do not require your immediate attention or decision. They are generally policy-setting groups, though you may choose to delegate executive functions to a few.

Ship's Regulations

Ship's regulations have traditionally been one of the most important elements in a ship's organization. Here, at least, is one thing that retains the flavor of tradition, many of its rules dating back to the days of wooden ships—though of course they have been brought thoroughly up-to-date where necessary.

Chapter 5 of the *SORN* contains a useful set of ship's regulations. This particular set may be obtained through the supply system and is printed on bulletin-board-sized posters.

You may be of the opinion, after a quick review, that they are too lengthy, too excessively detailed. Bear in mind, however, that they have evolved over many years, the product of the experiences of thousands of COs facing the same problems you are facing now. Most of them, in fact, started as navy regulations, and were gradually downgraded to ship's regs.

The range of subjects covered is peculiar, granted. They start with "Alarm Bells" and end with "Unauthorized Entry." They cover such diverse subjects as swearing, swimming, grooming, hitchhiking, and a host of other odd activities. But before you decide to cut some out, remember that if some of your sailors conduct themselves as you would not want them to, the court-martial or nonjudicial punishment hearing you convene will have to prove that they violated a law or regulation of some kind. The ship's regulations should, therefore, cover those rules of conduct that you want observed; and they must be *duly promulgated* to be legal. This means they must be *approved* by competent authority and *posted* in a place where the culprit could be expected to see them. Ship's regulations signed by you and posted on the division bulletin board in the sailor's living compartment constitute legal promulgation.

Bearing these considerations in mind, you will probably want to use the standard regulations as a *minimum* rather than as a *maximum*. Past COs have found each one to be necessary, or it wouldn't be there.

Organization for Embarked Staff

The chances are good that you will carry a permanently embarked flag or at some time carry one temporarily. Your organization should take both possibilities into account.

The basic guidance for relations with an embarked commander and accompanying staff is contained in *Navy Regulations,* Chapter 7. Articles 0710 and 0711 outline the organization of a staff and the authority and responsibilities of officers assigned to it. Article 0720 describes its administration and discipline. This article states that the staff of an embarked commander, along with the enlisted persons serving with them, are subject to the internal regulations and discipline of the ship. They will be assigned regular stations for battle and emergencies. Enlisted personnel are assigned to the ship for administration and discipline, usually as a flag division, under a flag division officer.

Additional details on accommodating an embarked staff are covered by the *SORN.* Basically, the organizational changes to take aboard a flag are relatively simple.

Ship's Routine

Establishment of a formal routine is essential to the smooth operations of any large organization—including a ship. If a daily routine is lacking, vital functions such as training and qualification, maintenance, and even watchstanding will suffer as surely as night follows day. This is especially true of periods spent underway and deployed. Officers and sailors must then attend to their departmental and divisional duties as well as stand watches, but it is hard for even the best-organized, best-motivated person to stand watch on a one-in-three basis if the daily routine is disorganized.

The plan of the day (POD) is the document that formalizes the ship's routine. The *SORN* addresses the plan of the day in detail in Article 510.46. This article provides that a plan of the day, published daily by the XO or an authorized representative, will constitute the primary medium for the promulgation of such orders and directives as the XO, or the duty officer when the XO is absent, may issue. The POD will be posted on all department and division bulletin boards, and will be read at quarters when the ship is in port. Each member of the crew is then responsible for obeying the orders it contains.

Your POD will prove most effective in administering the daily routine of the ship if it:

Is complete and addresses all shipwide major events.

Is published early (preferably the day before its execution) to allow departments to adjust to key events.

Is used to assist the ship's training program with training and qualification notes.

Is used to honor those awarded recognition for superior performance, recent promotion, or reenlistment.

Includes topics of general interest to the crew, such as upcoming port calls and mail deliveries.

Correspondence

Correspondence Accounting System. It is essential that you have an absolutely reliable correspondence system. All incoming matter must be opened and logged as soon as received, then routed promptly through the XO and you to action and information personnel. The routing sheets can be filled out by anyone of your choosing, depending upon the size of the ship. Large ships usually use the ship's secretary for the captain's correspondence and the XO's yeoman for routine correspondence. Small ships usually task a yeoman with all correspondence. In any event, make sure all correspondence is promptly put in the hands of the person designated to take action, and that a deadline for writing a reply is designated.

Part of this system should be a tickler file, preferably kept by the XO's yeoman. Many commanding officers keep a small personal tickler file on selected important correspondence. Having ensured that each piece of correspondence will reach a person who will present a proposed answer to you within the required time, you can now turn your attention to the content of the letters.

Command Communications Content. As CO, you should be conscious of your choice of words in all conversation and writing. Poor communications skills will handicap you in whatever you attempt. On the other hand, your chances are enhanced by the use of plain, forceful words, correctly chosen and arranged into well-composed sentences and paragraphs so as to convey your meaning directly, clearly, and unequivocally.

In addition to care in conversation and writing, you should always think at least one level above yourself. Try to imagine yourself as the senior officer who is receiving your request, answer, or statement. Is your case stated clearly? Will the problem be understood from what you have written, and have you made it easy for the senior officer to approve your request? Have you answered the simple questions of *How, When, What, Where,* and *Why?* Finally, if the written work is directed to an organization that may not understand shipboard terminology, have you completely explained or described the situation so that they can understand it? This last point is particularly important in communications involving investigations and fitness reports.

Tone. As commanding officer, you set the *tone* in which your command will speak. Your right to do so is obvious. Confusion and misunderstanding will occur, however, when you are unsure about the tone you desire or when your subordinates do not understand what you want. There are many examples of this. On one ship, officers had letters constantly returned for rewriting until they learned that their captain did not like to see the word "however" in the middle of a sentence. On another, the XO would not sign letters of fewer than two paragraphs. Misunderstandings like these waste time and are hardly good for morale. If you seem to be returning a lot of correspondence for rewrite, the solution is to *make a list* of your pet words and expressions and circulate it for the wardroom to see. Such a list of fifteen or twenty desired and "forbidden" items can save much writing and rewriting.

Guidance. A substantial part of your job as CO is the training of your officers. This training should include showing individual subordinates how to express themselves on paper. Many otherwise excellent young officers have failed to learn this aspect of their profession along the way, and have as a result been less effective at the XO level than they might have been.

If the "list" approach mentioned above does not result in acceptable correspondence, then you will have to devote more attention to this aspect of their training. Bear in mind, however, that harsh actions and words are rarely of value in teaching the art of corresponding and communicating. Stern discipline and quick censure may keep a person alert on a bridge or boiler room watch, but they are ineffective in stimulating someone to think and write with enthusiasm and imagination.

Another approach to training young officers to write is the "sigh and sign it" system. It is best understood by reading the description of it by one destroyer commanding officer, who said, "Sure, the junior officers on my ship write some clumsy letters, but unless they are in error or could cause a misunderstanding, I let them go as written. The young officer gets a feeling of accomplishment out of seeing his letter go off the ship to carry out the ship's business. Next time he does it better because he has had more experience. However, if his work shows no improvement, then the executive officer or I talk to him and give him a few hints about what a good Navy letter should look like." You might keep this advice and this system in mind the next time you are tempted to "nitpick" a letter. Who will read it? What harm can it do if it is less than perfect? Is it really written badly, or is it just written differently from your style?

You will now have established a workable system for receiving, routing, and processing correspondence and for producing satisfactory answers. You can afford to pass on to solving some of the administrative problems that correspondence will bring you.

Make sure you have a copy of *A Guide to Naval Writing* by Robert Schenck handy. It is published by Naval Institute Press.

Investigations

From time to time, even in the best-run ships, incidents will occur that require investigation. These may range from minor injuries to personnel or damage to equipment up to more serious matters. As CO, you should familiarize yourself with the investigation process and be prepared to carry it out properly. A carefully conducted investigation is not to be feared, and in most cases may be to your advantage.

The *Manual of the Judge Advocate General* (*JAG Manual*) explains the three types of fact-finding bodies in the Navy: courts of inquiry, boards of investigation, and one-officer investigations. While investigations conducted by a court of inquiry are always "formal," those conducted by the other two fact-finding bodies may be either "formal" or "informal." The difference is that the "formal" investigation is convened by a written appointing order, testimony is taken under oath, and the proceedings are recorded verbatim.

Only an officer authorized under the *Uniform Code of Military Justice* to convene a general court-martial (or other person designated by the Secretary of the Navy for the purpose) may convene a court of inquiry. You, as a commanding officer, may convene either a board or a one-officer investigation. The informal one-officer investigation, convened either orally or in writing, is the type most frequently used in small ships.

Whenever you have reason to believe that you may become a "party" (defined as a person whose conduct or performance of duty is "subject to inquiry" or who has a "direct interest" in the inquiry), ask your superior in command to order the investigation. This ensures objectivity and reduces the possibility of reinvestigation. Where reference to a superior is impracticable, however, or where the incident is of such minor nature that objectivity can be maintained in spite of an apparent personal interest of the convening authority, the *JAG Manual* states that the matter need not be referred to a superior in command, since one investigation does not preclude a subsequent investigation of the same subject by order of either the same or a superior commander.

Informal investigations are discussed in detail in the *JAG Manual,* which also includes required guides, forms, and checklists. You should be familiar with these provisions, since most of your investigations will be of this type.

Classified Information

Some of your correspondence will be classified, and your handling of it will have to conform closely to the classified information handling regulations. Violations can lead to serious consequences, both for the violator and his or her commanding officer. *Don't let this happen in your ship.* Understand the appropriate regulations, school your administrative personnel, and give the subject command attention.

Navy Regulations, Article 1121, states in part that no person in the Department of the Navy shall convey or disclose by oral or written communications, publication, graphic (including photographic), or other means, any classified information.

Security of classified information should be an integral part of your command philosophy. It is wrong to assume that mere promulgation of the regulations will guarantee protection. Such regulations cannot meet every situation and cannot possibly cover all ship's equipment and the many classified details of operations and performance capabilities.

One of your primary concerns, then, is to ensure that classified information is not revealed to those without a need to know. This subject is also part of the larger subject of ship's security, which we will now discuss in detail.

Ship's Security

The security of the ship is another twenty-four-hour administrative concern of the CO. In this case we are not talking about security in the sense of fire or flood prevention, but rather the protection of classified correspondence, materials, and equipment; unclassified but vital areas such as the engineering spaces; and other ship functions that might be the target of sabotage. This subject is so intermeshed with that of the preceding section that much of the information discussed will apply equally to both. Definitions of various levels of classification and some of the bills are the same for correspondence as for physical security.

Under the security program, your primary concern will be to develop several subprograms, which will:

> Control access to the ship and to specific areas within it by means of rules, alarm systems, locks, and guards.
>
> Ensure that classified correspondence and objects are clearly marked, strictly accounted for, used only by authorized personnel, and securely stowed when not in use.
>
> Ensure that all personnel are screened, instructed, and monitored to ensure their integrity, reliability, and understanding of the techniques for safeguarding classified information and nuclear weapons. (*OP-NAVINST 5510.1H*)

To accomplish the foregoing, you will need to establish certain regulations and bills.

Security Regulations. The *SORN* contains most of the information you will need to establish a strong security program. It prescribes the following bills for use afloat:

> *Security Bill,* which describes and assigns responsibilities for the handling and safeguarding of classified material and information.
> *Ship's Official Correspondence and Classified Material Control Bill,* which details procedures to be followed in handling classified correspondence.
> *Ship's Visitors' Bill,* which specifies procedures and restrictions for control of visitors.
> *Ship's Repel Boarders and Sneak Attack Bill,* which specifies procedures for defending the ship from external or internal attack.
> *Ship's Security from Unauthorized Visitors Bill,* which promulgates instructions for dealing with unauthorized visitors when "repel boarders" action is not required.

Ship Destruction Bill, which outlines the procedures for destroying the ship.

The Security Manager. Chapter 3 of the *SORN* prescribes that a security manager be appointed to assist the commanding officer. This officer can legally be appointed only by the CO or by a legally convened court-martial acting to safeguard security within the command.

An effective security manager is vital to the success of the command security program. The officer you assign to this post should be well versed in all aspects of classified material control and security regulations.

Classification Categories. *OPNAVINST 5510.1* and the *SORN* describe the various categories of classifications and definition of terms used in security programs. All crew members should be instructed in the different classification categories, and should understand how they are handled. This means indoctrinating them in the meanings of the following terms:

Need to Know. The need for certain information by an individual in order to fulfill his or her duties. A security clearance does not in itself establish a "need to know."

Personal Security Clearance. An administrative determination by competent authority that an individual is eligible, from a security standpoint, for access to classified information up to and including the designated category.

Top Secret. Information the unauthorized disclosure of which could result in exceptionally grave damage to the nation.

Secret. Information the unauthorized disclosure of which could result in serious damage to the nation.

Confidential. Information the unauthorized disclosure of which could reasonably be expected to cause damage to the national security.

Restricted Data. All information concerning the design, manufacture, or utilization of atomic weapons, the production of special nuclear material, and the use of nuclear material in the production of energy.

For Official Use Only. Information not requiring safeguarding in the interest of national defense but still not considered releasable to the general public.

Access. The ability and opportunity to obtain knowledge or possession of classified information.

Security Areas. In certain ships, equipment and material of different classifications create the need for defining security areas on a graduated basis concerning the necessary restrictions on access, control of movement within the area, and type of protection required. Security areas are categorized in *OPNAVINST 5510.1* as:

Exclusion Area. An area containing classified information of such nature that access to it means, for all practical purposes, access to such information.

Limited Area. An area containing classified information such that uncontrolled movement by a visitor would permit access to it, but such that while within it access may be prevented by escort and other internal restrictions and controls.

Controlled Area. An area adjacent to or encompassing limited or exclusion areas, but such that uncontrolled movement by a visitor does not permit access to classified information.

Public Relations

Public relations is a very important responsibility. You must be aware of its pitfalls twenty-four hours a day. At the same time, you must be ready to take advantage of every opportunity to make a contribution to the Navy's overall public affairs program.

You will be assisted by your public affairs officer (PAO). Nevertheless, you must personally oversee the administration of the public affairs program. The PAO needs your command interest, and you, in turn, cannot afford a major error in administration.

Much of your contact with the press and public will occur when you are on independent operations. On independent duty you will be conducting public relations on your own, with little help available. When operating as part of a fleet or when within the continental limits of the United States, you will be able to get help from staff public affairs officers, larger ships, and shore commanders.

The following discussion of the administration of public affairs includes those aspects which apply both to independent operations and to periods when you are under another commander.

Shipboard public relations is essentially the advancement of the proper interests of the Navy by putting forward the ship's "best foot," with due regard for the requirements of good taste, honesty, and security.

Visitors. In a small ship, most of the CO's "public relations" has to do with visitors. Visitors cannot be casually invited or lightly treated. Article 0714 of *Navy Regulations* makes you responsible for the control of visitors to your command. You must comply with the relevant provisions of the *Department of the Navy Security Manual for Classified Information* and other pertinent directives. *Navy Regulations* further requires that commanding officers take such measures and impose such restrictions on visitors as are necessary to safeguard the classified material under their jurisdiction. Finally, it requires that COs and other officially concerned personnel exercise reasonable care to safeguard the persons and property of visitors, as well as to take precautions to safeguard the property and persons within the command. The general visiting bill in the *SORN* describes visiting procedures in detail, and should be reviewed carefully prior to each "open house" or other visiting occasion.

When general visiting is permitted, encourage your officers and crew to entertain visitors with such general information about the ship and the Navy as they can without disclosing classified data. In addition to security provisions, warn your sailors to be alert for pilferage, theft, and sabotage. Always conduct tours as if foreign agents might be among the visitors. Set up clearly marked routes so as to avoid crowding, confusion, and possible injury. Limit the number of people in any one space at a given time, and have medical personnel available. Create a festive and welcoming air by arranging unclassified displays or exhibits with descriptive posters and by rehearsing escorts in the briefs they can give while conducting groups around the ship. Courtesy, patience, and tact are the keys to success during these tours.

Unclassified, controlled visits of foreign nationals, within the capacity of the ship to handle them, may be authorized by the commanding officer, subject to local restrictions. Classified visits must be authorized by the CNO in accordance with the *Security Manual*.

Dealers, Tradesmen, and Agents. *Navy Regulations,* Article 0811, prescribes that, in general, dealers or tradesmen or their agents shall not be admitted within a command. You may grant exceptions to this to conduct public business, to transact private business with individuals at the request of the latter, or to furnish services and supplies that would otherwise not be sufficiently available to the ship's personnel. Personal commercial solicitation and the conduct of commercial transactions are governed by separately promulgated policies of the Department of Defense. Never accept gifts or "special favors" from tradesmen in return for embarking the ship.

Although you should encourage your crew to make financial and insurance provisions for their dependents, you should never allow solicitation of them by a specific company. The purchase of insurance, mutual funds, and financial plans is the private business of the individual and must be dealt with as such. Unfortunately, salespeople are inclined to take advantage of various service connections and demand the crew's time for a "presentation," which sooner or later becomes a sales pitch. You have firm grounds for refusing any such request. Regulations prohibit commercial companies from soliciting participation in life insurance, mutual funds, and other investment plans, commodities, or services at any naval installation, with or without compensation. It also prohibits personal commercial solicitation and sale to military personnel who are junior in grade and rank. The intent is to eliminate any and all instances where it would appear that coercion, intimidation, or pressure was used because of rank, grade, or position.

Press Relations. Press personnel and correspondents occupy a unique place in our society. They are quite conscious of this position and of what they hold to be their prerogatives. Their need to produce interesting news and your requirements regarding security can conflict on occasion. This makes relations with the press an important business for the average CO.

Generally, press releases are not made directly to the press by ships, but there may be emergencies or special occasions where you will be authorized or even directed to make a press release locally. Ask for help from your type commander if you need it. If not, be sure you comply with the provisions of the *Public Affairs Manual*. You may originate hometown news releases, but these should be sent to the Home Town News Release Center for screening and release.

When direct contact with the press is authorized or directed by higher authority, you should review with your PAO the questions the press might ask and the areas of possible inquiry. Write down the details of the situation you are preparing to discuss and be sure of your numbers. Rehearse your answers if time permits. If your ship does not have a PAO of sufficient experience, ask help from the type commander or any nearby shore commander.

When you meet the press, try to be honest and forthright. If you feel you cannot furnish an answer for some reason, tell the press why. If you do not know the answer, say so and offer to provide it as soon as possible. Journalists are, for the most part, professionals. They are required by their editors to ask embarrassing questions, and they don't always expect an answer.

Command Interest

There are many details in administering a ship, and this chapter has touched on most key matters. Certainly the organization and administration of your ship are primarily the executive officer's functions, but never delude yourself that you can afford to neglect either. As in all areas of command, as soon as you fail to manifest interest in organization or administration, they will become of less interest to your officers and crew. Show an appropriate interest, and your officers and crew will do the rest, while you can concentrate on training the men and women under your command to beat any force opposed to them.

4

Executive Officer, Department Heads, and Wardroom

You will face—as you search that hidden terrain at the very heart of yourself—what your heart is all about. You will find yourself at the heart of an officer, and I truly hope you will like what you discover about yourself in that moment.

—Secretary of the Navy Sean O'Keefe

Taking Care of the Wardroom

Very little that you do as a captain is more important than taking care of the officers assigned to your command. Each of the men and women in the wardroom, from the executive officer to the most junior ensign, is a responsibility entrusted to you by the Navy and our nation. Your job is to train, lead, evaluate, and—perhaps most importantly—*inspire* them in the execution of their responsibilities. If you wake up every morning and ask yourself, "How can I best train and lead my wardroom today," you will be well on your way to a successful command tour.

Let's talk about the executive officer, the department heads, and the wardroom one at a time.

Executive Officer: Status, Authority, and Responsibilities

Title 10 of the *U.S. Code* states that the Secretary of the Navy may detail a line officer of the Navy as executive officer of a vessel. When practicable, the *Code* goes on, the XO shall be next in rank to the commanding officer. While executing the orders of the CO, the XO takes precedence over all other officers attached or assigned, and the orders given are to be considered as coming from the CO. The *Code* points out, however, that the XO has no independent authority. Any officer of a staff corps who is senior to the executive officer has the right to communicate directly with the commanding officer.

Prior to 1973, *Navy Regulations* amplified these provisions of the *U.S. Code* with a great many details. The present revision, however, is much less specific about the position of the executive officer. *Navy Regulations* states only that the XO shall be an officer eligible to succeed to command, and who, when practicable, will be next in rank to the CO. When the officer so assigned is absent or incapable of performing duties, the commanding officer shall detail the senior line officer in the command to succeed the XO. *Navy Regulations* goes on to say that the XO, while in the execution of duties as such, will take precedence over all other persons under the command of the CO.

In the *SORN,* OPNAVINST 3120.321C, we begin to find details—lots of them. According to this reference, the XO is to be the direct representative of the CO. All orders issued by the XO will have the same force and effect as though uttered by the captain, and must be obeyed accordingly by all persons within the command. The XO will be primarily responsible to the CO for the organization, performance of duty, and the good order and discipline of the entire command. The XO will recognize the right of a department head to confer directly with the CO on matters relating specifically to the department. It is clear, however, that the most important duties of the XO lie in the conforming to and carrying out of the policies of the commander and in keeping the CO informed of all significant matters relating to the ship and crew.

The *SORN* states that the acting executive officer will have the same authority and responsibility as the assigned executive officer, but that the acting XO will not make changes in organization or routine and will endeavor to carry out affairs in the usual manner.

Specific Duties of the Executive Officer

Under current regulations, the duties of the executive officer are, simply, such duties as the commanding officer assigns. However, the executive officer cannot literally "do everything." He, like the commanding officer, must delegate to his subordinates (in this case, the department heads). The wise commander will insist on this delegation and will support the results, good or bad. Further, he should encourage the XO to use the ship's organization, requiring that heads of departments delegate their authority downward in turn. The exec must use the abilities of all, coordinating their activities and correlating their purposes. If he does not, if he tries to run the whole ship himself, he dooms himself, his commanding officer, and his ship to failure.

One example should suffice. The XO must be the ship's planner, but he must subordinate to this function the larger everyday role of administrator and expediter. Administration and planning are important, but only when they implement larger goals. Delegation operates here when the XO originates the *overall* plan and requires subordinates to make *dependent* plans.

Remember at all times that being executive officer is no piece of cake. The XO must compose conflicts, establish unity of purpose, and mold the spirit of the ship; he must ensure that these duties are carried out within the policies you set forth, and everything must reflect your personality, rather than his own. This is a tall order, particularly for a relatively senior officer, one who has formed his own opinions and is preparing for his own eventual command.

Relationship with the Commanding Officer

Official directives make plain what the relationship should be. *Navy Regulations* provides that the commanding officer shall keep the executive officer informed of all policies, and normally shall issue all orders relative to the duties of that command through the XO. Accordingly, the CO will normally require that all communications of an official nature from subordinates be forwarded through the XO. The two exceptions to this, already mentioned, are the department heads, when necessary, and those senior to the executive officer (usually medical or dental officers). Even these officers, however, must keep the XO informed on matters related to the functions of the command.

Obviously, the executive officer must use the nicest sense of judgment in carrying out your policies. Equally obviously, you, as the commanding officer, must preside wisely. While you must require that your exec carry out the spirit and letter of the regulations, there will be times when you can learn from him, if you encourage his initiative and ask for his opinions and advice. This is particularly true if he has served in your ship type before.

There are ways you can help the XO to function more effectively. For instance, with regard to those provisions of the regulations which use the word "normally" when discussing communications "around" the XO, most senior officers counsel against permitting department heads too much latitude. Require them to communicate via the executive officer unless a real emergency exists.

Again, it is unwise to take upon yourself the executive officer's duties. This will be a specially inviting pitfall for you as a new commanding officer if you were XO in your last sea tour. In fact, it is doubly wrong. It occupies your attention uselessly and at the same time deprives you of your executive officer's best efforts.

Finally, keep your executive officer informed at all times of your changes of policy and schedule. He is only as good as the last information he has.

The commanding officer must ask himself throughout his tour—*How do I use my executive officer?* Is the XO an administrator, a policy-setter, or both? Is he really the assistant commanding officer? Do I have to lean on him to make him perform? Does he follow me or go his own way? How is our rapport? How much do we talk each day, and where? Is he strong or weak? What is my evaluation of his potential for command?

The answers to these questions provide a basis for judging whether or not your relationship is healthy and providing the results you want as far as proper administration of your ship is concerned, as well as whether you are giving him an adequate opportunity to demonstrate and extend his abilities.

In the last analysis, the XO's performance will depend on yours. The successful commanding officer will develop in his executive officer the ability to manage his own and the crew's time and effort to do the most for the ship. He will instill in his executive officer the most efficient methods of keeping him informed of every aspect of the ship's administration and operation. He will delve into details when necessary to ensure that correct action is being taken, but will not preempt responsibility or seem to run a one-man show. It is imperative that the commanding officer grant sufficient authority to his executive to enable him to carry out his responsibilities. He must set and make known his priorities. There is never enough time or money to do everything; the XO must know what you want done first. A continuous appraisal of "What have we accomplished? What do we intend to do next?" with the XO will ensure that you are both running on the same track. All these are things *you* must do to make *him* more effective.

One exception to this principle is punishment. Punishment is the prerogative and duty of the commanding officer, and cannot be delegated. Establish early with your executive officer what you consider punishment and what is only "completing a prescribed duty satisfactorily." Never tolerate unofficial extra duty, but do support his judgment of when required work has been completed so that liberty can begin. (On a small and busy ship duty often can seem like punishment.) Avoid like the plague any form of mass punishment. Either find the culprit or make known your displeasure in some other manner.

Try to find ways to break free time for your XO to work. As soon as you can establish his competence in ship- and linehandling, shift your training effort in these fields to more junior officers.

You will have a large amount of correspondence that your XO has to read, route, and designate for action or reply. Have it all routed to you first, but unless you like being bogged down, let it pass through you with minimal or no comment on the routing slip. Let your young action addressees develop their initiative. If you have phobias or idiosyncrasies about writing letters, do your best to curb them; or, if this is not practicable, get out a list of do's and don'ts (as suggested in the previous chapter) as soon as possible. Don't accept sloppy typing or English, but do accept neat erasures or corrections, especially on routine correspondence and forms where the addressee is impersonal. A good tickler system run by your executive officer is invaluable. Keep a selective tickler file for very important items for your own use.

Finally, even though your executive officer's only function is to be your *alter ego,* try to make more of him. Make him feel that he is part of your team, that you want and will use his suggestions and opinions. Use some of them now and then even though you may not like them all that much.

See that the XO has a share in the success of your command.

Training for Command

Navy Regulations states that the commanding officer shall afford frequent opportunities to the executive officer, and to other officers of the ship as practicable, to improve their skill in shiphandling, which is the first and most important aspect of qualification for command. There are many good books on the subject. The best is *Naval Shiphandling,* published by Naval Institute Press. Require that your executive officer demonstrate theoretical knowledge of the kind contained in *Naval Shiphandling* before letting her handle the ship. The next step (assuming she is new to your type) is to have her observe your shiphandling under a wide variety of conditions and maneuvers. Then allow her to take the conn under your supervision. Finally, place her on her own, with corrections given by you only to avoid damage.

The second important requirement for training of your executive officer for command is preparation for battle. Every general quarters drill, every emergency drill, and all exercises involving the ship's armament, engines, and equipment are opportunities to impart to her, and of course to the rest of your crew, your philosophy of fighting a ship.

With these two essentials in hand, all that remains is your assessment of the XO's overall character and potential command ability, and your efforts to correct any faults you might perceive in these areas. This task can be simplified by asking yourself, "What (in addition to professional competence) are the characteristics of a good commanding officer?" Here are several:

Common sense
Integrity
Enthusiasm
Command presence
Composure
Managerial ability

A similar listing made a century ago might have been somewhat different, leaning perhaps to physical courage, tenacity, and endurance. These qualities are still needed today, but emphasis has shifted over the years to the mental side. Very few of us are born with all the attributes of an outstanding naval officer, and your executive officer will probably lack some of them. She must learn this from your example and from her discussions with you. You must help her to explore herself, judge herself, and then to take advantage of her capabilities and compensate for her deficiencies.

The qualities of common sense and integrity are probably the most important of those listed. If an officer is to take actions that can affect the entire Navy or even the country, she must realize that help is available if she asks for it, but she must also be prepared to stand on her own. Similarly, when a problem arises, it must not be covered up. An officer of integrity will bring it out in the open, try to solve it, and report to higher authority if she can't, without fear of the consequences.

Command presences may be one quality an officer is born with, but it can be enhanced by careful attention to personal detail. Uniforms should be kept clean and neat and worn with pride. The appearance, conduct, and language of the commanding and executive officers should be the standard for the ship. Your XO will have many occasions throughout the day to address small groups of officers and sailors. Encourage her to take a few minutes before each one to organize her thoughts so that her communications will be coherent and firmly and clearly delivered. The industry, enthusiasm, and dedication which you demonstrate throughout the day, as well as in your contacts with your executive officer, will encourage her to display the same qualities she sees in you. If you are unenthusiastic and unprofessional, you will hardly convince your XO that command is the best job in the Navy.

Composure is generally defined as a state of mind in which an individual remains calm and efficient in spite of adversity. Most executive officers have many opportunities during an average day to show composure, or lack of it. When the 0730 boat is late returning with the liberty party, when the OOD drops his binoculars over the side while leaning over to reprimand the coxswain, and when the commodore wants to know why the colors were hoisted five minutes late, the XO's composure will be severely tested. If she can hear the stories of the individuals involved, resolve differences, and take appropriate disciplinary action, all without raising her voice or showing undue dissatisfaction, she has sufficient composure to meet almost any situation. A healthy sense of humor is an enormous plus.

The modern ship's executive officer, like her shore-based counterpart, must have managerial ability. The technical complexities of machinery and equipment, the large amounts of funds required for maintenance, supplies, and the general running of ships, and the massive amount of administrative matters generated by higher command need a firm managerial hand. Make sure your XO demonstrates that she can manage those assigned to solve these problems and does not attempt to take them on herself.

An impatient or intolerant commanding officer will often have such an uneasy and uncomfortable relationship with an executive officer that it detracts not only from the CO's daily performance of duty but also from efforts to prepare the XO for command. The wise commanding officer corrects and criticizes his executive officer in private and commends her in public, and requires, of course, the same behavior from her in relation to her own juniors.

If you can train your executive officer in this careful way, and end her tour by giving her good marks, you have helped produce a fine potential commanding officer. You may have improved your own style of command, too. Enjoy her performance while you can, before she goes off to her own ship. When she leaves, you will find your own task temporarily harder, but you will have made an important

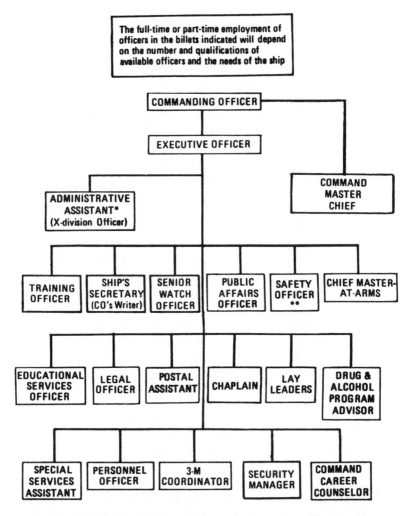

The full-time or part-time employment of officers in the billets indicated will depend on the number and qualifications of available officers and the needs of the ship

COMMANDING OFFICER

EXECUTIVE OFFICER

COMMAND MASTER CHIEF

ADMINISTRATIVE ASSISTANT* (X-division Officer)

TRAINING OFFICER

SHIP'S SECRETARY (CO's Writer)

SENIOR WATCH OFFICER

PUBLIC AFFAIRS OFFICER

SAFETY OFFICER **

CHIEF MASTER-AT-ARMS

EDUCATIONAL SERVICES OFFICER

LEGAL OFFICER

POSTAL ASSISTANT

CHAPLAIN

LAY LEADERS

DRUG & ALCOHOL PROGRAM ADVISOR

SPECIAL SERVICES ASSISTANT

PERSONNEL OFFICER

3-M COORDINATOR

SECURITY MANAGER

COMMAND CAREER COUNSELOR

* If approved by higher authority, the administrative assistant may be a department head and selected executive officer's assistants will report to him.

**In aircraft carriers, the safety officer heads the safety department and shall be listed on the ship's organizational chart with the other departments.

Figure 4–1. The executive assistants. These officers serve under the executive officer and carry out many of the ship's administrative functions.

contribution to the Navy. The instruction and qualification of future commanding officers is, next to command itself, the most important task a senior naval officer has.

The Executive Staff

The function of the executive staff is to assist the executive officer in the discharge of his administrative responsibilities. The duties of staff members are set forth in the *SORN,* Chapter 3. It is important, however, to work for a good *spirit* in the staff, as well as toward professional competence.

The size of your XO's staff will depend on the size of your ship. In a large vessel you will have officers assigned to each billet in the standard organization illustrated in Figure 4–1. In smaller ships, a single officer may fill more than one of them. In very small ships either some of them will be left vacant completely or they will be filled by petty officers. Your own desires will also determine how many of your personnel can be assigned full or part time. In general, the XO's office will include an administrative assistant (usually a junior officer or chief yeoman), the ship's secretary (an ensign or rated yeoman), and a personnel officer (an ensign or rated personnelman). Exact ranks and rates will depend on the size of the ship.

Other officers shown on the organization chart, if assigned, will usually have small offices, or will operate from their staterooms.

The master-at-arms force is also part of the XO's staff. In a large ship it can be quite extensive, including a chief MAA, a mate in each division, and brig guards. In smaller ships the force will be reduced accordingly; in a submarine, it may consist only of the chief of the boat. In all vessels, the chief MAA (or chief of the boat) should be a leader of impeccable record and outstanding capabilities.

The public affairs officer is shown in Figure 4–1 as being directly under the executive officer. You should make sure, however, that it is understood between you, the XO, and the PAO that he is to have *direct* and *instant* access to you on public affairs matters. (He should, of course, fill in the executive officer as soon as possible after he has found it necessary to contact you directly.) If you do *not* make this arrangement, your PAO, with a reporter in tow who has an important question and a deadline to meet, will cool his heels outside the XO's cabin someday. If the impatient reporter has to leave without an answer to his question, an unnecessarily adverse story may appear in the paper the next morning. *Public affairs will not wait on protocol.* It is your *personal* responsibility, and *no one* in your organization should be allowed to slow down the process, even inadvertently.

Chaplains, when assigned, are placed directly under the executive officer, as are combat cargo officers on amphibious ships. Enlisted medical personnel, when no medical officer is assigned, are part of the executive staff.

The senior watch officer on large ships is sometimes assigned under the navigator, but usually is assigned under the executive officer. The senior watch officer is the senior person standing deck watches. His job is to make up the watch list for officers at sea and the duty list in port. In large ships, the command duty list is handled by the XO or senior head of department. You should make the senior watch officer responsible for instruction of watch officers and recording of qualifications and practical factors for watchstanders. This arrangement not only reduces the executive officer's workload, but gives the senior watch officer good experience in conducting and administering.

In submarines, the chief of the boat is considered the senior enlisted person on board. As such, he is your principal enlisted advisor. He is responsible for keeping you aware of existing or potential situations, procedures, or practices which could affect the welfare, morale, job satisfaction, and efficiency of enlisted personnel. The *Standard Submarine Organization and Regulations Manual (SSORM)* addresses his duties in detail. In dealing with the chief of the boat, you and your XO must ensure that he is looked upon with respect and given the latitude, authority, and responsibility he needs to perform. A good rapport with him will go a long way toward improving the effectiveness of your chain of command.

The 3-M (Maintenance and Material Management) coordinator, an officer or senior enlisted performing collateral duty, is the XO's assistant for matters pertaining to the Preventive Maintenance System and the Maintenance Data Collection System. On a submarine, however, he will work more closely with and for the department heads.

The leading yeoman is also uniquely important in the submarine force. He assists the XO in all clerical and personnel matters, though he must also be available to other officers. His exact duties are set forth in the *SSORM*.

Temporary Succession to Command

Navy Regulations provides that in the event of the incapacity, death, relief from duty, or absence of the commanding officer, the executive officer shall succeed to command until relieved by competent authority or until the regular CO returns. If the XO is unable to take over, others then succeed to command by rank if attached to the ship and eligible for command at sea.

An officer who succeeds to command due to incapacity, death, departure on leave, detachment without relief, or absence due to orders from competent authority of the officer detailed to command has the same authority and responsibility as the officer he succeeded. However, his position is limited in that he is prohibited from making any changes in the existing organization, and he is required to carry out the routine and other affairs of the command in the usual manner. This is pointed up by the requirement that correspondence signed by this officer must carry the word "acting" below his signature.

Relieving Commanding Officer in Extenuating Circumstances

Occasionally an executive officer may have to relieve his commanding officer in extenuating circumstances. This should be done only after extremely careful consideration. *Navy Regulations* covers the subject completely and should be studied thoroughly before contemplating such a step. It is rare these days that a ship is not in radio communication with the fleet type commander, but it is possible in the case of a forward-deployed submarine that such communications could not be made because of intelligence reasons. In any event, the provisions of *Navy Regulations* must be strictly followed. The executive officer who relieves under this article must make sure that the case is documented and witnessed in such a fashion that it will stand up in a military court.

A good executive officer makes your job easy by getting the most out of your officers. He will indeed work them to their limit, but if he assigns work fairly, supervises well, and praises appropriately, they will produce beyond their expected capabilities.

The Ship's Officers

The officers of a ship are the driveshaft between the commanding officer, who holds supreme authority and responsibility, and the enlisted sailors, who man the watches, the weapons, and the equipment that give life, mobility, and power to the ship. Without officers, a ship would be a static piece of machinery without a transmission; with them, she can become a smoothly functioning weapon of war, capable of accomplishing as much as the captain can command and inspire.

Unfortunately, good officers do not come completely trained and ready to fit into the organization. You will have to take those ordered to your command and place them so that you get the maximum benefit from their abilities. Analyzing their potential is not an easy task, but you should work hard at it.

When you have finished studying your officers' professional and physical qualifications, and are ready to assign them, remember also the less apparent qualities of leadership every good officer must have. Sometimes character and intensity can overcome a lack of qualification. Robert E. Lee, in a letter to Jefferson Davis, said, "No matter what the ability of the officer, if he loses the confidence of his troops, disaster must sooner or later ensue."

It is important to look for confidence-inspiring qualities in your officers. Such men and women will *avert* disaster.

The selection and placement of your officers in the ship's organization is only the first step in their efficient use.

In this section we will review and examine the command authority given to your officers by *Navy Regulations* and other directives; the limits on their authority; their ordering and assignment; career patterns and broadening; the responsibilities and qualifications of officers for various positions in the ship's organization; additional responsibilities of department heads, division officers, and watchstanders; leadership training; social usage; and fitness reports.

Basic Authority and Responsibilities of Officers

Basic Authority. The authority and responsibility of a naval officer begins the day she accepts her commission or warrant. Its very wording, "Know ye that, reposing special trust and confidence in the patriotism, fidelity, and abilities . . ." of the person commissioned, is an inspiration to the new officer. This is followed by an equally moving occasion, when she takes the oath of office, swearing to support and defend the Constitution of the United States against all enemies, foreign and domestic; to bear true faith and allegiance to same; to take the obligation freely and without any mental reservation or purpose of evasion; and to "well and faithfully" discharge the duties of the office on which she is about to enter. This is indeed an oath not entered into lightly.

Thus, the day she accepts her commission or warrant and takes her oath, an officer takes on certain basic responsibilities by virtue of these actions. At this time, and later, other responsibilities and the authority to carry them out are given her by *Navy Regulations* and other directives. These sources should be examined carefully by all of your officers so that they will know the extent and limits of their authority, and by you as a commanding officer, so that you can instruct and guide them.

Authority and Responsibilities under *Navy Regulations*

General Authority. *Navy Regulations* is quite general in its regulations concerning officers. Every officer in the naval service shall acquaint herself with, obey, and, so far as her authority extends, enforce the laws, regulations, and orders relating to the Department of the Navy. She must faithfully and truthfully discharge the duties of her office to the best of her ability, in conformance with existing orders and regulations and her oath of office. In the absence of instructions, she shall act in conformity with the policies and customs of the service to protect the public interest. This requirement is very broad and covers a multitude of possible circumstances where an officer can, and should, take action. Every officer, then, upon acceptance of her commission or warrant, and upon taking her oath, accepts these general duties of all officers.

Required Conduct. *Navy Regulations* goes on to require all persons (including officers) in the naval service to show in themselves good examples of subordination, courage, zeal, sobriety, neatness, and attention to duty. All persons are to act to the utmost of their ability and the extent of their authority in maintaining good order and discipline, as well as in other matters concerned with the efficiency of the command. All persons in the naval service must obey readily and strictly, and execute promptly, the lawful orders of superiors.

Amplifying Directives Concerning Authority and Responsibilities

Authority from Organizational Position. While the basic authority for all officers stems from *Navy Regulations,* as discussed above, additional authority and responsibility come from the officer's organizational position.

The final fixing of responsibility has been a topic of interest in the military profession for thousands of years. One of the best discourses on the subject, however, is a recent one, by Admiral Hyman G. Rickover. Responsibility, he said, is

> a unique concept. It can only reside and inhere in a single individual. You may share it with others, but your portion is not diminished. You may delegate it, but it is still with you. You may disdain it, but you cannot divest yourself of it. Even if you do not recognize it or admit its presence, you cannot escape it. If responsibility is rightfully yours, no evasion, or ignorance, no passing the blame, can shift the burden to some one else. Unless you can point your finger at the man who is responsible when something goes wrong, then you never really had anyone responsible.

These are strong but true words. The concept is an almost sacred one in our Navy.

Organizational Authority. The *SORN* explains that organizational authority of an officer comes from his assigned billet within an organization. The command structure to which he is assigned is based upon guidance from this instruction as promulgated by command, department, division, and other instructions. The organizational structure sets forth the positions, duties, and responsibilities of all persons in the structure, and invests authority accordingly.

Limits on Authority: Lawful Orders

Injurious or Capricious Conduct. Notwithstanding the almost unlimited authority and responsibility of a naval officer, there are limits. They must be well known by you and your officers and carefully observed. *Only lawful orders must be given and obeyed.*

Most naval officers are familiar with the semi-fictitious examples of Captain Queeg of *The Caine Mutiny* and Lieutenant Roberts of *Mister Roberts.* These so-called stories drew upon true events. Other examples from history are difficult to bring to the attention of the reader and do not illustrate the point as well as the semi-fictional examples. Read both books; they will illustrate the points in question better than fact.

Navy Regulations, Article 0814, prohibits persons in authority from injuring their subordinates by tyrannical or capricious conduct, or by abusive language.

Limits on Organizational Authority. The *SORN,* Article 141.7 in discussing limitation of authority, points out that since it is given only to fulfill duties and responsibilities, only so much as may be considered necessary to fulfill responsibilities need be delegated beyond the lowest level of competence. This is limitation of authority by command. It is a vague and not often encountered concept, but it should be noted.

Contradictory Orders. *Navy Regulations,* Article 1024, covers contradictory and conflicting orders. If an officer contradicts orders given to another by a common superior, he must immediately report that fact to the superior whose orders he contravened, preferably in writing.

If an officer receives such a contradictory order he shall immediately exhibit his previous orders, unless instructed not to do so, and represent the facts in writing to the officer who has given him the latest order. If that officer insists upon the execution of his new order, it shall be obeyed and the circumstances reported to the officer issuing the original order.

Article 0824 prohibits an officer from placing himself on duty by virtue of his commission or warrant alone.

Unlawful Imposition of Nonjudicial Punishment. The giving of only lawful orders must be carefully understood by all officers. Most instances where there might be doubt as to the legality of orders occur in the area of nonjudicial punishment. The *SORN* spells this out in detail in Articles 142.1 and 142.2. You and your officers should be intimately familiar with them. Article 142.2 states that no order may be given that imposes punishment outside of the *Uniform Code of Military Justice (UCMJ)*. It further states that the administration of *UCMJ* nonjudicial punishment is carefully reserved to certain commanders, commanding officers, and officers-in-charge. This is generally well understood. What is *not* well understood, according to this article, is what measures may be taken by officers and petty officers to correct minor deficiencies not meriting *UCMJ* punishment, to correct a subordinate in a phase of military duty in which he may be deficient, or to direct completion of work assignments which may extend beyond normal working hours.

Extra Military Instruction. In an effort to clear up the foregoing uncertainty, Article 142.2 establishes policy guidance for extra military instruction (EMI). This is a much-needed step. More letters have been written to COs by parents, congressmen, and concerned citizens on this subject than on all others put together. Making sure your officers, leading petty officers, and enlisted personnel understand this subject will cut your administrative and letter-writing load drastically.

Article 142.2a defines "extra military instruction" as instruction in a phase of military duty in which an individual is deficient. The article states that EMI is sanctioned by paragraph 306c, *Manual for Courts-Martial (MCM)*, 1984 (Rev.), as a training device to improve the efficiency of a command or unit. It therefore must be used for this purpose and not for punitive actions which should have been taken under *UCMJ*. Article 142.2b then describes how to implement this form of instruction and states that it will not be assigned for more than two hours a day, may be assigned at a reasonable time outside of working hours, will be no longer than necessary to correct the deficiency, and will not be assigned on the sailor's Sabbath. Further, an individual who is otherwise entitled to liberty may commence liberty upon completion of EMI.

EMI assignment during normal working hours may be made by any officer or petty officer as part of his inherent authority. EMI after working hours should be assigned by the commanding officer but may be delegated to officers and petty officers. If it is so delegated, the CO must monitor the process. Commanding officers are advised that they *may* delegate authority to chief petty officers, and in some cases where trustworthy leading petty officers are filling organizational billets normally filled by chief petty officers, they *may* delegate authority to such petty officers.

Withholding of Privileges. Certain privileges may be withheld temporarily, and this act is sanctioned by paragraph 306(c)(2), *MCM,* 1984 (Rev.). This procedure may be used to correct infractions of military regulations or performance deficiencies of a minor nature where stronger action is not required. Examples of privileges which may be withheld are special liberty, exchange of duty, special pay, special command programs, movies, libraries, and off-ship events on base. The authority to use this procedure rests with the individual empowered to grant the privileges. Withholding of privileges of personnel in a liberty status is the prerogative of the commanding officer. This authority may be delegated, but it must not result in deprivation of liberty itself.

Additional Work Assignments. Article 142.2 is an important article and is usually the cause of most of the misunderstanding as to lawful or unlawful deprivation of liberty. It states that deprivation of liberty as punishment, except under *UCMJ,* is illegal, and therefore no officer or petty officer may deny liberty as a punishment for any offense or malperformance of duty. This is clear enough. The next part of the article then goes on to state that since it is necessary to the efficiency of the naval service that certain functions be performed and that certain work be accomplished in a timely manner, it is therefore not a punishment when certain men are required to remain on board and perform work assignments *that should have been completed,* for *ad-*

ditional essential work, or *to meet the currently required level of operational readiness.* This is the crux of the problem and is so recognized by the *SORN,* which then goes on to suggest that good leadership and management practices will cure any resultant problems. This means extending working hours for all hands or for certain selected persons *only when absolutely necessary.* When you do, or when your officers recommend that you do, you should make every effort to ensure that your crew understands the necessity for such action. If they understand it, they will carry it out readily and well; if not, you can expect some additional mail.

If these areas of questionable authority are clear in your mind, they will give you little trouble. If your officers understand the limits of *your* and *their* authority, they will perform more efficiently and with greater confidence, and your ship will benefit accordingly.

Assuming that you are prepared to evaluate and assign your officers to their proper billets when they arrive, and ready to supervise their use of their authority, it is now time to discuss their ordering and assignment.

Ordering and Assignment of Officers

Officer Distribution. The Commander, Naval Military Personnel Command, has the responsibility for assigning qualified officers to authorized billets. He has also the parallel responsibility of assigning each officer opportunities for the development of his professional and personal capabilities. The officer distribution system, in implementing these twin responsibilities, assigns officers according to the requirements of the service, the individuals' professional needs, their record and qualifications, and, where possible, their preference as to billet, ship type, and location.

The Officer Distribution System. The officer distribution system is organized under the Commander, Naval Military Personnel Command, as follows. A group of "placement officers" monitors ships and other organizations by types. Another group of officers monitors ranks. These officers are called "detailers." The placement officer posts his requirements for billets with the appropriate rank detailers, giving dates of expected rotation and qualifications. The rank detailer tries to fill the billet with an officer of appropriate rank and qualifications who is due to rotate at the proper time. The two officers then get together to work out details of orders to be issued. The placement officer usually informs the ship CO of the results, and the rank detailer contacts the officer to be ordered, giving advance notice.

The greatest help you can give the officer distribution system (other than patience and understanding) is to keep submitting up-to-date inputs for your Long-Range Officer Rotation, Training, and Readiness Plan (LORTARP). This document is used by the placement officer to monitor your present status and future needs. The most important entries on it are those indicating the billets for which each officer is in training and his qualifications to fill them. Back up your inputs with monthly phone calls.

Communications with Detailers. Encourage your officers to take care in submitting their preference cards. The detailer will generally follow their wishes if at all possible.

As commanding officer, your inputs to your officers' detailers can play a large part in retaining them in the Navy and furthering their professional development. For one thing, your involvement in the detailing process clearly displays your concern for your officers. It also tends to ameliorate the detailer-constituent disagreements that sometimes occur.

Career Patterns and Broadening

If you can do so without decreasing readiness, you should do all within your power to increase the professional competence of your officers by giving them opportunities to broaden their assignments and experience.

Career Patterns. Before you take any specific action, analyze the career patterns to date of each of your officers. Study their officer qualification jackets and past assignments and then call them in one by one and find out where each one thinks he or she is heading professionally. They may not know. If so, you will have to be a counselor. There are various books, documents, and directives bearing on the subject; unfortunately, they relate to the past, while you need to predict the future.

You will probably find that you know more about career counseling than anyone else aboard, simply by virtue of your experience. Read the directives concerning the subspecialist program. Read the latest letters of instruction (usually published in *Navy Times*) of the Secretary of the Navy to the presidents of the flag and other selection boards. These documents will indicate trends that will probably be valid for at least ten years. This information will be of value to your lieutenants. For your more junior officers, you and they will have to make educated guesses as to what experience and qualifications will be needed for promotion.

Importance of Command at Sea. Notwithstanding the pace of progress, there are certain essentials that will never change. Command at sea will always be vital for promotion to senior ranks. An officer may reach senior rank by other paths, but command at sea will always be the route for the majority of officers. Any officer aspiring to command at sea should begin by learning all she can about her command. This is best accomplished by serving in the three basic departments, operations, weapons, and engineering. In aviation squadrons, rotation will occur naturally, as it will in submarines.

Counseling. With these factors in mind, you can counsel your officers easily. You will not need to be an expert at this time about the details of the subspecialist program, for your officers will not have to face this until subsequent shore duty assignments. However, if you do have expertise, experience, or opinions in this area, it will be of help to your officers in making out their preference cards for future shore assignments.

Your most important role in their career advancement will be to assign them to as broad a span of billets as possible. Advise them to qualify in a second or third major departmental area. They may resist, since obviously they may perform less well in an unfamiliar billet. It will take a good officer with a long-range outlook to agree if he thinks he will have to accept lesser fitness report marks in exchange for a "broadening experience." You can help by promising to mark his fitness report indicating the efficiency of his performance considering his lack of previous qualification rather than his absolute performance.

Self-Improvement. Even though not assigned to a "broadening" billet, your officers can broaden themselves, especially with your encouragement. A selection board looks for these efforts, and you should make them more visible by including them in your fitness report remarks. More than one aviation captain has been selected as a carrier commanding officer because he took the trouble to qualify as an officer of the deck underway when serving in an embarked squadron. Give all of your officers a chance to handle your ship, including radical maneuvers.

With these comments concerning billet assignments in mind, let us now review the qualifications required to fill various billets. Since we are talking about all kinds and sizes of ships, you will find many positions described which do not apply to the ship you are commanding at the present time. We will discuss them by major departments.

The Executive Officer's Assistants

Chaplain. The chaplain is responsible for all religious activities, as well as such other appropriate duties as may be assigned to him. He may conduct worship according to the manner and form of his own church, but must do everything possible to provide for the other denominations, either by presiding himself, using lay leaders, or by arranging for visiting chaplains. He should make himself available for counsel on all matters and should be your liaison with the Navy Relief Society and the American Red Cross.

Command Career Counselor. The command career counselor is responsible for establishing a program to disseminate career information and furnish career counseling. Large ships may have an officer assigned full time to this billet. Others may assign an enlisted man. A limited duty officer with previous experience as a yeoman or personnelman is ideal. No matter who is assigned, he must be positively motivated, be thought of highly by the crew, and be a good administrator.

Drug and Alcohol Program Adviser. This officer's responsibility is to advise you on the establishment of a drug and alcohol abuse program, and then to establish and administer it.

Large ships may have a junior line officer assigned to this program full time. This is a line and not a medical function, although the medical department should be called upon for expertise and lecturing. Small ships will have to make this a collateral function. Junior officers from the Naval Academy, NROTC, and OCS will have had some grounding in this area, but may need further instruction if they are to do a satisfactory job.

Educational Services Officer. The educational services officer administers educational programs. He also acts as a member of the training board and assists the training officer. He may be assigned other duties in the educational and training area, and he usually administers examining boards and examinations.

Only very large ships can afford to fill this billet on a full-time basis. An officer from any source can be used, but he will require instruction.

Legal Officer. The legal officer is the staff assistant to the commanding officer and executive officer on all matters concerning the interpretation and application of *UCMJ* and other laws and regulations in the maintenance of discipline and the administration of justice. She should also make herself available to the personnel of the command for rendering legal advice.

On large ships a member of the Judge Advocate General's Corps is usually assigned to this billet. If one is not available, a graduate of the Military Justice School should be assigned, or a junior officer sent to this school prior to reporting.

On small ships the XO usually has to assume these responsibilities, unless the ship can spare an officer to attend school.

Personnel Officer. The personnel officer is responsible for the placement of enlisted personnel in accordance with the personnel assignment bill, and for the administration and custody of enlisted records. As with officer personnel, you will not receive enlisted personnel in the exact number of rates your ship's allowance calls for. Your personnel officer will have the same task you face with officers in fitting those personnel he actually receives into the listed billets.

On large ships a personnel officer is usually full time. On smaller ships a personnelman performs the job. You will be fortunate if you have a limited duty officer who was a personnelman.

Postal Officer. This officer supervises the postal functions of the command. It is an important billet in that accountability for postal funds is a sensitive matter. Obviously receipt of mail is important to the morale of your command. However, these duties cannot occupy an officer full time, and even on a large ship this duty is usually assigned collaterally. No particular schooling or qualification is required.

Public Affairs Officer. The PAO is charged with carrying out the public affairs program of the command. This billet is a sleeper and is more important than you may think when first considering it. As noted in the previous chapter, *you,* as commanding officer, are responsible for the public affairs program of your ship, and you cannot afford to delegate the function so completely that you lose control of it. You must employ the talents and capabilities of the PAO to the utmost, but she cannot assume your final responsibility, nor can the executive officer, under whom she nominally operates. It is important that you establish the fact that you are available to her at *all* times.

Large ships may have a full-time PAO, but small ships assign the duty collaterally.

Naval Academy graduates will have had a short course in public affairs and can fill the billet, but the important factor is that the officer should be able to write and speak well. Common sense and social ease are also important qualifications.

Safety Officer. On ships other than aircraft carriers, a safety officer is assigned the responsibility for the ship's safety program. He distributes safety information, maintains safety records, and carries out and monitors the safety program. On large ships other than aircraft carriers, this is usually a full-time billet. On small ships it is a collateral duty. In aircraft carriers and aircraft squadrons, it is a head-of-department billet. Any officer, preferably engineering-oriented, can be assigned.

Ship's Secretary. The ship's secretary is responsible for the administration of ship's correspondence and directives, for the administration and custody of officer personnel records, for the preparation of the commanding officer's personal correspondence, for the supervision of preparation of officers' fitness reports, and for the ship's nonclassified reference library.

In large ships the ship's secretary is an officer assigned full time. On small ships a rated yeoman performs the job. An outstanding junior officer is usually assigned as ship's secretary. No specific qualifications are necessary, though the ability to handle English well is desirable.

Special Services Officer. The special services officer carries out the ship's special services program. This includes athletics, recreational programs, and entertainment. He is the custodian of the recreation fund and all special services equipment. Large ships have a full-time special services officer. Others assign it as a collateral duty. No special qualifications are required, but an ex-athlete usually gets the job.

Training Officer. The training officer is an adviser and assistant to the executive officer for training matters. He is a member of the training planning board, and prepares and monitors training plans and schedules.

On large ships a senior officer is assigned to this billet. On small ships the executive officer may assume it and assign a junior officer as her assistant, or assign it as a collateral duty.

3-M Coordinator. This officer is responsible for administering the ship's Maintenance and Material Management system. On large ships a fairly senior officer will be assigned to this billet. On small ships a junior officer or senior enlisted man will be assigned, usually full time. Whoever is assigned, he should have completed formal schooling in administration and operation of the shipboard 3-M system or have had appropriate Personnel Qualification Standards (PQS) qualification in the 3-M system.

Security Manager. The security manager is responsible for all matters concerning security of classified information. She prepares destruction bills, security procedures, clearance requests, and declassification plans. No specific qualification is required.

Collateral Duties. There are several other duties assigned as collateral duties to officers and sometimes to leading petty officers:

Athletics officer
Communications security material custodian
Crypto security officer
Library officer
Mess caterer
Mess treasurer
Movie officer
Naval warfare publications control officer
Nuclear handling supervisor
Nuclear safety officer
Photographic officer
Radiation health officer
Recreation fund custodian
Secret control officer
Security officer
Senior watch officer
Top secret control officer

Officers of the Operations Department

In addition to carrying out the duties of a head of department, the operations officer is responsible for the collection, evaluation, and dissemination of the combat and operational information required by the missions of the ship. This includes air, surface, and sub-surface search; control of aircraft; collection, display, analysis, and dissemination of intelligence; preparation of operating plans and schedules; meteorological information; and repair of electronics equipment.

The operations officer on all ships is a relatively senior officer and should be well qualified both by previous duties and by having completed as many applicable schools as possible. You will be assigned a qualified or nearly qualified officer of appropriate rank to fill this billet, unless your roster shows a person now assigned to you who is about to be declared qualified.

The following officers generally report to the operations officer (on large ships they may, where indicated, be separate department heads). On small ships, unless indicated otherwise, they will be part of the operations department.

Administration and training assistant
Air intelligence officer (supplied by the appropriate type commander)
Carrier air traffic control officer (supplied by the appropriate type commander)
Combat information center (CIC) officer
Communications officer (when not a department head)
Computer programmer
Cryptologic officer (on those ships which have a special intelligence capability)
Electronics warfare (EW) officer
First lieutenant (when the ship has a combat systems department but not a deck department)
Intelligence officer
Meteorological officer
Photographic officer

You will do well to review the responsibilities and duties of your operations officer, and his relations with you. He will be close to you many hours of the day.

Officers of the Navigation Department

The navigator is the head of the navigation department and is responsible under the commanding officer for the safe navigation and piloting of the ship. The custom of ordering officers by name as navigator of ships is no longer followed. The CO may choose his or her own navigator, but he should be a senior and well-qualified officer, preferably senior to all watch and division officers. In small ships this is not always possible.

The assistant navigator, if assigned, reports to the navigator. The engineering officer reports to the navigator concerning steering matters.

The navigator's relationship with the commanding officer is, like that of the executive officer, close. For this reason, you should select as navigator an officer whom you trust personally, one who will tell you promptly and honestly when he doesn't know where the ship is, one who will make accurate and frank recommendations.

Require him to check all chart corrections entered by the quartermasters, and to keep clean and neat navigation workbooks and bearing books. These are official and important records, and if they are ever needed at an investigation, their neatness and correctness will pay dividends. He should in turn require the watch officers to write proper logs.

Officers of the Communications Department

In ships with a communications department, the communications officer acts as its head. He is responsible for visual and electronic exterior communications systems and the administration of the interior systems supporting them.

Assistants to the communications officer include the radio officer, the signal officer, the custodian of CMS distributed material, the crypto-security officer, and the communication watch officers.

You will have to train your own communications officer. You will be fortunate if you have an officer of appropriate rank with some communications experience.

Communications, like navigation, is very much a part of your everyday affairs. You should make every effort to master it. It is just as important in port as underway. The success of all your efforts depends upon knowing *what* your ship is to do and *when* it is to do it; thus, you can succeed only if communications with your seniors are fast and reliable. There is nothing that makes an officer in tactical command (OTC) unhappier than a ship with bumbling communications. You may have the best ship in the unit, but if the OTC can't get the word to you, you are useless to him.

Efficient communications can be achieved. Success starts with knowing your equipment. Both you and your communications officer should know the location, characteristics, capabilities, and limitations of every transmitter, receiver, and transceiver on your ship. Know the effective range, frequency range, power, tuning capabilities, and frequency-shifting speeds of your equipment. Send for the manuals and study them. Ask questions. You will find out what your subordinates know about the equipment and what they *don't* know. Require frequent and accurate tuning and the use of the most efficient internal transmission and switching setups. If you display such interest and knowledge, your communications officer will try to equal or excel you, and your enlisted personnel will love it. When you go to a presail conference for an exercise or deployment, be prepared to make sensible and informed decisions about the communications plan to be used. If you know your equipment, you won't be trapped into agreeing to guard more circuits than you have equipment or watchstanders, which is always embarrassing.

When your equipment is working at maximum efficiency you can turn your attention to other matters. The "word" is no good if it arrives on your ship and you never hear it. Consequently, you must ensure that the communications department has a rapid and accurate system of writing up incoming messages, routing them, and filing them for future use. The same is true for the outgoing system. Good drafting is a matter of knowledge ingrained by habit. Make sure your messages are concise, clear, and free from "overkill." Obviously precedence, classification, and need-to-send-at-all should be considered.

Have your communications officer read the fleet broadcast schedule. Sometimes the best watch can miss a call decode.

A ship's most obvious interfaces with higher authorities (and other ships) are its voice radio circuits and its visual communications. Visual communications are relatively easy to set in order. Sharp lookouts for incoming calls, willingness to relay, and prompt to-blocking of flag hoists all contribute to your ship's reputation. The more difficult task is to excel at voice communications. This is the one most critical indication of the success of your communications department, and even of the overall competence of your ship. *You and your communications officer must work at it continuously.* We have already emphasized the careful and frequent tuning of your equipment. Next, be sure you, as commanding officer, know and observe circuit discipline, proper procedure, correct vocabulary, and authentication and numeral coding procedures. If you demonstrate expertise and concern, your watch officers and enlisted operators will try to rise to your level. Insist on clear diction, prompt responses, correct phraseology, confident tones of voice, and avoidance of slang or redundancy. Monitor your ship's air control circuits from time to time; they are the most frequent sources of violations.

In essence, after safe navigation, communications is probably the most important area for your personal concern. The communications officer and other officers of this department should be carefully chosen and schooled.

Officers of the Combat Systems Department

Ships having a combat systems department will have a combat systems officer serving as its head. He will be responsible for the supervision and direction of the ship's combat systems, including ordnance equipment. Under the combat systems officer, if assigned, are the following assistants:

ASW officer
Department administrative assistant
Electronics material officer
Fire control officer
Ordnance officer or gunnery officer
Strike officer
System test officer
Weapons officer

Most of these officers will be partially qualified. Ask your detailer to order them to additional schools en route, or send them yourself at the next opportunity.

Officers of the Air Department

On ships with an air department, the air officer is assigned as its head. He is responsible for the supervision and direction of launching and landing operations and for the servicing and handling of aircraft. He is also responsible for salvage, fire fighting, aviation fuels, aviation lubricants, and safety precautions.

He will not be ordered to the billet by name, but there will be only one such qualified officer sent to your ship.

His assistants will include the assistant air officer, the catapult officer, the arresting gear officer, the aviation fuels officer, and the training assistant (air). Most of these officers will be qualified by schooling or previous experience before their arrival aboard.

In ships without air departments, where a Navy helicopter detachment is embarked, an aviation department should be organized with an aviation officer as its head. He should have under him a qualified helicopter control officer.

Officers of the Embarked Air Wing

The air wing commander of an embarked squadron has the status of a department head. He is responsible for the tactical training and indoctrination of the air wing and for the coordination and supervision of its various squadrons and detachments.

He will be ordered to this billet by name.

Officers of the Deck Department

In ships with a deck department, the first lieutenant will be the department head. He is responsible for the supervision and direction of the employment of the equipment associated with deck seamanship and, in ships not having a weapons or combat systems department, of the ordnance equipment.

He will not be ordered by name. Most likely, there will be a senior officer ordered to your ship with previous experience in your type whom you can assign.

The following are his assistants, if billets exist: combat systems or gunnery officer, cargo officer, ship's boatswain, and boat group commander.

Officers of the Repair Department

In ships with a repair department, the repair officer will be its head. He is responsible for the accomplishment of repairs and alterations in those ships and aircraft assigned to the repair ship.

Although not ordered by name, there will be an officer on your ship whose experience will indicate he is meant to be your repair officer.

The repair officer will have as assistants the assistant repair officer, the electrical assistant, the hull assistant, and the machinery assistant, as well as other assistants, depending upon the class of repair ship or tender.

Officers of the Engineering Department

The engineering officer heads the engineering department. He is responsible for the operation, care, and maintenance of all propulsion and auxiliary machinery, the control of damage, and, upon request of the head of department concerned, those repairs beyond the capacity of other departments.

The chief engineer is a very important officer in your organization. He will have great influence over the other officers in his department in building their approach toward good engineering practices and procedures. In small ships this influence is at a maximum, since the officers under him usually will have had no other exposure to engineering. Other officers not in his department will also be influenced. You should do everything possible to encourage officers in other departments to learn all they can about engineering. Have your executive officer and chief engineer set up tours of the plant, lectures, and opportunities to examine machinery when open for inspection or overhaul. In small ships, and even in large ones, officers who really want to broaden themselves can do so by volunteering to stand instruction watches in engineering spaces, taking qualifying courses, and otherwise trying to qualify for engineering. Make notes in the fitness reports of such officers, including their attitudes, accomplishments, and status of qualification. It will help them later. Such entries have been significant in selection for promotion in the past.

Keep abreast of proceedings in the engineering department through your engineering officer. An engineering night order book is not required by higher authority, but you will do well to require one yourself and approve it personally. *Engineering Administration* has samples of engineering night orders. This is a sound practice from an administrative point of view, and provides for continuity of control in the absence of the engineering officer. Having such a night order book is also a help in indoctrinating young officers in proper engineering procedures.

The advent of nuclear power has required many changes in ship organization. If a nuclear-powered warship does not have a separate reactor department, the chief engineer will be detailed as the reactor officer. Under this arrangement, the duties of the reactor and mechanical assistants devolve upon the main propulsion assistant, and an additional billet for reactor control officer is provided. The *SSORM* for SSN/SSBNs amplifies this organization.

The following are assistants to the engineering officer, where billets are assigned: main propulsion assistant, reactor control assistant, damage control assistant, electrical officer, and other assistants as provided in nuclear-powered ships.

Submarine Ship's Diving Officer. In submarines a ship's diving officer is assigned under provisions of the *SSORM*. This function may be a collateral duty handled by the chief engineer personally, or by his damage control assistant, if so qualified.

The diving officer is listed here with officers of the engineering department, but he is not a part of that department. He reports directly to you in matters concerning the safe submerged operations of the ship, and to the XO concerning the administration and training of personnel. He keeps the engineering officer informed of technical matters concerning submerged operation, but is not otherwise under his control.

Officers of the Reactor Department

In ships with a reactor department, the reactor officer is the head of the department. He will be ordered by name, and will be senior to all engineering watch officers and engineering and reactor division officers. He will be responsible for the operation, care, maintenance, and safety of the reactor plants and their auxiliaries. He will receive all orders concerning these responsibilities directly from you and will make all corresponding reports directly to you. He reports to you for reactor matters and acts as your technical assistant. He reports to the XO for administrative matters.

The special nature of a nuclear plant requires that the reactor officer and the engineer officer cooperate very closely. The reactor officer and his assistants are responsible for some duties (as prescribed by their specific duties) normally prescribed for the engineer officer and his assistants on non-nuclear-powered ships not having separate departments.

Assistants to the reactor officer are the reactor control assistant, the reactor mechanical assistant, and the reactor watch officers. The reactor officer and his principal assistants will be qualified before arrival aboard.

The reactor officer will be ordered by name to that billet. Specific responsibilities of the reactor control assistant and the reactor mechanical assistant are described in the *SORN*, Article 325.

Officers of the Research and Deep Submergence Departments

In ships having research as their mission, a research officer is assigned as head of department and carries out responsibilities regarding research. In ships having deep submergence as their mission, a deep submergence officer serves as head of department and carries out appropriate responsibilities.

Officers of the Supply Department

In ships having a supply department, its head is designated as the supply officer. He is responsible for procuring, receiving, storing, issuing, transferring, selling, accounting for, and, while in his custody, maintaining all stores and equipment of the unit.

On large ships and most medium-sized ships an officer of the Supply Corps is ordered as supply officer. On very small ships the CO must designate a line officer as supply officer. The supply officer of a large ship will have as assistants a commissary officer and a disbursing officer.

Officers of the Medical and Dental Departments

Medical Officer. The senior medical officer is the head of the medical department. He is responsible for maintaining the health of all personnel, making appropriate inspections, and advising the commanding officer on hygiene and sanitation.

Almost all large ships will have a medical officer ordered. Smaller ships without them will have a hospital corpsman qualified for independent duty, who will function under the executive officer.

First aid instruction is an important duty of medical officers. In battle, damage control requirements for closed doors and restricted access will result in many isolated areas. Prompt first aid until the wounded can be moved to battle dressing stations can save many lives.

Dental Officer. The dental officer is the head of the dental department. He is responsible for preventing and controlling dental disease and for supervising dental hygiene.

Small ships without a dental officer have their dental affairs overseen by the leading hospitalman, who arranges periodic dental checkups and other care at nearby facilities.

Department Heads

The duties of officers assigned as heads of departments in various ship organizations have been outlined in previous pages. Those who are so designated have certain other duties by virtue of that designation.

As stated before, heads of departments may confer directly with you concerning matters within their department if they believe such action to be necessary for the good of their department or the naval service. This right should be used carefully, and in any event the executive officer should be brought up to date as soon as possible.

The head of department is responsible for organizing and training his department for battle, preparing and writing bills and orders for his department, and for assigning and administering all of its personnel.

A detailed description of all his responsibilities and duties is contained in the *SORN*.

The head of department on a large ship may have an assistant department head and an administrative assistant. On almost all ships he will have a department training officer and division officers.

Division Officers

Division officers are assigned to major groups of personnel within each ship's organization. They train, supervise, and administer all personnel assigned to their division, and are responsible for their total performance. They assign division personnel to watches, battle bills, other bills, and nonrecurring assignments. Their detailed responsibilities are outlined in the *SORN,* Article 350. Division officers usually have other duties assigned collaterally, and have assignments in the battle and other bills.

Division officer billets are filled by junior officers ordered to you without specific qualifications. If you want them to be schooled, you will have to make arrangements with the placement officer for them to be ordered to specific schools en route. Alternately, you may send them on temporary additional duty at first opportunity after they have reported, when you can spare them.

Division officers are your direct contact with the enlisted personnel of your command. Time spent in observing, training, and encouraging them, done in concert, of course, with their department head, will be time well spent.

The detailed duties of the division officer are outlined in the *SORN.* The *Division Officer's Guide,* published by Naval Institute Press, is a bookshelf must for all division officers. It merits your reading also. It translates the cold listing of duties into chapters and paragraphs that tell the division officer *how* to carry them out.

Watchstanding

The preceding paragraphs have set forth the duties of officers with regard to specific billet assignments and the administering organization. However, your ship won't move far or accomplish much without a watch organization.

Senior Watch Officer. A watch organization begins with a senior watch officer. The senior watch officer, under the XO, is responsible for the assignment and general supervision of all deck watch officers and enlisted watchstanders in port and underway. He maintains records concerning the qualifications of all deck watchstanders, coordinates their training, and prepares appropriate bills.

Deck Watchstanding. The *Watch Officer's Guide,* published by Naval Institute Press, is a good source of information on deck watchstanding. It covers the deck watch in general, log writing, shiphandling, rules of the road, and other safety at sea problems. It also covers the duties of the OOD in port.

CIC Watchstanding. The duties, responsibilities, and requirements of the CIC watch officer and his subordinates are set forth in *The Ops Officer's Manual,* also published by Naval Institute Press. CIC is a vital part of a ship's operations. You should delve deeply into the details of CIC and its watches. Familiarity will pay dividends.

Engineering Watch. The chief engineer is responsible to you for preparing and administering the engineering watch bill and for qualifying all watchstanders. Ensure that he is strict in his qualifying procedures and that he maintains adequate records of those qualified.

Cooperation between your OODs and your engineer officers of the watch is essential. In order to be sure that your OODs understand the problems below decks, insist that they be familiar with *Engineering for the Officer of the Deck,* published by Naval Institute Press. This publication describes, in easily readable form, "what happens below" and why.

Communications Watch. As stated above, you should keep a close eye on your communications watch. *With* a good one, you will be informed rapidly of the requirements of your superiors, and can make correspondingly rapid responses and reports. You will live a satisfying and relaxed life. *Without* one, you will run scared, never sure you're up to speed. Work with your communications officer, his coding board, his communications watch officers, and your signal officer and his gang. It will pay dividends.

Leadership Training

After your officers are placed in their proper billets, qualified and trained for their primary responsibilities, and integrated into a viable watch bill, your ship should be properly officered.

It is time now to turn to improving your officers as individuals. This starts with leadership training. You, as commanding officer, must lead in this effort. You can get help from your XO and your heads of departments in organizing and carrying out a leadership training program, but you need to spark this effort with your own personal interest and drive. Even if you are blessed with these personal qualities, you will need external help. There are many fine texts that you can use. One good one in *Naval Leadership,* compiled by a group of officers at the Naval Academy and published by Naval Institute Press.

The discussion of leadership training for officers falls into six easily identifiable categories: personal characteristics, moral leadership, personal relations with seniors, personal relations with juniors, techniques of counseling and communication, and the role of the officer in training. Let us examine each of these aspects of leadership in more detail.

Personal Characteristics. First, an officer must *want* to be a naval officer. A person who doesn't want to go to sea, command, fight, and lead ought to seek another profession. This does not mean being overly aggressive personally. Some of our greatest naval officers have been quiet individuals who preferred peaceful solutions if possible, but who fought hard and aggressively when necessary.

Moral Leadership. Moral leadership has always been important in our navy. Americans have long felt that the first essential for a leader is self-confidence, a strong moral position, and a sense of self-worth. In this area "moral" means what is *right,* considering integrity, sense of duty, and obligation to one's country. Flowing from a sense of self-worth is the attribution of equal worth to others. Any person with this attitude cannot be bigoted, partial, or unfair toward other people. Integrity and honesty are paramount.

Personal Relations with Seniors. No officer can be an effective leader if he cannot first be a good follower. Simply put, this means being loyal to seniors, but not blindly loyal. Encourage your juniors to question in their own minds your decisions and the decisions of all seniors. They need not be outspoken about their disagreement, or contentious, or overly aggressive. In most cases only the mental process needs to be followed and no expression of it is necessary. In those cases where there is definite disagreement, juniors are duty bound to express their honest opinion to their seniors. Explain carefully to your officers the classic procedure of military dissent: if one disagrees with an order or decision of a senior, one should say so, privately if possible, but promptly, frankly, and fully. Once the decision is explained or reaffirmed, one must, then, immediately and loyally proceed to carry it out. If you find young officers who are inept in their relations with seniors, counsel, instruct, and correct them.

Personal Relations with Juniors. Once a junior officer learns to follow, he is ready to learn to lead. His own personal characteristics are the basis of this ability. He must also learn to communicate, for no one can know what his leader wants him to do if he does not receive a lucid and correct order. Communication means the ability to speak (and write) clearly, logically, plainly, and promptly. It means giving orders impersonally, yet leaving no doubt that they are to be obeyed. It means talking before small and large groups, both extemporaneously or from a prepared text, using proper, simple language, free from slang, idiom, and obscenity.

Other characteristics will help a senior lead well. A senior must learn not to be tolerant of small deficiencies, but to correct them patiently and in a low key, and not to accept large deficiencies at all. He must plan ahead to ensure that his juniors do not do useless work that foresight could have avoided. He should know all of his sailors, but should avoid using first names, nicknames, or taking other familiarities. He must be considerate, fair, and tactful, but still firm and exacting. Above all, if he knows his job, his machinery and equipment and tactics, he will be respected by his juniors and they will probably forgive or tolerate any deficiencies.

Technique of Counseling. A leader must gain the confidence of his subordinates to be able to counsel them. This means finding out as much as possible about their families and relationships in order to analyze their problems and provide help. He can begin this by examining their service records. After this grounding, discreet questioning can add to knowledge without invading privacy. If each division officer has a basic knowledge of the record and personal situation of each sailor, he will recognize when someone appears to be troubled, and will be able to help with problems beyond his capability to handle alone. The Navy Relief Society, the American Red Cross, and various legal aid societies can be called upon for assistance. After learning as much as he can about his subordinates, an officer will find, however, that most problems can be solved by cultivating the art of listening and by learning to analyze character.

The Role of the Officer in Training. Most of an officer's career is spent in training. No sooner is a sailor, a gun crew, or a CIC team trained adequately than ends of enlistments, transfers, or illnesses start the training cycle all over again. An officer must recognize that training is both never-ending and important. Sailors must first be trained to fill the ship's billets. Next they must learn the administrative duties of their rates, and then they must know the duties of their battle stations, emergency and other bills, and their watchstanding duties. In addition, they must be trained for advancement in rating and to further their general education.

For the officer this means formulating a plan, procuring manuals, training aids, course books, and other materials, and then preparing lectures, on-the-job training sessions, discussions, and examinations. This is an endless task, but a satisfying one if done well. Make sure your officers do it well, and encourage them by your example.

Other Characteristics. There are many other necessary personal characteristics of a leader than those we have discussed above, including loyalty to country, command, and associates, both senior and junior; courage, both physical and moral; honesty; sense of humor; modesty of mind and demeanor; self-confidence; common sense;

judgment; enthusiasm and a cheerful demeanor; tact; self-control; and consideration of others. You can't teach these qualities, nor any of the others; but you can recognize them, provide an example of them, encourage them, and provide a climate in which they can flourish.

Professional Competence

In the context we are using it in, professional competence starts with general education and includes qualifications to fill billets, other technical qualifications (such as air controller), watchstanding qualifications, and general professional capabilities.

When officers report for duty their general education may be well advanced, but it is *never* completed. Officers should be encouraged to take university extension courses, to read in disciplines other than their educational majors, to read widely in the liberal arts, and to prepare for future postgraduate formal education. You can help by encouraging them and by making time available.

All officers must be required to master their billets. This can be done by reading manuals and publications, taking on- and off-ship qualification courses, asking questions, and receiving instruction from seniors. When their services can be spared, officers should be sent to shore-based schools to increase their knowledge and prepare them for more important and demanding billets.

Cross-training should be accomplished whenever the ship can afford it. In most cases junior officers can be rotated without impairing the efficiency of the ship too much. Where this cannot be done, encourage your officers to complete courses of instruction in other departments, to stand qualification watches, and to examine equipment and machinery when it is opened for overhaul or repairs. Follow up with entries in fitness reports to reflect the initiative of the officers and the status of their progress.

Qualification in such specialties as air control, catapult operation, and other areas not primary duties should be encouraged. When possible, officers should be sent to school in excess of the numbers you require. This gives you flexibility in future assignments and broadens the professional competence of the officers involved.

In a very real sense, a ship's wardroom is an extended family.

Watchstanding should be made to seem a privilege rather than an onerous chore. To do so you will have to set the tone. Good watch-standers should receive your approbation in public and your private acknowledgment in the form of good fitness report entries. Encourage junior officers to qualify in other areas, such as deck watch-standers qualifying in engineering, and vice versa. This broadens professional competence.

Finally, encourage your officers to prepare for eventual attendance at war college by taking correspondence courses in strategy and tactics, and in other useful subjects such as naval justice.

Your involvement, example, and encouragement will help your officers to enlarge their areas of professional competence. If you find officers who are not interested in doing so, counsel them, for otherwise they have little future in the Navy.

This fine-looking wardroom is the first requirement for a satisfactory onboard social life for the officers of this ship, but to make it a home will require the courtesy, hospitality, and friendliness of all the members of the mess.

Social Customs

As commanding officer, you also have the responsibility of guiding the social development and conduct of your officers, and by example and advice of influencing the involvement of their spouses.

The first essential of social presence of an officer is that of being considerate of others. This single, simple quality is the basis for correct social usage. With this quality in hand, the mechanics of proper social behavior can be learned; they are not difficult.

General Social Conduct. *Naval Ceremonies, Customs, and Traditions,* published by Naval Institute Press, covers the general conduct expected of officers in the wardroom, ashore, and in the messes of other navies. Some of the history behind these customs is included, and the explanations of their origin help the young officer to understand them.

Social Usage and Protocol, OPNAVINST 1710.7, is the Navy's official and very adequate guide for invitations, seating, dining, receptions, calls, ceremonies, and almost any social event which would involve your ship or any of your officers. Any officer, armed with a sense of consideration for others, and having reviewed the contents of these two publications, can move in any social circle in the world with confidence and success.

Wardroom. Your wardroom (and other messes on a larger ship) is the center of social usage for your ship and should receive your personal attention. If you command a large ship and have your own mess, you will have to depend on your XO to set the tone of the wardroom mess. Correct social usage begins here. Make sure it is clean, well run, correct in all respects but not stuffy, and that it is a place where your officers will be proud to bring their guests.

Help the wardroom to extend its social presence ashore by making it easy to have wardroom-sponsored social affairs.

The subject of social calls and visits is fully covered in *Naval Ceremonies, Customs, and Traditions.*

The Captain's Role with the Wardroom

As commanding officer of a ship or submarine, or as skipper of an aircraft squadron, you have several important roles you must execute with regard to your wardroom or ready room. First, you are the leading planner, tactician, and mariner/airman of your command. Take every opportunity to share your experience and knowledge. This can be done formally through classroom sessions and discussions; during extended planning sessions and briefings for upcoming events; and, most effectively, "on the deckplates" during the execution of actual operations. Step up to the plate! Your team expects to see you take the lead and orchestrate events running the gamut from a simple anchoring to a complex anti-air warfare exercise.

Second, you are the "voice of experience" in terms of the career patterns of your officers. Shortly after taking command, you should have a detailed conversation with each of your officers concerning his or her goals, aspirations, and current level of qualification. Work out with them a career plan, and try to provide a focused set of alternatives that covers the next five years. Find out what your officers want to do, and try to guide them into the kind of assignments that will be best for both them and the Navy.

Third, when it comes time for them to shift assignments within the command, you should work with the exec, the appropriate department heads, and the officers themselves to make sure they move to good new jobs. For example, you may want to shift your younger DOs between engineering and combat systems/operations jobs. In an aircraft squadron, you must orchestrate the movement among your department heads.

Lastly, when your officers approach the end of their tour with your command, you must work with both them and BUPERS to find them the right job. This is not always the job they want, and you must help your officers understand that any new assignment is a balance between the needs of the Navy and the desires of the individual. But you should always work hard on behalf of your officers, calling the detailers if you believe it warranted to try and adjust assignments to best balance the requirements of the situation.

As a flip side to working for your current officers, you must also work with the bureau (this time with the placement side instead of the detailers) to ensure that you get the right kind of officers assigned to your command. This does *not* mean you should attempt to manipulate the system to obtain a handpicked group of officers. Rather, you should work with the placement officer to make sure the bureau understands the unique needs of your command, the implication of your particular schedule, where your command is in the training cycle, and the many other variables that go into assignment of officers to your ship, submarine, or squadron.

Fitness Reports

There is no magic answer here. Writing good, accurate FITREPs is challenging; and above all, making decisions that rank your officers is hard work. Start by reviewing the well-written FITREP instructions before you work on individual fitness reports. Require your XO to carefully review the entire package of drafts by your department heads. Make sure no one in your command is ever asked to "write up his or her own FITREP," but make sure that the officer about whom the report is being written has the opportunity to provide comprehensive inputs to the process.

When it comes to ranking, there is no easy answer. The bottom line is that you, as commanding officer, must make the tough calls. You should make those calls on the basis of performance, long-term potential for naval service, and the specific qualities described in the FITREP itself: professional expertise, equal opportunity, military bearing/character, teamwork, mission accomplishment/initiative, leadership, and tactical performance. Avoid a system that is based on seniority, length of time in the command, or any other artificial discriminator. And it goes without saying that personal favoritism has no place in a fair system of evaluation. In the end, you must remember that you were placed in command because of your judgment, fairness, and balance. Rely on those traits and make the best call you can on ranking. Don't ever try and rig the system.

When you are relatively new in command, you may want to discuss in general terms the subjects of FITREPs, rankings, and wording with your immediate superior or other COs "on the waterfront or flight line" who have been around a little longer. They can give you a steer on any particular nuances in your community. But don't over rely on any one individual's opinion or view—except your own, Captain.

Conclusion

As Secretary of the Navy Sean O'Keefe correctly said in 1992, what matters in the end is what your officers carry in their hearts. As their captain, you will have the opportunity to influence every aspect of their lives during their assignment to your command. You will be an endless source of information, inspiration, and leadership to each of the young men and women with whom you serve. It is the highest responsibility you will execute in command, and you should cherish it.

Be honest, friendly, and interested in your wardroom—from the seasoned executive officer who should be your closest counselor to the most junior ensign who spends most of each day learning his or her new trade. Take care of them. Help them. Correct them when you must, praise them whenever you can. Above all, Captain, listen to *your* heart in all of your dealings with your officers—it will not fail you.

5

Master Chief of the Command, Chief Petty Officers, and Crew

Men mean more than guns in the rating of a ship.

—Captain John Paul Jones

Leading the Crew

It is really very simple. Your job as commanding officer will be to instill pride and professionalism in each and every crew member. Success in this endeavor will depend in large measure on the personal attributes you bring to command and the degree to which you give your subordinates responsibility and require that they perform. You must ensure that the entire crew—from the command master chief to the newest seaman recruit—seeks success, that they desire to be part of a winning team. No sailor in the Navy would leave a demanding winning command to serve in a permissive loser. Remember: your crew will perform and serve at the level you demand.

The command atmosphere you set will determine the nature of your crew's efforts. Integrity, especially, is a quality which you must demonstrate. The crew has opportunities each day to measure it, and they will set their standards by those you show in your own behavior. Your impartiality, a component of integrity, is a necessity in building a good crew. The old expression "a taut ship is a happy ship" is true largely because in such a ship there is impartiality of treatment, fairness, and thus justice; crew members know where they stand and what is expected of them.

Another factor involving command integrity is loyalty. The commanding officer has every right to expect the crew to be loyal to the ship—and to the CO personally because he represents the ship. Loyalty, however, must be worked for; it does not come automatically. Along with being solicitous of the well-being of his officers and crew, the captain inspires their loyalty by exhibiting his own, not in words, but in deeds. As commanding officer they expect him to be loyal to the chain of command, to "make the best of what you have," as Admiral King phrased it in his famous *Order to the Atlantic Fleet* of 24 March 1941. When—as sometimes happens—the "best you have" is not good enough for readiness, or where the process of achieving readiness works real hardship on your sailors, you must do what you can to alleviate their problems while making suggestions for bettering the situation up the chain of command.

A crew considers a captain loyal to them when he stands up for them. Sailors who brag about their ship are beyond price, but they do not come to think of their ship as a "good ship" simply by being told it. Integrity, impartiality, and loyalty of command bind the captain, wardroom, and the crew into an effective fighting unit.

The Command Master Chief

Function. The command master chief, or chief of the boat on submarines, is the principal enlisted adviser to the commanding officer. He keeps the CO aware of existing or potential situations, procedures, and practices that affect the welfare, morale, job satisfaction, and effective employment of crew members. The CMC reports directly to the commanding officer.

Duties, Responsibilities, and Authority. The command master chief will take precedence over all other members of equal or subordinate pay grades within the command during the tenure of his assignment. The *SORN* assigns the CMC the following duties and responsibilities:

To act at all times to maintain and promote the effectiveness of the chain of command.

To advise the commanding officer in the formulation of and changes in policy pertaining to enlisted members.

To ensure that established policies are adequately explained, understood, and carried out, by inspiring subordinates to develop and use basic leadership principles, and to encourage other enlisted members to maintain the highest standards of conduct and appearance through effective middle management.

To routinely attend department head staff meetings, and, when invited, participate in wardroom discussions in order to promote communications between the officer and enlisted communities.

To assist in the preparation for, and participate in, ceremonies concerning enlisted members.

When appropriate, to represent or accompany the commanding officer at official functions, inspections, and conferences.

To participate in the reception and hosting of official enlisted visitors to the command.

Upon invitation, to represent the command and the Navy by participating in community and civic functions.

To act as a member of, or function in close coordination with, the following boards, committees, and other groups:

Command Retention Team
Career Counselor
Quality Control and Retention Board
Awards Board
Striker Board
Sailor of the Quarter Board
Human Relations Council
Enlisted Advisory Council
Welfare and Recreation Committee
Commissary, Navy Exchange, and Berthing Advisory Boards
CPO, PO, and All Hands Club Advisory Boards
Navy Wives' Club and Ombudsman

Importance of the Command Master Chief. To a large degree, the morale of your crew and therefore the success of your command will depend on the effectiveness of the CMC. As the *key* link between you and the crew, he expedites the execution of command policy and advises you when that policy requires redirection. If he doesn't carry out these important functions, command communication will be slowed, resulting in a ship less able to fulfill its assigned missions. He does *not,* however, take the place of the normal command system; he assists its functioning, as we will point out later.

A good command master chief will make it his responsibility to know what is going on in the command. On smaller ships he should be aware of all personnel problems and should ensure that proper action is being taken to correct them. For example, if your drug abuse program fails to the point that the ship experiences a major "drug bust," you should consider carefully the effectiveness of your CMC. It is his responsibility to sense and ferret out those indicators which normally precede such personnel problems.

Your relationship with the CMC must be one of total openness and frankness. It does little good for morale for him to become a "yes man" and a "rubber stamp" for all command policy. Yet, when policy is set he must support it thoroughly and ensure that his subordinates do so as well. He must carefully consider the comments of the crew regarding policy and forward them up to you when appropriate.

Command Master Chief and the Chain of Command. The command master chief position was created to strengthen the chain of command, *not* to replace it! As CO, you must therefore ensure that the role is used as a command strengthening mechanism. It is not a vehicle for bypassing the chain of command with petty gripes and complaints. You must ensure that all hands understand the CMC's role as that of principal enlisted adviser to the commanding officer.

Chief Petty Officers

The Navy chief petty officer continues to occupy a position of general respect unmatched by comparable ratings in the other services. This distinction is fundamental to the way our ships operate at sea. It is your business to recognize the importance of the chiefs, to protect and enhance their prestige, and to use all your authority to ensure that their ranks include only well-qualified officers.

The importance of the CPO has never been greater than today. Under the division officer, he is responsible for young, inexperienced personnel who must operate equipment of increasing complexity. The pivotal point of the chain of command is the individual chief. He must be made a *participating* member of your chain of command. He must clearly understand his authority as well as his responsibilities to you.

You should quickly put to rest any chief's concern regarding authority. This concern often appears as complaints about the "diminishing authority" of senior POs. For example, a brainstorming session between the chief petty officers of a frigate and their commanding officer resulted in a list of those *authority* areas in which they considered their present involvement inadequate. It covered three typewritten pages. Among them were:

Scheduling of maintenance activity for their divisions
Assignment of enlisted evaluation grades
Issuance of EMI
Scheduling of divisional training
Preparation and approval of personnel for advancement in rate
Use of the nonjudicial punishment system
Award recommendations
Supervision of maintenance
Supervision of cleanliness and preservation
Senior supervisory watchstanding

At the end of the meeting, after the CO had made it clear that they would participate more fully in these activities in the future, he stated, "Now you all know more regarding your *authority*. It is *your responsibility* to see that each item is carried out to the best of your ability. It is *my responsibility* to see that you do."

Retention

Command Retention Team. Retention will be one of your prime responsibilities in command. The retention team concept was initiated to foster a career "satisfaction environment" within all commands and to develop a means of strengthening policy and programs designed to increase retention. The command retention team on each ship is organized as follows:

Commanding officer. Serves as the senior career counselor aboard.

Executive officer. Serves as retention team coordinator.

Command career counselor. Works directly for the commanding officer, serving as his principal adviser on policies and regulations related to Navy career planning matters. The command career counselor serves as a primary technical assistant in support of the command's retention team and maintains an awareness of revisions and innovations in retention programs through his access to directives, reference materials, experience, and training.

Command master chief. Works in close association with the career counselor to support the command's retention team efforts. Works with senior petty officers to enhance the retention and counseling effort, and to motivate the Navy's number one asset—the senior petty officer.

Department head. Serves as retention team coordinator for his department.

Division officer. Serves as retention team coordinator for his division.

Service-oriented divisions/departments. Personnel, disbursing, medical, and dental departments support the retention team as required, and provide personalized services to enhance the climate in support of retention.

As the senior counselor, your specific responsibilities are to:

Pursue a vigorous retention program utilizing the retention team concept.

Frequently measure command retention effectiveness.

Ensure that the command career counselor is properly trained.

Actively involve every level of the command structure in the unit retention program. An effective retention program requires the support and active participation of all levels of supervision.

Ensure that the proficiency and motivation of the team members is maintained at a high level.

Accord appropriate ceremony and attention to reenlistments, advancements, awards, and other ceremonies and special occasions.

In establishing or updating your own retention program, beware of blindly following retention program policies. The overall Navy program was designed to give latitude to each command in formulating its own program. Each ship will face a unique situation because of its own homeport, deployment schedule, facilities available, and other factors. Your initial objective should be to identify those areas that adversely affect retention so that you can deal with them. Each person counseled will reveal problem areas. Once you identify them, you can begin to eliminate these problem areas. For example, the command's first-term retention may be excellent, but the second- and third-term reenlistments can be down. In this case, your program should place increased emphasis on second- and third-term personnel.

Keep in mind always that *all* retention areas must be considered. It's easy for one facet of the program to absorb your attention when other problem areas may be as bad or worse. To meet the needs of the command as a whole, the system you establish must "police" itself through appropriate control or feedback designed to ensure that *all* elements of the problem receive the necessary attention.

Specific Aids to Retention

Advancement. Advancement is one of the primary reasons enlisted personnel stay in the service. Moving up the ladder, making more money, having more responsibility, and having more benefits are things that everyone seeks as measures of a successful career. Without the command's use of available service schools and correspondence courses, however, advancement becomes difficult for your crew. Approval of travel to service schools and provision of assisted study hours and on-the-job training will assist an individual's quest for advancement and thus improve his or her dedication to a career. It will also help those of your crew who desire specific training for striker designation and change of rating. Another useful technique is the publication of lists of personnel who are eligible and ineligible for advancement-in-rate examinations. This can help motivate both groups.

After advancement results are published, hold individual or group ceremonies, with the entire department or crew attending, depending on the size of the group and the desires of the individual. Such ceremonies will not only give recognition to those advanced, but may "light off" those who have previously lacked motivation.

Education. Although it is not a written rule, we generally assume that higher education will provide better career opportunities. Although benefits change with the years, there will always be *some* educational program available to your enlisted personnel. The *Retention Team Manual* describes the current programs in detail. By providing flexible hours and command recognition of the importance of the various educational programs available, you will generate interest and involvement—and enhance your retention climate.

Dependents' Organizations. The welfare and happiness of your crew's dependents is an important element of morale. You can reach dependents in many ways, but one of the best is through dependents' organizations. The following programs can be presented to the ship's spouses' club and other dependents' organizations for consideration:

Welcome aboard packages

Designated sponsor (if a member's sponsor is unmarried)

Ensuring that the spouses' club president and ombudsperson contact all newly reporting families

Luncheons for new families and departing families

During deployments, the organization of potluck suppers, picnics, card games, bazaars, swimming parties, sightseeing tours, bowling leagues, and other recreational activities

Welcome home parties for the command, using Navy clubs and facilities

A list of educational institutions available in the area with points of contact so dependents can continue their education

Reenlistment. There is no guarantee that your command retention efforts will produce "Golden Anchor" results. However, by having an effective retention program, by providing an atmosphere of genuine interest in each individual's desires, and by showing command concern for the family unit, you can strengthen your reenlistment program significantly.

At set intervals have personnel office staff provide the other retention team members with a list of personnel who do not meet the professional growth requirements for reenlistment. They can then contact the ineligible members and encourage and help them to meet the requirements.

Finally, if the reenlistee is agreeable, hold a reenlistment ceremony with all hands present. This serves a fourfold purpose:

It provides recognition to the reenlistee.
It displays the results of the retention team and command efforts.
It may encourage others to reenlist or to work on eligibility.
It reemphasizes the solemnity of the "Oath of Enlistment" to all hands.

Though not all-inclusive, the following is a list of additional benefits you may want to provide the reenlistee:

Photograph of the ceremony
Letter of congratulation to spouse or parents
Reenlistment day liberty
Reenlistment leave
Command plaque with name and date of reenlistment
Head of line privileges for a given period of time
Reenlistment Benefit Book

Request Mast. When an individual submits a special request form (chit) through the chain of command, *it will be the most important thing on his mind until he gets an answer.* Resentment sets in rapidly if the chit is slowly or sloppily handled, or if it disappears in someone's pocket or in-basket. Few things say so clearly to a person that he isn't very important as a badly handled request chit. Remember, that chit is his own, personal, *formal* test of your personnel management standards. It isn't a "yes" answer that is important, it is that the command cares enough to give him *some answer quickly!*

Welcome Aboard/Sponsors. This is an area where many commands fail in their retention efforts. Some years ago, a young second class petty officer assigned to a fast attack submarine stopped to chat with the CO prior to his discharge. The captain asked him if there was anything he personally would recommend to improve the retention climate onboard. The petty officer replied, "I'm grateful for the education and I liked my shipmates, but I knew the day I reported that I'd leave at the completion of my obligated service." When questioned further he said, "When I reported aboard I got absolutely no assistance in settling into my new job. When I asked the chief of the boat about a place to sleep, he assigned me to a temporary bunk in the torpedo room next to a torpedo, and I was never assigned a personal locker. From that first day I knew that if the system cared that little for me I did not want to be part of it." The CO learned from this unfortunate episode, but the Navy lost a fine young petty officer. Ensure that your welcome aboard practices are formalized and *always* carried out. Sponsors should be intelligently chosen and should contact the new personnel before their arrival in the area. Send spouse-to-spouse notes when this is possible. Publishing a "welcome aboard" note in the plan of the day, introducing the crew to each newly reporting individual, can also prove highly beneficial.

The Family. Family happiness is vital to continued career satisfaction. There is no way a command can solve all family problems, but concern for them can go far in easing the difficulties of service life and can certainly improve your retention program. Some thoughts in improving your practices in this area are to encourage spouses to come aboard often, both for ceremonies and formal counseling and presentations on Navy Career Benefits. Make the spouse a "co-star" in award, advancement, and reenlistment ceremonies. Scheduling a few minutes for coffee with the CO can often turn a spouse into a real booster of the command and its programs.

Dependents living overseas will help the morale of your officers and men, but you will have to be concerned with their welfare.

Striker Selection Board. Establishment of a Striker Selection Board can provide significant motivation for the nondesignated community. Recognition for professional achievements and initiative through designation as a striker can be decisive in a further reenlistment decision. This is not to imply that all nondesignated personnel should be designated through this process. Only those who have shown a sincere desire and personal initiative in preparing for a particular rating should be designated.

Recognition. This is the most important ingredient in a successful retention program. Recognition is a measure of the command's care, concern, and appreciation for the efforts of an individual. The use of "all hands" quarters to recognize individual and group achievements is very important. "Positive strokes," when deserved, are a proven method of improving the morale of a crew.

There are other levels in the command, such as in work centers or divisions, where recognition ceremonies can also be carried out. The act of recognition is more important than the level of recognition.

Discipline

Aboard ship, discipline means a prompt, willing responsiveness to commands. The best discipline is self-discipline; individuals doing the right thing because they *want* to do it. You can create it in your command by building willingness, enthusiasm, and cooperation. It will then exist not only while sailors are under the eyes of their superiors, but while they are off duty as well.

Admiral Arleigh Burke wrote: "A well disciplined organization is one whose members work with enthusiasm, willingness, and zest as individuals and as a group to fulfill the mission of the organization with expectation of success. Lack of discipline results in loss of smooth, determined operating action and combat efficiency."

In striving for a high level of discipline, remember that sailors admire an individual who lives in accordance with the code he enforces. They will resent a CO who demands behavior from his followers which he doesn't exhibit himself. The captain who expects unflinching obedience and cooperation from his crew will do well to give the same obedience and cooperation to his own seniors. If he combines this with ability and a genuine interest in his sailors' well-being, he will eliminate many of his disciplinary problems.

Positive Discipline. *Naval Leadership,* published by Naval Institute Press, discusses positive discipline as follows:

> Positive discipline is the development of that state of mind in which individuals endeavor to do the right thing, with or without specific instructions. In order for positive discipline to operate most effectively, it is necessary that personnel *know* their jobs thoroughly. Training, therefore, is one of the basic factors involved in this type of discipline. The commanding officer must strive constantly to train his men to perform their duties in such a way as not to break regulations. In this way he is disciplining them just as surely as by punishing them after an infraction, but in a much more productive manner.

The following actions on you part will assist in the achievement of positive discipline. You must:

Maintain a general attitude of approval of the crew. A feeling of distrust on your part is soon transmitted to the crew, and causes a general sense of insecurity.

Let your crew know what is expected of them. This can be done by formal written directives and by clear verbal instructions.

Keep the crew informed of their mission. Sailors work better when they fully understand the relationship of what they do and how they do it to the whole task of the ship.

Let your crew know that their officers are behind them as long as they perform their duties to the best of their abilities.

Keep your crew informed of their progress. This is equally important whether their work is good or bad.

Keep your crew informed, within security restrictions, of any changes which will affect their future.

Assure the crew by your actions that each will receive fair and impartial treatment.

Improve your own professional ability. Enlisted personnel have been asked what they think makes a good leader. They say they like and respect professional competence more than any other single attribute.

Delegate authority, with corresponding responsibility, as far down in the organization as competence exists.

Punishment. Punishment, like positive discipline, which it is intended to uphold, is your personal responsibility. It cannot be delegated, since it can legally be awarded only by you or by a legally convened court-martial acting in accordance with the *Uniform Code of Military Justice* (*UCMJ*). No officer except the commanding officer has any authority to inflict punishment on any person he is assigned to control. Your subordinates must be careful not to assume this authority under the assumption that they will save time for you, or that the accused will get a fairer deal from them than from you, or for any other reason. You must ensure that your officers and chiefs understand they can only exercise *positive* discipline in guiding the offender's future actions. That failing, they must place them on report for you to deal with. Insist that all infractions are fully investigated before this is done. The mast process aboard ship should be a tribunal feared and respected by all crew members.

Military Justice. Present-day command qualification requires training and examination in military justice. It is essential that you review the *Manual for Court Martial* and *Judge Advocate General Manual* frequently, especially prior to any legal proceeding. The captain who relies on his past experience to conduct mast is being unfair to his crew and may find himself on the wrong side of the military justice system.

The American military justice system is designed as the last resort in enforcing standards of behavior and discipline in the services. It is governed by the *UCMJ,* which came into effect in 1951. The *UCMJ* is a compromise between the necessities of military discipline and the need to guarantee that this discipline does not hinge simply on the wishes of the commanding officer. As an added safeguard, an all-civilian Court of Military Appeals, insulated from military control, reviews the records of military trials to ensure due process.

The following constitutes a brief overview of the system, as an aid to you in explaining it to the crew.

The military justice system provides for three kinds of courts-martial. The most formal is the general court-martial. This court can impose any punishment up to and including death, subject to the limitations described in the *UCMJ*'s Table of Maximum Punishments.

The second type is the special court-martial. It requires no trained lawyer to serve as "judge," and is less formal than a general court. A special court-martial is convened for less serious offenses, and can impose up to six months' confinement and a bad conduct discharge.

The summary court-martial, now seldom used, is the third kind of court-martial. It is similar to a civilian police court: a one-person court, usually consisting of a field-grade officer. The maximum sentence it can impose is thirty days' confinement.

In addition to the three kinds of courts-martial, service members may be subject to nonjudicial punishments, called Article 15's, after the article of the *UCMJ* that governs nonjudicial punishment. All service members may be subject to Article 15 actions, but some types of punishments are applicable only to certain ranks.

Article 15 permits the commanding officer to impose such punishments as the following:

Restriction to the ship
Withholding of privileges
Extra duty
Reduction to the next lower grade, if the grade from which the accused would be reduced is within the promotion authority of the commanding officer
Forfeiture of pay
Correctional custody
Confinement for not more than three consecutive days on bread and water

The accused may submit matters in extenuation and mitigation to the commander, and may have counsel present when appealing. Further, the officer who imposes the punishment, or his superior, can suspend the punishment, set it aside, or remit any part of it. Any appeal or suspension of punishment does not affect the question of guilt or innocence, however.

Procedures of general or special courts-martial are somewhat different from civilian courts. For instance, the number of court members usually is smaller—at least three in a special and five in a general court-martial. The members of the court will be officers, unless the accused is enlisted and requests trial by an "enlisted court." In that case, at least one-third of the court must be enlisted personnel.

After an evidence-gathering investigation, the first step in the court-martial process is a so-called "Article 32" hearing. This is similar to a civil preliminary hearing or grand jury hearing. However, in contrast to civilian procedure, a defendant must hear the charges against him and may question witnesses at this time.

The results of the Article 32 hearing are then submitted to the "convening authority"—that is, the officer in the chain of command with the power to convene the court. In another departure from civil law, the convening authority then appoints the court's members.

As the judge does in civil courts, the law officer of a general court-martial gives detailed instructions of law for the court members to apply to the evidence before them. This "jury," in addition to determining guilt or innocence, imposes sentence.

The accused has the right to request that the military judge, or law officer, act as a jury. The accused may also request that the government produce witnesses he thinks essential, but the defense has no subpoena power.

The conduct of the court-martial is similar to that of a civil court, with the prosecution presenting evidence first, followed by the defense. If a guilty verdict is reached, evidence is presented before sentencing concerning the accused's general military record. The accused may give other evidence in extenuation and mitigation—for instance, proof of good character. If the court has several members, the law officer will then advise them as to the maximum penalty permitted.

Court members vote on sentencing. In most cases, two-thirds of the court must concur with the sentence, although three-fourths must concur if it calls for more than ten years' confinement. A sentence of death must be affirmed by unanimous decision.

The military justice system also has an automatic appellate review. In lesser cases, this is done by the convening authority and his staff judge advocate. The convening authority may reject a conviction or reduce a sentence, but cannot impose a harsher punishment.

In more serious cases, the Court of Military Review reviews the case. After this, the accused may appeal a case to the Court of Military Appeals, the three-person civilian court. Final appeal of a court-martial case is to the U.S. Supreme Court.

Passing and Getting the Word

It is worth your attention to determine how well the word is passed in your ship. It is often a shock for a commanding officer in talking to one of his younger sailors to find out that the individual does not know what the ship's operating schedule is, what exercises the ship is engaged in, or, for that matter, the name of his division officer, the executive officer, or the captain!

Making a habit of passing the word on policy and future expectations and inculcating the same habit in his officers and petty officers are two of the most important contributions a captain can make toward a successful command tour and a well-integrated crew. Various ways and means of communicating have been discussed in this chapter and elsewhere. Nothing is more destructive to a person's morale than not to know what is going on.

A corollary to "passing the word" is the commanding officer's "getting the word" about the policies and objectives of his superior in command. "Getting the word" in a timely manner allows you to efficiently implement policy from above. Failure to promulgate current policy changes and directives can result in a disorderly implementation, which displays to the crew the fact that the commanding officer is not running the ship efficiently.

Use of the 1MC

One of the best tools at your disposal in command for communicating with the crew is the 1MC. It is a "real time" means to let everyone in the ship know about events. While at sea, you should strive to get on the 1MC once or twice a day, providing the crew with a general update of the day's events and any late-breaking changes. Remember, this is not an opportunity to impart long ideas about philosophy or to direct traffic around the ship—you have other vehicles for such communications. The 1MC is all about short bursts of interesting information, ranging from port visit schedule changes to operational achievements. It is a good place to give out the occasional "BZ" to exceptional performers, and a little humor can go a long way. When you first take command, let the crew hear your voice a bit, then pulse the XO and the command master chief for an honest appraisal of your style: encourage them to be brutally honest.

Never forget that the hard work of any ship is performed by young sailors. A good captain will find ways to acknowledge and reward their contributions.

Some ships use a "morning report" format, which can be done either by you or the officer of the deck—a quick summary of major events, weather, and operational status. Keep it short. Another thing to consider is a late-evening "round-up" from you as captain, giving your quick impressions of the day's work and passing along a little encouragement. Be sure in both cases to consider timing—don't interrupt movies in the evening or start blaring too early in the morning.

Minority Affairs

Navy Regulations states that equal opportunity and treatment shall be accorded all persons in the Department of the Navy irrespective of their race, color, religion, sex, or national origin, consistent with requirements for physical capabilities.

The subject is covered in greater detail in the *Navy Equal Opportunity Manual (OPNAVINST 534.1)* and *Navy Race Relations Education (OPNAVINST 1500.42)* and should be well understood by all officers in command. The policy of equal opportunity has its roots in the Constitution, which all service personnel are sworn "to support and defend," and in the moral concept of human dignity. As commanding officer, you must instruct all those under your supervision in the concept of equal opportunity, and you must implement the equal opportunity program on your ship.

The problem of race relations is an offshoot of intercultural prejudices, stemming from widespread misconceptions regarding the capabilities, dignity, and worth of individuals of different races, creeds, or national origins. These prejudices have pervaded our society at many levels since well before 1776. The most notable abuses have been in black-white relationships. However, yellow-white, red-white, and even white minority group clashes have been present throughout our history. It is hard indeed to change the way people think, but if you fail to ensure the equality of treatment of all both morally and under the law, you will make a farce both of the Constitution and of the naval profession.

As commanding officer, you must ensure that every person meets the same minimums of performance for advancement. Similarly, each person appearing before you at mast must be judged solely on the merits of the case. Ethnic background, religious belief, and political persuasion must be separated from qualification and performance standards. By the same token, never think that you are obligated to compensate for previous racial injustices by using reverse discrimination. Rather, strive for *real* equality in all aspects of your command.

Families and Dependents

The welfare of dependents has been partially treated in our discussion of retention. However, there are other aspects of this problem which you should consider.

The importance of the family as a unit of the Navy team has been well established over the years. Morale, job performance, retention, and unit readiness are directly linked to the well-being of the families of those you command. The key to success here is *concern*. You must display your concern in your daily actions involving personal problems and hardships, and by your command's earnest efforts to inform dependents of their privileges and the services available to them.

Common Navy programs and dependent privileges and services are described in such publications as the *Retention Team Manual, Sea Legs: A Handbook for the Navy Family (NAVMILPERS 15309A)*, and the *Navy Times' Handbook for Military Families,* which is published annually. These publications should be made available to spouses of your crew members by means of seminars, welcome aboard packages, and individual counselor interviews.

Family Service Centers and Ombudsmen

Two of the best resources you have in the endless challenge of taking care of your command's families are the Navy's Family Service Centers and your own command ombudsman.

The Family Service Centers are located at major Navy bases all around the world. They provide an enormous array of services, information, and assistance to your command's families. Headed up by trained counselors and led by a Navy officer, the centers can provide classes in everything from parenting to financial planning; assist in spousal job hunting; give advice on moving and finding a place to live; provide welcome aboard packages describing the area; and refer your families to other services they may require. As a new commanding officer in an area, you should take the time to drop by the Family Service Center, perhaps with your CMC and ombudsmen, to see for yourself all they can provide.

The Navy's outstanding ombudsman program has been steadily improving over the past two decades. Today's ombudsmen are well-trained, motivated, and informed volunteers who can provide a bridge between you and your families. They serve as communicators, facilitators, and referral experts to your command's families. You will receive the pro forma resignation of the incumbent ombudsman when you take command; normally you will ask him to remain in the post until you decide on a new ombudsman. After consultation with your XO and CMC, you may want to ask the incumbent to remain indefinitely; or you may choose to appoint a new ombudsman.

If you are going to change ombudsmen, you should work closely with the XO and CMC on the selection process. Volunteers can be solicited in the plan of the day, but often a better approach is for the CMC to ask several spouses to apply. You should personally interview each of them, seeking to determine if they have the character, temperament, and available time to do the job properly.

Being an ombudsman is a demanding and challenging task. After a week of Navy school, the new ombudsman is expected to be able to field phone calls ranging from requests for information on the ship's schedule to advice on how to set up a move. The ombudsman should set up a "care line," which is a pre-recorded voice mail available to your command's families providing the latest information on the command. He must be able to refer your command family members to appropriate resources and keep you informed of any problems that arise.

Your relationship with the command ombudsman should be friendly and close. Invite him to a meeting, perhaps at breakfast, every couple of months, taking the time to talk about the situation in the command. You will be amazed at what you learn. You may want to invite the XO and CMC to the meetings. Make sure your ombudsman has all the resources necessary to do the job. These include a complete social roster of the entire ship, updated monthly; a separate phone line for official calls; an answering machine with the capability of playing long messages for the ship's "careline"; expenses for baby-sitting, travel, and administrative overhead; and anything else they need. The ombudsman should be encouraged to be in touch with the command's social side, generally through meetings with the chairman or president of the command's support group.

In general, as in so many things, you will get out of the ombudsman program about what you put into it. Properly executed, this program is a superb resource for you in taking care of your command's families. Good ombudsmen are worth their weight in gold to your command—treat them accordingly.

The Enlisted Performance Evaluation

Enlisted evaluations are vitally important for a person's promotion and for selection for special billets. You are responsible for ensuring that they are submitted on time and that they give a fair assessment of an individual's performance. In preparing these important documents, keep your comments succinct, objective, and consistent with the marks assigned. Outstanding crew members should receive marks and written evaluations that reflect their contribution to the command. Special accomplishments should be highlighted. Unique or difficult watch qualifications, performance as leading petty officer, assignment as command chief, contribution to a Ney Award, and so forth are accomplishments which each leading petty officer and division officer should include in evaluations. You must insist that your chain of command fully understands the importance of the enlisted evaluation system as defined in *NAVMILPERSMAN* Article 3410150, including the use of evaluations as described below:

To determine eligibility of a member for reenlistment, for honorable discharge, and for good conduct awards.

To permit the commanding officer to accelerate the advancement of outstanding members and to reduce those who show themselves incompetent.

To inform the various selection boards which select members for advancement, appointment to commissioned status, assignment to special duties, and for special education programs.

Adequate performance evaluations are essential for all the above reasons. Failure to objectively appraise a person's performance is a grave failure to meet a public trust, and could constitute an injustice not only to him but to his peers as well

As commanding officer, you must ensure that the preparation of enlisted evaluations is not lost in the welter of other required reports, inspections, and the other calamities that occur from time to time. It is no understatement to say that fitness reports and evaluations are the most important documents processed on your ship!

Performance Evaluation Hints. The comments and hints that follow, taken from senior and master chief petty officer selection board remarks regarding evaluation preparation and wording, are applicable to all evaluation reports. Study them and pass them along. They can help upgrade your enlisted evaluation system.

Once an individual is selected as a senior enlisted petty officer (E-6 through E-10), department heads and commanding officers should endeavor to give him a variety of assignments to evaluate his potential for further advancement. These can be made in such a way that they do not prevent him from demonstrating his ability to carry out his primary responsibility. Too many CPOs are content to remain within the confines of their work centers. In this capacity, however, they cannot be judged on their ability to function satisfactorily on department and command levels, as they will have to as E-8 and E-9 leaders.

The detailers sometimes have to fill the more difficult (less desirable) assignments with qualified personnel. This possibility should be considered and commented upon.

Don't waste narrative comments in describing how well the ship did on deployment, inspection, and so forth. Tell exactly *what* jobs the individual had and *how well* they were performed.

Eliminate flowery adjectives and get to the point in plain English.

Place your emphasis on the individual's ability, potential, and willingness to accept positions of leadership and management. Indicate *why* he should be advanced.

Take care to list all collateral duties, awards, education, and qualifications.

If an individual is marked higher or lower than his peers, explain the reason clearly in the narrative.

Don't recommend an individual for advancement just because he meets the time in service requirements.

School commands should not mark students. Their evaluations should read simply, "student under instruction."

Proofread the evaluation to ensure that no blocks are left blank. Do not leave the selection board to reconstruct the record.

Don't type over any of the block labels. This interferes with form-reading equipment.

Write succinctly, in organized paragraphs.

If your command is not composed of "highly selected" or "specially chosen" individuals, don't say that it is. The board will know better and your efforts will be discounted accordingly.

Fill in blocks on duties completely and specifically. Don't assume that board members know what duties specific billets in your unit entail.

Establish an evaluation review board or some other method of ensuring that correct evaluations are submitted.

Your enlisted personnel make your ship. Don't shortchange them!

The Captain's Role with the Crew

The best way to take the measure of your crew is simply to spend time with them. There is a great deal to be said for being the kind of captain who is well known for turning up at unexpected times. One way to look at this is that you are perpetually walking around your command trying to catch people doing something good!

Try and schedule at least one activity each day that will draw you to a part of the ship, submarine, or squadron where you do not normally go. A great choice on a surface ship, for example, is to do a planned maintenance spot check every day. Make it a surprise to the division concerned, take the 3-M coordinator with you, and enjoy the exchange with your people on the deckplates. You will demonstrate how important you think maintenance is to the command, have a chance to interact with your hardest workers, and get the opportunity to spot-check an important function.

Spend as little time as possible in your stateroom. Nothing happens there! As a default position if nothing else is going on, head up to the bridge. Talk to everyone on the bridge team. Then walk around the decks. And don't forget to tour one of your main engineering spaces each day. If you "take a spin around" at least once in the morning and once in the afternoon, you'll be amazed how much you pick up about what is happening in your world.

Bear in mind that you cannot walk past something that isn't right. The minute you do, you've accepted that standard—be it something as mundane as a dirty ladder back or as complicated as an improperly conducted signal processor check on the SPY-1B radar. Be especially vigilant for safety violations of any kind.

Sailors will work the hardest for commanding officers they like and respect. Know your job, interact with your people in positive ways, and keep everyone focused on safety and the mission at hand. You'll enjoy every day you spend with your sailors.

6

Maintenance and Logistics

If the equipment doesn't work in battle, it doesn't make much differ-
ence how much else the officers know, the battle is lost—and so
are the people in it.
So—it can be right handy to be a good engineer first—and a bril-
liant theorist after.

—Admiral Arleigh Burke, "Winning Naval Battles"

A Philosophy of Maintenance and Logistics

Navy Regulations, under the heading "Care of Ships, Aircraft, Vehicles and Their Equipment," states that the commanding officer shall cause such inspections and tests to be made and procedures carried out as are prescribed by competent authority, together with such others as he or she deems necessary to ensure the proper preservation, repair, maintenance, and operations of any ship, aircraft, vehicle, and equipment assigned to the command. Philosophically speaking, such a policy is certainly not unique to the Navy. Civilian engineers and industrial managers have emphasized such maintenance procedures for years. What is unique about the challenges you will face in the areas of maintenance and logistics is the requirement to take your systems into the unpredictable world of combat. Thus, as Admiral Burke said after World War II, "All that equipment has to work the way it ought to or it is simply excess baggage." Today, the Navy sends extraordinarily complex systems to sea as we prepare for potential combat operations. Your challenge is to maintain them in a condition to fight. That additional level of responsibility must form the basis of your command philosophy as it applies to maintenance and logistics. You should work hard to communicate that aspect to your crew.

Because your systems must go into combat, and because your people's lives may depend on your equipment, your maintenance and logistics team must approach the challenges they face with a "zero defects" philosophy.

Many senior engineering officers feel that mistakes are caused by a lack of knowledge on the part of maintenance personnel and by a lack of attention to the task at hand. The first condition can be corrected by testing all personnel to determine that they have the necessary knowledge to perform their tasks and stand their watches. The second condition, lack of attention, is a state of mind that can be changed. The supervisor must observe the sailor's mental habits. Is he or she mentally lazy? Uninterested? Overqualified, and thus bored? Your maintenance and logistics team must be reminded to watch each detail and maintain an orderly "scan" or examination of each indicator of success or failure of that responsibility. With concentration, they can reach the goal of zero defects in all things and at all times. You, as commanding officer, may have to accept some slowing down as your sailors get used to more thorough performance, but attainment of habit and development of confidence will soon bring them back to near their previous speed. Lack of defects will more than improve the overall performance.

Your insistence on accountability for maintenance performed and strict adherence to maintenance and operating procedures forms an essential part of the ship's general philosophy concerning the safe and proper operation of all equipment and the logistic support of the entire ship.

Emphasis on Maintenance and Repair Afloat

Realize this from the first: you will have to stress material readiness throughout your tour. Today's fleet consists of complex and highly capable ships. Any single casualty or material failure, if quickly corrected, will seldom detract from the ship's readiness for war. Those which are not quickly corrected, however, will usually precipitate an avalanche of problems which, once started, is very difficult to reverse. This snowball effect can result in a significant degradation of the ship's readiness, as well as an extraordinary amount of work. Careful attention to detail on the part of all hands is a necessity for all ships large or small. Demand uniform *formality* with respect to the definition, reporting, logging, and clearing of material deficiencies, whether large or small. Insist that identified deficiencies be pursued aggressively in accordance with the priorities you have established, and train your personnel not to learn to "live with" deficiencies. Similarly, you must attack your ship's established corrective and preventive maintenance routines with vigor and care. An unenthusiastic or careless attitude toward scheduled preventive maintenance will result in the certain degradation and failure of mechanical, electrical, and electronic equipment. These failures will affect operating time and cause the expenditure of large amounts of effort and money to repair.

The fleet can ill afford expenditures of time, money, and manpower to correct damage from improperly performed maintenance. Keep in mind that the improper maintenance your sailors perform today may have twenty or thirty years to catch up with your ship. You won't be there to see the result; but the Navy will suffer.

Training Junior Officers. Most maintenance errors can be prevented by conscientious planning and by supervision by officers and senior petty officers. Personnel reporting to a ship for the first time generally have little practical training in maintenance and test procedures. They can only gain competence through conscientious training aboard ship, by supervised on-the-job experience. It is false economy to assign inexperienced personnel to independent maintenance jobs without at least spot supervision.

To ensure that this supervision is effective, you must provide your junior officers with proper training in maintenance management and the need for material readiness afloat. Among the many duties of a commanding officer, there are few that have more lasting importance than the responsibility for the proper employment and development of junior officers. The influence and impact of your policies on the eventual development of these young men and women cannot be overemphasized.

Your division officers should not be confined solely to routine administrative functions and repetitive training tasks. They must be taught how to perform their divisional responsibilities, and then they must be *used* as division officers. They must know that they are held directly responsible for the repairs, maintenance, and equipment assigned to their division. All too frequently, when a problem occurs, the department head will bypass the division officers or usurp their authority. You should prevent this. The division officer must be required to work on these problems alone, at least initially. He will be consulted concerning, and held accountable for, all the material matters of the division.

In an effort to increase this awareness among their junior officers, some COs have instituted a policy of having a junior officer accompany them on at least one of their daily tours through the ship. They then discuss each of the discrepancies noted on the tour. As a result of these tours, these COs have noted a significant increase in awareness of conditions and responsibility for material readiness.

Material Readiness

Good Engineering Practice. "Good engineering practice" means the safe and proper operation of engineering plants. It is a philosophy based on a respect for, and an understanding of, the equipment being operated. It applies not only to shipboard propulsion plant operation, but to everyday operations and maintenance routine on all other shipboard systems as well. Good engineering practice begins with each watchstander. It means such things as feeling pipes and equipment for abnormal temperatures, listening to equipment for unusual noises, fixing minor discrepancies such as drips, packing leaks before they become more serious, keeping the bilges pumped down, and double-checking logs and records.

Good engineering practice recognizes that there is a "right way" and a "wrong way" to perform maintenance. Although written instructions and procedures usually specify the "right way" to maintain a piece of equipment, there are many instances for which specific guidance is not given. It is then necessary for the operator to use his judgment, experience, and knowledge of equipment to determine the action to take—in short, to exercise good engineering practice.

The exercise of good engineering practice is the essence of material readiness. The commanding officer will improve the engineering practice of the command by insisting on the involvement of subordinates (in particular, officers) in the material management of the command.

Officer Involvement. Obviously, officers are not trained as technicians, nor should they be so employed. As managers and trainers, however, junior officers must learn the practical aspects of their division's responsibilities. This includes the ability to recognize when proper tools and instruments are being utilized and when and how various tasks are performed by the division. This may require an officer to perform certain tasks himself to learn the required knowledge. It definitely requires his periodic, routine verification that his division is properly performing assigned maintenance functions, by his thorough review of required documentation.

Proper officer involvement in the technical supervision of a division requires a thorough theoretical and practical technical knowledge of appropriate operating and maintenance procedures. He acquires this by study of applicable documentation and by sufficient "on the job" practice and observation to understand the correct methods of operating and conducting maintenance procedures. For example, the DO responsible for a diesel engine should understand thoroughly each step in the diesel lineup and operating procedure. He must have the practical knowledge to recognize if the procedure is being conducted properly when he monitors the personnel actually performing the lineup and operation. He should know what inspections are required and how they are conducted.

He must actively direct the planning of division work to ensure that required maintenance is completed at necessary frequencies and in the required sequences, as set forth by Planned Maintenance Subsystem instructions.

He must review maintenance, alignment, and operational data to ensure that they are within allowed specifications, that trends are analyzed, and that they correctly reflect the readiness of the systems and equipment under his charge. He must have a thorough enough knowledge of the correct specifications to readily recognize abnormalities.

He must examine completed work and maintenance records and other data to ensure that they are maintained in accordance with applicable directives, that the operation or maintenance action has achieved the desired goal, and that the records reflect this.

He must establish and use checkpoints to ensure that complicated or lengthy work proceeds satisfactorily. Checkpoints are a technique of requiring periodic reports to determine that work is proceeding as planned. Prudent choice of checkpoints in a procedure or maintenance task keeps an officer informed about what is going on without the close degree of supervision implied by monitoring.

He must insist that his senior subordinates actively involve themselves in the planning, supervision, and execution of all divisional maintenance, training, and operational responsibilities.

Application of good engineering practices will enhance the professional development of the officer, improve the performance of the division, and result in increased material readiness of the entire ship.

Preventive Maintenance

The 3-M System. The Navy ships' 3-M (Maintenance and Material Management) system was created to help manage required maintenance in an atmosphere of growing complexity of equipment, increased tempo of operations, and decline in available resources. The 3-M system is an integrated system to improve the management of maintenance and provide for the collection and dissemination of maintenance-related information for use in developing better management, engineering analysis, and techniques of equipment maintenance.

The ships' 3-M system, when properly used, provides for the orderly scheduling and accomplishment of maintenance and for reporting and disseminating maintenance-related information. It is comprised of two subsystems—the PMS (Planned Maintenance Subsystem) and the MDCS (Maintenance Data Collection Subsystem).

The PMS pertains to the planning, scheduling, and management of resources (personnel, material, and time) to keep equipment running within its design characteristics. It defines uniform maintenance standards (based on engineering experience) and prescribes simplified procedures and techniques for the accomplishment of maintenance. The procedures and tools of the PMS are described in detail in *Planned Maintenance Subsystems, OPNAVINST 4790.4*.

When used properly, PMS improves maintenance practices and significantly upgrades equipment readiness. One of your most difficult challenges in command will be to utilize this vital system effectively. Over the years, type commanders have investigated the way it is used in the fleet. They found considerable differences between procedures on maintenance requirement cards (MRCs) and in equipment technical manuals; and, again, between the procedures on the MRCs and the actual performance of maintenance. In particular, they found that equipment guide lists were not always prepared properly, and that in several cases the preventive maintenance item they asked about had never been accomplished before. This was evident from failure to refer to technical manuals, the finding of errors in manuals and MRCs, the use of improper tools, identification of improper equipment wiring, identification of long-term equipment misoperation, and general unfamiliarity of personnel with maintenance procedures. In some cases, the type commander inspections showed that no preventive maintenance procedures at all were in effect and that no one had even requested the MRCs and manuals that would have been needed to institute them.

Testing Effectiveness. The simplest test to use to measure your preventive maintenance effectiveness is to select a single maintenance action and audit its performance from start to finish. The commanding officer can do this by checking:

The preventive maintenance card against the technical manual and feedback reports

The use of correct tools

The identification and use of proper repair parts

The use of correct safety procedures, tag-outs, and internal ship command control procedures

The use of proper work procedures

Corrective Maintenance

In the area of material management, you must strive to get deficiencies identified early, and develop a positive plan to correct them. The wise commanding officer will not tolerate the "it's always been that way" syndrome and will insist upon a strong corrective maintenance program. You must expect the sailors to attack every minor deficiency, before it becomes a major problem and results in a last-minute crisis before a deployment or other operational requirement.

Maintenance Training

In the area of maintenance training, you must ensure that ship's force personnel understand what is expected of them and of repair or maintenance activities. Furthermore, you must build in each of your sailors a desire to determine and correct the "fundamental cause" of equipment malfunctions rather than merely treating its symptoms.

Training on individual equipment must include formal presentations on maintenance procedures, hands-on training sessions, and formal examinations to determine effectiveness of the program.

Shipboard Training Program. In a more general sense, the program should ensure that all personnel understand these rules:

For each work item to be accomplished, specific procedures that define the system and component to be worked on, the work to be accomplished, and the desired results must be formulated and approved by proper authority. This is generally what has been done by the 3-M system.

Proper permission will be requested from higher authority prior to commencing maintenance work.

Systems will be tagged out properly prior to maintenance.

Watchstanders are responsible for monitoring work being performed by outside maintenance activities.

Watchstanders should report to duty officers any discrepancies they notice; for example, missing danger tags, or tags attached to the wrong components.

Safety precautions as outlined in the *SORN* will be strictly enforced.

Maintenance Records

CSMP. Over the past several years, type commanders have made significant progress in making the Current Ship's Maintenance Project (CSMP) a meaningful maintenance control document. The automated CSMP provides the depth of information necessary to evaluate and quantify the backlog and scope of work for ship's force, intermediate maintenance activity (IMA), or depot accomplishment, and to plan, schedule, and fund upkeeps, availabilities, and overhauls. As the Navy moves toward extended operating cycles between regular overhauls, with continuing reductions in overhaul funds, the automated CSMP becomes increasingly important as a controlling record at all levels of supervision. However, recent observations by type commanders indicated that the CSMP is not always maintained properly on all ships. Specifically, they identified these problems:

Junior officer and work center supervisors must develop a working knowledge of the CSMP.

The CSMP should be cleared promptly of deferred maintenance which is no longer required or has been completed.

Ships must identify deferred maintenance as it occurs and enter it into the CSMP.

Deferred maintenance documents must be prepared thoroughly to generate complete work requests.

Maintenance documents must be delivered to the designated CSMP maintenance activity on time.

CSMP accuracy, completeness, and management are important. If the ship's CSMP is not a valid assessment of material condition and maintenance requirements, you should examine internal handling of MDCS documents, internal CSMP distribution and use, and junior officer/work center supervisor knowledge and understanding of the CSMP. Upkeep and availability work packages can be significantly improved through advanced planning from an improved CSMP.

Testing

After most repair and maintenance work, equipment must be tested to see that it is working properly. Where these tests are not properly organized and supervised, the expression "give her the smoke test" may be more than a joke.

The basic assumption in the testing of equipment should be that it will not respond as expected (else why the test?) and that the personnel involved are unfamiliar with the procedures to be followed (testing is seldom a routine operation). Where a series of large, expensive, or inherently dangerous components are involved in a system test of one sort or another, poor procedures may have very serious consequences indeed.

Testing Guidelines. For such systems it is good engineering practice to follow, as applicable, the following guidelines:

The test must be properly authorized. For many components or systems this involves the approval of higher authority and perhaps the material command concerned.

The test procedures must be approved by an authorized source and reviewed for accuracy on board by the head of department (and in some cases, commanding officer) concerned. In most cases it is mandatory to commit procedures to writing.

Brief all personnel involved about the purpose of the test, prerequisites (i.e., steps to be taken before the test begins), step-by-step procedures in sequence, communications, precautions, out-of-commission indications, expected readings and results of the various test stages, and possible casualties.

A test station bill, separate from the normal watch bill, should be drawn up, with specific assignments of qualified personnel by name where tests of any complexity are involved. This bill should provide for personnel relief if the test is to be of appreciable duration. The relief personnel should be given the same briefing as the original test gang.

The station bill should include the communications circuits to be manned.

Make up proper data forms, where applicable, before the briefing. Operating personnel should not normally be assigned data-collecting duties. Data-gathering communications circuits should be separate from operating circuits.

Valve and switch lineups following the written test procedures should be made independently by two persons prior to the test. Double-check any changes made during the test as well.

Plan for a rehearsal, or dry run, before complicated or potentially dangerous tests. The officer in charge should check each station and each communications channel before the rehearsal and the actual test.

Testing is not comparable in urgency to operating. If anything "goes sour," the test should come to "all stop" and the equipment put in the safest condition possible while the difficulty is resolved.

Quality Assurance

All type commanders have issued detailed instructions regarding quality assurance. It is good engineering practice for the ship to have a strong quality assurance program in order to check maintenance and recertify repaired systems.

Importance of Inspection. Perhaps of even greater importance is inspection by the ship when outside activities conduct repair work. One of the weaknesses of our Navy repair and overhaul system is that the quality assurance system within the repair organization generally reports to the repair or production officer rather than directly to the commanding officer of the repair facility. This means that even with the best inspectors available, originally objective reports on quality are often considered subjectively if they might influence completion dates. Needless to say, it is up to you to look hard and long at the thoroughness and quality of the work completed by repair or maintenance activities.

Material Inspections

One of the characteristics of a good commanding officer is the ability to inspect. Whether material, personnel, or administrative, no inspection can be properly performed unless the inspector knows what to look for. This ability is not inborn, but comes through years of experience spent mostly on the receiving end of inspections.

If a captain really knows how to inspect, good things will happen in short order. A sense of pride will develop within the ship when previously unnoticed discrepancies are now noticed and quickly corrected. The commanding officer who knows how to conduct a material inspection will soon discover fewer items to comment upon unfavorably, as material readiness improves.

Use of Inspection Forms. In preparing yourself to do effective material inspections, you would be well advised to review the annual summaries of shipboard deficiencies noted by the Board of Inspection and Survey, the Type Commander Operational Readiness Examinations, and the Fleet Operational Reactor Safeguards Examinations. These summaries are provided to applicable ships and form a useful general index of where trouble can be anticipated.

Your Ship as Others See Her

The captain who serves the ship well is one who can stand back occasionally and see her as others do. This is not easy.

To start with, take physical appearance. The conduct of morning quarters on deck is the business of the executive officer; but you are in unfortunate straits if you are the only officer in the squadron who does not know that quarters on your ship is referred to in the flag mess as the "0800 mob scene." The military appearance of your formations, the smartness of your deck watches, the proper handling of colors, anchor lights, and absentee pennants, the cleanliness of your quarterdeck and topside areas—all these are taken by the rest of the fleet as outward signs of your ship's inward state; and more than likely, they are right.

Without deluding yourself that dressy show can long conceal less pleasant realities belowdecks, you will do well to make firsthand, periodic checks on how these outward symbols look from the flag bridge, as well as to check on the details of watchkeeping and maintenance below decks.

Since this chapter deals primarily with the subject of maintenance, it is also appropriate to consider at this point how a maintenance activity views your ship.

Little things mean a lot—and nowhere more so than on a modern warship. Proper maintenance of small boats can mean the difference between accomplishing your mission and failing to do so.

In the eyes of any maintenance activity, the best customers are those who solve problems during availabilities at the lowest possible level. You can do this by encouraging communications at every level in both chains of command. This occurs naturally once good relations have been established and ship's force and maintenance activity people know each other.

Maintenance activity COs appreciate the ship captain who keeps them informed. They will work closely with him to improve this type of relationship. The other end of the spectrum here is the commanding officer who cries "wolf" at every difficulty to the next senior in command (i.e., the commodore).

Ships that perform well during availabilities make use of the ship superintendent. They let him know what they need and keep him cut in on ship conditions that might preclude specific maintenance or testing.

Maintenance activities appreciate ships that react quickly to emergent work by rapid submittal of necessary work requests. Delay in this will only cause problems downstream, when many work items are simultaneously scheduled for completion. In this regard, maintenance activities also feel positively about the ship that does required testing right after repairs rather than waiting until the end of the maintenance period.

Maintenance activity COs feel secure when they work with a ship CO who is safety-conscious. They are particularly sensitive to diver safety and the fact that refit poses many hazards to men and machinery. The alert CO will concentrate his efforts on general safety, with particular emphasis on hull integrity and personnel safety.

Finally, maintenance activity sailors appreciate praise. This praise, where warranted, can inspire them to increase the quality of the refit or upkeep period.

By keeping this advice in mind, you can better the chances that your ship will receive a good availability.

Availability Planning

As "availability" is the period assigned a ship for the uninterrupted accomplishment of work that requires services of a repair activity ashore or afloat.

The key to success in availability or upkeep/refit planning is early and complete preparation. This starts by educating all work center supervisors in the proper preparation of work requests. This training must include the mechanics of filling out work requests but must, in addition, ensure that the following items will be clear to the maintenance activity when you submit the work package:

Accurate identification of the problem, including just what assistance is required

Inclusion of all necessary equipment nameplate data, reference publications, drawings, and repair procedures

Inclusion of equipment location

Identification of knowledgeable shipboard contact personnel

Assignment of correct level of maintenance assistance; intermediate maintenance activity (IMA), depot, or drydock

Identity of key events

Special controls identified, if applicable

Commanding officer or designated representative signature

Once the work center supervisors are well versed in work request preparation, you must ensure that your departments identify *all* work necessary prior to submission of the work package to the repair activity. Late submittal of known work items will degrade the effectiveness of the availability, and also will create ill-will between the maintenance activity and the ship.

At present, most maintenance activities also perform certain routine work items during an availability. These include lagging, sail loft work, and fuel and lubricant analysis, as examples. The well-prepared ship will ensure that work requiring lists, such as lagging, are properly prepared, indicating the problem and exact location.

Another significant input to availability planning is the CSMP. The end product of the CSMP is a listing of all ship's work items yet to be accomplished, including responsibility, status, and complete description. Ships with good maintenance programs work to keep the CSMP updated at all times. This provides the maintenance activity with a complete status of current work and allows them to plan most of the availability well before your work package arrives. The results are obvious. The better the planning input, the better the resulting work period.

Once the work package is complete, the next milestone in a successful availability is the arrival conference. The arrival conference permits the ship, the immediate superior in command, and the maintenance activity to discuss the work package in detail and to factor in controlling work items.

You can help your ship and your reputation by being prepared to discuss all work items in detail. You must have the facts regarding all work items in order to be able to make recommendations on management decisions. Furthermore, you must leave the conference with a clear understanding of the various actions taken on work requests, and must get this information to his crew. Since the arrival conference sets the tone for availability, you and your availability coordinator (usually the engineering officer) must attend. If possible, division officers and leading petty officers should be invited as well. They can learn from the experience and will be able to transfer firsthand information on the conference to their subordinates.

Most maintenance activities conduct periodic management or work review meetings throughout the availability. Generally, only you and your availability coordinator are invited. These meetings track work items with a view toward maximizing maintenance activity effectiveness. It is during these meetings that supply effectiveness is measured, emergent work is reviewed, and the critical flow points are checked for validity.

To be effective at management meetings, you must be well briefed on the status of all work items on the ship. You must do your homework and have the facts prior to the meeting. Some successful COs have used a technique whereby they discuss each pertinent work item with the respective department head in the presence of the ship's superintendent just prior to the meeting. This gives them the up-to-date job status as seen by the ship and the maintenance activity.

During the management meeting try hard to avoid placing others in an adversary position, particularly if you don't have all the facts. Likewise, if you feel it necessary to introduce a big issue at the meeting, it is wise to "grease the skids" with the maintenance activity and administrative seniors prior to it.

In summary, the success or lack of success that attends upkeep, availabilities, and overhauls depends greatly upon the relations established between the ship and the maintenance activity, whether afloat or ashore. Sources of friction often encountered are the lack of understanding on the part of the ship's officers and crew of the organization of the repair activity and the lack of knowledge about the differing responsibilities of the ship and the maintenance activity.

When going alongside a tender for upkeep or into a yard for availability, it is good practice to obtain an organization chart of the activity. Study it and promulgate its contents to the leading personnel in your ship. It can usually be assumed that the tender or yard knows what gear comes under this or that shipboard department, but a good many stumbles, fumbles, and grumbles come about from the ship's company thinking that one shop or office in the yard or on board the tender is taking care of something when actually it is the concern of another. Availability or refit period success is enhanced when ship managers know who in the maintenance activity hierarchy they interface with on repair management issues.

The communications network set up by the ship is all-important in establishing the proper rapport with the maintenance activity.

Repairs and Maintenance Advice

Over the past several years, several new concepts have reshaped the shoreside repair structure. All seem to be working reasonably well, and as CO you need to understand how they work in your homeport. The first is the creation of centralized organizations to control maintenance activities in fleet homeports. As an example, in San Diego there is a large supervisory organization working for the surface type commander called Southwest Regional Maintenance Center. Headed up by a very senior post–major command captain, this organization directs all maintenance activity in the homeport and for the surface force. They control maintenance dollars for all repair efforts, and the various Intermediate Maintenance Activities (IMA) report to them.

This centralization of this inport maintenance promises to create efficiencies in the process that will make your job as CO easier. In essence, it creates "one-stop shopping" for waterfront maintenance customers. Pay a call early on the CO of the regional maintenance organization as well as his subordinate commands. You should also meet the repair officer (essentially the "operations officer" of the regional maintenance organization) as early as you can.

A second change is the creation of "port engineers" for all seagoing units. These well-qualified civilians represent a long-term, shore-based adjunct to your own engineer officer. The port engineer works for the regional maintenance organization and provides day-to-day support for all repair work in the ship. Your chief engineer should be working on a daily basis with the port engineer, and you should get to know that individual very well too. When your port engineer is doing a good job, be sure to let his boss—the head of the regional maintenance organization—know that. Likewise, when you experience a problem or frustration in the world of maintenance, if your port engineer cannot solve the problem, ensure that his chain of command knows the situation as well.

A third factor at work on the waterfront in the world of maintenance is the increasing privatization of repair efforts. This is part of a national trend to permit private-sector competition to create efficiencies in government work activity. Tenders are being decommissioned, and their work in the homeport is generally taken up by private firms under contract to the regional maintenance organization. You can still affect the quality of work being done for you, but now you must work through the contracting agency (generally the regional maintenance organization) to do so.

If you are in O-5 level command, working for an O-6 (e.g., a destroyer squadron commander), you should avail yourself of the support of the staff in interfacing with the maintenance world. While you have considerable impact as CO of a destroyer, your commodore has considerably more when engaged in the problem. As always, it is a good idea to try to work things out at your level, but don't hesitate to call on the staff to support you if you need more or better attention to your maintenance needs.

Drydocking

Normal drydocking is scheduled during the regular overhaul period. Drydocking may also be accomplished between regular overhauls (interim drydocking) for routine maintenance or to repair propellers, replace propellers, repair shafting, sonar, or other underwater damage, or to examine the bottom for possible damage or deterioration.

Drydocking is accomplished in a navy yard or naval repair facility, or at a commercial yard under contract to the Navy. When docking at a commercial yard, arrangements will be made for the proceedings by an industrial manager.

Prior to docking, the commanding officer and the docking officer or commercial dockmaster should hold a conference to arrange for time of docking, tugs and pilots, the condition of the ship when entering, and the housekeeping arrangements for the visit. These consist of the brows to be furnished, utility services to be provided, sanitary services needed, garbage and waste removal arrangements, and other necessary services. Reactor safety provisions should be discussed for nuclear-powered ships.

At this same conference, provide the yard with any information about the last docking, the ship's docking plan, if not already held, and make arrangements regarding working and linehandling parties.

A similar conference is held near the end of work to set time and date of undocking and other events leading to it, such as flooding of the dock. Weight shifts must be reported and arrangements made for berthing.

Responsibility for Ship During Drydocking. Article 0752–4 of *Navy Regulations* prescribes that when a ship operating under her own power is being drydocked, the CO is fully responsible until the extremity of the ship first to enter the dock crosses the sill and the ship is pointed fair. The docking officer then assumes responsibility, and retains it until the dock is pumped dry. In undocking, the docking officer assumes responsibility when flooding commences, and returns it to the CO when the last extremity of the ship crosses the sill and the ship is pointed fair. In a commercial drydock the responsibilities are the same, with the supervisor of shipbuilding being responsible for ensuring that the contractor performs satisfactorily.

Safety in Drydock. In drydock, the CO is responsible for ensuring closure when unattended of all valves and openings in the ship's bottom on which no work is being done by the repair facility. The CO of the repair facility is responsible for closing at the end of working hours all valves and openings in the ship's bottom being worked on by the repair facility. Prior to undocking, the CO of the ship shall report to the docking officer any material changes in the amount and location of weights on board made by the ship's force and that all sea valves and other openings in the ship's bottom are closed. Flooding will not commence until the CO has made this report.

Preparation for Regular Overhaul

Experience with ship overhauls indicates that their success depends in large measure on the preparations made by the ship's CO during the pre-overhaul period. During the overhaul, heavy demands are placed on the crew for auxiliary and propulsion plant operations, preventive maintenance, ship's force overhaul work, monitoring of shipyard work, and training. Ships that have prepared for these demands during the pre-overhaul period have more time during the overhaul to meet them.

In order to assist you in preparing for your next overhaul, we will now discuss the areas requiring special attention before overhaul begins.

Pre-overhaul Testing. Since the results of pre-overhaul tests are used in determining the scope of work required, accurate recording of data and expeditious completion of these tests are important.

Overhaul Work Package Planning. One of the key elements in the successful accomplishment of shipyard overhaul is planning. Years before the overhaul or conversion starts, representatives of the fleet, shipyards, and technical commands work together to define the desired work package. As a result of approved alterations, deferred maintenance actions, and improved repair techniques, this package is periodically refined. Ideally, as the shipyard period begins, overhaul planning is complete and a workable schedule exists for the accomplishment of the required package. Realistically, this is not a totally achievable goal. Additional work will result from arrival inspections, open and inspect deficiencies, and equipment breakdowns during the overhaul. Aside from this, though, any other major deviations from the initial work package will confuse orderly planning and can eventually destroy even the best schedule. In this case much shipyard effort is wasted and delays become inevitable, with a resultant rise in total costs.

Ship's force can significantly affect the impact of "new work" on planning efforts. It is your responsibility to prepare thoroughly for the shipyard overhaul. This is accomplished by reviewing the proposed work package and by submitting work requests for *all* necessary items not included.

The earlier you identify this work, the more easily it can be assimilated into the package and thus minimize disruption. Recent reviews of supplemental work packages submitted after overhaul commencement have shown that pre-overhaul preparation was inadequate. In addition, a shipyard can refuse to do new work identified after the overhaul starts, based on its total workload. This rejection leaves only two options for the ship's type commander: (1) designation of the work as mandatory and acceptance of a schedule slip, or (2) disapproval of the work.

Review of Operating Procedures and Instructions. While they are doing pre-overhaul and overhaul tests, the ship's force will be exposed to infrequently used operating procedures and instructions. Ships must utilize the period prior to overhaul to familiarize themselves with these procedures and instructions.

Preventive Maintenance. Preventive maintenance must be kept current before and during the overhaul. Numerous delays in post-overhaul test programs can be avoided if equipment is properly maintained during the overhaul.

Watchstanding and Surveillance of Shipyard Work. During overhaul, the combination of abnormal shipboard conditions and the presence of shipyard workers not familiar with the ship makes it imperative that ship's force maintain close surveillance to ensure safety. The crew must be indoctrinated well before the overhaul in the following areas:

The necessity to tag out systems in accordance with shipyard procedures prior to the commencement of work.

The necessity and procedures involved in providing adequate support for fire protection and keeping the number of fire hazards to a minimum.

Maintenance of proper standards of system and component cleanliness.

Contacts with the Overhaul Shipyard Prior to Overhaul. During upkeeps prior to overhaul, shipyard personnel may visit the ship to check alteration plans to verify that all interferences have been identified. This can save a great deal of wasted time. The yard may also ask to review shipboard records to aid their planning and material procurement. You can use these contacts with the shipyard to obtain documents to familiarize the crew with shipyard administrative procedures, such as rip-out control, tag-out of systems, and verification of valve line-ups prior to the start of overhaul.

In summary, know your job, work hard, and conduct good follow-up inspections, and you can get as effective and efficient overhaul in these days of complex equipment as was common years ago. The conduct of proper overhaul preparation and the overhaul itself are not new to the Navy.

Joint Fleet Maintenance Manual (JFMM)

In 1996, CINCPACFLT and CINCLANTFLT jointly issued a new five-volume maintenance manual, *CPF/CLF Instruction 4790.3*. This new *JFMM* is the best single source of information on maintenance issues produced in several decades, and should be readily available to every ship, submarine, and aircraft squadron commanding officer in the U.S. Navy. As soon as you take command, ensure that all your officers and sailors involved in maintenance are fully conversant with the *JFMM*, and that copies are available in every departmental office for quick reference.

In broadest terms, the manual serves as a standardized, basic set of minimum requirements to be used by all type commanders and subordinate commands; provides clear and concise technical instructions to ensure that maintenance is planned, executed, completed, and documented within all fleet commands; acts as a vehicle for implementing regional maintenance policies across all platforms; and includes a comprehensive set of process descriptions for use by Navy schools engaged in training officers and sailors involved in maintenance.

Let's take a closer look at what is contained in this excellent "one-stop shopping" guide to maintenance.

Volume 1: New Construction. Information in this volume covers everything a commanding officer would need for the overall program of new construction, including detailed discussions of responsibilities for NAVSEA, the building yard, the design/planning yard, the CO, and various support activities. It also includes specifics on pre-delivery activities such as shipbuilder's test program, equipment load-out, logistic support, and the various trials (dock, fast cruise, and sea). The volume also has information on post-delivery deficiencies and the post-shakedown availability.

Volume 2: Integrated Fleet Maintenance. The second volume is the "heart of the matter," and covers the fundamentals of executing both CNO-scheduled and type commander–driven availabilities. This section of the *JFMM* contains superb information on the planning, execution, and documentation of repair periods as well as day-to-day maintenance activity.

Volume 3: Deployed Maintenance. This section of the *JFMM* focuses on the execution of maintenance during forward deployment, and includes a remarkably well produced section of information on maintenance support in each of the forward deployed areas—the Mediterranean, the Arabian Gulf, and the western Pacific. There is also a specific section for maintenance activity involving Military Sealift Command and U.S. Coast Guard vessels.

Volume 4: Test, Inspections, and Special Application Maintenance Programs. In this volume, detailed information on technical specifics is found for a wide variety of programs, including boilers, diesels, industrial plant equipment, marine sanitation devices, shipboard elec-

tromagnetic systems, INSURV issues, small boats, oxygen and nitro-
gen systems, degaussing, corrosion control, elevators, and maintenance of technical libraries. There is also a section specific to naval
air issues, including a carrier systems like catapults and aircraft
launch/recovery. A final section looks in detail at submarine systems,
including submarine salvage, submarine batteries, Trident system issues, noise reduction, and operating depth policy.

Volume 5: Quality Maintenance. Also referred to as Quality Assurance, or QA, the idea of "quality maintenance" is thoroughly ex-
plored in this final volume of the *JFMM.* It includes wide-ranging
discussions of personnel qualification systems, welder requirements,
work procedures for specific systems, departures from specification
requests, audits and surveillance, testing requirements, material control, and quality assurance records. There is also a set of blank repro-
ducible forms and form instruction in this final volume.

Frankly, it is difficult to envision a question that could not be answered by a quick perusal of this superbly organized five-volume
work. It should be a familiar reference to your department heads, and
you may find yourself dipping into it from time to time as you work
on your command's maintenance program.

Afloat Logistics

The science of logistics has for many years been an important part of
our mobility-conscious armed forces. Ashore, at headquarters, it
means determining the needs of all elements of our Navy and then
procuring and supplying these requirements worldwide. Solving
these complicated problems requires the best talent the Navy has.

Afloat, logistics is the determination of what individual ships need
to carry out their projected tasks, and the supply of these items and
services both before they leave port and on a continuing basis by replenishment underway.

Afloat logistics is carried out on the individual ship level by the
commanding officer and his supply department. In large ships, the
commanding officer will be assisted by a well-qualified Supply Corps
officer. In small ships, you may have either a newly commissioned
and schooled officer of the Supply Corps or a line officer. This sec-

tion is intended to help the CO with the demanding task of running a small ship with an inexperienced supply or junior line officer. It will also be of assistance to the captain of a large ship in monitoring the performance of the supply system.

The supply officer of a small ship has one of the most difficult jobs the Navy can offer. This officer is responsible, often singlehandedly, for administering all ship's supplies and equipage, coordinating a budget of millions of dollars, and providing food and personal services for the entire wardroom and crew. The billet appears even more difficult when one considers that the average supply officer assigned to such a ship has had little or no prior experience in supply matters and that her seniors, the commanding officer and executive officer, can often provide only cursory direction in the daily management of the department.

Ship Supply Officer's Responsibilities

OPNAVINST 3120.32C, the *SORN,* states that in addition to her duties as head of department, the supply officer is responsible for procuring, receiving, storing, issuing, shipping, transferring, selling, accounting for, and, while in her custody, maintaining all stores and equipment of the command.

Specifically, depending on the size and organization of the ship, she is responsible for the following:

The operation of the general mess, including the preparation and service of food.

The wardroom mess, on those ships where a billet has been established for a supply officer to be wardroom mess officer, or where the wardroom dines on food prepared by the general mess.

The ship's store and the subsidiary activities and services thereof.

Disbursing government funds; although where there is an assistant for disbursing, the supply officer will be relieved by that officer for responsibility for the procurement, custody, transfer, issue of, and accounting for funds. In such case the supply officer will exercise general supervision over and inspect the accounts of the assistant for disbursing.

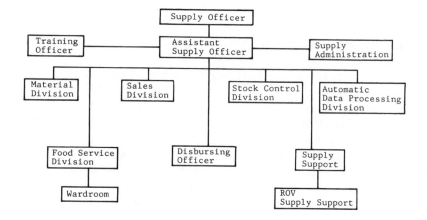

Shipboard supply organizations can be as large as that shown
above for a tender and as small as that shown below for a
submarine. Each, in its own way, performs a vital logistics
function in support of its ship.

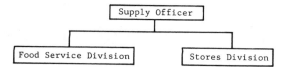

Figure 6–1. Typical supply department organization.

When there is an assistant for food service afloat or for the ship's
store, that officer may relieve the supply officer from personal financial accountability and responsibility for food service or ship's store
material. The supply officer must request such relief in writing, and it
must be approved by the CO. It is terminated upon relief or detachment of the supply officer or her assistant. In any case, she will continue to be responsible to the commanding officer for the overall administration of the supply department.

Supply Department Personnel

The Supply Officer. On a large ship the supply officer will undoubtedly be an officer of many years' experience in all aspects of logistics. On the other hand, the supply officer on a frigate or submarine is likely to be a young ensign directly out of the Naval Supply Corps School at Athens, Georgia. This discussion, as we stated earlier, is directed *specifically* to the small ship with a first toured or junior supply officer.

Your young supply officer was specifically chosen for her assignment as an independent duty department head as a result of her outstanding performance at supply school. She reports aboard technically qualified as supply department head, but with no previous experience whatsoever. In order to make up for this she will need strong support and counseling from you and your executive officer. She may also require some help in establishing herself in the wardroom with her contemporaries, who often tend to be overly critical of the "chop" and her apparent inability to meet their divisional supply needs and their culinary desires. Problems such as these can make life uncomfortable for your supply officer, reduce her effectiveness, and make her resignation certain at the end of her obligated service.

Supply Department Enlisted Personnel. Your young supply officer's lack of experience would be a minor liability were her subordinates well qualified. Today, however, more than ever before, the Navy suffers from severe shortages of senior storekeeper personnel and mid-grade mess management specialists. These shortages only complicate problems. In order to adjust for this you will have to ensure that an adequate training program is established. This is difficult to accomplish aboard a small ship, and it behooves you to take advantage of the excellent tender and shore establishment training programs established for storekeepers and mess management personnel. The monthly training schedule is usually published in advance by the tender, and ship personnel are always invited to participate. Use of this convenient formal training will not only help the ship, but will also help your enlisted personnel in their advancement.

Repair Parts and Material Management

Coordinated Shipboard Allowance List (COSAL). The COSAL shows the repair parts, special tools, and other material required on board to support installed equipment. All of your onboard parts are based on the COSAL. Over the past decade it has become a highly effective repair parts management tool.

Your ship's COSAL is complete at initial outfitting and is checked at every supply overhaul, but an active COSAL maintenance program is necessary to maintain supply efficiency while the ship is operating. Maintenance actions regarding the COSAL occur when equipment is added to or deleted from the ship. Parts for most new equipment changes are funded by the Naval Sea Systems Command COSAL allotment, so the ship is not charged. Failure to update the COSAL can only result in out-of-commission time for critical equipments, failure of your ship to meet its commitments, and unhappy unit and type commanders.

Inventory Maintenance. Your onboard repair parts are determined by your allowance (COSAL) and are adjusted by demand (usage). When discussing usage, the term "selected item" (SIM) is often used. A selected item is one which is required twice or more within a six-month period. The idea here is to spotlight material in regard to its inventory, control, and need to be reordered. A SIM is inventoried semiannually and, it is recommended, also before deployment. Stock items which are not designated as SIM will be completely inventoried only at the time of the ship's supply overhaul.

You can upgrade your inventory control system by tasking the supply department to spot-inventory a designated number of parts each week. However, many ships have been lulled into a false sense of security by spot-inventorying from stock records rather than actually locating the parts. A more effective method is to insist on actual location using stock record inventories. In addition, this is a good way to find and identify parts your crew may have hidden in lockers without stock records.

On the other hand, your inventory control system will lose effectiveness if you *permit* or are *perceived to condone* "deployment" spares. The use of "deployment" spares breaks the system's feedback link, hides the need for greater repair part support for certain equipment, and will frustrate your efforts to improve inventory control. Your attitude toward deployment spares should be: *if we really need it, submit an allowance change request.*

Repair Parts Maintenance. Many a ship has been forced to interrupt scheduled operations because a normally carried critical spare was not onboard. This tale becomes tragic when investigation shows that ship's force realized the problem but failed to take proper action to correct it. There are different versions to the story, but in almost every case the error was a lack of management of repair parts.

Each head of department is responsible for maintaining a full allowance of repair parts, and for requesting the supply officer to replace damaged, worn out, or missing items. Depending on ship size, the CO can require either the heads of departments or the supply officer to maintain stock records. In either case, repair part petty officers must be assigned from each division to assist in the work. Repair part availability is directly proportional to the degree of strictness of accounting for each part.

To make things simpler, storekeepers on small ships should be required, except in genuine emergencies, to make *all* issues of onboard repair parts at sea, and while in port to make *all* issues during normal working hours. Time and time again, supply inspection teams report that generally those ships that allow division repair parts petty officers to draw parts from the individual repair parts lockers are those ships with poor stock record validity. Ships without a full allowance of storekeepers should leave the assigned storekeepers off the underway watch bill. In addition, specific procedures requiring the command duty officer's approval should be adopted for issues of repair parts in port after normal working hours. On larger ships, where it would be difficult for a storekeeper to make each and every issue, the command must ensure that the repair parts petty officers are thoroughly trained in stock record keeping, allowance lists, and location of material, and that *they alone* have access to the lockers for their divisional parts.

Regardless of whether the ship is large or small, you must train supply personnel to take rapid replacement action on every repair part issued from stock. The supply officer should take follow-up action on all requisitions more than three months old.

Cannibalizations. There will be times when the ship will need to "cannibalize," or take a critical part or component directly from the physical plant of another vessel. (Note here that stock transfers from one ship to another are not cannibalizations.) You must submit requests through your commodore for both inter- and intra-squadron cannibalizations. It is wise to keep in mind that fleet commanders are generally opposed to cannibalization, and have controlled such material transfers very closely. When considering whether cannibalization is warranted, keep in mind that only mission-essential transfers will be approved, and that if your request is not backed up by a CASREP you are probably overreacting. In any case, review your type commander's directives to understand fully the policy on cannibalization.

Consumables. In small ships, consumable material is not controlled by detailed stock records but rather in a running account. Most smaller ships have found that the "commodity manager" concept for consumables is sound. Under this concept, one division or department is responsible for providing a particular commodity to the entire ship. This system precludes wholesale duplication of stock where space is in short supply and also improves consumable financial management. Where the commodity manager concept is used, it is essential that the ship devise consumable load lists from actual usage. These load lists should be refined often to support actual usage of an item through a deployment. Periodic informal reports from commodity managers to the CO or XO may prevent a minor disaster during independent operations. There have been several classic consumable problems over the years—the ship on independent operations that reaches the low level alarm on toilet paper, for example, or the ship which runs out of machinery-wiping rags with six weeks of independent steaming to go—these are problems you don't need, and won't have if your system is set up properly.

Controlled Equipage. Controlled equipage is given extra management control afloat because of high unit cost, vulnerability to pilferage, and importance to the ship's mission. Over the years the number of required controlled equipage items has been reduced to make management simpler. You should review additions carefully so as not to dilute the system's effectiveness. Modern power tools and portable test equipment are two categories that should definitely be included, though. In maintaining your controlled equipage inventory, require that all *signature required* material be accounted for. Most ships have found that the use of custody cards is the best way to maintain the system. Remember that if culpability is suspected for a controlled equipage item, you must require a formal survey.

Requisition Management. You must imbue your officers with a strong sense of responsibility regarding requisition prioritization. The priority of any requisition must be carefully determined, for the shore supply system can act only on the priorities ships assign it. Improper priorities are like false fire alarms; abuses only erode prompt and proper operation of the system.

Many operational commanders use "hot" or critical list systems to highlight command concern for certain items. These lists, if used efficiently by minimizing their length, can guide the supply officer in her efforts to obtain critical spares. This is made easier by keeping onboard status records up to date through a reconciliation process with the IMA. The supply officer should reconcile her outstanding requisitions and financial status with the tender at least weekly. Deployed ships should mail error lists to the tender so that support personnel stateside have a proper picture of their requisition and financial accounting status for spare parts. This reconciliation process, plus constant monitoring of requisitions, will also identify overage requisitions. This is important since some old, unfilled requisitions are probably no longer needed and should be cancelled. The present fleet commander Material Obligation Validation (MOV) program strives for a goal of 98 percent validity of all outstanding requisitions. One hundred percent is a reasonable goal; less than 80 percent is UNSATISFACTORY on an annual supply inspection.

Financial Management. Budget planning for spare parts and supplies is a valuable tool for all ships, and promotes foresight among the different shipboard departments. Your financial account for spare parts and supplies is termed your Operating Target (OPTAR). On a small ship, your commodore maintains the account and you do the spending. On a large ship you will maintain your own. You can avert embarrassing situations if you observe your budget, make your personnel aware of constraints, and insist upon frequent reconciliation of your account with the squadron and tender. You will find that your parent squadron or type commander will invite input on your needs, but be ready to back up your requests with facts. Most COs have maintained control of OPTARs by personally reviewing requisitions above a particular threshold value.

Supply Readiness Monitoring and Supply Assistance

There are several methods for you to monitor your ship's supply readiness. The most obvious is to learn the details of the supply system and ask your supply officer the *right* questions. All too often, line officers take on a supply system problem without adequate knowledge of basic inventory control, financing, and prioritization. Several years ago, a young supply officer in the process of being relieved for his displayed inability to operate his department described his problems to his commodore. He said that he couldn't dine in the wardroom for fear of being ridiculed by his peers and the commanding officer. He described how his critical list of needed repair parts had grown to well over one hundred and that he had not had time to perform COSAL maintenance in over six months. The lesson here is obvious. Your young supply officer needs the same support (and probably more) that you give your other junior officers. His responsibilities must be clearly defined and given priorities. You can never accept substandard performance, but you must be alert to see that your supply officer is not placed in a "reaction mode" and that he doesn't react to every comment, request, and gripe from the wardroom and crew. A proven way to build your young supply officer's confidence and performance is to ensure that the executive officer supports him, much like a "sea daddy" would help a young enlisted sailor, until he is clearly capable of taking charge.

Supply inspections also provide an excellent assessment of the ship's internal supply management. These inspections, normally conducted at eighteen- to twenty-month intervals, will bring out any major deficiencies. The wise commanding officer will review the inspection report with a critical eye toward *trends,* as well as absolute grades, and will set up a continuing program to solve identified deficiencies.

Supply Overhaul

Background. Supply overhauls are designed to upgrade supply effectiveness by establishing proper repair parts support for the ship's current configuration. A successful supply overhaul requires the combined efforts of shore-based support activities, fleet staffs, and ship's force. Normally, supply overhauls are conducted in conjunction with shipyard overhauls. In view of the number of activities involved, they are generally not conducted without prior approval and planning of your type commander. Supply overhauls are called "Integrated Logistics Overhauls," because they encompass a complete audit and update of not only the ship's supply package, but also the preventive maintenance support system and all technical manuals, and have also provided training to all hands in COSAL maintenance. This system has proven worthwhile, improving the coordination of preventive maintenance requirements, technical manual support, and the COSAL.

Supply Overhaul Events. A schedule of milestones for your supply overhaul is generally promulgated about a year prior to the scheduled start. To establish an accurate configuration baseline and effective COSAL, a validation baseline of all shipboard equipment must be completed well before the overhaul starts.

During your overhaul, the initial allowance of onboard repair parts for newly installed equipment and components and new items appearing in the COSAL as a result of Allowance Parts List (APL) revisions will be provided, using Commander Naval Sea Systems Command (COMNAVSEASYSCOM) funds. Funding for deficiencies other than these is the responsibility of your type commander. As you can see, failure to record consumed spare parts prior to overhaul to conserve OPTAR funds will only catch up later when the type commander has to pick up the tab for needed spares.

During your overhaul, numerous configuration changes will be made to the ship. The Naval Supervising Activity (NSA) has responsibility for all COSAL changes during overhaul. You and the Supply Operations Assistance Program (SOAP) team are responsible for forwarding COSAL change data to the NSA for all configuration changes made by the ship's force and by special assistance teams outside the shipyard overhaul effort. Your supply officer must be alert to identify these and to provide the information to the allowance section of the shipyard. Continuous liaison with the allowance section, and careful review of alterations conducted by your crew, are required throughout the overhaul to ensure that your COSAL reflects the final configuration of the ship.

In conclusion, then, to ensure that complete equipment support is achieved during your supply overhaul, you must carry out the following responsibilities:

Sufficient enlisted personnel must be assigned to support the supply overhaul.

Applicable instructions and procedures must be fully understood by ship's supply support personnel.

Written procedures must be established to coordinate the issue, control, accounting, and replacement of allowance list material withdrawn during the course of overhaul work. Issue of material from your ship should be made only in cases of urgent need and where the material is not readily available from other sources. Such issues should require the approval of the supply officer as a minimum.

You must ensure that prompt follow-up action is taken for all shortages. Prior to departing the shipyard, you must ensure that your current status is provided to the parent tender for continued monitoring and expediting.

Alterations and Improvements

Background. We have discussed the necessity of keeping your ship's COSAL up-to-date. This section provides a summary of the Navy's Alteration and Improvement Program, to enable you to understand better the forces behind equipment modifications on your ship.

Definitions. It is hard to understand the Alteration and Improvement Program without some knowledge of the term used in it.

Military Improvement of Ships. Changes to military or operational characteristics, qualities, and features that increase the capabilities of ships to perform their approved missions and tasks. These are approved by the CNO.

Technical Improvement of Ships. Changes to improve safety of personnel and equipment, increase the effectiveness of equipment, improve system performance, and increase reliability and maintainability.

Alteration Equivalent to a Repair (AER). An alteration that meets one or more of the following conditions:

(1) The substitution, without change in design, of different materials which have prior approval of the cognizant systems command for similar use and which are available from standard stock.

(2) The replacement of worn-out or damaged parts, assemblies, or equipments with those of later and more efficient design previously approved by the cognizant systems command.

(3) The strengthening of parts which require repair or replacement in order to improve reliability, provided no other change in design is involved.

(4) Minor modifications involving no significant changes in design or functioning of equipment, but considered essential to eliminate recurrence of unsatisfactory conditions.

Ship Alteration (SHIPALT) Categories. Alterations on Navy ships are assigned the following categories:

(1) *Title A.* Assigned to alterations requested for certain ships under construction, in which authorization is anticipated during the obligation period under construction funds. Title A

ship alterations are funded under Ship Construction Navy (SCN) funding. On expiration of these funds, Title A alterations may be classified as Title K alterations, discussed below.

(2) *Title D*. Assigned to alteration equivalent to a repair. These are authorized by type commanders and funded under Other Procurement Navy (OPN) funds as operating expenses.

(3) *Title F*. Assigned to alterations that can be accomplished by forces afloat. They are authorized by type commanders and require no industrial assistance.

(4) *Title K*. Assigned to all other type ship alterations authorized by NAVSEA as specified within the Fleet Modernization Program (FMP) and funded under OPN.

(5) *Title K-P or Title D-P*. Assigned to those alterations designated for inclusion in the SHIPALT Package Program of the FMP.

(6) *Type Commander Alterations and Improvements (A&I)*. Used by some type commanders for the following reasons:

   (a) To authorize accomplishment of alterations equivalent to repairs.

   (b) To authorize accomplishment of interim corrective action for recognized problems prior to the issuance of a ship alteration.

   (c) To maintain accountability for various required inspections, tests, and modifications.

Alteration and Improvement Programs. Each type commander administers an alteration and improvement program. This lists the various approved alterations, field changes, and AERs that apply to ships of the type. Your type commander's program is based on the Navy's FMP. The FMP is an integrated program that combines ship alterations of a technical and military improvement nature and lists them based on scheduled ship overhauls. The Navy's FMP consists of all alterations applicable to specific ships on a yearly basis within a five-year period. The current year program then becomes the schedule for implementing presently funded ship alterations. Future year programs form the basis for annual Navy budget submissions. Based on the FMP, material managers budget and procure supporting material and identify COSAL support as needed.

In support of the shipboard alteration program, you must ensure that your department heads keep abreast of information on package alteration kits that are, or will become, available for the ship. You must ensure that package alterations are installed expeditiously after receipt and that proper COSAL maintenance is conducted to support the change. Finally, you must ensure that completed installations are reported in a timely manner and that feedback is provided to Navy technical agencies when difficulty is experienced in completing any alteration.

Food Service

Food Service Officer. Although you may assign a separate food service officer, the more common practice in smaller ships is to have the supply officer carry out this function. In most ships the wardroom eats from the general mess, and no provision is necessary for a separate wardroom mess. The young supply officer will probably have little or no experience in the management of messes. Thus, it behooves you to keep a close eye on his operation of both the general and wardroom messes. You should review the menu carefully before approving it, and should insist that deviations be approved by you in writing. Make it clear to the food service officer that you expect a high level of performance from each person assigned food service responsibilities. If a meal is not palatable, find out why. You should not sit in the wardroom and eat poorly prepared food. If it doesn't taste good to you, it doesn't to the crew. As commanding officer you should strive for the reputation of being the best feeder in the Navy. Getting this reputation does not take as much money as it does attention.

An important corollary to rejecting substandard performance in the food service area is to recognize outstanding work. On the mess decks, the junior mess cook is of equal importance to the leading mess management specialist. These personnel and those who work with them should be publicly recognized for superior work. This type of recognition pays dividends. Recognition is directly related to

Recognizing outstanding food service management is directly related to improved morale.

morale, job satisfaction, and retention. Additionally, it sets the tone for all food service operations, and will result in improved relations between the mess management specialists and the rest of the crew.

Food Service Personnel and Service. At the present time, a shortage of experienced mess management specialists exists in the fleet. Improved retention of food service personnel will, in time, raise experience levels in this vital area. In the meantime, you should strive to improve the skills of food service personnel. In doing so, you must work to improve both management and the personal desire for excellence of your subordinates.

An example of improved food service management is in the area of menu planning. Some ships continue to require the leading mess management specialist to write a menu from scratch each week rather than using a five- or six-week cycle menu. Significant time can be saved on this job if your ship adopts a cycle menu. Each week the cycle menu is reviewed to reflect special events and seasonal fruits and vegetables, but the basic foods are fixed. A cycle menu will not hurt quality or variety if properly managed.

In the area of motivation, you must use technical training and your own support to strengthen the food service organization's morale. Your food service division will respond in a positive manner to frequent sanitation inspections and insistence on attention to detail. Obviously, these rules apply to wardroom service as well as to the enlisted dining facility. The key to success in food service throughout your tour will be consistent *attention to detail* and *prevention of deterioration of service* afforded your officers and crew.

Accountability. *NAVSUP* publications set forth stringent requirements regarding financial accountability files. Improper accounting and procedural control in the food service area can ruin a career. As commanding officer, you must involve yourself in food service accounting to the degree necessary to ensure *its* effectiveness and *your* peace of mind.

It is not necessary that you become a *full-time* food service or commissary officer to monitor properly the food service operation of your ship. It does take some knowledge, however, to ask the proper questions and conduct necessary audits. More importantly, it takes some of your time and interest to get the point across to food service personnel that you will accept nothing less than strict adherence to food service accounting.

Replenishment at Sea

Each ship should leave its base, tender, or port as fully provisioned and supplied as possible. Normal fleet operations provide for further replenishment, when needed, at sea. Each fleet unit must be ready to use the U.S. Navy's outstanding system of extending almost indefinitely the time and range of operations.

First, each ship must know how to communicate its requirements to replenishing ships. *Operational Reports* (*NWP 1-03.1*) stipulates that UNREP requirements be submitted twelve to twenty-four hours in advance of the rendezvous. Complete instructions for submission of these reports is contained in *Replenishment at Sea* (*NWP 4-01*).

Personnel assigned to the supply department are poised to collect a vertical replenishment delivery.

Second, each ship commander must be skilled at bringing the ship alongside promptly and accurately, and maintaining it there. The crew must be skilled in rigging replenishment systems and receiving and striking below provisions, ammunition, and fuel received by all means, including helicopters.

Submarines replenish at sea only in emergencies, and must be particularly careful to set out on patrol or on operations fully supplied.

The Captain's Role in Maintenance and Logistics

You must take some time as you approach the assumption of command and outline for yourself what you think your appropriate role should be in the interrelated challenges of maintenance and logistics. The first consideration is your own background. Whether you are about to take command of a ship, submarine, or aircraft squadron, you will have had at least some grounding in both maintenance and logistics. Take some time and think through your own skills and how applicable they will be to the challenges at hand. Were you the chief engineer of a nuclear attack board? In your squadron XO role, were you heavily involved in the supervision of the maintenance officer and the maintenance department? When you were in your department head tour on a destroyer, were you the operations officer, with very little interaction with either maintenance or logistics? Start by setting out your own experiences in these two areas.

Next, shortly before taking command, you will be afforded an opportunity to visit with the applicable type commander's staff, as well as the ISIC staff. Pay particular attention to what you hear from the staff personnel in the logistics and maintenance shops. Hopefully you will hear a candid assessment of the strengths and weaknesses of your command from an outside and relatively dispassionate source. Key indicators you should focus on are readiness statistics, operational availability percentages, length of time between CASREPs, budget trends, cannibalization requests, inspection results, food service reviews and participation in the Ney Award competition for food service, and general reputation. Normally you will be provided with "hard copy" printouts of your command's situation in both maintenance and logistics.

Armed with a review of your own strengths and weaknesses and the status of your command, you are ready for turnover. During the turnover, take a hard and thorough look at all of the indicators discussed previously in this chapter. Bring to bear the information you've obtained from you staff visits as well as your personal experience and expectations. Naturally, during the turnover week you should refrain from making any policy statements or giving any orders; a command has only one skipper, of course!

Once you have relieved, you should be in a reasonably good position to discuss your philosophy on both maintenance and logistics with your wardroom and your chief's mess. You may want to consider drafting a short, one- or two-page statement of your approach in these areas, or your thoughts could be included in a broader "command philosophy." You could also choose to include your thoughts in another document. Whichever approach you take, it is wise to provide your team with something in writing that lays out the basics of your feelings on maintenance. Some good things to address include standards for notification of department head, executive officer, and commanding officer; policies on CASREPs; expectations for supplies (e.g., "never out" lists, goals for restocking); desire to compete for the Ney Award; mess deck standards; relationships with outside repair activities (e.g., times when only the CO will speak for the ship, guidelines for peer relationships with staffs); and general repair philosophy and adherence to good engineering practices. An excellent source of thoughts for the maintenance portion of your statement is the *Naval Engineer's Guide,* published by Naval Institute Press. From a logistics perspective, you may want to rely on a discussion with your type commander's assistant chief of staff (ACOS) for supply matters, a very senior and experienced supply officer. Naturally, the key source of information is your personal experience and philosophy.

A central element of your philosophy will be an understanding, shared by everyone in the ship, of the CO's role in maintenance and logistics. In general, you will want to be very involved in maintenance and logistics issues that directly affect the maneuverability and combat capability of your ship at a command level—essentially everything that warrants a CASREP or has immediate impact. You will also probably choose to be fairly closely involved in the PMS, probably wanting to undertake two or three checks a week where you actually watch the maintenance personnel work—on some ships and submarines, the CO does one every day! Most captains find it helpful to be involved in the mess decks in some way each day, at least dropping by between meals or walking through the galley. You will be amazed how the crew appreciates your interest in their well-being as reflected in time spent in the galley. Plus, you may walk in just as the chocolate chip cookies come out of the oven!

Conclusion

Maintenance and logistics: they are truly the twin pillars upon which the day-to-day capability of your ship rests. Admiral Burke, as usual, had it exactly right—all the brilliant tactical thoughts in the world won't matter if you don't have working equipment. This is an area in which experience will help, but the real determinant is command attention. Walk your decks, talk to your maintainers and logisticians, and never, ever take them for granted—your command will prosper. It is surprising how a ship that is a good "feeder" always seems to score well on the gunfire range; how a squadron with high maintenance results drops ordnance on target time after time; and how the submarine with the best engineering practice is always the one launching green flares signifying a hit in the JTFEX. A coincidence? Hardly. War is won by those who get there first with the most, as a Confederate Civil War general said well over a century ago. You should strive to be that commander who gets there first with the most—by building a winning team in the world of maintenance and logistics.

7

Safety

The mark of a great shiphandler is never getting into situations that require great shiphandling.

—Fleet Admiral Ernest King

Prior to World War II, safety at sea was a relatively simple matter. All of shipboard safety could be treated under only three major categories. First, the ship had to sail safely, which meant avoiding grounding and collision by good navigation and proper shiphandling. Second, fireroom casualties, mainly boiler explosions and fires, had to be avoided by the observance of traditional precautions and the careful use of checklists. Third, ammunition had to be received, stored, moved, and fired safely. This task was the subject of elaborate, almost sacred safety precautions, which were observed to the letter. As for minor hazards, most ships had a paint locker, which occasionally produced a rousing fire (and a resultant flurry of corrective instruction), and a five-inch loading machine, which amputated at least one finger a year. Other than these small irritants, the safety program, then not yet dignified by a name, was simple, straightforward, and effective.

Today, safety is a much more complex subject. Nuclear power, nuclear weapons, high-pressure steam plants, exotic missile propellents, more powerful conventional explosives, aviation fuels, automatic gun and missile loading machinery, complex replenishment systems, the threat of biological and gas warfare, the possibility of nuclear contamination, toxic chemical concerns, and a host of other developments make a far-ranging, integrated, formal safety program necessary. The safety program now must cover almost every function of your ship, from the location of your brow to the storage of special weapons.

Many of the areas that require safety bills and programs are peculiar to each type of ship. Many are simple and require no discussion. These latter will be found in *OPNAVINST 3120.32A,* the *SORN.* Those general programs of the greatest importance, however, will be discussed in the following pages.

Accident Prevention Education

Responsibility. The *SORN* assigns the commanding officer the ultimate responsibility for all safety matters within his unit. To help him carry out his responsibilities in this area, the CO may appoint a safety officer to provide day-to-day staff assistance. The *SORN* also requires that a command safety program be built on policies and goals established by the captain. A typical safety organization is shown in Figure 7–1.

A good safety program must imbue the crew with the understanding that *safety is an all-hands responsibility.* All crewmen must develop an attitude which makes them stop and think before they make, or allow another person to make, that one wrong move that can bring disaster. In light of current shipboard manning problems, and the declining level of supervisory experience in the fleet, you must aim for this attitude in every sailor, down to the rawest seaman recruit.

Safety Officer. You will have to use insight and judgment in appointing your safety officer. Assigning this program to the "boot ensign" will guarantee its failure. This officer will serve as your principal adviser on all internal safety matters, and her relationship with you, the executive officer, and the crew is the key to success.

A successful safety program does not have to mean extra work for the crew. The most successful programs, in fact, are those which have been incorporated in the ship's normal training and qualification procedures. This can be done by concentrating safety training efforts in

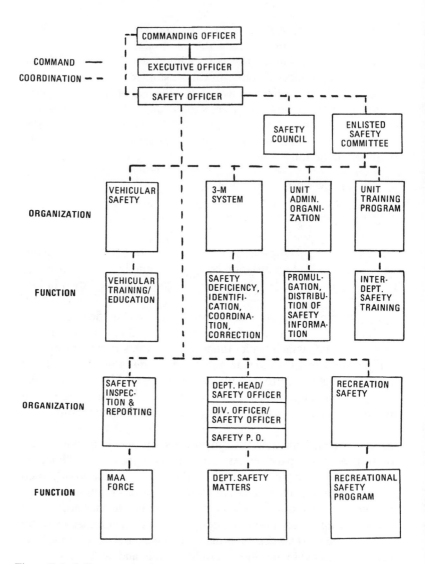

Figure 7–1. Safety organization.

areas that complement shipboard operational and administrative training.

As an example, accident prevention education can be presented as part of the ship's general military training. This can be done in a painless way by proper dissemination of pertinent safety bulletins. The Navy spends thousands of dollars annually publishing such fine periodicals as *Fathom* and *Safety Notes,* as well as defective material reports, lessons learned, and many other items. The wise will learn by the mistakes of others; the foolish are destined to learn by their own bad experiences. Needless to say, these publications should also be routed and reviewed by all supervisory personnel.

Routine Inspections. Another safety-related training vehicle is the use of routine inspections to highlight safety hazard awareness, as well as material conditions. Daily inspections of spaces by division officers and leading petty officers should be directed to instill hazard awareness in their personnel. Your periodic inspections, and those by the other senior officers assigned, can emphasize the same points. In addition, selected monitoring of hazardous evolutions will tell you much about your ship's safety awareness.

Naval Safety Center. Your command accident prevention program can get off to a good start by inviting the Naval Safety Center inspection team aboard to perform a safety survey. Safety Center surveys are completely informal. They are designed to provide the ship with the latest safety information and to discuss hazard identification and safety management techniques with your key personnel. No preparation is required other than making time and personnel available.

Most surveys consist of several elements. First, an all hands accident briefing is generally presented, detailing current accident prevention methods. A wardroom briefing is conducted simultaneously with the all hands briefing. Next, the survey team conducts a hazard review. This passes the latest safety programs and accident prevention methods to each division. The team will, if you desire, also conduct a hazard identification walk-through with key personnel. This is carried out using a checklist derived from hazardous items identified by INSURV inspections and through the SAFETYGRAM system.

Your ship's safety program should also be reflected in the watch station qualification program and in the formal certification of watchstanders. This can readily be done by promulgating standard procedures to cover all operational, maintenance, and repair evolutions, and by making use of these procedures mandatory.

Safety Investigations. Finally, your safety program should provide a way to analyze accidents afloat and to report them properly when necessary. Ensure that your safety officer is thoroughly versed in the conduct of investigations. Particularly, direct her to place her emphasis on determining *why* the accident happened. She should also be familiar with material damage and injury reports, the use of accident reports for accident analysis, and hazard reporting.

All this might seem like a large load for one junior officer. However, familiarity with the references below will provide her all the information necessary to do the job properly:

OPNAVINST 3120.32C, Standard Organization and Regulations of the U.S. Navy, Chapter 7
OPNAVINST 5100.21B, Afloat Mishap Investigation and Reporting
OPNAVINST 5102.1, Investigating and Reporting
OPNAVINST 5100.19, NAVOSH Program Manual for Forces Afloat
The Watch Officer's Guide, published by Naval Institute Press

You can give your program another boost by sending your safety officer to the unit safety supervisor's course, taught at the fleet training centers on both coasts.

Watch Officers and Safety

Watch Officer Responsibilities. A ship is administered departmentally, but her operation at sea is directed on a watch basis. Watch officers assigned directly assist the captain with the safe navigation and operation of the ship. The *SORN,* Chapter 4, authorizes you to establish such watches as are necessary for the safe and proper operation of the command. In addition, it directs that the watch of the officer of the deck and of the engineering officer of the watch be regular and continuous while underway.

The remarks below amplify those watch officer responsibilities and relations provided by *Navy Regulations* and the *SORN*, especially as they relate to safety underway.

Officer of the Deck (OOD). The officer of the deck underway is that officer on watch designated by the commanding officer to be in charge of the ship. He is primarily responsible, under the captain, for the safe and proper operation of the ship and for the safety and performance of her personnel. The OOD must keep continually informed concerning the tactical situation and geographic factors that may affect the safe navigation of the ship, and must take appropriate action to avoid grounding or collision in accordance with tactical doctrine, the rules of the road, and the orders of the commanding officer or other proper authority.

The OOD reports directly to the CO for the safe navigation and general operation of the ship; to the XO for carrying out the ship's routine; and to the navigator for sightings of navigation landmarks and course and speed changes.

Engineering Officer of the Watch (EOOW). The engineering officer of the watch is the officer or petty officer designated by the engineer officer to be in charge of the engineering department watch. He is responsible for the safe and proper performance of the engineering department watch, in accordance with the orders of the engineer, the commanding officer, and higher authority. The EOOW reports to the OOD for the speed and direction of rotation of the main engines and for direction as to standby power requirements and other services anticipated or ordered. He reports to the engineer officer for technical control and on matters affecting the administration of his watch.

Command Duty Officer (CDO). The *SORN* also provides for an inport watch organization, led by a command duty officer, to ensure the security and safety of the ship. The CDO is responsible for security, for the conduct of routine, and, in the absence of the regularly responsible officer, for the supervision of all ship's activities. He succeeds to the responsibilities and authority of command when all eligible ship's officers senior to him are absent or incapacitated.

As head of the inport watch organization, the CDO must ensure that all hands are continuously alert to their responsibilities while in a duty status. Fire, flooding, sabotage, and enemy attack are always possibilities. Early detection will prevent or minimize damage. The CDO is your direct representative.

Watchstanding Principles

Procedures for safety at sea and in port are clearly defined in the *SORN*. In addition to the formal organizational requirements of this instruction, you must stress proven watchstanding principles to your subordinates as prerequisites to the safe and efficient operation of the ship and for its security from all hazards.

Watchstanders must clearly understand that their effectiveness is a function not only of their basic understanding of operations and equipment, but also of their watchstanding habits and regard for safety. Even the best operational and safety training program will only be as effective as the standards they keep. The following paragraphs briefly describe those attributes required by the members of a watch section to enable them to maintain the ship in a safe manner.

Attention to Duty. Watchstanders must be vigilant and attentive to all details. The appearance of normal, steady state conditions should never be an excuse for relaxing attention. Watchstanders should never conduct business except as required by the duties of the watch.

Conduct While on Watch. Each individual must stand watch in a smart military manner. In doing so, loud conversation and unnecessary noise are never appropriate. Reading of any material not directly pertinent to the watch should never be allowed.

Physical Condition of Watchstanders. No individual should be allowed to relieve the watch unless physically and mentally able to stand an alert, effective watch. Watchstanders whose abilities are impaired by sickness or exhaustion should inform their supervisors and request a relief.

Congestion. The conduct of any watch requires proper access to equipment and clearly defined duties and responsibilities. Spectators should never be permitted at any station or in any space where they might obstruct or distract the watch.

Communications. All watchstanders must conduct communications in strict accordance with the ship's interior communications bill.

Casualty Action. Watchstanders should read and understand all casualty procedures pertinent to the watch station. They should review these procedures periodically as necessary to ensure complete familiarity. While on watch, they should be encouraged to review mentally the actions they would take under various casualty conditions.

Log Keeping. Keeping logs and data sheets, while important, must never be allowed to interfere with the effective and *safe* operation of the ship and its equipment. If it does, the watchstander should report it immediately to the next senior in the watch organization.

All watchstanders must understand the significance of log entries and trends evident therefrom. A review for trends at the time of recording hourly readings may indicate a system change which can be diagnosed and rectified before the situation deteriorates into a casualty.

Instrumentation. Experience with naval machinery and equipment has emphasized the importance of instrumentation and records. In general, it is best to proceed by assuming that all instruments are reading correctly, or operating on the safe side of the worst indication of the instrument. Never blame the instrument until investigation has proven it defective.

Relieving the Watch. Relieving the watch should be a controlled and precise procedure. The ability to handle casualties and tactical decisions is significantly reduced during the transition period between watches. Accordingly, observe the following procedures during watch relief:

1. The relieving watch should be on station sufficiently early to become familiar with equipment conditions and the overall situation and still relieve on time.
2. The relieving watch must make a thorough and complete inspection of all spaces and equipment under his cognizance *before* relieving the watch. This is particularly applicable to engineering and weapons areas, but is not limited to them.
3. Both the relieved and the relieving watch are responsible for ensuring that the relieving watch is completely aware of all un-

usual conditions that exist. These include the tactical situation, equipment out of commission or being worked on, outstanding orders, deviations from normal "line up," forthcoming evolutions, and any other matters pertinent to the watch.

Underway Operational Safety

Underway Safety Directives. *Navy Regulations* and the *SORN* both state that the commanding officer is responsible for the safe navigation of his ship or aircraft, except as prescribed otherwise for ships at a naval shipyard or station, in drydock, or in the Panama Canal. In time of war, or during exercises simulating war, the provisions of these references pertaining to the use of lights and electronic devices may be modified by competent authority.

The commanding officer of a ship and, as appropriate, of an aircraft, shall:

Keep informed of the error of all compasses and other devices available as aids to navigation.

Ensure that efficient devices for fixing the ship's position and for ascertaining the depth of water are employed when underway on soundings, entering or leaving port, or upon approaching an anchorage, shore, or rock, whether or not a pilot is aboard. If circumstances warrant, speed must be reduced to the extent necessary to permit these devices to be operated efficiently and accurately.

Observe every precaution prescribed by law to prevent collisions and other accidents on the high seas, inland waters, or in the air.

When underway in restricted waters or close inshore, and unless unusual circumstances prevent, steam at a speed that will not endanger other ships or craft, or property close to the shore.

Take special care that the lights required by law to prevent collisions at sea, in port, or in the air are kept in order and burning in all weathers from sunset to sunrise, and that means for promptly relighting or replacing such lights are available.

Piloting Errors. Failure to heed these regulations has resulted in disaster at sea as a result of collision or grounding. In the matter of grounding, a review of investigations over the past one hundred years has clearly pointed out that one or more of a group of common piloting errors have been found to be the cause of each disaster. Yet these errors still occur all too often. The wise commanding officer will review the below list often, asking, *Does my organization suffer in any of these areas?*

Failure to obtain or evaluate soundings.

Failure to identify aids to navigation.

Failure to use available navigational aids effectively.

Failure to correct charts.

Failure to adjust a magnetic compass or maintain an accurate table of corrections.

Failure to apply deviation, or error in its application.

Failure to apply variation, or to allow for change in variation.

Failure to check gyro against magnetic compass readings at frequent and regular intervals.

Failure to keep a dead reckoning plot.

Failure to plot information received.

Failure to properly evaluate information received.

Poor judgment.

Failure to do own navigating (following another vessel).

Failure to obtain and use information available on charts and in various publications.

Poor ship organization.

Failure to "keep ahead of the vessel."

In addition to reviewing your organization for these errors, you should ask yourself the following questions each time you review the navigation picture with the navigator or the OOD:

What is the reliability of the present indicated position? How was it obtained?

Does the OOD clearly understand his responsibility under *Navy Regulations* to positively establish the ship's position and track as being safe?

Where do the greatest hazards lie on the track ahead?

What is the bottom contour along the track?
Will there be adequate warning of approaching danger?
What would the worst conditions of set, drift, and position mean?
Am I rushing the ship at the expense of safety?

Training OODs. The effective commanding officer will train officers to ask themselves these same questions prior to relieving and while on watch as OOD or JOOD.

All to often, grounding investigations determine that the OOD did not clearly understand the burden on him regarding the safe navigation of the ship. The *SORN* clearly describes his obligations in regard to navigational safety. *The officer of the deck underway must keep continuously informed concerning the tactical situation and geographical factors that may affect the safe navigation of the ship, and must take appropriate action to avoid the danger of grounding or collision.*

Investigations have also shown that often the OOD took insufficient interest in navigation simply because the navigator or one of his assistants was on the bridge. Each OOD must understand that the navigator's position as the authoritative adviser on the safe navigation on the ship does not relieve him of any of his responsibilities.

Navigational Readiness. Procedures for checking your ship's navigational readiness are important, and proper use of them will pay you dividends. An excellent resource is the conduct of frequent (at least semiannual) navigation check rides. These one-day events can be done by your ISIC or the Afloat Training Group (ATG) in your homeport. Your own experience and attention are, of course, the key here.

Collisions. Thucydides, in the fifth century B.C., said, "A collision at sea can ruin your entire day." This witticism has been repeated in some form by each generation of seamen since. Analysis of collisions over many years has shown that one or more of the following mistakes caused each incident:

Failure to realize in time that there was a risk of collision.
Failure to take timely avoiding action.

Failure of a darkened ship to turn on running lights in an emergency.

Failure of a watch officer to notify the commanding officer of a potentially dangerous situation.

Failure to check for steady bearing in a closing situation until too late.

Reliance on CIC to the exclusion of a common-sense evaluation of the situation being made on the bridge.

Poor judgment in evaluating the effects of wind and tide.

Failure to understand the tactical characteristics of the ship.

Injudicious use of the power available in the ship.

Bridge and CIC radars both on long-range setting, thereby making the detection of close-in targets difficult, or bridge and CIC radars both on short-range setting, resulting in a failure to detect distant targets on a collision course until very close in.

Failure of bridge personnel to keep sharp visual lookout.

Failure of CIC and the bridge to ensure that the commanding officer understood tactical signals.

Making a radical change in course without informing ships in the vicinity.

Failure to use whistle signals.

Failure to make the required checks between gyro and magnetic compasses.

Failure of a ship in formation to broadcast a warning by voice radio when contacts are seen to be merging.

Failure of the bridge to check maneuvering board solutions provided by CIC, and vice versa.

Deck watch officer's lack of familiarity with the rules of the road and with accepted procedures for preventing collisions.

Failure to execute tactical signals correctly.

Most of the errors above are elementary, but still they are made all too often. In addition to training your officers in the academics of watchstanding, you must imbue them with a general attitude of vigilance, a highly developed sense of responsibility, and the faculty of good judgment. You must stress the value of mental review of casu-

Even in the calmest weather, anchoring is a potentially dangerous evolution.

alty actions while the watch is slow, and insist upon formal communications by watchstanders. Failure to use proper phraseology and to preserve strict formality of address among members of the watch is asking for trouble.

Underway Operational Safety. Safety at sea is enhanced by emphasis on all of the areas mentioned above. By such emphasis, safety becomes command philosophy and policy. You must avoid letting the routine performance of safety measures deteriorate into carelessness.

Many COs tend to standardize the procedures they use to approach channel entrance ranges and make turns and speed changes in proceeding to or from their berth. This standardization can help the captain in the development of his supervisory ability on the bridge by shifting some of his concentration from decision-making to supervisory observation.

Supervisory ability is distinct from the ability to conn the ship or, specifically, to conduct any evolution personally. It involves keeping in mind what the OOD is doing, where the navigator wants to go, what lookouts are reporting, what signals are in the air, what is happening on the forecastle, who is at quarters aft, whose barge is passing down the side, and whether or not the ship ahead is turning early—*but without being directly involved.*

Cultivation of this faculty permits overall observation of the ship's performance, avoidance of dangers that more preoccupied personnel may miss, and, finally, the ability to handle the ship successfully in combat. When the captain's personal skill must be applied to the conn, or when he has to concentrate his attention on any other one facet of operations, something vital may be missed. In contrast, the captain who insists on navigational and piloting briefs before entering restricted waters, who ensures that his subordinates plan and brief supervisory personnel prior to any non-standard or complicated evolution, will be better prepared to practice overall supervision. This is particularly true when the risk of overlooking something important is increased by several days of strain, lack of sleep, and physical "pounding."

A Pacific Fleet letter by Fleet Admiral Nimitz has a bearing on this:

There are certain psychological factors which have fully as much to do with safety at sea as any of the more strictly technical ones. A large proportion of the disasters in tactics and maneuvers comes from concentrating too much on one objective or urgency, at the cost of not being sufficiently alert for others. Thus, absorption with enemy craft already under fire has led to being torpedoed by others not looked for or not given attention; while preoccupation with navigation, with carrying out the particular job in hand, or with avoiding some particular vessel or hazard, has resulted in collision with ships to whose presence we were temporarily oblivious. There is no rule that can cover this except the ancient one that eternal vigilance is the price of safety, no matter what the immediate distractions.

No officer, whatever his rank and experience, should flatter himself that he is immune to the inexplicable lapses in judgment, calculation and memory, or to the slips of the tongue in giving orders, which throughout seagoing history have often brought disaster to men of the highest reputation and ability. Where a mistake in maneuvering or navigating can spell calamity, an officer shows rashness and conceit, rather than admirable self-confidence, in not checking his plan with someone else before starting it, *if time permits*. This is not yielding to another's judgment; it is merely making sure that one's own has not "blown a fuse" somewhere, as the best mental and mechanical equipment in the world has sometimes done.

Who Has the Conn?

Distinction between Conn and Deck. When underway, you must ensure that the OOD is thoroughly aware of the distinction between the conn, which is the actual control of the movements of the ship, and the deck, which is the supervisory authority of the watch as outlined in the *SORN*. A conning officer who is also OOD has all the responsibilities imposed by the *SORN,* as well as those imposed by the directives of the commanding officer.

Changing the Conn. In order to ensure that no confusion exists over who has the conn, a definite routine of taking it over and relinquishing it must be followed. The status of the conn must be clearly understood by the OOD, verbally acknowledged, and, most important, loudly brought to the attention of all personnel who perform manually the orders given by the officer who has the conn. A considerable measure of responsibility for the ship's safety remains with the OOD even when he is relieved of the conn by the CO or other qualified officer.

Although there is no official set of rules about the conn, the following principles have been evolved through the experience of seamen. You may relieve the OOD of the conn at any time. In addition, you may instruct the OOD how to proceed without previously assuming the conn. Any direct order to the wheel or engine order telegraph will, however, in itself constitute assumption of the responsibility for direction of the ship's movements—the *conn*. Under these conditions, in order to ensure efficient response and eliminate the possibility of conflicting orders, the OOD should announce to the bridge watch, "The captain [or other officer as appropriate] has the conn," and immediately thereafter report to that officer, "Sir, I have relinquished the conn."

Involuntary Relief of the Officer of the Deck. In the previous section it was pointed out that you could relieve the OOD of the conn at any time. Over the years the authority of the XO and the navigator with regard to involuntary relief of the OOD has changed. Prior to 1973, the XO and the navigator could relieve at any time. At present, Article 323, *SORN,* states that the navigator may relieve the OOD as authorized or directed by the CO in writing.

The authority of the XO is less clear. The general authority of the executive officer delegated by the commanding officer would seem to cover the matter, but it is advisable, in order to avoid misunderstanding, to give the same authorization in writing to the XO to relieve the OOD. Both officers should be instructed to inform the CO as soon as practicable after relieving.

Good Sea Manners and Shiphandling Tips

Naval Shiphandling, by Captain R. S. Crenshaw, USN (Ret.), published by Naval Institute Press, should be read by every officer who goes to sea. In addition to a comprehensive explanation of the principles of shiphandling, this excellent book includes most of the information and advice which makes up its "folklore." These are little rules that are picked up as one's experience broadens at sea, and which in total are the wisdom that prevents one from repeating mistakes. They might be called the safety precautions or "good manners" of shiphandling.

In listing these tips, Captain Crenshaw made no attempt to record them in order of their importance. We reproduce them here to provoke thought for safety at sea.

Keep your ship's stern away from danger. If the propellers and rudders become damaged, you are crippled. If the stern is free to maneuver, though, you can usually work your ship out of trouble.

Don't take a chance. If you recognize it as a chance, it is probably too risky.

When ordering rudder, look in the direction you intend to turn. This is as wise at sea as in a vehicle ashore.

Check to make sure that the rudder moved in the direction you ordered. Watch the helmsman move the wheel if you can. Check the rudder position indicator to see what the rudder actually did. Check the compass for direction. On a surfaced submarine, check the rudder.

When ordering rudder, tell the helmsman your intended final course. You may be distracted during the turn, and the ship will continue to swing.

When swinging to a new course, bring the rudder amidships a number of degrees before reaching the new course equal to one-half the rudder angle being used. When using thirty degrees of rudder, order the rudder amidships when you have fifteen degrees yet to go. This works remarkably well for coming smartly to a new course.

Beware of a ship lying to. She is often moving imperceptibly.

Don't trust your sense of distance in a flat calm. This sense is undependable under any conditions, but is at its worst across a glassy sea.

Don't attempt precise maneuvers when going astern. Ships handle awkwardly when backing, and occasionally veer erratically.

Give buoys a wide berth. You can't see the cable to the buoy anchor from the surface. Many a screw has been damaged on a buoy that had been "cleared."

If you are confused, consider that the other ships in the formation are, too. When the situation seems confused, a normal maneuver by another ship may catch you by surprise.

When uncertain what to do, come to formation course and speed. This will give you time to clarify the situation.

During a complex formation maneuver, remember the direction toward open water. This is the avenue to safety; you may need it.

When collision is imminent and a safe course of action is not apparent, back emergency and turn toward the danger. The backing will delay the collision and reduce the impact. The turn toward the danger will reduce the target you present, and a ship can withstand impact better forward. A head-on collision will crumple the bow, but the ship can be cut in two if hit from the beam.

Never trust a compass or a chart. Keep checking the ship's heading by landmarks and auxiliary compass. A compass doesn't announce its departure when it goes out. And all charts have minor inaccuracies; some have major ones.

If blown against a ship or pier when going alongside, stay there until you have made complete preparations to get clear. The ship is normally quite safe resting there, but can sustain major damage trying to pull clear without assistance.

Never trust a mooring; check it. Anchor chains part, mooring shackles break, buoys break adrift, even bollards pull out of piers. Check the position regularly.

In low visibility, keep the radar tuned for short range. The power setting and tuning of the main control console should be selected for best coverage of the band 0–5,000 yards. Though you can expand the presentation by changing the scale setting on the remote scope on the bridge, you can't get optimum results unless the main console is properly adjusted. Remember, it is the contact at short range that presents the danger!

When sounding fog signals, shorten the interval once every few minutes. You may be synchronized with another ship and not hear her signal because of your own.

Sound the danger signal early. This is legal, and it declares that you do not understand the other ship's intentions. It will prompt her to commit herself and thus clarify the situation.

A ship on a steady bearing is on a collision course. Take precise bearings on approaching ships, and check the trend.

Avoid passing starboard-to-starboard close aboard. The other ships may evaluate the situation as being nearly head-on, and cause a collision situation by altering her course for a port-to-port passage. It's safer to alter course to starboard at an early stage and pass port-to-port.

Join other ships by coming up from astern. Relative speeds will be lower and the whole maneuver will be more comfortable for yourself and your formation mates.

The faster the ship is moving through the water, the better control you will have. Both rudder force and hull stability improve with speed, and wind and current are felt less.

When adjusting position alongside with the lines over, don't wait for the ship to begin moving before stopping the engines. The time lags are too long for this.

Steer your ship as you would a boat. Look ahead and steer where good sense indicates. Orient to the real world of landmarks, channels, buoys, ships, and obstructions. Keep your head up and your eyes open. Charts, maneuvering boards, and compasses are aids, not substitutes. If the navigator's recommended course doesn't look right, stop your ship and "let her soak" until you are sure that the course you are taking corresponds both with the indications of the chart and the physical situation you see.

When following a tortuous channel, or the movements of another ship, steer with rudder angles instead of ordering successive courses. You are fitting curves to curves and you must adjust as you move along the curved part.

When entering a narrow channel, try to adjust your heading to compensate for cross wind and cross current before getting into the narrow part. This can be deceptive visually and very tricky.

When required to maneuver by the rules of the road, turn early and turn plenty. Make your intention completely clear to the other vessel; you can refine your course later.

When the bow goes to port, the stern goes to starboard; make sure to allow room for it. In a tight place, where even a small drift in the wrong direction spells trouble, leave a spring line secured to check a faulty movement until the ship is actually moving in the right direction.

If your ship loses power or steering, notify any other ships in the vicinity immediately so they can stand clear. Be prepared to drop anchor immediately and indicate your change of status with appropriate day shapes.

Keep the jackstaff up when maneuvering in port. It is a valuable aid in verifying the ship's head with respect to other ships and landmarks, and in judging the rate of swing of the bow in a turn.

Shiphandling in Heavy Weather

Crenshaw's *Naval Shiphandling* provides excellent information on handling a ship in heavy weather. All members of your wardroom should be familiar with it.

It is one thing to pass the word "secure ship for heavy weather," and another to have it done effectively. You would be wise to order a thorough inspection each time the ship is preparing for a storm. Hatches, lifelines, storerooms, holds, and engineering spaces should get special attention. The more effort spent in preparing for heavy weather, the less damage the storm can cause.

As opportunity permits during bad (but not dangerous) weather, experiment to determine the best courses and speeds for the ship during rough seas. The average and extreme rolls of the ship on courses into and with the seas should be compared, and any tendency to pitch severely or to pound noted. Prove to yourself and to your crew the capabilities and limitations of your ship, so that when actually faced with a hurricane or typhoon you can have confidence in your ability to cope with it. Decide firmly the best method of handling the ship in a hurricane or typhoon and make sure that all conning officers are acquainted with this decision.

The Commanding Officer's Role in Safety

As you begin a command tour, whether of a ship, submarine, or aircraft squadron, you should outline a few very basic goals. Whether you commit these to paper and keep them to yourself, incorporate them into a written "command philosophy" to share with your shipmates, or merely think them through in a quiet moment is completely up to you—it is the process of focusing on your ultimate goals that matters most.

Certainly at the very top of your list of command goals should be a commitment to do all within your power to minimize risk to personnel and equipment. *In peacetime, there is no higher goal.* As you prepare for command, and indeed every day you spend as captain or skipper, you should think about your *specific* role in accomplishing this worthy goal.

Perhaps the first thing to consider is the old standard of personal example. Ensure that every aspect of your personal behavior in the command sets the standard, including safety checks on personal electronics, safe equipment in your stateroom, safety glasses and earplugs worn whenever necessary, fire-retardant uniforms, steel-toed shoes— if you "drop by" the engine room in a pair of docksiders and don't bother to put in earplugs because you're "just sticking your head in," a very bad signal is sent to your sailors. Your stateroom on the carrier, for example, should have strict adherence to safety checks for all electronics, from your electric razor up through the television set. When you walk by a rig during an evolution, you should be the first one wearing a safety helmet properly. Rank does have some privileges, even in today's Navy, but safety violations are definitely not one of them.

A second place you can have a positive impact with your crew from a safety perspective is in the area of command communications. You have all the tools: 1MC, plan of the day, perhaps a monthly command plan. Part of your daily message to your team should focus on safety. Occasionally sport a "safety button" with the green cross on your uniform or ball cap. Make sure you personally attend all the safety council meetings, and come up with at least one good idea to throw on the table. You may want to consider having the safety officer start up a monthly "safety newsletter" for your command—there are dozens of easy-to-use desktop publishing products that can make this a fun and enjoyable publication for the crew, complete with a monthly message from the CO, an XO's focus "issue," a few words from the ship's safety officer, a "dumb move of the month" (with names changed to protect the not-so-innocent), and so forth. Encourage your safety team to share their good ideas by submitting articles on safety to *Fathom, Proceedings,* or *Surface Warfare.*

A third high-impact area for you as CO in the safety world is driving the command toward appropriate recognition and awards. This should be as important in your command goal focus as the Ney Award for food service, the Battle E, or any of the Combat Systems Awards. Appoint a smart, articulate officer to the program—normally the operations officer in a ship; and of course the designated safety officer department head in a squadron. Make him or her outline a plan to establish, improve, and maintain the highest level of safety. Use the type commander's annual safety award program as a specific goal, and insist on regular reports on how your command is improving in all areas of safety management. Insist that you review the list of safety petty officers, and ensure they are well respected, articulate, and good examples. You can't do it yourself—but you can ensure you have a top-flight team moving toward a specific goal.

Recognize that shiphandling and flight safety are your special province. As the leading mariner or aviator in your ship, submarine, or squadron, take every opportunity to inculcate an attitude of safe shiphandling and airmanship in your subordinates. In this day of billion-dollar warships—many with deep and sensitive sonar domes—and multimillion-dollar aircraft, there is no excuse for putting your ego ahead of the safety of your ship, submarine, or aircraft. Never hazard your ship, submarine, or aircraft for the sake of showy shiphandling or flashy airmanship. Take the assistance of professional pilots in shiphandling, listen to experienced controllers in the air, utilize tugs when available, and always select the safest way to handle the expensive asset the Navy has placed in your care. Any other approach is simply wrong. In this regard, you may want to call upon the expertise of the pilots in your homeport for coming to your ship or submarine and discussing shiphandling with your wardroom. They will make more landings in a month than you will in a career—use them as a resource to help train and educate your wardroom. Senior aviators from outside the squadron can also be used in this regard.

Finally, you should be the leader in making use of outside resources. In addition to taking advantage of the excellent support from the Naval Safety Center, think about how you can use other waterfront assets to help you out. You may want to consider setting up a mutual "safety check" with a sister ship, submarine, or aircraft squadron—outside eyes are always the best in seeing the safety issues you may be walking by day after day. Additionally, your staffs will all have designated safety personnel who can help by doing informal "walk arounds." You can bring in organizations from outside the Navy as well, perhaps a police or fire department. Don't forget that part of your safety responsibilities extends to your crew's home life and time away from the command as well as within the lifelines or on the flight line. Set up programs that reflect safety in the home, both for your sailors and their families.

Conclusion

In the end, safety is the area where you, as commanding officer, must find the time to rise above the day-to-day fray that absorbs your XO and department heads. In their press to get everything done on time and perfectly, they will be highly tempted to cut corners from time to time. You are the safety conscience of your command! Remember that the minute your immediate subordinates get the impression that you are willing to cut a few corners, stand by: a true disaster is just over the horizon.

Admiral King, in the quotation at the head of this chapter, had it exactly right—and not only for shiphandling. In the world of safety, you avoid trouble by looking downrange for potential problems, and avoiding them altogether. You have no role more important than protecting your crew and your command.

8

Training and Inspections

To lead an untrained people to war is to throw them away.

—Confucius, *Analects*

Let such teach others who themselves excel.

—Alexander Pope, *Essay on Criticism*

Building Your Team

As the leader of a combat organization, you are the captain, not only of a ship, but also of a team of individuals who must be prepared to undertake the Navy's fundamental mission: to conduct prompt and sustained combat operations at sea.

Building that team is the heart of your command responsibility, and everything you say and do is in furtherance of that overarching mission. To help you accomplish the building of a first-rate fighting team, you will have the tools you developed in the years leading up to your command—judgment, professional skill, knowledge, common sense. You will also find that the Navy provides a myriad of helpful assessments and inspections that will test your team in demanding conditions short of combat. At times, the seemingly endless march of requirements that stem from training will stress you and your team to an extraordinary degree. Yet you must always remember that what you undergo in the training cycle is only a small percentage of the true stress of combat operations. You must exhibit an

A proud moment in the life of one comanding officer as his ship, the USS *Valley Forge* (CG 50), steams up to "join the fleet."

attitude of excitement and anticipation during training and inspections. All those serving in your command will take their cue from you, and if you seem apprehensive, nervous, and unprepared, so will your entire team. If, on the other hand, you take the attitude that training evolutions and inspections are your command's chance to shine, your enthusiasm will communicate itself quickly to every corner of your ship, submarine, or squadron.

The same things you learned in sports about how teams succeed manifest themselves in the building of a combat team. You will be as strong as the weakest link; superstars help, but they cannot carry the day alone; the sharing of credit is a crucial element in promoting team unity; pulling together in unison, your team is far stronger than the sum of its individual elements; teams need good leaders at every level; and it is a combination of heart and head that wins in the end. Remember to play with courage, and don't overestimate the views of those who endlessly take counsel of their own fears. Fortune usually does favor the bold. And while the race is not always to the swift, that's usually a good way to bet.

The Training Cycle

Admiral Chester Nimitz, in addition to being a superb wartime commander, was an expert on training. He once made the following observation in describing the fundamentals of training: "First you *instruct* men, then you *drill* them repeatedly to make the use of this knowledge automatic, then you *exercise* them, singly and in teams, to extend their individual abilities ship-wide; then the authority one level above the person who trained them *inspects* to insure that the desired results have been achieved."

In a broad sense, this is what you must do. Early in the training cycle, you must form a *training organization,* prepare a *training program,* and under this program and using this organization, instruct your individuals and teams. When instruction is completed, *drills* are used to assure the thoroughness and quality of instruction and to instill automatic reactions. *Ship exercises* then extend the drilling of individuals to drilling ship's teams. These intra-ship exercises then progress to intership exercises to bring the unit up to fleet standards. Finally, administrative seniors make *inspections* to determine the state of training of each ship. Inspections can cover a wide range of administrative and operational areas. All of these areas of preparation will be described in subsequent sections; but before getting too involved in them, you should be in touch with your type commander.

A Typical Inter-Deployment Training Cycle

While there is naturally a great deal of variability between the inter-deployment training cycle of different ships, submarines, and squadrons, it is still useful to look at a typical cycle for a surface combatant. Doing so will provide a frame of reference that will be roughly applicable for every type of Navy command at sea. All of this is referred to as the Tactical Training Strategy, or TTS.

A good reference for constructing such a typical inter-deployment cycle is the combined COMNAVSURFLANT and COMNAVSURFPAC Instruction 3502.2C, the *Surface Force Training Manual*. This detailed and excellent publication provides a superb summary of overall inter-deployment training, as well as a wide variety of broad training information. It includes extensive sections on the training cycle, unit training and qualification programs, team training, unit competitions, training reporting, and readiness reporting. Of note, there are equivalent manuals and instructions available from the aviation and submarine type commanders for submarines and aircraft carriers and squadrons as well.

After reviewing the applicable type commander training manual (in our example, the surface force version), it is possible to construct a hypothetical inter-deployment training cycle:

Return from Cruise. During the midpoint in the cruise, the commanding officer has conducted a Command Assessment of Readiness and Training (CART I), which provides a rough training "road map" to wrap up the cruise and line up required schools, services, and scheduling in preparation for executing the inter-deployment cycle.

Month 1. The key event is a post-deployment upkeep in homeport, a thirty-day period that lets the crew recharge their batteries, get reacquainted with their families, and return refreshed to begin the challenging inter-deployment cycle. You will probably undertake an initial offload of your cruise levels of ammo and fuel, depending on your upcoming schedule and the requirements of your Selected Restricted Availability (SRA).

Months 2–3. You will conduct an SRA, which is a medium-length industrial availability, normally conducted in the ship's homeport. Of note, there is a current movement toward shorter (nine-week) SRAs, which will be of benefit in maintaining cruise-level readiness throughout the inter-deployment cycle. You will conduct a Light-Off Assessment (LOA) during this part of the cycle. This evolution ensures that the ship is ready to operate propulsion, includes a short sea trial, and permits completion of the SRA. The LOA is conducted by the ship's ISIC, supported by the Propulsion Examining Board (PEB) and the Afloat Training Group (ATG).

Month 4. The next step is initial training activity, including a limited ammo onload, the next Command Assessment of Readiness and Training (CART II), and initial team training in naval surface fire, undersea warfare, and other specific warfare areas. The CART II is the most important early event at this point in the cycle, because it provides you the opportunity to review the readiness level of the command and tailor a training plan for the rest of the inter-deployment cycle. The command works closely with the ISIC—in this example, a DESRON commander and staff—and the ATG, which will provide assistance and training throughout the cycle.

Months 5–7. This portion of the training cycle provides the command with the opportunity to complete initial basic phase training, primarily unit-level training in which the command's various training teams come "on line" and prepare to take over the training function. This occurs across all areas of command endeavor, including combat systems, operations, navigation, engineering, and supply. The periods are divided into various phases referred to as Tailored Ship's Training Availabilities (TSTA I through IV). The highlight is the engineering certification (ECERT), which is conducted by the ISIC, supported by the PEB and the ATG. This important event is completed during TSTA II, which completes the certification of the engineering plant.

Months 8–9. This portion of the training cycle includes such important events as the Cruise Missile Tactical Qualification (CMTQ), the Logistics Management Assessment (LMA), and the Final Evaluation Problem (FEP). The CMTQ (which can be included as part of the FEP, but is often done as a stand-alone evaluation) qualifies a ship to launch cruise missiles (i.e., Tomahawks and Harpoons). The LMA is the overall supply, logistic support, and maintenance inspection of the ship, while the FEP is a kind of "final exam" in which the entire ship's fighting, damage control, and readiness is assessed. Completion of the FEP frees the ship to proceed into the more complex battle group portions of the training cycle.

At this point in the cycle, the ship will "chop" from the type commander (COMNAVSURFLANT or COMNAVSURFPAC) to the operational fleet commander, that is, Third Fleet or Second Fleet.

Months 9–15. While there is a good deal of variability in this portion of the schedule depending on the command's relationship with the battle group, in general there will be four to six months between the end of the FEP and the departure for the next deployment. This period includes Carrier Battle Group (CVBG) or Middle East Force (MEF) preparations. A wide variety of other activities occur, including testing, loading, fueling, gunfire qualification, and several short (two- to four-week) maintenance availabilities.

Final Month. The final month before deployment is a Preparation for Overseas Movement (POM) month, which permits granting liberal leave and liberty to the crew, conducting any final logistic preparations, and making final arrangements to depart homeport.

Some key terms to bear in mind as you look at the inter-deployment cycle:

TSTA:	Tailored Ship's Training Availability
TSTA I:	Develop training teams, work on basic warfare skills.
TSTA II:	Integrate watch teams and develop complex training scenarios.
TSTA III:	Commanding officer's time to practice and refine skills.
FEP:	Final Evaluation Problem. Evaluate all reportable mission areas, with ship emerging as at least "M-2" in all areas before proceeding to next phase. ISIC reports to type commander.

Shipboard Training Program

The Importance of Training. The basic directive for shipboard training is Chapter 8, *Standard Organization and Regulations of the U.S. Navy, OPNAVINST 3120.32C* (the *SORN*). The *SORN* points out that the training of personnel to operate and maintain shipboard equipment and systems is one of the prime factors contributing to battle readiness. This training requires instruction of operator and maintenance personnel in the requirements of their rates, as well as the additional requirements of their Navy Enlisted Classifications (NEC).

The *SORN* further states that for purposes of orientation, training can be characterized as follows:

1. Individual in-rate maintenance training, normally conducted at a shore facility as a prerequisite to assignment of personnel to a fleet unit
2. Individual in-rate operator basic training, traditionally accomplished ashore
3. Individual watch station qualification, normally accomplished in the command
4. Systems training for individual operators and teams which includes subsystem training (undersea warfare, air warfare, repair party, etc.) and total integrated systems training (combat systems, damage control, etc.), traditionally ashore, with training to maintain efficiency accomplished in the fleet. Integrated systems training must necessarily be conducted at the unit. This unit training as discussed in the *SORN* concerns individual watch station qualification and operator and team proficiency in subsystems and integrated systems.

Requirements for Effective Training. The *SORN* states that to be effective:

1. Instruction must be dynamic and progressive, with repetition avoided except for emphasis.
2. Instruction must be regularly scheduled, daily if possible.
3. The instructor's degree of preparation and method of presentation must reflect his deep interest in the subject.
4. Persons in authority must show interest in the progress of individuals in self-education and in all other forms of education.

This last requirement is aimed directly at you as commanding officer. If you show interest and concern, all those under you in the training organization will follow your lead.

Formulating a Training Program. Training without a firm, sound program is wasted. Thucydides, as far back as 404 B.C., recognized this when he said, "The Persians' want of practice will make them unskillful, and their want of skill timid. Maritime skill, like skills of other kinds, is not to be cultivated by the way or at chance times." This is just as true today as it was 2,400 years ago. Put your strongest efforts into the development of a training program.

Your shipboard training program should be created while your ship is still under construction or early in its yard overhaul, and it must be based on Chapter 8 of the *SORN*. This publication and the parallel supplements put out by each type commander should become your "bibles" for training.

The *SORN* covers training in detail. It gives general guidance for the establishment of a training program as follows:

1. Establish long-range goals to cover the periods between over-hauls and short-range goals which recognize scheduled operational commitments. These should be expressed in terms of achieving and maintaining the highest possible readiness for each assigned mission area.
2. Develop resource requirements in terms of personnel/NECs, shore training site curricula, watch station qualifications, and subsystems and systems proficiency.
3. Identify deficiencies in resources and take action to correct them.
4. Identify factors in the unit's schedule that clearly will affect established shipboard training goals.
5. Establish a schedule for the conduct of unit training, including:
   a. Specific accomplishments.
   b. Means of conducting the training.
   c. Means of evaluating the training.

Your training program must include the formation of a shipboard training organization, the carefully considered appointment of a training officer, the constitution of a planning board for training, the formulation of a set of detailed training plans, and the creation of a comprehensive set of training records; and then, with these preliminary organizational steps accomplished, the use of these tools to instruct, drill, exercise, and inspect your crew. We will take up each of these steps in turn.

Forming a Training Organization. The backbone of your training program must be a strong and effective training organization. A typical organization is shown in Figure 8–1. Yours will vary somewhat according to your ideas and the numbers and qualifications of personnel assigned. *No* organization will work, however, unless those assigned to it are instructed as to what is wanted and how you want them to carry out their missions. This means instructing the instructors, making sure adequate teaching materials are on hand, and ensuring that lesson plans are prepared and made available.

The key person in this organization is the training officer. Give careful consideration to choosing and assigning this individual and make sure he fits the organization you have formed.

Training Officer. Large ships can afford to assign as training officer a fairly senior individual, who can exert a goodly amount of authority, but small ships must depend upon the XO. One course of action is to appoint him as training officer and to assign a junior officer to assist. Another is to assign the task to a junior officer and then direct the XO to oversee and support his efforts. A third is to assign the task to the operations officer, with assistance from a junior officer. Of these choices, the soundest seems to be to assign the operations officer as training officer and to assign a junior officer as assistant training officer. Remember, however, that in training, the full authority of the XO is needed, and his every action should take into account the training of the crew.

When the XO blows his horn, everybody listens.

Planning Board for Training. Regardless of your decision with regard to the training officer, it can be retrieved by your next action, which is to form a planning board for training, as required by Article 812 of the *SORN*. You must include on this board the executive offi-

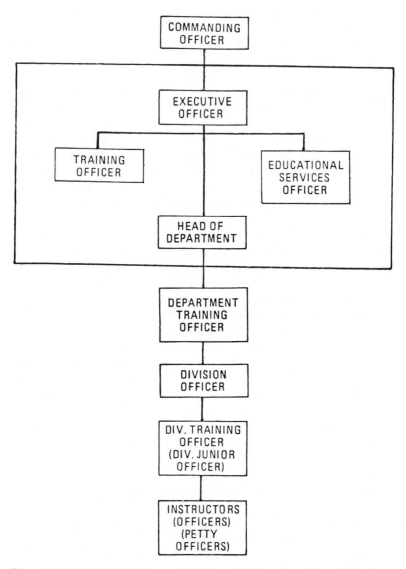

Figure 8–1. Shipboard training organization showing composition of the planning board for training.

cer as chairman, the heads of departments, the educational services officer, and the training officer. Figure 8–1 shows the relative position of the planning board for training in the ship training organization. If you have decided to appoint the operations officer as training officer, ensure that the XO applies firm direction as head of the board. His interest and direction can buttress the efforts of the operations officer, counteracting the tendency of more senior department heads to put other activities ahead of training.

Training Plans. With a training organization in being, headed by a well-chosen officer, your next step is to develop a series of training plans. These start with a long-range training plan, which is the basic plan for all training and for keeping personnel informed of projected training aims and operating schedules. It should contain enough information to ensure that the training effort can be made effective. The quarterly and monthly training plans, which should go into more detail, can be formed from it. Minor details should not be included in the long-range training plan.

This plan should cover the battle efficiency competition cycle (if in effect) or other training cycle, such as between deployments. The *SORN* gives the following considerations you should use in preparing this plan:

1. *Training during overhaul.* For most ships, the overhaul period provides an opportunity for sending personnel to schools. However, shipyard overhaul periods also impose heavy workloads of repairs, tests, fire watches, and supervision of shipyard work. On-the-job training, inport fire drills, self-study courses, and drills by rating must also be pursued during this period.
2. *Training during leave and upkeep periods* following deployment is usually limited to formal school attendance and onboard damage control drills.
3. *Coordinating training and maintenance* should be done by allotting the available work hours in accordance with the requirements for maintenance and training. Accordingly, major maintenance should be shown in the plan.

MONTHLY TRAINING PLAN

JULY

SUNDAY	MONDAY	TUESDAY	WEDNESDAY	THURSDAY	FRIDAY	SATURDAY
OPPORTUNE: Z-26-S(R) Z-28-S(O) Z-29-S Z-13-CC	1 G.Q. Z-10-D NBC Lecture Intelligence Briefing UNREP: 3 DER	2 DIVISIONAL SCHOOL J.O. School Crypto Drill UNREP: 2 MSO	3 DIVISIONAL SCHOOL J.O. School INREP: An Thoi	4 Hand grenade & small arms training all day for Deck and Ops	5 Field Day	6 G.Q. Battle Prob Z-6-D Z-11-S(R) Z-10-D Z-14-S Z-24-D Z-27-D Z-52-D Z-111-E(R)
7 Arrive Subic Z-27-D	8 Z-20-C(O) Z-27-D(Sec I)	9 GMT III DIVISIONAL SCHOOL J.O. School Crypto Drill Z-27-D(Sec II)	10 GMT III DIVISIONAL SCHOOL J.O. School Z-27-D(Sec III)	11 Lookouts lecture (Steaming Watches) Z-27-D(Sec I) PAY DAY	12 0500 Depart SUB G.Q. Gun Shoot Z-20-S Z-14-CC(R) Z-1-AA(R) Z-1-N(R) Z-3-AA(O) Z-5-N(O) Z-29-G(R) Z-110-E(R) Z-21-S(O) Z-1-E(R)	13 SF-1, 6-M(R) for all departments GQLT NBC Lecture Training Board Z-27-D(Night)
14	15 Mil/Lead Exams E-3 Exams	16 Arrive YOKO DIVISIONAL SCHOOL J.O. School Crypto Drill Z-27-D(Sec II)	17 DIVISIONAL SCHOOL J.O. School Blood Donations Z-27-D(Sec III)	18 Z-27-D(Sec I)	19 Field Day Z-27-D(Sec II)	20 DEPART YOKO C.O. Pers Insp. C.O. Zone Insp.
21	22 G.Q. Battle Prob. Z-6-D Z-10-D Z-24-D Z-27-D	23 DIVISIONAL SCHOOL J.O. School Crypto Drill	24 DIVISIONAL SCHOOL J.O. School	25 Telephone Talker Drill (GQ talkers) PAY DAY	26 Field Day SF-2, 5-M(R) for all departments	27 GQLT NBC Lecture Training Board Z-27-D(Night)
28 Arrive PEARL Z-27-D(Sec III)	29 COMSERVPAC visit G.Q. Z-10-D NBC Lecture Z-27-D(Sec I)	30 Depart PEARL DC Lectures DIVISIONAL SCHOOL J.O. School Crypto Drill	31 DC Lectures DIVISIONAL SCHOOL J.O. School	1 AUG Hand grenade & small arms training for Supply & Engineering	2 AUG Field Day	3 AUG C.O. Zone Insp. C.O. Pers Insp. 5 AUG Arrive SFRAN

Figure 8–2. Sample monthly training plan.

The *SORN* also gives these instructions for preparing the long-range training plan:

1. Schedule fleet exercises, trials, inspections, and other major evolutions required by type or fleet commanders.
2. Schedule all required exercises in kind and frequency required by the type commander to maintain C-1 readiness.
3. Schedule other applicable unit exercises, keeping in mind the considerations above.
4. Schedule all unit training (damage control lectures, counter-insurgency, security orientation, boat crew training, telephone talker training, military training, etc.).

The quarterly training plan is extracted from the long-range training plan. It can be prepared on a single sheet of paper and should be kept updated. It should contain more detail than the long-range training plan.

The monthly training plan gives a daily schedule of training, evolutions, and operations for each month. Figure 8–2 shows a typical plan. It should be prepared by the training board, and should show all unit training, evolutions, and operations scheduled in the quarterly plan, expanded with necessary detail.

The *SORN* points out that no information classified higher than confidential should be included in these plans. The crew should be able to guard this level of classification, if properly instructed.

A plan should also be prepared summarizing the scheduling and completion of drills, exercises, and inspections required by the type commander. When the battle efficiency competition is in effect, one plan will probably suffice for both these purposes.

Each division officer should prepare a division officer's plan and keep records of all operational drills, team training periods, and instructional periods in the division. Your training officer should require that all division officers keep these records. Proper instruction on the division level is the final payoff for your program. Without it, all the plans are just pieces of paper.

You must also plan for the training and indoctrination opportunities that do not occur as part of your planned program. This includes a variety of presentations for all hands, such as career benefits, minority affairs, drug and alcohol abuse, and safe driving.

Newly arrived personnel, particularly recruits and class "A" school graduates, will need special consideration and careful indoctrination. This is important, and it deserves the personal attention of the commanding and executive officers. Recruits are graduated in a state of mind that needs to be seen to be appreciated. They have been taught patriotism, respect for themselves and others, and exemplary conduct, and are eager to join their ship and become part of the active Navy. If they join a crew whose morals are suspect, whose love of their ship, navy, and country is low, and whose language and appearance mark them as poorly disciplined, the shock and disappointment can be devastating. These young recruits need not be pampered, but they must be encouraged to maintain their high standards.

Training Records

It is important that you set up a comprehensive record-keeping system, one that will show at any instant the exact status of all phases of training. The training officer and department head might well keep the long-range (annual and quarterly) training plans, the monthly training plan, and the record of exercises, trials, and inspections required by the type commander. On small ships this might be done with one set of records, but on a larger one an overall record might be required, with additional records kept by heads of departments.

The senior watch officer should keep records of deck watchstanding officer and enlisted assignments and qualifications and deck watchstander's courses and training record. Similarly, the chief engineer should keep the same records for engineering watchstanders, and the communications officer should maintain records for the communications and coding watch. The division officer should keep a record of drills and instructions, formal school training, and a personnel record. The chief or leading petty officer of each rating should keep a record of practical factors completed, and a Personnel Qualification Standards progress chart.

The foregoing record program is only a minimum; you will find additional records desirable, depending upon your ship type. Record forms for most programs are available from your type commander. Others can be easily drawn up.

The *SORN* provides a simple and workable training record program that you can vary to suit your needs and preferences. It includes nine standard forms, as follows:

1. Long Range—Quarterly Plan
2. Monthly Training Plan
3. Type Commander's Required Training Exercises, Trials, and Inspections
4. Division Training Schedule
5. Group Record of Practical Factors
6. Record of Qualifications at Watch and Battle Stations
7. Personnel Qualification Standards
8. Formal School Training Records
9. Division Officer's Personnel Record Form

A well-established system of training records will be of great value. For you, it will provide an instant overview of the state of training of your crew. For your officers and petty officers, it will be both a reminder of past accomplishments and a record of tasks still pending. It may seem at times like useless paperwork, but you will find in the end that your training program will be no better than its records. See the section at the end of this chapter on "Innovation and Training" for some ideas on record keeping.

Personnel Qualification Standards

In earlier days, junior officers and senior petty officers had ample time personally to train and qualify junior petty officers and nonrated personnel. Following World War II, however, the steadily increasing sophistication of ships, submarines, and aircraft, and the ever more rigorous demands placed upon their personnel, have combined to require a formalized system of training for personnel.

This system is known as Personnel Qualification Standards (PQS). It is now the heart of the training program, and we will, therefore, discuss it now in detail.

The PQS System. In essence, PQS is a listing of the knowledge and skills required for a sailor to qualify for each watch station, to maintain a specific equipment or system, or to perform as a member of a given team. It is a qualification guide, one that asks the questions trainees must answer to prove their readiness to perform a given task. It also provides a record of progress and final certification. PQS is an *individualized* learning process. Trainees have the complete program in their hands. The supervisor serves both as a source of assistance to the trainee and as a quality control over the learning process by certifying the completion of each step.

Standard lesson plans are provided by bureaus and offices, training commands, and type commanders. They provide a detailed, step-by-step breakdown of the requirements of each task and watch.

The PQS system does not completely replace normal division training. Rather, it is the key element of that program.

PQS Handbook. Every commanding officer should be familiar with the *PQS Handbook*. It begins with an introduction to the theory, format, and organization of the system. A glossary defines PQS words, phrases, and terms. The main portion of the *Handbook* discusses theory, system, watchstanders, and qualification cards.

PQS Progress Charts. The PQS progress chart shows which persons are in training for each watch and major task, their progress toward qualification, and the watch on which each person is qualified, together with the date of qualification. The *SORN* has a good sample chart which you can use.

PQS Qualification Card. The PQS qualification card is carried by each learner. It is a record of the completion of each item required for qualification for that task. The card is given to each trainee to be used by him to train himself with minimum supervision.

A typical card contains these items:

A *final qualification page,* identifying the long-term goal. Final commanding officer certification is placed on this page.

A *qualification summary,* giving the subordinate qualifications necessary to achieve total qualification within the specialty.

A *theory and systems summary,* which is a record of completion of the various theory and system requirements for qualification. Many of the systems are required to be completed for more than one watch station. If so, they are summarized on these pages, so that only one signature is necessary.

A *watch station checkoff* section, giving all the various duties that a trainee must complete to achieve qualification.

Properly administered and used, the PQS system is a valuable adjunct to your training system. Let your crew know that you support it, demand progress, and they will produce corresponding results. Inspect it personally during the "Division in the Spotlight" review.

Routine Drills

You may think that after completing TSTA you can forget drills and exercises for a while. Unfortunately, this is not the case. Drills must be as much a part of your ship's daily routine as instruction, exercises, and inspections. Refresher training just gets you into the swing of things.

Drills are conducted to prepare a ship's crew to meet any conceivable requirement or contingency. The basis of drilling is ship's bills, each of which is designed to meet one of these contingencies. Your ship's bills, as we have said before, must stem from the basic bills in the *SORN.* This publication contains sample bills in four categories: administrative, operational, emergency, and special. Type commanders augment these with additional and modified bills peculiar to their types.

Those bills requiring action by the crew also require *drill.* Drill allows those in authority to determine that qualified personnel are assigned, that requirements of bills are correct, and that equipment is in working order and on hand. Once this is established, repeated drills produce a set of automatic responses that will carry over under the most stressful conditions. All personnel should be able to perform their part even though wounded, in the dark, or if gas or nuclear fallout is present.

Once individual teams, such as damage control teams or gun

Frequent and thorough damage control drills will prepare your crew for any eventuality—collision, fire, or war damage.

crews, are organized and drilled, you may shift emphasis to larger groups such as gun batteries, boat loading teams, or missile firing teams, culminating in exercising the ship as a whole. Drills must be repetitive, thorough, and short. Obviously, drilling of a prize crew can be done infrequently, but the fire party must be drilled often and thoroughly, and it is important that this be done for each section.

This is of special importance during overhaul, when daytime debris and welding sparks may be smoldering at night in spite of the best efforts of your fire watches. You will sleep better if you require the CDO to report to you each day when under overhaul that he has mustered and instructed the fire party.

General quarters is the most important underway drill. If you make GQ frequent, interesting, and as short as possible, it will then be most productive. A good procedure is to plan a short battle problem for each drill, followed by imposed damages which will require the execution of various bills such as nuclear attack or collision.

In all your drills, remember that modern ships depend on internal communications (IC) systems. If you have a real collision, however, you may find a ship's bow in the middle of your IC panel with no means of communications left to you except word of mouth and messenger. Condition your crew to this and other unpleasant eventualities. In World War II some ships steered in battle at night by chains of messengers. Try it. You may have to be even more inventive. Make repetition work for you, not against you. Simple repetition induces boredom, but repetition tempered with imagination produces both rapid response and the ability to react to the unusual.

Exercises

By dictionary definition, *drilling* is "instructing thoroughly by repetition" and *exercising* is "training by practice." These terms are frequently used interchangeably, but in this discussion we will adhere to the proper meanings.

Exercises, then, are used to put the knowledge given by instruction and ingrained by drilling to a more practical use. A telephone talker is *instructed* as to how to use a battle telephone, *drilled* in its use by transmitting and receiving many made-up messages, and then *exercised* in its use by manning and using the telephone when the gun battery conducts a firing exercise.

Exercise Direction. Major exercise programs are set forth in the FXP series of fleet tactical publications and the AXP series of allied tactical publications. Key publications include:

FXP 1, *Submarine and Antisubmarine Exercises*. Establishes tactics and procedures for conducting submarine and antisubmarine exercises, with criteria for evaluating results.

FXP 2, *Air and Antiair Exercises*. Presents procedures and tactics for conducting aircraft exercises, as well as criteria for evaluation.

FXP 3, *Ship Exercises*. Provides exercises for all types of surface ships and guidance for observers in evaluating them.

AXP 1, *Allied Submarine and Antisubmarine Exercise Manual.* Establishes tactics and procedures for conducting Allied antisubmarine exercises with criteria for evaluation.

AXP 2, *Allied Tactical Exercises Manual.* Contains standard seamanship, gunnery, torpedo, and miscellaneous exercises for use by NATO navies in training their forces for participation in Allied operations.

AXP 3, *Allied Naval Communication Exercises.* Presents standard instructions for the conduct of communication exercises by the Allied navies.

AXP 4, *Allied Naval CIC/AIO and Radar Calibration Exercises.* Presents general instructions for the conduct of Allied naval exercises to prepare the CIC/action-information organization for performing its functions. An appendix provides guidance for evaluating the results of the exercises.

AXP 5, *NATO Experimental Tactics and Amplifying Tactical Instructions.* Provides a means of testing new naval and maritime/air tactics and exercises developed by a NATO nation, group of nations, or NATO Commander. AXP 5 has a mine warfare supplement and a secret supplement.

Type Commander's Supplements. Each type commander issues an exercise publication modifying or supplementing the FXP series. Where FXP 3, for instance, sets forth the goals, scoring, observation requirements, and reporting for a surface ship gunnery exercise in general terms, the type commander describes these criteria in exact terms for each type and subtype of surface ship.

Exercise Designation System. A self-translating, short-titling system is used to designate exercises for ease in communications. A typical title is Z-24-G. "Z" means an exercise for surface ships, "24" is a particular exercise, and "G" means it is a gunnery exercise.

Advanced and Inter-type Exercises. Advanced and inter-type exercises are usually conducted by unit commanders using a written operation order or a letter of instruction (LOI). The operation order is used for more complicated exercises and can be quite lengthy. The LOI system is used when the unit has a standard operation order already in existence or when the exercise is relatively simple. The LOI can be nothing more than a schedule of exercises.

Advanced exercises are usually given self-descriptive titles, such as ASW Hunter-Killer Exercise (ASWEX), Amphibious Fire Support Exercise (FIREX), Composite Training Unit Exercise (COMP-TUEX), Fleet Readiness Exercise (FLTEX), and Joint Task Force Exercise (JTFEX).

An ASWEX may last up to three weeks. Forces will include a land-based patrol squadron, a destroyer squadron, other ASW surface ships, shore-based surveillance systems, and several submarines. The operating area may cover thousands of square miles.

A FIREX is a shorter exercise designed to exercise ship and air portions of the fire support system of an amphibious force. Exercises are limited to areas where firing and bombing may be done.

A COMPTUEX may last one or two weeks. This is a relatively simple exercise arranged to combine available forces due for training so as to use them most efficiently. A unit commander usually operates under an LOI and schedules exercises using areas and services available.

A FLTEX is a fleet problem type of exercise in which available forces are split in two and exercised against each other. Forces involved can be quite large, often including all those available and due for advanced training or deployment. They usually include units of all types. Extensive advanced planning is required, and pre-sail and post-exercise critiques are always held.

Larger fleet exercises are occasionally scheduled. Each of these is different, and their planning, preparation, and execution can run into months.

A JFTEX is the "final exam" for a battle group prior to deployment. It incorporates all service assets, including Navy, Marines, Army, and Air Force, as well as international allied players. It is a complex war-fighting scenario off the U.S. coast for ten to fourteen days.

It is Navy policy to include UNREP in each of the above exercises, using whatever replenishment units are available. UNREP is such an integral and important part of our operations that unit commanders and commanding officers should make every effort to keep ship skills at a high level. If service force units are not available, replenishment and other alongside maneuvers should be scheduled using other units of the exercise force.

Inspections

Inspections are a means of ascertaining the state of battle readiness, administration, preservation, and training of your ship and its crew.

Inspections can be divided into two categories: those which you make, or cause to be made, under your authority as commanding officer (internal inspections); and those imposed on you and conducted by higher authority (external inspections). We will treat internal inspections first.

Internal Inspections.   The longest-established inspection in the Navy is the weekly captain's inspection. Article 0708-1 of *Navy Regulations* directs you to hold periodic inspections of the material of your command to determine deficiencies and cleanliness. If the command is large, you are permitted to designate zones and delegate assistants to inspect them, alternating the inspections so as to cover the entire command at minimum intervals. This has become known as "zone inspection" and is generally held on Friday afternoon.

Weekly inspections offer you an excellent opportunity to impress your policies on the crew. When you inspect, tell them what you want, what is wrong, and, more importantly, what is right. If they know what you want, then they will give it to you. It is also wise to require your XO to make a daily topside and living space inspection to see that proper cleanliness and maintenance plans and techniques are being used. The surest incentive for daily work is the knowledge by those doing it that it will be seen *every* day. Be circumspect about making daily inspections yourself, though, for too much "presence" can undermine the confidence and authority of your division and petty officers. They expect the XO, but they don't expect you. When you *do* inspect during the week, consider confining your efforts to trouble areas or special projects. This is a time to show interest, to bestow praise if warranted, but not to find too much fault. If you do find errors, have the XO correct them privately later. You must presume that the XO, the division officer, or the leading petty officers would have found the fault in due time if you had not preempted them.

There are other internal inspections you can make by means of boards. You can form a board or group to inspect any aspect of your administration. However, the *SORN* requires you to form certain boards which, in effect, make inspections even though they may be called "audits." The most important are:

Communications Security Material Board. Conducts audits, or inspections, of the records of the communications security material custodian.

Hull Board. Inspects the hull, tanks, free flood spaces, outboard fittings, valves, and appendages at times of drydocking and prior to undocking.

Flight Order Audit Board. Inspects and audits to ensure that all requirements concerning hazardous duty pay are met as per instructions.

Mess Audit Board. Audits the various messes on a monthly basis to ensure that they are correctly administered.

Monies Audit Board. Inspects to determine that all government properties and monies are present and accounted for, are properly protected and disposed of, and are otherwise properly administered. Audits disbursing cash verification, post office funds, imprest funds, and recreation funds.

Naval Commercial Traffic Funds Audit Board. Audits the account of the naval commercial traffic fund.

Personnel Reliability Board. Screens and continuously evaluates personnel assigned to duty with nuclear weapons.

Precious Metals Audit Board. Audits precious metals in the custody of the dental officer.

Ship Silencing Board. Assists the commanding officer in the development and execution of long-range plans for reducing the acoustic signature of the ship.

The best approach to internal inspections is to perform a weekly "Division in the Spotlight." See Appendix 3 for an example.

Inspections by Higher Authority. Over the years, higher authorities have formulated and imposed more and more outside inspections. This started in World War II, when the Training Command was created and refresher training was established. The large number of ships being commissioned, the relative inexperience of many commanding officers, and the preoccupation of type commanders with wartime operations made a system of outside inspection necessary. After World War II the use of formal inspections remained high as administrators sought a substitute for wartime motivation. They felt that competition, in combination with graded inspections, would be an incentive to superior performance.

Command Inspection. One important inspection is the command inspection. Some type commanders give it annually, while others give it twice a year, once on a scheduled basis and once by surprise. It is generally given in port over a twenty-four-hour period. The unit commander is usually the chief inspector, augmented by an inspection team from another ship. The inspection starts with a formal personnel and upper decks inspection, sometimes in a variety of uniforms. Some lower decks and machinery spaces are inspected. A standard type inspection form is used to record the results.

You would be wise to procure this form at an early opportunity and organize and administer your ship to pass a surprise command inspection at any time. The checklist requirements are not that difficult, though there will always be differences of opinion as to interpretation. The biggest problem, mostly found on small ships, is that in time of busy employment, or when shorthanded, personnel tend to let required records and procedures lag. You will have to make it clear that just the reverse should happen, even if you have to arrange temporary help. The records setup and administrative procedures are designed to keep people (and your ship) *out* of trouble, not *in* it. A properly administered ship can pass a command inspection at any time.

Should you fail a command inspection, sit down in the wardroom with your administrative personnel and test the advice given above against the record. Ninety percent of the time you will just have to start doing what you should have been doing all the time. The other 10 percent of failures probably will fit within Murphy's law or some variation thereof. Ever-ingenious bluejackets can find a hundred ways to avoid paperwork. It is up to you and your XO to keep their marvelous energies directed where *you* want them. Do so before the inspection and you will pass; do so after a failure, and you will quickly become satisfactory.

Medical Readiness Inspection. The unit commander will make a comprehensive inspection of the medical department either at or near the same time as a command inspection. This inspection determines the qualifications and state of training of personnel, the adequacy of medical procedures, both peacetime and wartime, and the completeness of medical material allowances.

Propulsion Examining Board. The PEB supports the ship's ISIC (along with the Afloat Training Group) in conducting engineering assessments.

The mission of the PEB is to assist the fleet commanders-in-chief in verifying that steam and gas turbine propulsion plants in certain conventionally powered ships are safe to operate. The fleet commanders also use it to promote improved engineering training and readiness within the fleets. This includes coordination of program evaluation, drill criteria, and standardization of procedures among the various training and inspecting commands.

The PEB has the following responsibilities:

1. Examine propulsion engineering personnel to determine their state of training and qualification. The appropriate engineering Personnel Qualification Standards are used to evaluate the level of qualification of all propulsion plant personnel.
2. Witness and evaluate the conduct of propulsion plant drills and evolutions, employing the installed Engineering Operational Sequencing System (EOSS) as a guide.
3. Inspect the material condition of the propulsion plant to ascertain its state of readiness, preservation, and cleanliness.

4. Review and evaluate the administration of the ship's engineering department and the completeness and accuracy of all ship's records relating to propulsion.

The Atlantic and Pacific Fleets both have boards of twenty officers. Each officer is well qualified and schooled in at least one of the three types of installations. Inspections are conducted by sub-boards of varying numbers of members depending upon the size of the ship inspected.

The PEB supports two main types of assessments. The first is the light-off assessment (LOA), conducted prior to lighting off the first fire in any boiler (or first light-off of a main or auxiliary gas turbine) during a regular overhaul (ROH), major conversion, fitting out availability, or restricted availability (RAV) in excess of four months in length. In the case of new construction ships, the LOA will be conducted following delivery and prior to initial light-off by ship's company. The second class of assessment is the engineering certification (ECERT).

The LOA can be divided into three parts. First, the PEB verifies that the propulsion plant is in a material condition which supports safe operation. Associated auxiliaries are included in the examination; that is, ship's service and emergency electrical plants, air compressors supporting propulsion plant operation, and any other equipment located in the propulsion spaces and/or normally operated by propulsion personnel.

The PEB also determines the adequacy of the administrative/operating procedures directly related to the propulsion plant, and the capability of shipboard personnel to safely operate and maintain equipment, systems, and spaces; for example, logs and records, liquid programs, hearing and heat stress programs, equipment tag-out procedures, and training.

Lastly, it determines whether engineering personnel have the knowledge to operate the plant safely. For a satisfactory finding, the ship must present at least two qualified watch sections with the proficiency to support safe auxiliary steaming. A capability for self-training of watchstanders and watch teams in the safe control of routinely encountered casualties must also be evident, for example, proficient engineering casualty control teams (ECCTT). Propulsion plant drills are not required as part of this examination. However, simple evaluations, such as boiler- and feedwater, or fuel sampling and analysis (as applicable), and casualty control walk-through drills may be conducted at the discretion of the senior member of the examining board.

During an ECERT:

1. Those areas discussed above under the requirements for an LOA will be examined.
2. The PEB will evaluate propulsion plant casualty control drills. The EOSS, where installed, will be the basic guide in evaluating the conduct of equipment light-off/securing and casualty control drills. The inspectors will require demonstration of these capabilities:
   a. The capability of at least two watch sections to support safely underway steaming.
   b. The capability of self-training, that is, the proficiency of ECCTT and of watchstanders and watch teams in the control of routinely encountered casualties.
   c. The capability to combat effectively a major fire in a main propulsion space.
3. Boiler flexibility tests (automatic boiler control [ABC] configured plants) on those boilers normally on the line to support the examination will be conducted to evaluate the ability of the plant to respond to changing power demands.
4. The board may, if examination circumstances warrant, witness and evaluate a high power demonstration.

Prepare for these examinations as the assessments direct. Drill often and prepare well and you should have no trouble. Fail to do so and the board will find you out.

Board of Inspection and Survey. INSURV is given basic duties in *Navy Regulations*. The president of the board, assisted by the other members and by permanent and semipermanent sub-boards as designated by the Secretary of the Navy, is required to:

1. Conduct acceptance trials and inspections of all ships and service craft prior to acceptance for service.
2. Conduct acceptance trials on one or more aircraft of each type or model prior to acceptance for service.
3. At least once every three years, if practicable, inspect each naval ship to determine its material condition and, if found unfit for continued service, report this to higher authority.
4. Perform such other inspections and trials as directed by the CNO.

Higher authority schedules INSURV inspections. Article 0850, *Navy Regulations,* provides one other means of scheduling an INSURV inspection. If you feel that the condition of your ship, or any department therein, is such as to require an inspection by INSURV, you may request it through official channels. This does not occur very frequently.

The best time for an INSURV is four to six months before the commencement of your next yard overhaul. This gives you time to translate those deficiencies either found by the board or confirmed by them into yard work requests. An INSURV-confirmed deficiency gets top attention from all the intermediate authorities who act on or make recommendations regarding your requests.

Preparations for INSURV are discussed in the *Naval Sea Service Command Technical Manual.*

The primary aim of the INSURV inspection is to determine the condition of your machinery and equipment, and then to recommend steps necessary to correct deficiencies and return unsatisfactory items to a satisfactory condition. This means it will be necessary to inspect the inside and all working parts of boilers, pumps, turbines, and other pieces of machinery. The president of the board will tell you in advance which machinery is to be opened. If the carrying out of these instructions leaves you without propulsion or auxiliary power, you must make arrangements with your type commander or other administrative authority to have your ship placed in a safe mooring condition and furnished with necessary services while it is undergoing inspection.

Intense training and frequent inspections give U.S. submarines superb readiness and performance.

Your engineering records will also be an important item of the inspection. Make sure your 3-M system is up-to-date and that all records are complete and accurate.

Finally, most members of the board feel that a good indication of the condition of the engineering plant and its past maintenance is the cleanliness and preservation evident to the eye. This does not mean that your *spaces* must be spotless. It means that *working machinery* must be clean, lubricated, and immaculate.

Propulsion Examination (Nuclear) Board. A propulsion examination board for nuclear-powered ships is established by *OPNAVINST 3540.4j.* The boards, one in each fleet, are maintained within the organizations of the fleet commanders-in-chief, and assist them in ensuring that naval nuclear-powered ships are operated by qualified personnel in accordance with approved procedures. The Commander, Naval Sea Systems Command, and the Director, Division of Naval Reactors, Department of Energy, provide technical assistance to the commanders-in-chief and to the boards.

Each board has a senior member (captain) who has served as CO of a naval nuclear-powered ship, and usually also has an engineering officer. Deputy senior members have the same qualifications, and other members are nuclear-power qualified. Normally four members constitute an inspection team.

The responsibilities of the board are:

1. Examine personnel assigned responsibility for supervision, operation, and maintenance of the propulsion plant to determine their state of training.
2. Witness and evaluate the conduct of propulsion plant drills.
3. Inspect the material condition of the plant to ascertain its readiness, preservation, and cleanliness.
4. Review and evaluate the engineering (reactor) department administration, and the completeness and accuracy of all records relating to the propulsion plant.

The board gives the following types of examinations:

1. *Pre-Critical Reactor Safeguards Examination* of nuclear-powered ships prior to initial criticality of a newly installed reactor core, including new construction ships and ships completing refueling.
2. *Post-Overhaul Reactor Safeguards Examination* (PORSE), prior to initial reactor operation after an overhaul without refueling, but lasting more than six months. The board will ascertain the state of training of the propulsion plant crew, the adequacy of administrative procedures, and the material readiness of the propulsion plant and spaces as they affect impending reactor operations and propulsion plant power range operations. Appropriate evolutions and casualty drills may be conducted as part of this examination.

3. *Operational Reactor Safeguards Examination* (ORSE) of ships in an operational status. These are conducted no more than one year after the last pre-critical or post-overhaul examination, and thereafter at intervals of approximately one year, as close to the anniversary as practicable. Approval of the CNO and the Director, Division of Naval Reactors, is required to extend the interval between examinations beyond fifteen months.

4. *Radiological Control Practices Evaluation* (RCPE) of those reactor support facilities in tenders authorized to handle radioactivity associated with naval nuclear plants. This evaluation is conducted at intervals not exceeding a year. For tenders in overhaul, if the yearly interval will be exceeded during overhaul, an evaluation will be conducted before the end of the overhaul, after work in the nuclear support facility is essentially completed.

An ORSE is conducted on each nuclear-powered ship (and each of the crews of a fleet ballistic missile submarine) at approximately one-year intervals, and more frequently if the fleet commander-in-chief or the Director, Division of Naval Reactors, so desires.

Following examination, the board submits a written report to the appropriate commander-in-chief, with copies to interested commands. It submits reports of corrective action in the same way. If the board finds the ship unsatisfactory, it submits its findings by immediate precedence message. The ship is then returned to port and shut down. The sequence of actions following such a finding is quite involved and will not be described here. Briefly, though, the crew is retrained until all discrepancies have been corrected. The ship is then reexamined, and if satisfactory, the restrictions are lifted. Obviously, failure has personal consequences for the commanding officer.

Annual Competition

In peacetime, annual competitions are a means of attaining and maintaining battle and administrative readiness by using the stimulation of competition. The intratype competition was established in 1953 by the Secretary of the Navy's *Instruction 3590.1*. It provided for payment of prize money to enlisted members of the crew from the Marjorie Sterrett Battleship Award Fund for attaining certain scores in battle practices. Qualifying crewmen wore E's on their jumpers, and ships attaining certain scores displayed E's on gun and director mounts. In later years, the competition was expanded to an Intratype Battle Competition conducted in accordance with *OPNAVINST 3590.Sr.* Present regulations authorize type commanders to make awards to ships, submarines, and aircraft for attainment of certain standard scores in overall battle exercise competition. The awards start with individual gun, missile, and department crews, including departments such as communications and minesweeping, and culminate in ship awards. E's of various colors are authorized for display on ships, weapons, and assault boats, and the Efficiency "E" ribbon is worn on the uniform.

The Admiral Arleigh Burke Fleet Trophy was established in 1961 for the ship or aircraft squadron in each fleet achieving the greatest improvement as measured by the criteria of the Battle Efficiency Competition.

Other annual competitions include the Battenberg Cup (top Atlantic Fleet ship), the Spokane Trophy (top combat readiness in Pacific Fleet), the Arizona Memorial Trophy (top strike ship in the Fleet), and the Ney Award for the best general mess.

The annual competition is a powerful stimulus to your crew. The display of an E ribbon on the uniform, or the E on gun, sail, bridge, or stack is highly prized in the fleet.

Final Fleet Preparation for Deployment

Following completion of refresher training, you will most likely have to begin preparing for deployment. Your preparation may be short in the event of crisis, or may take several months, if scheduling permits. The final period of preparation will normally be from 60 to 120 days, and will be listed in the annual employment schedule as Preparation for Overseas Movement (POM).

Written Requirements. Usually the ship you will replace will forward you a "turnover letter" sometime during POM. This should give you an insight into the small day-to-day matters of preparation. The larger areas will be taken care of by your type commander's checklist and by the large packages of operation plans and orders you will receive from your future chain of command. Between the turnover letter, the POM checklist, and the operation plans and orders, you should have all the written guidance you'll need. The rest of your preparation is making sure you have achieved the necessary training and qualifications, personnel, material, and supplies, and are in a state of readiness adequate to carry out the tasks set forth in the written requirements. To do this you will need to carry out the following detailed preparations.

POM Checklist. Obtain a POM checklist from your type commander as early as possible. When you can answer all its questions satisfactorily, you are ready to deploy; and just as importantly, you will be able to pass the POM inspection. The chances are that you will have to carry out many of the following tasks before being able to pass the inspection.

Equipment Calibration. Have all of your equipment that requires calibration checked as completely as possible. This includes magnetic and gyrocompass systems, sonar equipment, communications equipment, radars, electric countermeasure equipment, and missile and gun battery alignment.

Combat Systems Readiness Review. If you command a modern ship, with complicated combat systems, you will be scheduled for a Combat Systems Readiness Review (CSRR). This inspection will test all aspects of the readiness of your combat systems. Prerequisites for the CSRR are proper alignment and calibration, presence of full spare parts allowance, and presence of the specially trained personnel required.

Logistics. Obviously you should be at 100 percent of allowance in all areas. Top off all your consumables before sailing. Make sure the key items in your allowance are *sighted* by responsible officers or petty officers.

Advanced Training. If you are just coming out of refresher training, your type commander will schedule you for advanced training. Additional advanced training is usually possible during transit to the forward areas. The type commander will work closely with the fleet commander responsible for assisting in your preparation. You can expect to participate in exercises appropriate to your type. Cruisers, destroyers, and carriers will take part in air attack–air defense exercises and submarine-antisubmarine exercises. If time permits, they will also take part in an amphibious exercise. Submarines will be worked up by their type commanders and will participate in advanced hunter-killer exercises where possible. The goal, of course, is to prepare your ship or submarine for forward deployment with the Sixth or Seventh Fleets or for independent missions.

POM Reports. Some type commanders require weekly progress reports on POM readiness. You may consider this just so much paperwork and further encroachment on your already eroded authority, but if you look at it objectively you will find that the report will be a help to you as well as to the type commander in monitoring your progress.

Crew Briefings. You will need to schedule many briefings for various groups of your officers and crew and some for all hands. These will range all the way from review of operations orders for officers to cultural and drug abuse briefings for the entire crew. Working out this schedule without interfering with other preparations can be challenging for your executive officer.

POM Inspection. Most type commanders schedule POM inspections so as to give you as much time as possible to prepare, and yet allow some time for correction of deficiencies. Passing your POM inspection means that you will be, and feel, ready for deployment. Fail it and you and your crew will be in for some night work. We have no specific good advice; just try to remedy each discrepancy as soon as you can.

If you have planned well, worked hard, and been fortunate in finding a recently returned ship to brief you, you should be reasonably ready. You should also be able to avoid the frantic urgency displayed aboard some ships in the last few days prior to departure. Make sure that you and your crew will spend these last few days at home, and not in line at the supply depot.

Innovation and Automation

You should always be alert for ways to improve the overall administration of your training programs. The Navy provides some automated means of tracking training in the SNAP II/III programs embedded in most ships, but there are many good programs available that can help.

One such example is the Compass program, developed by an East Coast department head in the mid-1990s. Compass is a software product designed to manage all of a ship's administrative, training, PQS, school, and watchbill functions. It integrates many stand-alone applications into one user-friendly program and functionally replaces the Admin module of SNAP II/III while adding significant capability.

Compass does not simply automate manual processes; more importantly, it allows for process reengineering, and in so doing, the command realizes a significant savings in man-hours devoted to administration. For this reason, many ships on both coasts are using the program for training and most facets of shipboard administration.

Compass is widely used today as an interim solution to shipboard training and administration until the next generation of SNAP, the Naval Tactical Command Support System (NTCSS), is fully fielded.

Compass has five major modules: Admin, Training, PQS, Schools, and Watchbill. Use of Compass for ships, submarines, and even aircraft squadrons has been shown to be a significant hourly time-saver on both coasts.

You should take a good look at your entire training (and administrative) process shortly after taking command and ensure that you have the optimal solution. In your search, talk to other commands as well as your type command. If Compass is not already installed at your organization, you may want to consider it, as well as other innovative solutions and ideas from your training and administration teams.

The Captain's Role in Training and Inspections

We started this chapter by saying that training of your combat team and the related skill of passing inspections with them were at the very heart of your command responsibility. In what practical ways can you accomplish these key objectives?

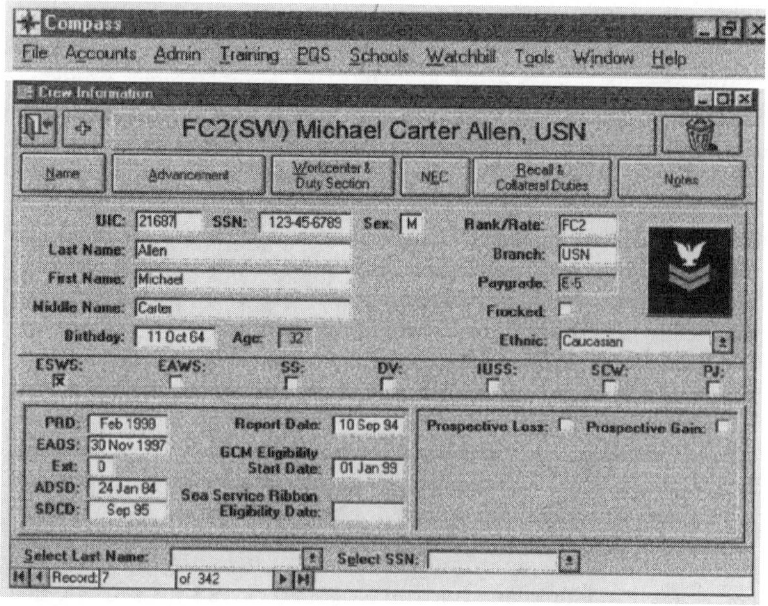

Figure 8–3. Compass

First, you must show your people that training matters deeply to you. The most effective means of doing this is to personally and enthusiastically participate in every element of shipboard training. Naturally, your executive officer is the nominal head of training for your organization; but it should be clear to everyone that the XO is operating with your direct charter and under the philosophical guidelines that you establish. This can be done through your written command philosophy, via your reviews with the XO and DHs following the planning board for training (PBFT), during wardroom or ready-room discussions, informally as you react during the day-to-day situations that present themselves, by what you say on the 1MC or at meetings, and how you structure the schedule of your ship, submarine, or squadron.

A related aspect of your role in training is the recognition that you are the ship's chief mariner (or airman) and tactician. No one else on board will have your breadth of skill and experience in these areas. You should personally be part of the training process in these two important areas. This must include getting on your feet in the wardroom or ready room and teaching your officers what you know of tactics, shiphandling (or airmanship), and maritime operations. You should also be involved in every aspect of drills and discussions involving tactics, particularly in the CIC in surface ships. Don't become a mysterious force who suddenly descends into drills or exercises wreaking havoc and then vanishing to your stateroom or the bridge—rather, you should be part of the planning, practicing, and executing of what your team is learning to do, throughout the training cycle.

In the crucial area of relations with outside entities, it is wise to establish a few basic guidelines regarding training and inspections. The first and most frequently observed problem area is the occurrence of conflicts between your team members and the inspection party, assessment group, or chain-of-command at the staff level. Your team is justifiably proud of their own way of doing business and their own experience. This can cause conflict with outside experts who have different (and generally better, frankly) methods of accomplishing certain tactical, navigational, or material feats. The best way to approach this potential problem is to train your team to accept the methods and suggestions of the outside experts, but to quickly and privately express their reservations up your organization's chain of command. A good approach to take is that *only* the CO (or possibly the CO and XO) is permitted to "argue" with the inspectors. This will ensure that there are very few arguments at the deckplate level, which—when they do occur—can and often do lead to bad feelings and emotional reactions. Naturally, when your team really does have either the *right* answer or even a *better* answer, you should plead the case strongly. But remember that the inspectors, although occasionally irritating in their manner, have a wealth of knowledge, resources, and experience; perhaps more importantly, they have the luxury of devoting all their time to the particular issue at hand—be it how to run a dead reckoning tracer, fire a torpedo, or perform aircraft maintenance. They will be right far more often than not, and if it is simply a matter of preference, your team is usually well served in the long run to opt for the "suggested" improvement. You can lose the war even while winning some very small battles in the world of training and inspections. Be perceived as the cooperative organization that "listens to experience" whenever possible.

One thing every command can do to ensure a coherent approach to training is to publish a training plan, get it out to the team at least monthly, and include a list of active plans to pass upcoming inspections. This document, often called a "Command Plan," is really a top-level management tool for the commanding officer. It should be promulgated over your signature. Use it to track upcoming key events, particularly training and inspection evolutions. By glancing at it, you should be able to see what all the upcoming command-level training and inspections are over the next twelve months, along with the lead responsibility, and the date of the published Plan of Action and Milestones (POAM). This will cue you to have the XO set up a review at appropriate periods. For example, if you are in command of a destroyer with a final ECERT coming up in six months, you should be meeting with the ECERT team to review that POAM about every two weeks; while the upcoming FEP in two weeks may demand a review every couple of days while final milestones are accomplished. With the new TSTA cycles of training, this is often more difficult to sort out than it was when inspections were discrete events. Nonetheless, you should be able to use the Command Plan to ensure that the "big ticket" items are all covered.

A real skill for a CO is running a POAM review. You should insist that the XO assemble all participants in a clean, well-lighted wardroom. Everyone should have a complete copy of the POAM in front of them. When all the players are in place, you are called in and the review commences. Either the XO or the DH responsible for the evolution should run the actual meeting. Listen carefully as each task is reviewed, and ensure that it is fully accomplished. This is an excellent opportunity for your prior experience and personal skills to come to bear, as you "ask the second question" and request to actually "see a copy of the reference." Your personal interest will generally ensure a high level of enthusiasm on the part of your team. This is also your chance to see exactly what *you* need to be doing to support the effort:

calling the local repair facility to bump up the priority on a key job, working with the chief staff officer at the squadron to facilitate delivery of a key part, obtaining more trainer or simulator time for your combat tacticians, finding an extra practice torpedo at the weapons station for the exercise—the influence of a call from a ship, submarine, or squadron CO is very high in every Navy port. Use your calls sparingly, but remember that the squeaky wheel really does get greased more often, and when you are in the crunch—with the exercise or the inspection looming close to the hull—you are expected to roll up your sleeves and pitch in. BUPERS didn't send you to your ship to sit in your stateroom detached from the action. Never underestimate what you can accomplish in a few polite phone calls that start out with, "Hello, this is the captain of the *Fiske,* and I was wondering if . . ."

9

Independent Operations

A Man of War is the best Ambassador.

—Oliver Cromwell

I wish to have no connection with any ship that does not sail fast, for I intend to go in harm's way.

—John Paul Jones, Letter to le Ray de Chaumont, 1778

Joining the Fleet for Initial Independent Operations

In every commanding officer's tour, one highlight is the opportunity to take your ship, submarine, or aircraft squadron out of a period of inactivity—perhaps due to a yard period, a post-cruise stand-down, an industrial availability, or initial construction—and join the fleet. While your efforts during stand-down, construction, or repair are important, they are certainly not as professionally fulfilling as taking your command and heading out to sea. In this chapter, we'll discuss the kind of independent operations you will conduct after initially joining the fleet, as you prepare for the more complex fleet and joint operations to come.

Discussions with the Wardroom, CPO Mess, and Crew

Emerging from a period of time in port, for whatever reason, is a good time to review with your entire team the basics of the command's philosophy. You should think about what are the most important aspects of your "message" at each level in your command—that is, what you need to say to the wardroom or ready room, to your chief petty officers, and to your crew. While the message must obviously be very consistent, it should be varied as is appropriate to these three audiences. You may want to meet in a "sit down" session with the wardroom or ready room, and then have an all hands call with the entire command. Alternatively, you may choose to meet with each level of the crew separately, perhaps with the E-6s, E-5 and E-4s, and E-3 and below. Doing so will encourage more discussion and questions. Another approach possible in larger commands is to use the installed closed-circuit television systems and go out initially to everyone at once, then follow up with smaller discussions with the officers and chiefs.

At a minimum, you must do three things in the "coming back on line" discussion: outline the upcoming schedule, focus your team on safety, and lay out some specific goals for your command. Discussing the schedule is your easiest task, and you can generally help by using some simple graphics—perhaps a calendar laying out the next six to twelve months. You should reinforce the schedule information by providing a monthly "command plan" that outlines your schedule and goals, as well as ensuring that the information (in a nonclassified format) finds its way into the command newsletter mailed to the families. It is not a bad idea to keep the schedule updated in the plan of the day and plan of the week as well. Focus on the positives and the challenges in the schedule, and let everyone see how excited and enthusiastic you are about the schedule.

Your second goal at this point should be to focus everyone's attention on safety. For obvious reasons, many serious accidents and mistakes occur when a command has not been operational for some time. This message is a challenging one to deliver without being boring or appearing to simply preach to the crew. You should try and incorporate some "real world" examples of commands who have experienced problems at a similar point in the operational cycle; include some specific things you want to have done (e.g., safety briefs on station prior to all evolutions, written plans for complex evolutions, pre-briefs for certain situations, post-action critiques); and try to incorporate some human interest in the presentation. Let everyone know that your top priority during the initial time at sea is to come back to port with a safe crew and working equipment.

The third major portion of your message at this point should be a discussion of your goals for the command over the upcoming year. These should be discussed at a high level, but should be specific in character. As an example, simply saying "We want to operate smoothly during COMPTUEX" doesn't say much to the crew, but if you said "During the COMPTUEX in October, we want to shoot over 95 on the naval gunfire range, score hits on 100 percent of our missile shots, and conduct every UNREP safely in less than sixty minutes," you have painted a far more specific picture for the crew. You should also mention some of the awards and competitions you are interested in, such as the Spokane Trophy on the West Coast, the Battenberg Cup on the East Coast, the Ney Award for food service, the Battle Efficiency E, and the Topgun Award. Try to select goals that are realistic and attainable by your command; and make an effort to get the entire crew, regardless of rate or pay grade, involved in the process.

In addition to those minimum points of discussion, there are many other things you may choose to discuss at this stage of your command's life cycle, including specific personnel issues (advancement, retention, male-female relations); policies on drug or alcohol use; ideas about family support and community responsibility; command atmosphere; current events and the world situation that might affect your command's schedule; or any other particular point of importance to you and your team. You should also make an effort to look back over the activity that has kept your command from operating at sea (construction, repair, stand-down) and identify those individuals who worked hard to maintain the readiness of the organization.

Getting Back in the Saddle

The first underway period after an extended period away from operations is always a little exciting. Take some time before it happens to go over the ways you as the CO can make it smoother. A few ideas:

Conduct a fast cruiser. Whether you are in command of a ship, a submarine, or an aircraft squadron, having a period of time when your organization shuts down the phone lines, bars outside contact, and completely focuses on doing what you need to do to operate safely at sea has immense value. This can be a complex three-day affair, complete with watch bill changes, drills, exercises, communications drills, and all the panoply of actually going to sea; or it may be as simple as a two- to three-hour series of lectures, discussions, and rehearsals. You and your leadership team can best decide what to do based on the needs of your command. Whatever you choose to do, insist that a formal schedule be developed and distributed under your signature, and that your XO is driving the problem.

Pick a good time to get underway. While this is not always something within your control, it is generally better to select a morning departure at a reasonable hour, preferably no earlier than 0900; an ideal first underway is usually around 1000. This gives all your people plenty of time to get to work, park the car, have a decent breakfast, find the keys to the underway gear lockers, and get on station. Trying to jump underway at 0600 the first time out simply fails the common sense check.

Start with the basics. As you build the schedule for the first underway period, set yourself up for success. Pick out some drills and exercises that are neither complex nor dangerous. Single-ship operations, easy day flights, and basic drills should be the order of the day. No point in beginning day one with a dawn UNREP and moving into a gun shoot. As you succeed throughout the day, get on the 1MC and let your people know how quickly everyone is moving up the learning curve. Let confidence grow by remembering to crawl and walk a little before you break into a run.

Go easy for the first few hours. Everyone (including the CO!) needs to become reacclimatized to a moving environment, and about 40 percent of the crew will be at least somewhat seasick. People tend to make mistakes in a period of initial underway as a direct result of the tiredness and headache that can afflict many of your crew, even if it doesn't develop into a full-fledged case of "mal du mar." Virtually everyone will recover fully by the evening meal, but the first eight hours can be rough. Recognize this and give the team a chance to simply get their "sea legs" back.

Don't take outsiders. No assist teams or inspectors if you can possibly avoid it. A few yard workers may be unavoidable, but hold the presence of anyone outside the command to an absolute minimum. This is not the time to invite the commodore along for a navigation check ride!

Keep your sense of humor. Losing your temper, or permitting those in the organization to do so, seldom has any positive impact. People are almost always trying very hard to do the right thing, and yelling at them only decreases the chances that they will succeed. Be reasonable and sensible in your expectations and recognize that things will improve rapidly. Don't be afraid to laugh at the non-dangerous but funny occurrences that will inevitably be a part of that first day at sea.

Keep Seniors Informed

In all of the independent operations about to be discussed, one principle is all-important: *keep the chain of command informed.* You will find specific requirements for reporting in *NWP 1-03.1, Operational Reports,* which summarizes the reports required. Part II of *NWP 1-03.1* promulgates movement report requirements for reporting locations and movements of Navy ships and aircraft, Marine ground units, and VIPs. Details include preparation of forms and reports and responsibilities of movement report centers and officers.

Amplifying orders to *NWP 1-03.1* will also be issued by administrative and operational commanders above you.

All of this may turn out to be a sometimes bewildering array of requirements, but the aggregate demand is to *keep them informed.* Unless your ship is very small, you will have the communications equipment to reach your seniors, and they in turn will be in instant contact with superiors all the way to the White House. In these days of critical international situations, a single ship halfway around the world may find herself involved in search and rescue, asylum, collision, or other events of interest to the chain of command. You will find sometimes that *what* you are doing is not nearly as important as how you *describe* it. Indicate the *what, when, where, how,* and *why* of what is happening. If you can predict the next event, do so. Tell them when you will report next. Try to include everything you might want to know if you were a senior commander.

The Chain of Command

The old days of truly independent operations, when naval vessels disappeared into the South Seas for a year or so without being heard from, are gone. Even the pre–World War II shakedown cruise to foreign ports is no more. Today a ship on independent operations, and even SSBNs sixty days submerged, are firmly a part of the chain of command.

NDP 1, Naval Warfare, describes the basic command organization, the chain of command of the shore organization, and the dual lines of authority to the operating forces. You should master this publication. Note that the CNO, as such, has no operational authority. He or she is, however, in the administrative chain of command. If you are discussing a developing asylum case with the CNO's Duty Captain, you will have to keep these distinctions straight. Fortunately, the Duty Captain will have a good grasp of them. *NDP 6, Naval Command and Control,* is a simplified discussion of command and control matters and should be of great assistance to you.

Preparation for Independent Operations

You may, at times, be detached suddenly from your fleet assignment and ordered to proceed on independent ops. If this occurs there is little you can do to prepare. Either you are ready or you aren't. If you are given advance warning, however, or are going on a scheduled cruise, there is much preparation to be done.

If you did not do so before deploying, or if your independent operation begins from homeport, start with personnel preparation. Be sure you are up-to-date on inoculations and dental work and that all of your sailors have taken care of their financial affairs. Consider family issues, working with your command master chief and ombudsman.

If you have the opportunity, top off logistically before departing. This means fuel, ammunition, provisions, and spare parts. It also means many smaller but important items that you have been used to getting from supply sources. Things that gave you little concern before will suddenly loom large. U.S. stamps, mail order forms, and other postal supplies cannot be found in Australia. Ship's store items, particularly everyday necessities like razor blades and toothpaste, will be needed for a long period. Your supply officer will need extra cash for several paydays. When you reach port he or she will also need to know supply procedures for letting provision contracts, if none are in force for that port. You will be fortunate in this regard if your ship is big enough to warrant the assignment of a Supply Corps officer. A line officer who is doing this job will need help and your patience.

When you have a few minutes, have your XO survey the language abilities of your crew. Find out which of your officers and crew are qualified to act as interpreters, and which can help with a smattering of a language. You will need their help in SAR operations, contacts with merchant vessels, port visits, and on other occasions.

Special Submarine Preparations

Submarines normally operate independently. This provides exceptional training opportunities for our submarine force. For the fast attack force, independent ops provide training conditions not unlike wartime operations. In both SSBNs and SSNs, deployed operations are as independent as any command today, with the commanding officer given much latitude in his decision making.

SSN deployed operations are usually announced through the chain of command some nine months prior to deployment. As a surface counterpart does, the submarine CO will review in detail the administrative and logistical requirements prior to the deployment. In addition, the SSN commanding officer will review *NWP 3-21* in detail in order to indoctrinate thoroughly the wardroom and crew in tactical procedures to be conducted while on station. As in all operations, indepth planning is the key to success. During the nine-month preparation period, the SSN commanding officer will also be offered the services of the various training commands and technical agencies. Failure to accept their training offers can result in missed opportunities once deployed.

In these times of reduced manning, training deficiencies must be identified and corrected early in the preparation period. The tactical equipment a submarine carries must be used effectively to carry out its mission. If its personnel cannot support the technology, they must

Independent duty has its problems, but as you head off on your own, you will enjoy your command independence to the utmost.

be either trained or replaced. There is too much at stake to deploy to a forward area when mission success probability is lessened by lack of experience or technical ability.

The final process in preparing an SSN for deployment is the deployment workup and certification by the squadron commander. *NWP 3-21* is your guide in preparing for these events. During the entire workup, stress the importance of the mission to the crew. Conduct all preparations as if the ship were deploying in time of war. If you conduct your training and preparation in this spirit, your ship will

The Navy's mail service is outstanding, but it will only be as good for your ship as your routing instructions.

be successful during its truly *independent operation,* and every sailor will relish the experience.

SSBN preparations are similar to the SSN workup, except that the off-crew trains in homeport without the ship. The successful SSBN captain will set training goals for the crew and for each individual, and will monitor progress toward these goals throughout the nine-week off-crew training period.

Movement Report. Whether in a submarine or a surface ship, the movement report is probably the single most important report you will make on independent ops. The movement report system is responsible for your continuing safety when you are moving alone. The movement report system is designed to provide all necessary authorities with a dead reckoning position for all units at any time. If because of weather, engineering casualty, or other reason, your progress along your track varies at any time by more than four hours (100 miles for carrier operations; two hours for submarines), you must submit a report of change. *NWP 1.03, Operational Reports,* describes the entire movement report system. Be completely familiar with it.

Mail. A movement report provides information to appropriate naval area postal officials, who then verify the routing information on file. You must still, however, submit separate mail routing instructions to the appropriate fleet commander.

Underway Independent Operations

Presumably you are as ready now as foresight and a good foraging group of CPOs can make you, and are probably headed for a foreign port visit. During your transit to this port, or just on a simple independent operation, many things can happen to you. When you were part of a task group you could expect the task group commander to take care of each crisis. Now *you* are in charge. To assist you, we will now review some of the most common problems you can expect to face.

Weather. The crisis most likely to strike is heavy weather. Prepare your ship by reviewing your heavy weather plan and making sure all hands know how to implement it. Check your bill against the standard heavy weather bill found in the *SORN*. At a minimum, your bill should include all the points given there. If you carry out your bill properly, and ballast correctly, you should be able to handle any heavy weather situation if you maneuver your ship correctly. One exception might be if you command a *very* small ship. Small ships can survive by early avoidance of the dangerous portion of storms, and in some cases are safer than larger vessels.

A *good* ship captain always knows what the weather *is* at any moment. A *very good* one also knows what the weather *will be*. An *outstanding* one also knows what the weather *might be* in the future.

The most important factor in surviving heavy weather is the captain's ability to recognize its existence, its probable movement, and its development.

Your studies of weather should start with the basics of worldwide weather formation, and then proceed to the patterns of your particular area. A good text is *Weather for the Mariner,* published by Naval Institute Press. The piloting instructions for your area also cover local weather patterns and storm tracks.

These studies will enable you to interpret most weather predictions and weather advisories. The information in these messages will tell you what the weather is now, near you and over a wide area. It will also tell you what the weather *probably* will be, based on past history of weather development and movement, and using the skills of highly trained meteorologists.

This is not enough for your safety. You will remember from your shore duty listening to the evening television weather forecast giving you a forecast of fair weather, and then walking out to the first tee in the rain. Forecasters simply cannot forecast accurately. The movement of weather masses is, at this point in the study of meteorology, not completely predictable even with the finest computer systems. The movement of air masses over the irregularities of land and island chains is particularly unpredictable. Movement over the open seas is somewhat more uniform, and therefore somewhat more predictable. The point here is that you cannot place the safety of your ship in the hands of a meteorologist, no matter how skilled. In the final analysis he or she must *guess,* and you must always take this into account. You must learn enough about the science of weather, and, more importantly, the homely, practical knowledge of close-in weather prediction, to know when the forecast you received is wrong or when the weather is refusing to follow it.

Weather for the Mariner is technically correct in as much depth as you will need, and it is written in a readable style. It covers the general theory of weather, the generation of worldwide weather, and the standard patterns of weather to be found throughout the world. It is relatively short, non-mathematical, and its photographs and illustrations will help you make local predictions.

A hurricane off the coast of Florida.

Tropical Cyclones. The most dangerous weather disturbance you will encounter is the tropical cyclone. This type of storm is known as a hurricane in the Atlantic area and as a typhoon in the Pacific. Ships of all sizes are in for trouble during hurricane or typhoon season, which lasts roughly from July to December. There are also tropical cyclones in the Southern Hemisphere, which rotate clockwise, instead of counterclockwise as in the Northern Hemisphere. These storms are given different names, such as the Indian Ocean cyclone and the Australian willy-willy, but are essentially the same.

To learn more about these dangerous and unpredictable disturbances, read the chapter on weather disturbances in *Weather for the*

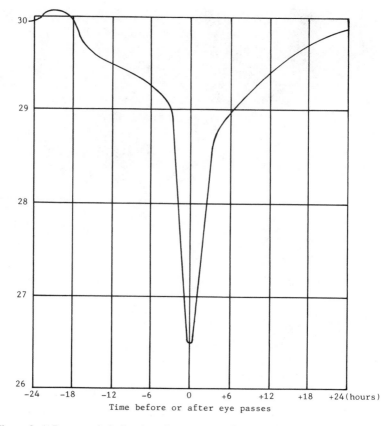

Figure 9–1. Barometric indication of movement of a typhoon or hurricane over a ship or station.

Mariner, particularly the section on precautions and disengagement. Another good text is *Heavy Weather Guide,* also published by Naval Institute Press. You, as commanding officer, are the final authority on the safety of your ship, and as such must know both her capabilities and her limitations, as well as the environment she will travel in— wind, water, and storm. In this age of worldwide satellite weather observation and reporting, you will have advantages that World War II

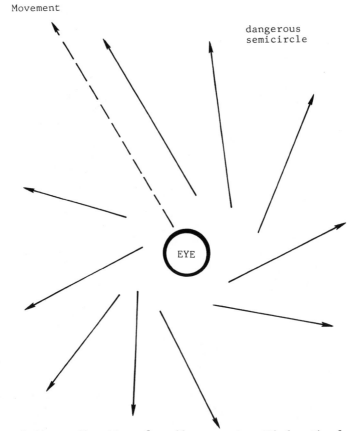

Movement

dangerous
semicircle

EYE

Arrows indicate direction of swell movement, with length of
arrows showing relative height of swell. Largest swells
are along direction of movement. Swells in dangerous semicircle are highest.

Figure 9–2. Swell directions and heights surrounding a tropical storm.

commanders and ship COs never had. You should have ample warning of typhoon and hurricane formation, movement, and prediction.

This said, we will now quickly review our storm precautions.

In essence, a hurricane or typhoon is a large mass of water-laden

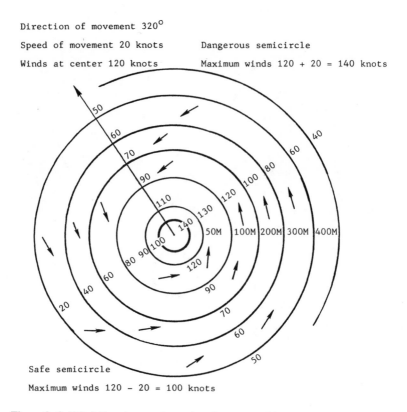

Figure 9–3. Wind directions and speeds to be expected in a typhoon or hurricane with eye wind speeds of 120 knots and a speed of advance of 20 knots.

air, rotating counterclockwise (in the Northern Hemisphere) about an eye of low pressure of from twenty to fifty miles in diameter. As one approaches the storm center, air pressure decreases gradually until one enters the eye, when it decreases dramatically, as illustrated in Figure 9–1. The whole mass is hundreds of miles in diameter and moves forward at speeds of up to fifty miles per hour. Occasionally it will remain stationary, though, and may even back up for short periods before resuming forward movement. Rotational wind speeds in

Hurricane winds of 100 knots. Tops of long swells are flattened, but the direction of the swell is still apparent, and helps to locate the center of the storm.

the right-hand semicircle (looking along the direction of movement) are added as vectors to the forward speed. Rotational wind speeds in the other semicircle are subtracted from the forward speed. Hence, the right-hand semicircle with its higher wind speed is known as the "dangerous semicircle," and the left-hand semicircle is known as the "safe semicircle." The direction in which the storm lies from you can be predicted fairly accurately by looking back along the direction from which the swells are coming. The storm center will be within a few degrees of the direction of swells, as indicated in Figure 9–2. Distance away can be predicted roughly by the speed with which the barometer is falling. Sudden falling to very low levels indicates the center is near, as indicated in Figure 9–1.

Wind speeds of over 200 knots have been experienced in hurricanes, and seas can be mountainous. Ships must avoid being caught broadside in the troughs of the seas, particularly destroyers and smaller ships. Hurricanes and typhoons form in tropical latitudes and move west. As they progress they tend to head more northwesterly and finally recurve to the northeast. Predicting the exact track is very difficult.

It is interesting to note that with only primitive prediction services in the period from 1920 to 1940 the ships of the Asiatic Fleet never suffered any serious damage from typhoons. During this period hundreds of typhoons of great violence swept through the Philippines area, but never managed to catch any of the thirteen old destroyers of the Asiatic Fleet. The reason was that the commanding officers of these ships soon learned to use some simple rules of typhoon prediction and avoidance that had been handed down from captain to captain. You will want to review the more complete rules in *Weather for the Mariner,* but it is interesting to note how simple they can be made and still be effective. The following rules were taped to the bulkhead of the emergency cabin of the commanding officer of an Asiatic Fleet four-stacker (in this class the emergency cabin was also the chart house):

1. If the barometer falls below 29.50 inches start worrying.
2. If the barometer falls below 29.35 *really* worry.
3. If you are in port, hoist in all boats, move to typhoon anchorage, put a second anchor down, and be prepared to steam at anchor.
4. If you are at sea watch out for long swells. The direction from which they approach is within 15 degrees of storm center.
5. Observe the direction of the wind. In the Northern Hemisphere the storm center will be 120 degrees to the right of the direction from which the wind is blowing.
6. Never try to outrun or pass ahead of a typhoon unless you are very close to its path. If you can, avoid the dangerous semicircle (left side looking toward eye.)
7. If the wind shifts clockwise you are in the dangerous semicircle; if it shifts counter-clockwise, you are, if in the Northern Hemisphere, in the safe semicircle. If the wind direction stays steady and the barometer continues to fall, you are directly in the path. Bug out to the west as fast as you can.
8. In the southern Philippines most typhoons are moving in a northwesterly direction. By the time they reach the northern Philippines, friction of land masses and their natural tendency to curve to the northeast will change their direction of move-

The calm inside the eye of a hurricane.

If the typhoon is astern and headed away from you, make best speed and hold divine services.

ment to northeast. One in ten will continue northwest to the China coast.

9. If you cannot evade completely, take the following actions:
   a. In dangerous semicircle bring wind on starboard bow. Make all speed possible.
   b. In safe semicircle bring wind on starboard quarter. Make all speed possible.
   c. If directly ahead of storm bring wind 160 degrees on starboard side. Make all speed possible, slowing as storm approaches. As eye approaches wind will decrease and then shift to opposite direction as eye passes over you. Keep turning to port to keep sea astern. Do *not* get in troughs.
   d. If behind storm go anywhere you want to go. Hold divine services if you feel sufficiently grateful.

The same instructions taped to the bulkhead of the sea cabin of a more modern destroyer enabled its commanding officer to leave the Third Fleet formation in the second typhoon experienced by Admiral Halsey's fleet and survive easily with no casualties or damage. Others were not as fortunate.

Hurricanes in the Caribbean and the Gulf of Mexico follow similar patterns and can be handled with the same rules of thumb. The island chains of the Caribbean and the large land masses surrounding the Gulf of Mexico influence storm buildup and movement differently from the western Pacific, but in either area simple principles of physics apply. Water areas add to storm energy and water content; land areas subtract. Storms move more easily over water, and the greater friction of land slows that portion of the storm passing over it. Storms, therefore, veer in the direction of that portion of them passing over land. As they pass over land, rainfall increases, energy lessens, winds decrease, and forward movement slows. The reverse happens if the storm passes out to sea again.

Keep your radars operating. Radar information can define storm center position and will show its movement accurately. This is of great assistance when maneuvering close to the storm's center. Antennas may be damaged by high winds, but you must balance a few thousand dollars' worth of repairs against the safety of your ship.

Frontal Systems. Most of the area of the earth, both sea and seacoast, over which you will operate lies in the northern mid-latitudes. The weather of this area is dominated by frontal systems. You should have a good understanding of what fronts are and how they are formed, travel, interact, and dissipate. They will control 90 percent of your weather. *Weather for the Mariner* has an excellent discussion of this subject, written in an understandable style and accompanied by photographs and diagrams.

There are two principal types of frontal systems, cold and warm. When moving in an orderly fashion and not otherwise influenced, they produce predictable weather. *Weather for the Mariner* contains a set of tables showing weather you can expect at each stage of the approach and passage of both cold and warm fronts. When they are occluded (occlusion occurs when a cold front overtakes a preceding warm front) the occlusion literally lifts up the boundaries of both fronts and weather becomes much more violent and unpredictable. Fronts can also be thrown off their orderly progression from west to east by low- and high-pressure cells, which can cause them to stall and remain stationary, to change direction, or to speed up. As with hurricanes and typhoons, weather prediction with frontal systems is sometimes educated guesswork. Still, an educated guess is better than an ignorant one. A small investment in the study of frontal weather systems can pay big dividends. A modern naval vessel is not usually vulnerable to frontal storms if properly moored or anchored in port or if well handled at sea, but ship's boats can suffer if not properly secured or hoisted early enough.

Local Storms. Other forms of local storms can be dangerous. The williwaws of the Aleutians, the Santa Anas of southern California, and the sandstorms of the Red Sea and the Persian Gulf must be understood and prepared for. The onslaught of local storms is usually sudden and without warning.

Fog is to be expected in various parts of the world at certain seasons. Check piloting instructions and your low visibility bill before entering such areas.

When thoroughly prepared for the vicissitudes of weather, though steaming peacefully under fair skies, you can concentrate on preparing for other emergencies.

Search and Rescue. After heavy weather, the crisis you will most likely encounter will be some form of search and rescue (SAR). Spend a little of your time reviewing your responsibilities in this area. They stem from *Navy Regulations,* and are spelled out in Article 0925, "Assistance to Persons, Ships, and Aircraft in Distress."

You are required, as far as you can do so without serious damage to your ship or injury to your crew, to proceed with all possible speed to the rescue of persons in distress. You must render assistance to any person found in danger at sea and must give all reasonable assistance to distressed ships and aircraft. Should you be so unfortunate as to collide with another ship, you must render assistance to that ship and her crew and passengers. As you would expect, you must report all SAR action to the chain of command as soon as possible.

Article 0925 ends with the reassuring statement that the accounting for rendering assistance and making repairs pursuant to the provisions and directions of the article shall be as prescribed by the Comptroller of the Navy. These instructions are somewhat complicated, but they do provide for your reimbursement. Maintain a good count of blankets, crew's clothing (if you command a small ship and do not have ship's store clothing to use), food, and other equipment and supplies used in rescue operations. Your crew and your ship will be repaid. You are enjoined specifically, however, *not* to effect repairs to a merchant vessel in distress or in collision with you unless in your capacity as senior officer present you feel such repairs are necessary to save life or to prevent the merchant vessel from sinking. If you do provide such assistance you must report the cost of labor and materials in your subsequent report.

Now that you know *what* you are supposed to do, and what *not* to do, a review of *how* you will do it is in order. The *SORN* contains sample bills which, when implemented, will enable you to meet most requirements. Article 630.15 provides for the rescue and assistance detail. This bill provides for rescue of survivors of plane crashes, ship sinkings, and other similar accidents. Article 630.16 describes a rescue of survivors bill and provides procedures for rescuing large numbers of survivors from the water. Article 640.2, aircraft crash and rescue bill, is a specific bill for the purpose of rescuing aircraft survivors. There is no specific bill provided for submarine rescue. If you are requested to assist a surfaced submarine, treat it like any surface ship in distress. If it requires a tow, the submarine CO will be careful to warn you what underwater portions of the submarine to avoid while passing the line. If it is submerged you will have to try to find it by sonar search. If you are not so equipped, there will help on the way soon. In the meantime you can search the area for evidence such as smoke flares or a communication buoy. Ships equipped with sonar can communicate with the submarine. The submarine may also have a wire antenna system, which may usable for radio communication if it is undamaged and the water is shallow enough.

Refugees. The refugee situations in southeast Asia and the Caribbean present a problem that will persist for many years. If you are transiting these areas you may encounter small boats and even fair-sized freighters loaded with refugees. These unfortunate people may have gone for days without food and water and will present all forms of sickness and physical disability. A small ship may be hard pressed to provide the medical care and space that they will require. This kind of contingency has become commonplace in the Seventh Fleet, and there will be annexes to the standard Seventh Fleet operation order telling you exactly what to do, what reports to make, and how to get help. Your standard bills will suffice unless you are overwhelmed by sheer numbers.

The standard *NWP* publications are implemented by the commanders-in-chief of the Atlantic and Pacific Fleets. They have SAR annexes to their standing operating plans. The commanders of the numbered fleets also have such annexes. With all of these publications and the fleet plans appropriate to your area and chain of command, you have all the guidance you will need as to what to do. Your bills will tell you how to do it.

The remaining element of SAR is *when* to do it. You may simply run across someone at sea in need of help. If so, your course of action is obvious. However, most SAR incidents in which you will be involved will be initiated by someone else. The communications plan under which you will be operating will require that you guard the international distress frequency. You will hear calls for assistance directly on this frequency. Report these calls up through the chain of command, stating what action you intend to take. You will have to make a judgment as to whether you can reach the scene in time to help and whether your mission will permit you to divert. Usually the chain of command will know the location of other forces available and will quickly take over and decide what to do. You may also get orders directly from a senior who has received information by some other means than the distress frequency, such as by aerial sighting. In this case he or she will know the location of all available forces and will issue appropriate orders.

Man Overboard.   One of the most common SAR efforts is a very short-range one: that of recovering a man overboard. If you are part of a formation, finding someone else's sailor becomes a problem of avoiding other units nearby, maneuvering in accordance with directions from CIC or by visual observation, and bringing the sailor aboard. Since we are discussing independent operations in this chapter, we will concentrate on the problems of a single ship.

The *SORN*, Article 640.5, contains a bill that covers training, responsibilities, actions, and many other details of man overboard procedure. You should, of course, have a complete man overboard bill patterned after this bill and adapted to your type. CIC and bridge watch personnel should be well qualified and instructed, and exercised frequently at drill.

The one area in which the standard bill is weak is in maneuvering advice, particularly for small ships. Lowering a boat for recovery is feasible less than 50 percent of the time at sea. Thus, the usual method of recovery for small ships is by maneuvering close to the

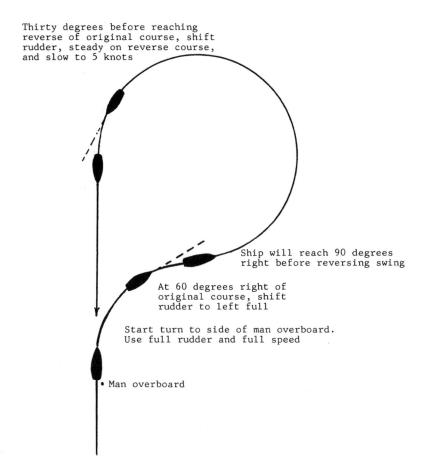

Thirty degrees before reaching
reverse of original course, shift
rudder, steady on reverse course,
and slow to 5 knots

Ship will reach 90 degrees
right before reversing swing

At 60 degrees right of
original course, shift
rudder to left full

Start turn to side of man overboard.
Use full rudder and full speed

• Man overboard

Figure 9–4. The Williamson turn can be used with modifications by any type of ship. If a sailor is overboard to port, reverse the procedure shown.

sailor, throwing a line over the bow or side, or, if he or she is weakened, by sending a strong swimmer over the side with a line attached.

There are many methods of returning your ship to the person's location. The three most widely used methods are the Williamson turn, the Anderson turn, and the Y turn. Regardless of the method you use,

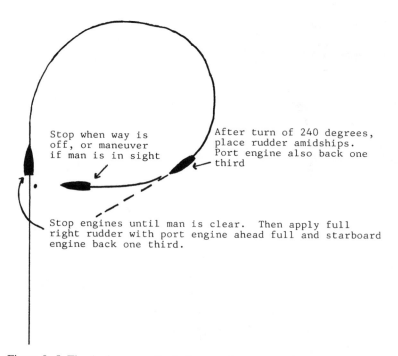

Stop when way is off, or maneuver if man is in sight

After turn of 240 degrees, place rudder amidships. Port engine also back one third

Stop engines until man is clear. Then apply full right rudder with port engine ahead full and starboard engine back one third.

Figure 9–5. The Anderson method of recovering man overboard, designed for use in cold weather, low visibility, or rough weather. Average time to complete the maneuver is three minutes and forty-five seconds.

an immediately established, meticulously kept CIC dead reckoning plot of the 200-yard scale is mandatory. If your special maneuvering method fails, CIC should then be able to assist you.

The Williamson turn is illustrated in Figure 9–4. This maneuver can be used by any type of ship, including carriers, cruisers, destroyers, submarines, amphibious ships, and single-screw vessels. As the diagram shows, it is well adapted for use when the exact time a sailor fell overboard is not known, since after making the turn you can continue back along the previous track indefinitely. Its disadvantage is that it takes a long time to execute, and the ship moves so far from the sailor that sight of him or her may be lost. Practice making the turn with your ship, for variations in maneuvering characteristics may require some adjustment.

The Anderson turn, illustrated in Figure 9–5, was developed in 1952 by the CO of the *Richard B. Anderson,* then-Commander W. P. Mack. It was promulgated to the destroyers of the Pacific Fleet and tested extensively by them both before and after promulgation. It was designed to be used by twin-screw destroyers, and it is still widely used by them. Its main purpose is to bring the ship back to the sailor in a short time in cold weather or reduced visibility. The ship is kept as close as possible to the person, and the maneuver ends with the ship stopped and its bow usually within fifty to one hundred feet of the sailor. The average time for the turn is three minutes and forty-five seconds, well within survival time in cold water. The Anderson turn also provides a simple set of maneuvering instructions readily mastered by inexperienced OODs. After the sailor is overboard and the initial orders are given to commence the turn (right full rudder, port ahead full, starboard back one third) the OOD has about two minutes to give the necessary orders to make sound signals, pass the word, notify the captain, and otherwise prepare for recovery. The next step is a simple order, given when the ship has swung 240 degrees, to bring the rudder amidships and back all engines one third. The third and equally simple order is to stop all engines when way is off. The ship can then do further maneuvering, if required, but it is not usually necessary. One destroyer, in an actual recovery, sent the boatswains mate of the watch and a messenger to the forecastle. They made the recovery using a line over the bow in three and one-half minutes.

The Y turn, illustrated in Figure 9–6, is intended for use by submarines, but may be used by any type. It permits the submarine to stay as close as possible to the person without losing sight of him or her (this is important because of the submarine's low height of eye). This method is not adapted to low visibility, and for some surface ships, backing into a heavy sea can decrease control. Of all types, the submarine is best able to back into wind and sea because of low freeboard and small sail area.

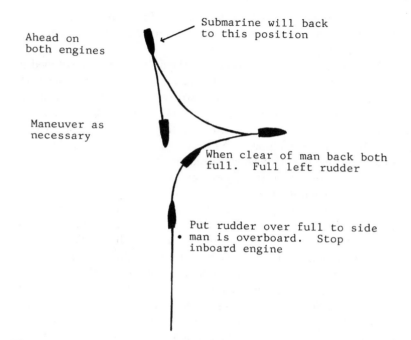

Submarine will back to this position

Ahead on both engines

Maneuver as necessary

When clear of man back both full. Full left rudder

Put rudder over full to side man is overboard. Stop inboard engine

Figure 9–6. Y-backing method of man overboard recovery designed for submarines.

There are other recovery methods in use, notably the racetrack method, described in the *Watch Officer's Guide,* published by Naval Institute Press. This method is designed for use in column, but in our opinion the Anderson turn is superior for this purpose.

You should experiment with your own ship to find out which method is best and to determine what modifications you should make to the standard methods.

Asylum. Our asylum policy reflects the case of Simas Kudirka, a seaman serving in a Soviet fishing trawler off Martha's Vineyard. A Coast Guard cutter was alongside the trawler conducting a routine search for compliance with fishing regulations when Kudirka came topside, jumped over to the deck of the cutter, and asked for asylum. The trawler captain then asked that he be returned. The Coast Guard captain asked via radio for instructions from higher authority, and was told to allow the return of Kudirka. A party from the trawler was then allowed to board the cutter, bind and gag the man, and return him to the trawler. A subsequent investigation found serious errors in the proceedings and violations of strict standing instructions. Guilt assessed and punishment made is past history, and is relatively unimportant to this discussion. What is important is for each CO to fix the proper asylum procedures in his or her mind.

As a result of the Kudirka incident, *Navy Regulations* now has much more specific instructions regarding asylum. Article 0939 states that any person requesting asylum on the high seas shall have it granted, and shall not be surrendered except at the personal direction of the Secretary of the Navy or higher authority. When in a foreign port, a request for asylum shall be granted only in extreme humanitarian cases, such as pursuit by a mob. Such protection can be terminated only by the Secretary of the Navy or higher authority. A request by foreign authorities for return of a refugee will be reported to the Chief of Naval Operations by immediate precedence message. However, though persons must be protected, the regulations state clearly that they shall not be *invited* to seek asylum.

The information and direction in Article 0939 should be adequate to handle any situation regarding asylum either ashore or afloat.

Harassment. Harassment by foreign forces may occur. The most common are direct overflights by aircraft, ships coming close aboard or shadowing closely astern, and shadowing by surveillance ships, either naval ships or trawlers. Harassment occurs most frequently when U.S. or NATO ships or groups of ships are engaged in exercises or other pursuits of technical interest to other forces, such as missile test firings. They will try to interfere in any way possible. While you are on independent duty you may be overflown by long-range reconnaissance aircraft. Take pictures, if possible, and report the incident to the chain of command.

Attempted Boarding or Capture. This sounds like something out of the nineteenth century, but it is more likely than you may think. We hope that *Pueblo*-style incidents are no longer possible, but they must be considered and planned for.

The *Pueblo* incident in 1968 is well known. There are many opinions regarding the action taken by Commander Loyd Bucher, the CO of the *Pueblo*. The official opinion, as expressed by the findings of the Board of Investigation, were, in simplified form, that his actions were incorrect. The final action of the Secretary of the Navy in setting aside these findings is not pertinent, since the rationale for doing so was based on factors extraneous to the principles involved. The opinions expressed as to what action Bucher should have taken range all the way from approval, with the rationale that resistance was useless and fighting the ship to the end would have resulted in the loss of many of the crew and the ultimate capture of any survivors, to the other end of the spectrum, that he should have had his guns ready (and not covered in iced canvas) and should have fought to the end.

The latter is the opinion held by most naval officers. Their reasons are best expressed in Article 0828, *Navy Regulations,* which states straightforwardly and unequivocally that you shall not permit a ship under your command to be searched on any pretense whatsoever by any person representing a foreign state, nor shall you permit any of the personnel within the confines of your command to be removed by such person, so long as you have the capacity to repel such act. If force is used in an attempt, you are to resist to the utmost of your power. This leaves no room for doubt. You are to resist *to the utmost.*

Crossing the Line. Several ceremonies, including crossing the line, may be necessary if operations cause you to cross the equator or the international date line. The crossing the line ceremony can be as elaborate as you and an enterprising and inventive crew want to make it. *Naval Ceremonies, Customs, and Traditions* contains a history of the ceremony and a sample scenario to help you make plans for your own. The ceremony of crossing the international date line is also described, and this too has a special certificate.

Other ceremonies can be held for those visiting the Arctic and the

Antarctic, and for those who become golden shellbacks by crossing the intersection of the equator and the international date line.

Review current directives and closely monitor the proceedings to ensure that an enjoyable and safe time is had by all. Remember that participation is voluntary.

Visits to a Foreign Port (Single Vessel)

Taking a Pilot. As you approach port, your next problem will be taking a pilot. *Navy Regulations,* Article 0856, covers your responsibility with regard to pilots. This article states that they are merely advisers. Pilots do not relieve you or your officers of any responsibility for the safe handling of the ship. The one exception is the Panama Canal, where the pilot does have control of the navigation and movement of your vessel (the Suez is *not* an exception). However, there have been occasions in the Panama Canal when COs took over from the pilot in the lake and channel sections to avoid grounding, and had their actions subsequently upheld. Nevertheless, be sure you are prepared to support your action if you relieve a Panama Canal pilot.

You may allow the pilot to handle your ship much as you would the OOD, but you must maintain your own navigational plot and make sure that your helmsman and engine order telegraph operator are alerted to respond to your order if and when you feel it necessary to take over the conn. You may also simply use the pilot as an adviser and keep the conn yourself. Many pilots do not speak good English, and you will have to stand by to clarify their orders. Also, foreign pilots are accustomed to merchant ships and tend to give orders in their parlance. "Ahead slow" can be interpreted as "ahead one-third." Be careful with "ahead full" if you are a destroyer type. The pilot doesn't *really* want twenty knots, so be sure you settle ahead of time as to what he wants when he asks for "full." He or she generally is thinking about ahead standard, or fifteen knots. Orders to the helm may not be familiar to you, but these can be interpreted fairly easily.

Pratique. *Pratique* is a French word meaning "the privilege of going ashore." The port health officer may board you either with the pilot or shortly after you are berthed. Remember that you are quarantined until he declares otherwise. U.S. Navy ships can request, and often receive, "free pratique."

Navy Regulations requires that you comply with all quarantine regulations for your port, and that you cooperate with the local health authorities and give them all health information available subject to the requirements of military security. Quarantine will remain in effect, as far as you are concerned, as long as you have doubt as to the sanitary regulations or health conditions of the port—and, from the health officer's point of view, if you have a quarantinable disease aboard or if you came from a port or area under quarantine. You must not conceal such conditions. Assuming that none of these problems exists, you will be granted pratique.

If, during your stay in port, a quarantinable condition arises aboard ship, you must hoist an appropriate signal to notify port authorities and the chain of command.

Boarding Officer's Call. A boarding officer will call on you at the first opportunity. Occasionally he will board with the pilot, or by separate boat as you are proceeding up the channel, but most frequently he will board just after you anchor or moor. In some ports he will have to wait until after pratique is granted. If there is another U.S. ship in port senior to you, he should still send a boarding officer to you with information and instructions. If you are senior, the other ship should send a boarding officer to you to ask when it would be convenient to turn over the SOPA files and duties, and for the commanding officer to call.

The more likely possibility is that you will be the lone U.S. ship in port. If so, the boarding call will come from one of several authorities, perhaps from several. If there is a U.S. naval attaché ashore, he will usually call or send someone from his office. If there is no such naval presence, the consul or a representative will call. If there is a naval command of the host country, either ashore or afloat, it will usually send a representative. The mayor or his representative may call.

In any event, there will be one or more persons who will welcome you and your ship and from whom you can obtain information necessary for the implementation of your responsibilities as SOPA, or for your own ship if you are alone.

Relations with U.S. Governmental Officials Ashore

Early in your port visit, and on the occasion of your boarding call, you will make contact with U.S. governmental officials ashore. The exact organization and size of the U.S. mission will depend on the rank of its head. If the port is the capital of its country, the mission will be headed by an ambassador. This official is appointed by the President and is his personal representative to the head of state. If the port is not the capital, the mission will be called a consular office, and will be headed by a consul. This individual will be a member of the U.S. Foreign Service, if the city is large, and will be seasoned and skilled in his profession. If the port is small, the mission will be headed by a consular agent, appointed by the Secretary of State. He will usually be a local businessman, not necessarily a U.S. citizen, and his primary duties will involve administration of shipping affairs.

Your duties as SOPA will probably require that you visit the mission frequently. A short description of the people you will meet will help you to seek the right persons to solve your problem. The ambassador, if you are involved with one, may be a political appointee with no previous diplomatic experience. He will, however, be a person of individual achievement and probably will be knowledgeable and communicative.

If not a political appointee, the ambassador will be a career member of the Foreign Service. The Foreign Service is the sixth federal service, and is a professional corps of men and women specially selected and trained to carry out the foreign policy of our nation in day-to-day relations with other countries. There are approximately 8,000 members serving abroad in 300 posts in 100 countries. The Foreign Service officer has a basic designation known as his "class." Class establishes seniority for internal purposes. He also holds a title, which is his assignment. You will also encounter Foreign Service staff officers and employees who are clerks or typists, and other administrative personnel. Local people will also be employed in supporting roles.

You will enjoy your relations with the embassy or mission personnel. They will be anxious to help, and will in turn ask for your help in furthering the good image of the United States in the port. This can be done by a people-to-people program, by allowing general visiting, or by personal relations with local governmental and business people.

The Statesmen's Yearbook, published annually by St. Martin's Press of New York, is a compendium of information about foreign countries, including descriptions of each, starting with the name of our ambassador and other U.S. governmental officials in that country, and covering the culture, religions, economy, demography, and other aspects. A study of the writeup for each country before you visit will be of great help.

Duties as SOPA

Once you have anchored or moored your ship and have received pratique, customs clearance, and your boarding call, you must get on with your duties as SOPA. These are covered in *Navy Regulations.* You might wish that all you had to do was look out for the safety of your own crew and ship, arrange liberty, and look forward to a pleasant visit, but this is only the beginning. As SOPA, you are the representative of your country and your Navy in that port, and you can be called upon to execute a great many duties.

Security. Your first duty is to look out for the *safety of your ship.* Ensure that you have a safe mooring, access to weather reports, an assigned typhoon or hurricane mooring if applicable, a method of recalling your crew, and adequate internal security, including sentries, watches, locked limited-access doors, and proper boat landing and securing facilities, if anchored out. With this done you can turn to your next priority, liberty arrangements.

Leave and Liberty. Article 0921 of *Navy Regulations* requires you as SOPA to regulate leave and liberty in conformance with any orders you may have, such as from a fleet commander or a local U.S. military authority. If you have no specific guidance or authority, issue your own, having due regard to information obtained from local officials as to vice and dangerous areas and local curfews.

Shore Patrol. With the privilege of leave and liberty goes the requirement to establish a shore patrol. Article 0922 of *Navy Regulations* requires that a shore patrol be established whenever liberty is granted to a considerable number of persons, except in an area that can absorb them without danger of disturbance or disorder. The purpose of a patrol of officers, petty officers, and noncommissioned officers, if Marines are embarked, is to maintain order and to suppress unseemly conduct. A lesser but not specifically stated reason is to provide for the safety of your crew ashore. This article goes on to require that the senior shore patrol officer communicate with the chief of police or local officials and make such arrangements as may be practicable to aid the patrol in carrying out its duties. Such duties would include providing assistance to your crew in their relations with police and local courts, including release to your custody.

With regard to the first requirement, which seems to require a patrol only if the liberty area cannot absorb your crew, it is wise to establish a small patrol even though your ship is small and the port is big. Any sailor getting into trouble usually ends up at the police station, and it is good to have a representative there, even though no street patrols are thought necessary.

You must, of course, obtain permission from local authorities to land the patrol, and if permission is denied you must restrict the size of liberty parties accordingly. Overseas the patrol must not be armed, but some countries will permit them to carry nightsticks. Remember to have your XO warn the members of the patrol that they may not indulge in intoxicants at any time when assigned to shore patrol.

Provisions and Supplies. Presumably your supply officer will be off attempting to obtain fresh provisions and stock for your ship's store. He should check first with the U.S. military force present or with the embassy or consulate to see if any contracts exist for this purpose. If they do, paperwork and time spent are very much reduced, and he can get on with ordering. If not, the supply officer will have to go through the time-consuming process of soliciting bids, awarding contracts, and then placing orders. Even these longer processes will be worthwhile, though, for the fresh produce will be welcome and the "exotic" ship's store stock can be sold at sea to produce added profits for recreation funds.

Calls. All of these arrangements sound complicated, but they actually proceed together and do not take too much of your time. Your personal occupation this first day will be to find out from the boarding officer which calls you should make and to get on with arranging them. Since we have assumed that there are no other U.S. ships present, your attention will be ashore first. Article 9011, *Navy Regulations,* requires that the SOPA preserve close relations with the diplomatic and consular representative of the United States. You must consider requests, recommendations, and other communications from such individuals, although the final responsibility for your acts as SOPA is yours. Obviously you should call on the ambassador, if there is one, or the consul at the earliest opportunity.

Article 0912, *Navy Regulations,* requires that you communicate with foreign civil, diplomatic, and consular officials through the local United States diplomatic consular representatives. You are not *required* to communicate or call, but it will be helpful if you have time to do so.

You should make arrangements through the embassy or consulate to call upon senior governmental officials of the host country.

If there are host country military forces present ashore, ask the advice of the embassy or consulate regarding calling.

If there are host country naval forces afloat, arrange a call on their SOPA. They will probably already have sent a calling officer to see you with the boarding officer.

If there are other foreign naval vessels present, use your own judgment about calling. Allied commanding officers will probably receive you enthusiastically. Other nations' COs are unpredictable. When you ask by message to call you may either be ignored or receive a warm invitation. If you are invited, by all means go; you will learn a lot.

You and your officers may receive invitations to use military messes and civilian clubs ashore. If so, arrange to have one or more of your wardroom officers call at the messes and clubs and leave cards. A letter of thanks after departure is also in order. Wardroom-to-wardroom calls are common in the British, Canadian, and Australian Navies. This is a fine custom, and your officers will enjoy it. They can expect a liberal alcoholic welcome anytime after noon. A word to your officers on what to expect would be wise. The Commonwealth officer is long conditioned to handling liquor on board ship. His mess will have an open bar, but if he is observed carefully it will be noted that even though he may drink *often,* he does not drink *much* at a time. He will always be ready for duty. American guests, however, will be plied with strong drinks under the guise of hospitality. Your young officers will do well to follow their hosts' example. *Drink often,* but not *much,* and stick to the soft stuff if possible. British beer is warm but good. Canadian naval messes are somewhat sedate; Australian, just the opposite. The French and Italian naval messes are less outgoing, as is their peoples' nature, but their hospitality will be worth enjoying. The Japanese Navy will be cordial, but formal, and will serve tea rather than strong drinks.

Finally, read Articles 1240 through 1249 of *Navy Regulations.* These cover in great detail your responsibilities regarding calls in a foreign port, and fill in some of the details omitted in the preceding summary of calls.

Honors and Ceremonies. Honors and ceremonies are particularly important to foreign navies. We tend to play them down, under the theory that sheer power is the most important ingredient of any navy. Foreign navies, lacking in power, depend instead for prestige on the careful and exact carrying out of ceremonies and honors, which they look upon as the true indicators of a respectable navy. We can play in this league, too, and we should. *Navy Regulations,* Chapter 10, sets forth the honors and ceremonies required in foreign ports. Careful study of them and instruction of your quarterdeck crew, boat crews, officers of the deck, and signal gang can ensure that your ship excels.

By now your initial duties will have been completed and your calls will be well on their way. You will also have taken care of all the miscellaneous duties of the SOPA. Try to get ashore for a little personal recreation and sightseeing before the rest of the social routine closes

A ship is evaluated, particularly in foreign ports, by the smartness of its quarter-deck, and the manner in which it renders honors.

in on you. You will soon be receiving return calls and accepting invitations ashore. These will lead in turn to the possibility of scheduling lunches aboard to return hospitality. Some ships have an open house aboard the last day before leaving port as a convenient way for all hands to return favors.

This is an appropriate time to suggest that you research the *Supply Manual* and appropriate type and fleet directives to find out what source of funds you have to help defray these entertainment costs. A little research and a few message requests will "pay off."

There are many other occasional but important duties that you will fall heir to as SOPA. If there are other ships present you will be responsible for the coordination of all the foregoing actions for all ships. You must also take command if concerted action is necessary for mutual defense or for safety against weather.

Using Military Force. With regard to the use of military force within the territorial waters of another nation, Articles 0914, 0915, and 0916 of *Navy Regulations* are very specific. When injury to U.S. citizens is committed or threatened in violation of a treaty or international law, the SOPA must consult with diplomatic or consular representatives if possible, and shall take such action as is demanded by the gravity of the situation. In time of peace, action by United States Navy personnel against any other nation, or against anyone within the territories thereof, either an actual use of force or a threat to use force, is illegal unless as an act of self-defense. You are required to exercise sound judgment and to assert this right only as a last resort.

Landing Forces for Exercise. In a more peaceful vein, you may not, in a foreign country, land a force for exercise, target practice, or funeral escort unless permission has been granted. You may not land a force to capture deserters. You may not conduct target practice with guns, torpedoes, rockets, or missiles at any point where these can enter territorial waters.

Medical and Dental Assistance. In a more routine vein, you are required by Article 0924 to render medical and dental assistance to persons not in the naval service when such aid is necessary and demanded by the laws of humanity or the principle of international courtesy.

Marriage Abroad. While you are attempting to relax, you may find the interlude broken by some of your other SOPA duties. One of them will occur when one of your officers or sailors conducts a romantic campaign ashore and comes to you asking to be married. Fleet regulations will cover the subject; refer first to them. If your ship is big enough to have a legal officer, you are in clover. If not, you or one of your officers will have to visit the embassy or consulate to determine the local laws and to help your sailor fill out the necessary forms. Hopefully ardor will cool when he or she sees the paperwork difficulties and delays, or, if not, he or she will take charge and get them done without involving too much of your time.

Marriage Aboard Ship. If still in the ball game, your sailor may ask to be married aboard ship. This matter is regulated by Article 0716,

Navy Regulations. This article is somewhat peculiarly phrased. It starts out by flatly prohibiting you from performing marriage aboard ship. It then, in a rather awkward and negative way, states that you may not *permit* a marriage to be performed aboard ship when outside the territory of the United States, but it then gives certain exceptions. The ceremony must be in accordance with the local laws and the laws of the state, territory, or district in which both parties are domiciled, and must take place only in the presence of a diplomatic or consular official of the United States who has consented to make the certificate and returns required by the consular regulations. From the tenor of the article it can be assumed that the Secretary of the Navy takes a negative view of marriage performed aboard ship. Be very sure you want to do so before going through the bureaucratic necessities involved. Your sailor will probably be just as happy being married ashore.

In summary, you as commanding officer *cannot* yourself conduct a marriage ceremony aboard ship. A chaplain, if you have one or can borrow one, *can* perform a marriage ceremony aboard if you comply with Article 0844.

SOPA Files. The boarding officer, if a U.S. naval or consular person, will probably have delivered to you the SOPA file of previous visitors. It will be of help to you. Update it and return it to the same person or to the senior U.S. commanding officer remaining in port after you depart.

People-to-People Programs. From time to time fleet commanders require that ships conduct people-to-people programs. You may also want to conduct one independently. You will find that your crew will be responsive and even enthusiastic if it is suggested that they visit orphans ashore or invite them aboard ship, donate food to the poor, or take other, more innovative action. Your crew will do best if they are allowed to initiate the kind and amount of response. Be sure that you check any proposed actions with embassy or consular officials ashore before carrying it out. You will avoid possible embarrassment to both of you if there is a political situation ashore that only the embassy or consular staff is aware of.

Community relations are an important part of a captain's job. They help build confidence in, and admiration of, the entire Navy—not just your own ship.

Hopefully, as part of your POM preparation, you will have been told about the various programs such as "Project Handclasp," which provides materials and gifts such as toys, food, and supplies for unfortunate foreign nationals. The best material you can have, however, is the enthusiasm and friendliness of the American bluejacket.

Conduct of Officers and Crew. *Navy Regulations* requires you to instruct your enlisted personnel as to their conduct ashore. They will stand out from the locals in their uniforms and even in their civilian clothes, when they are permitted to wear them, and will bear the brunt of any criticism for misconduct ashore. It is especially important, and many times overlooked, to instruct your junior officers as well. They will all be in civilian clothes and will therefore think themselves less obvious. In fact, because of their neat haircuts, clean

American bluejackets are our country's best ambassadors. Prepare them to carry out this role by thorough briefings in the culture of the area to be visited.

clothes, and generally excellent appearance, they will be recognized in every port. Counsel them to use the utmost discretion, particularly in public places, and to conduct themselves as they would in their own home towns. Foreign ports offer every kind of vice known to man. Your officers must lead the way in setting a good example in practicing restraint, if not abstinence.

Article 0917, *Navy Regulations,* enjoins you to uphold the prestige of the United States. Impress upon your officers and crew, when in foreign ports, that it is their duty to avoid all possible causes of offense to the inhabitants; that due deference must be shown by them to local laws and customs, ceremonies, and regulations; that moderation and courtesy should be displayed in all dealings with foreigners; and that a feeling of goodwill and mutual respect should be cultivated. Your crew will represent our country well if you have instructed them.

Ship's Boats. Article 0855, *Navy Regulations,* states that ship's boats shall be regarded as part of their ship in all matters concerning the rights, privileges, and comity of nations. In ports where war, insurrection, or armed conflict exists or threatens, you must have an appropriate and competent person in charge of each boat, and take steps to make the nationality of your boats evident at all times. This translates into flying a flag whenever the boat is away from the ship and having a boat officer or competent petty officer assigned. On some occasions the coxswain, if rated and competent in your eyes, may be enough. A deck chief petty officer is appropriate in most circumstances, particularly in small ships with few officers. The rank or rate of your boat officers is purely a matter of your judgment of their competence and the seriousness of the situation ashore and afloat.

Admiralty Claims and Reports. If a U.S. naval or merchant vessel collides with or otherwise damages a foreign vessel or pier in the port where you are SOPA, you will have certain responsibilities with regard to processing claims against the United States and rendering consequent reports. Article 0926, *Navy Regulations,* states that you shall process claims in accordance with the procedures set forth in the *Manual of the Judge Advocate General of the Navy.* If you have a legal officer assigned, you will be fortunate. If not, you may seek legal assistance from the embassy or consulate. You have limited authority to institute libel proceedings against a foreign vessel in a collision case. However, the *Manual* points out that the matter is within the primary cognizance of the Department of Justice. In view of your limited legal knowledge and experience and short time in port, you will do well to heed this advice and leave it to the professionals.

Relations between the SOPA and the SOP. In a few foreign ports, but in many U.S. ports, you will find U.S. military forces ashore. This brings up the subject of the relations between you, as SOPA, and the SOP ashore. Article 0901, *Navy Regulations,* states that in a locality within an area prescribed by competent authority the senior officer present shall be the senior line officer of the Navy on active duty eligible for command at sea, who is present and in command of any part of the Department of the Navy, except where both Navy and Marine Corps personnel are present on shore and the Marine Corps officer is senior. In such cases the officer of the Marine Corps shall be the senior officer present ashore.

Article 0903 then gives the senior officer present the authority to assume command and to direct the efforts of all persons in the Navy Department present, when, in his judgment, the exercise of authority is necessary. He must exercise his authority in a manner consistent with the full operational command vested in the commanders of unified or specified commands.

The import of these articles is that you must maintain close liaison with the SOP ashore. Commanding officers afloat tend to continue the independence they exercised at sea when they are in port. While you are still independent in certain matters, you must recognize the limitations upon you. Article 0930 specifically states that you must refer all matters affecting the afloat units under you to the senior officer present, either Naval or Marine Corps, ashore. This officer will not, however, expect literal interpretation of the requirement.

In the event that you as SOPA are senior to the SOP ashore, you must take other considerations into account. Article 0930 describes your general duties and states that as the common superior of all commanders of all naval units in that locality, except such units as may be assigned to shore units by competent authority, you are responsible for matters which collectively affect these commands. You are charged not to concern yourself with administrative matters within other commands, except to the extent necessary to secure uniformity and coordination of effort. You will assume command of all units of the operating forces of the Navy present in case of emergency or enemy attack.

Article 0932 then elaborates on relations with commanders ashore on the level of the Commandant of a Naval District. You are not likely to be senior to such a commander and will not be concerned with this problem.

Powers of Consul. If you are in a foreign port small enough not to have a consul, you may be required to exercise these powers. Article 0934, *Navy Regulations,* states that when upon the high seas, or in any foreign port where there is no resident consul of the United States, the SOPA has the authority to exercise all powers of consul in relation to mariners of the United States.

Article 1244 gives you the authority to issue rations to destitute sailors and airmen. The supply officer making such issue shall do so pursuant to an order in writing from you and shall procure receipts for such supplies in accordance with the *Naval Supply System Command Manual.* Article 0848 permits you to receive distressed sailors on board for rations and passage to the United States provided they agree to abide by *Navy Regulations.* You may also accept merchant seaman prisoners for transport provided that the witnesses against them are also received or adequate means are adopted to ensure the presence of such witnesses at the place where the prisoners are to be detained. Article 0926 states that you may not authorize repairs to a merchant vessel in collision with a Navy ship unless the exigency of war or national defense so requires. You may, however, authorize or perform repairs to save lives or prevent sinking. If you do so you must submit a report of repairs including labor and material costs and a certification as to why repairs were undertaken.

Protection of Commerce. Today, when the mission of the Navy seems to all of us to be the maintenance of the national security of our country, we tend to forget that historically the Navy was created to protect commerce. Article 0920 will remind you that you are required, while acting in conformity with international law and treaty obligations, to protect, insofar as it lies within your power, all commercial craft of the United States and to advance the commercial interests of your country.

International Law and Treaties. Article 1125 requires that in your relations with foreign nations, and with governments and agents thereof, you shall conform to international law and to the precedents established by the United States in such relations. You are separately enjoined to report to higher authority any violation of international law or treaty both by U.S. citizens and by foreign nationals and their governments. Your reports in these matters should go to the Fleet Commander and the Chief of Naval Operations, and as a matter of courtesy should also be reported to the local ambassador or consul.

NWP 1–14, Law of Naval Warfare, presents and amplifies international law as related to naval warfare, and legal restriction on methods and weapons. It provides guidance on the legal status of ships, aircraft, and personnel engaged in naval warfare, and the actions permitted against them under international law. The legal divisions of the sea and air are described, as well as areas in which belligerent naval operations are permitted, and the restrictions on belligerents in neutral jurisdiction. Those treaties which are the principal sources of the laws of naval warfare and the U.S. armed forces code of conduct are presented in appendices to this publication.

Foreign Civil Jurisdiction. The United States Senate, in giving its advice and consent to the NATO Status of Forces Agreement, resolved that safeguards would be provided to protect persons subject to U.S. military jurisdiction who are to be tried by foreign authorities. In implementing the resolution, the Department of Defense directed that in each unified command the commander would designate within each member country a "commanding officer" to ensure that such safeguards are provided. Both fleet commanders-in-chief also have issued instructions on this subject. This practice was first started to cover the needs of NATO members, but has now been enlarged to extend the same protection to all U.S. personnel serving abroad, as far as is possible.

Local SOPA regulations should normally cover the basic procedures for dealing with a foreign jurisdictional problem, but in small ports, where such regulations may be sketchy, you will have to take steps on your own. You should first require your officers and those of any other U.S. ship in port to report to you instances where personnel have become subject to foreign jurisdiction. When this occurs you should request a waiver of criminal jurisdiction and release of the person involved. Do so through the standing shore patrol organization, if one exists, or through your own. Notify your next senior in command and other seniors as high as necessary to reach one who has authority to convene a general court-martial. Make sure a U.S. observer attends the trial. This should be one of your own officers if you are still in port. Otherwise, ask the consul to observe and report to you. You should advise and assist the person concerned, helping him or her to retain counsel, paying the trial expenses, and paying bail. You may pay for these contingencies. The Act of July 24, 1956 (*10 U.S. Code 1037*) authorizes the Secretary of the Navy to employ counsel and pay counsel fees, court costs, bail, and other expenses required for representation before foreign tribunals and agencies of any person subject to the *Uniform Code of Military Justice*. In all cases, message reports up through the chain of command are required, with the Judge Advocate General an information addressee.

U.S. Civil Jurisdiction. Article 0822, *Navy Regulations,* prohibits you from delivering personnel serving under you to U.S. civil authorities except as provided by the *Manual of the Judge Advocate General*. Study it carefully and abide strictly by its provisions. There will probably be a large ship or station nearby where you can seek legal help. This same article authorizes you to permit the serving of a subpoena or other legal process as provided by *Manual of the Judge Advocate General*. There will frequently be occasions where your sailors will be detained by civil authority ashore. Usually you can seek legal help from other naval sources. Make every effort to see that your sailors get help. If possible, one of your officers should appear at the jail and in court.

Public Relations. Public relations is a major personal responsibility of every commanding officer. We discuss it in this chapter on independent operations because it is most likely to be a problem when you are operating independently. You will have to deal with both the positive and negative aspects of public relations in any situation that develops, not only with your own ship, but with regard to any situation involving the Navy or the United States. This translates as follows. If something *bad* happens (negative aspect), you will have to explain what happened and what is being done to correct the situation. Further, if something *good* (positive aspect) *doesn't* happen in the normal course of events, it will be up to you to *create* some positive situation, such as a people-to-people program or a press tour of your ship, so that the U.S. Navy will be seen in a good light.

When you are operating independently this responsibility will devolve upon you. When you are operating under another commander, it will be your responsibility to assist in the unit's public relations effort, and at the same time to carry out your ship's responsibilities even though you are part of a unit. In other words, public relations is always a problem for, and a responsibility of, every commanding officer at all times.

Your basic guidance for public relations is the *Chief of Information* (CHINFO) *Manual*. It covers every aspect of public relations, which, by definition, is the total of your relations with the public, including your relations with the press, public, families, congressmen, and other groups. *Public information* is a limited part of public relations, involving the giving (or withholding) of information to the various media (television, radio, newspapers, and magazines) and to those parts of the public who either want it or, in your judgment, or the view of CHINFO, should be exposed to it. The *Manual* will tell you how to approach the mechanics of public information.

Your public affairs officer (PAO) is responsible to you for carrying out the ship's public affairs program. The *SORN* outlines the PAO's duties, responsibilities, and authority. In describing this officer's organizational position, it states that he reports to you via the executive officer. This is certainly organizationally correct for all of the other ship's officers, but for the PAO it is wrong. Public affairs officers at all levels, from the White House to the Secretary of the Navy's office to your ship, must have direct and instant access to the commander. Put your PAO in the prescribed organizational box for normal routine, but if you want to avoid disaster, make sure that he and the executive officer both understand his authority to consult with you and to advise you directly at any time of the day or night. He should, of course, fill in the XO at the first opportunity after seeing you.

These visitors observing flight operations will carry away a good impression of the Navy.

Now that you understand this, you are ready to consider a few simple rules that will keep you out of trouble.

First, don't be afraid of reporters. They have job to do and will ask frank and sometimes embarrassing questions. Treat their questions as opportunities to get across the points that you want to make. You do *not* have to answer every question. You may decline to answer and give a reason for not answering, or you may simply move on to the next question. Second, if you have bad news to present, give it all at once and as fully and frankly as you can. If you don't, and it comes out piecemeal, the effect on the media will be to intensify and prolong the negative atmosphere. Third, if you want to tell a positive story about your ship's or crew's activities, carefully prepare a release, give it your personal attention, and make sure your public affairs officer gives it to the press and other local media at a time that allows them to meet their deadlines.

This may seem like a lot of detail to devote to this subject, but we want to underline the increasing importance of telling the Navy's story to the public. The public and the Congress must know what the Navy does and what it needs, and must feel a personal relationship with us. It is your responsibility to produce these results, and you must take part personally and enthusiastically in the public affairs program, afloat, ashore, and overseas.

Asylum. Earlier in this chapter, we outlined the requirements for a commanding officer to grant asylum at sea. The same requirements exist in port and are covered completely in Article 0940, *Navy Regulations*. Be conversant with them. If an incident occurs it will happen quickly and without warning. Your actions should be both informed and automatic.

As your port visit draws to a close you have, we hope, carried out your social responsibilities, fulfilled your duties as SOPA, looked out for the many and varied interests of your navy and your country, withdrawn your shore patrol, paid all of your ship's bills, and squeezed in a little personal recreation and sightseeing. Now you are more than ready to get underway. Both independent duty and being SOPA are rewarding experiences, but they are also demanding. Rejoining the fleet or visiting your next port with other, bigger ships will now have a sweeter taste than ever.

The Rewards of Independent Operation

As you steam quietly out of the harbor and set course to rejoin, take time to recall the contingencies you either met or avoided on your independent duty. You can return to your unit secure in the knowledge that you have met the same physical challenges mastered by generations of mariners, as well as some more modern administrative challenges they never dreamed of. The commanding officer of a naval vessel is truly "a mariner for all seasons" and fits Theodore Roosevelt's description of the individual who dares great things:

> The credit belongs to the man who is actually in the arena, whose face is marred with sweat and dirt and blood; who strives valiantly; who errs and comes short again and again; who knows the great enthusi-

asms, the great devotions, and spends himself on a worthy cause; who, if he wins, knows the triumph of high achievement; and who, if he fails, at least fails while daring greatly, so that his place will never be with those cold and timid souls who know neither victory nor defeat.

With the fleet you are, unfortunately, part of the herd. You will have the protection of the herd, but fewer challenges. Independent duty places upon you, and you alone, the responsibility for meeting challenges with determined, positive action. Accept responsibility; enjoy it; it is what your profession is all about.

10

Forward Operations and Combat Philosophy

Whosoever can hold the sea has command of everything.

–Themistocles (524–460 B.C.)

War teaches us to lose everything and become what we were not.

–John Milton

Your Role in Our Nation's Armed Forces

Having taken your ship, submarine, or aircraft squadron through training, inspections, and independent operations, it is time to discuss the truly critical importance of how to best integrate your command into the Navy–Marine Corps team and the larger organizations of joint task forces, interagency operations, and coalition warfare. We will conclude with some thoughts on the unique character of combat operations.

Naval Strategy, Planning, and Operations

Every commanding officer in today's world should be familiar with basic naval strategy, operational art, and tactics. While a detailed discussion of all of this is beyond the structure of this volume, a few key points are worth highlighting.

First of all, you should make an effort to be conversant with the basic Navy and Marine Corps doctrine publications, which provide a great deal of the philosophical underpinning to our nation's approach to sea power. These include ". . . From the Sea," the initial document that appeared in 1992 and shifted naval focus to the littoral region following the end of the Cold War, and "Forward . . . From the Sea," which continued the discussion through the mid-1990s. Both are available from the Commander of the Naval Doctrine Command or via the Department of Defense website at www.defenselink.mil. Additionally, two of the most fundamental naval doctrine documents are NDP-1, "Naval Warfare," published in 1994, and NDP-5, "Naval Planning," published in 1996. These two relatively concise publications provide an excellent overview of sea power's application to modern warfighting and the basics on planning for naval operations.

Second, remember that the United States is a maritime nation that relies on transoceanic trade. Our primary Navy–Marine Corps missions of sea control, power projection, strategic deterrence, and sealift will always be required given the global nature of U.S. interests. In your dealings with the public, seek to make the point that the sea services (Navy, Marine Corps, and Coast Guard) all conduct maritime operations in the world's oceans and littorals as part of fundamental U.S. strategy.

Third, the increasingly joint character of all operations is an important component to our approach as a Navy–Marine Corps team. Particularly since the 1986 Goldwater-Nichols legislation, all of the services have sought to work more closely together in meeting the complex demands of national security. You will find that virtually every aspect of your command's operational activity will have a joint component to it, and you should be alert to improve your ship, submarine, or squadron's ability to integrate and perform well in joint operations. In preparing for joint operations, you should review the publications discussed below, as well as the terms discussed in the Glossary following this chapter.

Fourth, you will find that interagency activity is an important and challenging part of your role today. In addition to working with the other services in joint operations, your command will interact with an extraordinarily wide range of interagency actors. A few of the ones you will most frequently work with include the Department of State, the Department of Energy, the Department of Transportation/Coast

Guard, the Drug Enforcement Agency, the CIA, the Department of Justice, and the Federal Emergency Management Agency. You may also work with private voluntary organizations and nongovernmental organizations (NGOs). Virtually everything you need to know about interagency activity can be found in an excellent joint doctrine publication, Joint Publication 3-08, "Interagency Coordination during Joint Operations." It is available at the defenselink website, and is well worth reading as you complete your workups and begin joint operations.

Finally, be aware that there is an increasing emphasis on coalition warfare throughout all forward deployed areas today. Since the end of the Cold War and the collapse of the Soviet bloc, the bipolar character of the global environment has given way to a far more fluid situation in which ad hoc coalitions are formed to deal with emerging situations. The prime example of this, of course, was the coalition formed in 1990–91 to defeat Saddam Hussein's aggression into Kuwait. Additional coalition activities have been conducted throughout the world, including sanction operations directed against Serbia and United Nations activities in a wide variety of locales from Africa to Southeast Asia.

Welcome to the Joint World

Since joint operations are by far the most common form of activity today for your command, we'll focus on preparing for those in additional detail. The first step for a commanding officer in understanding the position that his or her ship, submarine, or squadron plays in the world of joint operations is to comprehend the language associated with it. There are several key publications that should be mastered, including the "bible" of joint operations, "Unified Action of the Armed Forces." This short, easy-to-read publication is available on the Internet at www.defenselink.mil, along with essentially the entire joint library of tactical publications (unclassified, of course). Spend some time browsing through the defense link site, where you will find a wide assortment of key documents and publications.

A few key concepts and actors first—very basic, but you must hold them in mind as you review the joint world:

Unity of effort requires coordination among government departments and agencies within the executive branch, between the executive and legislative branches, between NGOs, and among nations in any alliance or coalition.

The President of the United States, advised by the National Security Council, is responsible to the American people for national strategic unity of effort.

The Secretary of Defense is responsible to the President for national military unity of effort for creating, supporting, and employing military capabilities.

The Chairman of the Joint Chiefs of Staff (CJCS) functions under the authority, direction, and control of the National Command Authorities (NCA) and transmits communications between the NCA and combatant commanders and oversees activities of combatant commanders as directed by the Secretary of Defense.

In a foreign country, the *U.S. ambassador* is responsible to the President for directing, coordinating, and supervising all U.S. government elements in the host nation except those under the command of a combatant commander.

Commanders of combatant commands exercise combatant command (command authority) over assigned forces and are directly responsible to the Secretary of Defense (although all communications go through the CJCS) for the preparedness of their commands to perform assigned missions. Referred to as "CINCs," these are the four-star officers who run the armed forces day-to-day on operational missions. In accomplishing the missions your command will undertake, it is important to know they generally do so by forming *joint task forces (JTFs)* to conduct operations.

All joint force commanders, be they CINCs or lower-echelon commanders, have the authority to organize forces to best accomplish the assigned mission based on their concept of operations. The organization should be sufficiently flexible to meet the planned phases of the contemplated operations and any development that may necessitate a change in plan. A JTF is a joint force that is constituted and so designated by the Secretary of Defense, a combatant commander, a subordinate unified command commander, or an existing JTF commander.

A JTF may be established on a geographical area or functional basis when the mission has a specific limited objective. Of note, your Carrier/Amphibious Battle Group is also a Joint Task Group.

With those basics in mind, you are ready to do some reading in the Joint Publication library. As you read through these materials, you will be helped by immediate familiarity with terms defined in the Glossary following the end of this chapter. In addition to the many joint publications available on the web, you should use the defense link site to review the current Navy strategic and tactical publications. Armed with this overview of the joint world, you should be more than ready to engage in the naval aspects of campaign planning and operations.

Naval Warfare and the Principles of War

A very fundamental publication that should find a permanent place over your desk is NDP-1, "Naval Warfare." If there is a "bible" for naval operations at sea, this is it. Derived from the long-standing Naval Warfare Publication 1A, this is the document that lays out, in clear, systematic prose, the reason the U.S. Navy exists. You should be conversant with it for several reasons. First, it is an excellent summary of what naval missions you will be called upon to undertake. Second, as commanding officer you must be able to articulate to your crew their role in the defense of the United States as part of the Navy–Marine Corps team. And third, when your duties bring you to interact with both the American public and the international world, you must be an articulate, informed spokesperson for our Navy–Marine Corps team.

One key section of this brief and easy-to-read publication includes a discussion of the principles of war, which are summarized here:

Objective. Direct every military operation toward a clearly defined, decisive, and attainable objective.

Mass. Concentrate combat power at the decisive time and place.

Maneuver. Place the enemy in a position of disadvantage through the feasible application of combat power.

Offensive. Seize, retain, and exploit the initiative.

Economy of force. Employ all combat power available in the most effective way possible; allocate minimum essential combat power to secondary efforts.

Unity of command. Ensure unity of effort for every objective under one responsible commander.

Simplicity. Avoid unnecessary complexity in preparing, planning, and conducting military operations.

Surprise. Strike the enemy at a time or place or in a manner for which the enemy is unprepared.

Security. Never permit the enemy to acquire unexpected advantage. Protecting the force increases our combat power.

These principles of war, identified by Clausewitz and validated in battle for centuries, should be considered in every aspect of your command's employment.

Other key sections in "Naval Warfare" include a discussion of the Navy and Marine Corps' roles in today's potential combat scenarios. The publication focuses on the Navy–Marine Corps involvement in command, control, and surveillance; battlespace dominance; power projection; and force sustainment. These twenty-first-century naval warfare concepts are balanced with a discussion of enduring naval roles in deterrence; forward presence; sealift; and joint operations. Taken together, the material included in "Naval Warfare" is well worth sharing with your wardroom as part of general discussions of strategy and tactics.

Planning

In many ways, the key to your command's operational success lies in the effective execution of planning. And you, Captain, are the chief planner for your command. Your operations officer will be a great help to you; but only the CO can bring the right mix of operational experience, depth of tactical knowledge, and hard-won perspective to the table.

An excellent resource for you in your role as planner for your command is NDP-5, "Naval Planning." It is not a detailed, "nuts and bolts" guide to planning; rather, it is a general overview that will refresh you on the key elements to be borne in mind as you sit with your ops boss and other key planners and put together exercises, tactical engagement plans, and your battle orders. In it you will find a discussion of the basic planning principles: relevance, clarity, timeliness, flexibility, participation, economy of resources, security, and coordination. Each and every time you plan an event, whether it is a complex missile shoot, a multi-day transit, or a dependent's cruise, you should methodically work through each of the principles of planning. Is the plan clear? Have we most effectively applied resources to the event? Is there flexibility (i.e., a Plan B and a Plan C)?

"Naval Planning" also includes a discussion of the linkages between our own Navy–Marine Corps team planning and the larger joint world. It discusses the three types of joint operation planning: campaign planning, deliberate planning, and crisis action planning. Reviewing this portion of the publication and keeping these separate processes in mind will be helpful as you work your ship through battle group and joint operations.

Finally, "Naval Planning" also includes a good discussion of the Maritime Tactical Messages used to standardize the general operating instructions—for example, Operational General Matters (OPGENs), Operational Tasks (OPTASKs), and Operational Status (OPSTATs) messages. All of these are structured in formats that are compatible with the Joint Operation Planning and Execution System (JOPES) which drives the joint world. You will also see a discussion of Marine Corps planning, which is important for today's world of combined Carrier Battle Group and Amphibious Readiness Group activities. The Marines use a fifteen-step process (which will be streamlined to a six-step process), as well as a Rapid Response Planning Process (R2P2), which is also increasingly in use by Navy units.

Study this publication and keep a copy handy in your "desk load." Your ops officer will want to keep equally familiar with Naval Warfare Publication 5-01, "Naval Operational Planning," which contains a more detailed, format-oriented discussion of the same topics. For your level of participation at the command level, though, NDP-5 is perfect.

Interagency Operations

An area of increasing emphasis in which your command may find itself playing a role is interagency operations. Examples of scenarios that may require interagency coordination include humanitarian response, natural disaster relief, noncombatant evacuations, migrant control, and many others. The key definition of interagency operations is simply that they are activities requiring the active participation of more than one governmental organization.

Some of the typical partners with whom you may work in the world of interagency operations include the Departments of State, Treasury (Drug Enforcement Agency), Commerce, Energy, Transportation (Coast Guard), and Justice (FBI), as well as the CIA. You may also find yourself involved with international actors, including the United Nations, allied civilian and governmental organizations, private voluntary organizations, NGOs, the Federal Emergency Management Agency, and a host of others. While a discussion of each of these organizations is beyond the scope of this work, there is an excellent two-volume publication that should be on every CO's desk: Joint Publication 3-08 (two volumes), "Interagency Coordination during Joint Operations." In it you will find solid information about each of the organizations you may come in contact with, the command relationships, the organization of the Civil-Military Operations Center (CMOC), and many of the other details of conducting joint operations.

In the course of your workups for forward deployment, you will conduct several exercises with interagency challenges embedded in them, typically a noncombatant evacuation operation and possibly some type of humanitarian response.

Forward Deployment Preparations

As the commanding officer, you will be deeply involved in every aspect of deployment preparations. One of the most important things you should do is help your command leadership focus on the potential challenges for the deployment.

The first and perhaps most important tool is the pre-deployment checklist, provided by your type commander. It typically starts about 180 days prior to cruise, and contains a detailed series of hundreds of specific items your team should accomplish—everything from dental surveys to the loading of storerooms, from preparation of required reports to ensuring that the right communication crypto is onboard. Take the time each month to sit down and review progress on the checklist with your XO and department heads.

Second, you should be personally helping your officers, chiefs, and sailors focus on the tactical and operational challenges ahead. Brief each group on your ship about the upcoming deployment at about the 90-day point, focusing on the very real possibility that your cruise will entail "real world" operations. Discuss likely scenarios for employment of your unit, with frequent references to the front pages of the newspapers. The odds run about 50–50 that any given forward deployed Navy unit will participate in a crisis of some kind, and about 70 percent are involved in either a Noncombatant Evacuation Operation (NEO) or a UN sanctions deployment. These are dangerous, challenging evolutions involving every man and woman in your crew. They need to understand how important their cruise is to the national security of the United States, and your personal involvement should be part of that understanding.

Third, ensure that your families are well taken care of in the deployment preparations. You should form a separate "family team" composed of the command master chief, XO, supply officer, chaplain (if assigned), legal officer (collateral duty), and other individuals in the crew or squadron who have an impact on family support activities. They should be working closely with the Navy Family Services Center, the command ombudsman, and the chairperson of the Family Support Group. Meet with them frequently and monitor their progress. They should set up pre-deployment briefings for the families, arrange support mechanisms in the homeport, line up services, ensure that the command ombudsman has a care line installed, and generally work to make sure that problems are headed off in the homeport. Every sailor whose family has a problem while you are forward deployed will sap the combat efficiency of your unit, and anything you can do to stop problems before they happen will make you more capable while forward deployed.

Another important aspect of making a forward deployment is encouraging all the members of your team to think about how they can best improve themselves during the six months. They should have ideas and goals for such self-improvement, with appropriate support from the command. Physical fitness is a great place to emphasize self-improvement, and the addition of new workout equipment before cruise is a must. Set up a means for your sailors to work on educational self-improvement as well, through the PACE system of embarked instructors for college credits. Have a strong educational service program in place, and your personal attention to the entire area of crew goal attainment will pay dividends.

Lastly, try and specifically articulate your goals for the command as a whole on the cruise. Naturally, you should start with safety and mission accomplishment. Then think about what innovative tactical concepts your command would best pursue. Set a goal that each department complete a draft TACMEMO, for example; or ask each division to complete one major project that will improve the command in some way during the six-month period. And don't neglect the good your command can do in various ports around the world. Painting orphanages may seem a little bit of a cliché, but it is a very real and tangible way for your sailors to light a candle of hope in an occasionally dark and turbulent world.

All of these areas are places your personal involvement will have a great and positive impact on forward deployment for your command.

Another major aspect of forward deployment preparations is the workup period. Most Navy ships, submarines, and aircraft squadrons currently deploy with either a Carrier Battle Group (named after the CVNs, e.g., Abraham Lincoln Battle Group) or an Amphibious Readiness Group (named after the large-deck amphib, e.g., Essex ARG). Some units do deploy independently, such as P-3C Orion squadrons, occasional submarines conducting special operations, or small groups of ships deploying the Fifth Fleet in the Arabian Gulf.

As part of your preparations for forward deployment, your command will be part of a designated workup sequence, normally orchestrated either by Third Fleet on the West Coast or Second Fleet on the East Coast. This workup sequence will commence when you complete the initial portion of the training cycle described earlier in this volume. When you "chop" from your type commander (COM-NAVSURFLANT or COMNAVSURFPAC in the case of surface combatants, for example) to Third or Second Fleet, you will begin a series of conferences, training exercises, war games, and at-sea exercises (e.g., COMPTUEX, FLTEX) culminating in a Joint Task Force Exercise (JTFEX) that is the "final exam" prior to deployment. This is a very strenuous and challenging exercise undertaken in the OP-AREAs off the U.S. coasts and will put your command through its paces in terms of virtually every type of contingency you can expect to encounter on deployment. Observers will be stationed in the Fleet Commander's flagship to observe the activity and ensure you are prepared for the rigors of forward deployment.

In terms of preparing for these evolutions, the best approach is to seek the advice of a ship that has recently completed the pre-deployment workup cycle and can give you a blow-by-blow description of the training packages. This kind of advance information will be very helpful in shaping your preparations. You should build on the information you receive from a recent "graduate" and develop a sort of tactical Plan of Action and Milestones (POAM) that will ensure that your team is ready to go. Items in the POAM should include combat and operational training scenarios run within your lifelines, time for tactical training for all watchstanders, as well as in-port lectures on the sorts of operations you will encounter (Maritime Interception Operations training, for example). Set up a two- to three-day block of time for your wardroom and CPO mess to prepare for the COMPTUEX, FLTEX, and the subsequent JTFEX. Brief the events for which you hold PRE-EX messages, go over the known portions of the schedule of events, discuss your own battle orders, review shiphandling and formation steaming issues, and have a safety brief. Each of your department heads and division officers should be encouraged to perform similar briefings for their individual portions of the command.

Forward Deployed Operations

It is a proud and exciting day in every CO's tour when you forward deploy. You can look forward to six months of dedicated training, operations, port visits, and challenge. Whether or not you face a "real world" crisis, you can take pride in the knowledge that your deployment is a significant factor in U.S. national security policy, beginning with the significant deterrent value every U.S. Carrier Battle Group, Amphibious Readiness Group, and independent deployer makes.

Each of the three forward deployed Fleets has a different set of challenges, and as you transit from Third and Second Fleet areas of responsibility (AORs) into the forward world of Sixth, Seventh, and Fifth Fleets you should be working to ensure that your entire team is well briefed and ready for anything.

Certainly a good place to begin is conducting a daily operations brief. This can be done in the morning, at noon, or after the evening meal. The best approach seems to be around 1800, after everyone has had dinner, but before the mid-watchstanders and the late-night fliers need to be turning in. Use a standard format for each brief, perhaps beginning with the weather, position, current intelligence, and upcoming events for the next twenty-four hours. This should be followed by specific briefs on any complex events, as well as a "topic of the day" on an individual issue—perhaps an intell report on a new type of Iranian cruise missile tactic. As CO, you should try to be part of the briefing lineup every evening. Remember, you are the leading tactician and mariner or airman of your command—get up every night and share a little of your experience with your team!

These daily briefs are an excellent place to provide training and information to your wardroom or ready room and combat team on the challenges in the individual theater. You will find yourself facing the continuing crises on the Korean peninsula and wondering about Chinese intentions in the Seventh Fleet AOR; studying the challenges of dual containment of Iraq and Iran in the Fifth Fleet; and thinking about the delicate Arab-Israeli peace process, the turbulence in Bosnia, and the potential dangers in Algeria in the Sixth Fleet—just to name a few issues. Your team should be "up to speed" on these and any other major potential operational challenges. They should have an appreciation for the threat, our allies, and neutrals in each region in which you operate.

Keep your team training, training, training throughout the deployment. Meet the challenges as they arise. And keep a weather eye on the longer-range issues that might be bubbling in your current AOR.

Liberty Call

One of the most important jobs you will undertake is that of being a good ambassador for your country. The actions of your crew ashore are a direct reflection of the United States, and you must take every opportunity to emphasize that to your crew. The days of tolerance for the "ugly American" are long since past, and public intoxication, creating disturbances, or interfering with the good order of a host nation will land your individual sailor in local jail and send your entire ship packing in the blink of an eye. A few keys to having a safe, productive liberty call overseas include the following:

Emphasize the message to the crew. Get on the closed-circuit television the night before every port call, go around to divisions at quarters, get on the 1MC, and do anything you can to get the word out that only good citizens are going ashore.

Use the "liberty risk" program. When you identify someone who is a potential problem, don't let him or her ashore. The forward Fleet Commanders all authorize a "liberty risk" program, which gives you the authority (and the obligation) to completely curtail or partially restrict the liberty of anyone you suspect will not be a good ambassador for the United States.

Offer good alternatives to the bars. Task your command master chief, chaplain, and welfare and recreation team to come up with athletics, picnics, tours, and other alternatives to "hitting the bars." Give your sailors good options, and in most cases they will make good choices.

Be consistent in the treatment of any and all violators. This is particularly necessary in the case of an officer or chief who gets out of line, as the whole crew will be watching for equity in their treatment.

Keep the chain of command informed. The absolute worst liberty incident is the one the Sixth Fleet Commander reads about from someone besides you. Don't think you can hide a problem or incident that involves local police. Tell what happened, what you did to resolve the incident, and what you have done to make sure it doesn't happen again.

Televise the port briefs. Whenever you arrive in a foreign port, you will be greeted by a group of officials, with representatives from the senior Navy people in the area, the American embassy, and local officials. Have the XO quickly put together a fact-filled brief, and present it to the crew before anyone leaves the ship.

Give everyone who goes ashore a "liberty safety card." This card should include the ship's phone number and location (in both English and the local language). Also insist that each person take a simple map of the area around the ship, which can be photocopied and handed out.

Insist on the buddy system. No one should go on liberty alone, ever.

Hold your chiefs accountable for their sailors' plans. Every CPO should have a pretty good idea of what his or her division is doing on liberty, and be able to move people into more productive activities.

Avoid mass punishment. It doesn't work.

Does all of this sound a little threatening? It shouldn't. Almost all of your people want to go ashore, walk the port, do a little shopping, call home, and have dinner and a couple of beers before returning to the ship. Your job is to facilitate that program, perhaps with a tour and a ship's picnic thrown in.

And it goes without saying, but you are the commanding officer. Your behavior ashore must be above reproach, as must that of every leader in your command. Focus there and you probably won't have a problem to begin with.

Enjoy your liberty call!

The Captain's Duties Ashore

One of the most interesting aspects of foreign port visits is your own participation in formal calls. These are normally arranged by the local Navy representative, and they may range from no calls, as perhaps in a frequently visited port like Naples, to many, many calls in a high-visibility port like Cannes on the Fourth of July. If you are going on calls, it is wise to ask about the custom of exchanging gifts; these can range from a ship's ballcap or lighter to a bottle of Kentucky bourbon or California wine. Another nice touch is an inexpensively framed photograph of the ship or a plaque, although it is increasingly difficult to obtain brass plaques at reasonable cost. Be prepared and you won't be embarrassed.

If you are in a port in which it is appropriate, you may be able to obtain a rental car for official business. Be very careful about using such a vehicle for private means, which you may not do; although in certain ports, the need for your instant access to the ship or for security reasons may make it acceptable. In this day of careful scrutiny for ethics, you should check with a Navy lawyer if you have any questions concerning this issue.

Combat Philosophy

This portion of this book is the most important part of our discussion on the art of command at sea. In modern times, we are prone to think that a naval vessel is built and manned for a variety of reasons, ranging from protection and promotion of commerce to carrying out "presence" visits. All of these peacetime occupations are important, but they sometimes obscure the fact that navies exist primarily to protect national security. Even this description of the Navy's mission is not clear, for the phrase "protect national security" is a euphemism, coined to avoid offending the political sensibilities of congressmen and the moral feelings of citizens. The plain, brutally frank truth is that naval vessels exist to *fight*. We must never forget this fact, even though we must always be aware of the other functions and responsibilities we are called upon to carry out.

Effectiveness for Service.   This is an unfamiliar and slightly misleading subtitle, but it is the title of Article 0737, *Navy Regulations,* which states that you shall exert every effort to maintain your command in a state of maximum effectiveness for war or other service consistent with the degree of readiness prescribed by higher authority. Effectiveness for service is directly related to the state of personnel and material readiness.

Article 0739, titled "Action with the Enemy," is equally low-key. Its first paragraph requires you to communicate to your officers information which might be of value to them should they succeed to command. The next paragraph then gets to the point. It requires you to engage the enemy to the best of your ability during action, and forbids you, without permission, to break off action to assist a disabled ship or to take possession of a captured one.

These are the only words of advice to you in all of *Navy Regulations* regarding your conduct in battle. We can only assume, from the simplicity of the words and the restraint of the rhetoric, that this is deliberate, and that this language must be fleshed out with advice handed down over decades by naval commanders and distilled from the naval tradition of centuries.

U.S. Navy Combat Tradition.   The foregoing is a reasonable assumption, and is certainly not contradicted by any written information or directives. Therefore, let us examine the U.S. Navy traditions of the past, and recent additions to them during modern times, from World War I to the Gulf War. These traditions are *use of the initiative, boldness and daring, tenacity, courage, aggressiveness, ingenuity,* and the *ability of our young junior officers and enlisted men to carry on and display their own initiative when their seniors are dead or incapacitated.* You, as a commanding officer, may *add* to these traditions or originate others, but you must never *subtract* from them.

The Athenians most prized in their naval officers and men high enthusiasm or spirit, courage, the ability to innovate or solve problems, and the willingness to work long and hard. Our own prized characteristics are, therefore, not new. We have also learned from the British, who have had centuries of a sound naval tradition. The qualities they prized most were courage, aggressiveness, tenacity, and coolness under fire.

Our own American traditions are outstanding. They have produced the world's finest naval officers, from John Paul Jones to Chester

Nimitz. In between came such leaders as David Glasgow Farragut, of whom Admiral Mahan wrote:

> It is in the strength of purpose, in the power of rapid decision, of instant action, and if need be, of strenuous endurance through a period of danger or of responsibility, when the terrifying alternatives of war are vibrating in the balance, that the power of a great captain mainly lies. It is in the courage to apply knowledge under conditions of exceptional danger; not merely to see the true direction for effort to take, but to dare to follow it, accepting all the risks and all the chances inseparable from war, facing all that defeat means in order to secure victory if it may be had. It was upon those inborn moral qualities that reposed the conduct which led Farragut to fame. He had a clear eye for the true key of a military situation, a quick and accurate perception of the right thing to do at a critical moment, a firm grasp upon the leading principles of war; but he might have had all these and yet miserably failed. He was a man of most determined will and character, ready to tread down or fight through any obstacles which stood in the path he sought to follow.

Farragut's other characteristics are well known. He sought responsibility where others shunned it. Above all, he *liked* being a naval officer, as witnessed by his oft-quoted statement, "I have as much pleasure in running into port in a gale of wind as ever a boy did in a feat of skill."

We can learn from those nations who were our predecessors upon the sea, and we can benefit from studying and observing various countries and their cultures and traditions; but in doing so, we must maintain our own established, successful, and honored traditions.

Use of the Initiative.   Probably the most distinctively American naval tradition is the use of the initiative, and we will discuss it first.

There is a fine line of distinction between the use of the initiative and the display of boldness, daring, and aggressiveness. Fortunately, the enemy won't know the difference, and will be at a disadvantage if you display any or all of these characteristics.

The dictionary states that *initiative* means to be the "first mover," and to have the ability for original conception and independent action. A commanding officer who takes the initiative is usually also being bold and daring, but not necessarily so. In any event, don't be too concerned about the exact description of what you are about to do. Just do it *first*. Taking the initiative should be a principal part of your combat philosophy.

Boldness and Daring.   Charles Lindbergh had a fine feeling for boldness and daring. He said, "What kind of man would live where there is no daring? And is life so dear that we should blame men for dying in adventure? Is there a better way to die?" Still, the ideal is to be bold and daring and *not* to die. Even more ideal is to make sure the *enemy* dies and that *you* survive.

John Paul Jones epitomized boldness and daring. He sailed in fast ships and in harm's way, and would not tolerate any captain or subordinate who was not equally bold. Boldness was his legacy to those who would follow in his footsteps.

Modern American naval officers have been equally daring. In the opening weeks of World War II, when the Japanese were overrunning the Philippines and landing large forces in Lingayen Gulf, Lieutenant Commander Wreford "Moon" Chapple took his submarine, the S-38, into the Gulf via a poorly charted and shallow side channel, and for over twenty-four hours did his best to attack Japanese ships. He was harassed and attacked repeatedly by Japanese escorts, and discouraged by the repeated failure of the defective torpedoes he was firing, but he managed to sink and damage some shipping and to slow the landing process markedly. His boldness was inspiring to those who were doing their best to hold the Philippines against overpowering odds.

Later, his contemporaries of Destroyer Squadron 29 conducted an equally daring attack on another Japanese landing operation, at Macassar in the Dutch East Indies. Four of these decrepit old four-stackers steamed at twenty-seven knots in the dark of night through a cruiser and destroyer screen into the middle of the Japanese landing area and sank five Japanese landing transports and escorts with torpedo and gunfire. They made repeated passes at high speed until all torpedoes were expended and then retired under cover of darkness and their own gunfire without damage. This was the first such surface action for the United States Navy since the Spanish-American War.

Only boldness and daring made these efforts successful. You will do well to give those characteristics a prominent place in your combat philosophy. They are distinctively American in character.

Tenacity. Tenacity has been a characteristic of our Navy for years. Farragut's order to "Damn the torpedoes; full speed ahead" is a classic example of refusing to fear what *might be*. Don't be put off by small failures; instead drive *tenaciously* forward. You, as commanding officer, will do well to emulate Admiral Farragut. Washington Irving once said, "Great minds have purpose; others have wishes. Little minds are tamed by misfortune; great minds rise above them."

Lest you think tenacity is an old-fashioned quality, remember the advice given in World War II by Commander "Mush" Morton, a superb submarine commanding officer, to Lieutenant Commander Richard O'Kane, who would go on to become an equally famed CO: "*Tenacity,* Dick, you've got to stick with the bastard until he's on the bottom." O'Kane did, repeatedly.

In World War II, other naval officers also continued this tradition of tenacity. Admiral Arleigh Burke's operations repeatedly demonstrated this characteristic. He believed in hitting the enemy hard and fast, delivering repeated blows until the enemy's will to resist collapsed. Admiral William Halsey was as tenacious as any officer who ever went to sea.

It can be argued that the Japanese were equally tenacious. They were, but it was a tenacity without purpose, almost a religious belief. They repeatedly lost large numbers of men, aircraft, and ships long after they should have known that a particular battle was a losing strategic or tactical situation. Tenacity of this kind, without the ability to change direction or to modify operations to suit changed conditions, is a losing cause. The Americans probed, jabbed, kept moving forward, but changed the direction of thrust and the magnitude of their efforts to take advantage of uncovered weakness and to avoid strong points. This kind of tenacity is one of our traditions.

"I have not yet begun to fight" is not a failure to hear the starting gun, but a stern statement of tenacity of purpose which has become a part, not only of the traditions of the Navy, but of the personal philosophy of combat of every naval officer. Preserve and use it.

Courage. Courage comes in many varieties, and it has been the mainstay of the combat philosophy of all peoples and services for centuries. It can be wasted, though, as it was in the charge of the Light Brigade at Balaclava, when the Brigade went to certain destruction, knowing that its effort was useless.

American naval officers and sailors have performed many courageous acts in our relatively short history. Unfortunately for history, the most courageous individual acts are seldom recorded, and are known only to those who performed them. This is the most superb kind of courage: where one does one's duty in the full understanding that no one else will ever know.

There are many kinds of courage, and some in new settings. In Vietnamese and Iraqi prison camps our prisoners of war demonstrated new kinds of courage when they withstood to the death the torture of their captors.

Physical courage will be commonplace in the next war, given the moral upbringing and characteristics of our countrymen. You, as a commanding officer, will find the personal exercise of physical courage easy. The stimulus of command will make you forget your own personal safety. The more difficult assignment for you will be the proper exercise of moral courage. Situations calling for moral courage will not have the stimulus of combat. It will be necessary when you demand top performance from your officers and crew; take steps to correct or punish those who do not perform; make honest reports of your or your ship's failure, should such occur; and when you are completely honest in all of your command relations.

Courage, then, must be part of your combat philosophy, to be expected and required of others, and one which you demonstrate automatically as commanding officer.

Aggressiveness. The aggressive commanding officer is one who wants to win so much that he or she *will* take vigorous action to attain the objective. The key is to determine the right and appropriate action and to pursue it to the utmost, but not to the point of foolhardiness, or of being led into an adverse situation such as an ambush. Normally an aggressive fighter has the advantage, and will win unless the defender has had the time to arrange his or her defenses so that attacking becomes a disadvantage.

One key element of aggressiveness is speed of attack. Admiral Arleigh Burke was known for his high-speed attacks. Burke was usually in the middle of the enemy's formation before he had a chance to retaliate. There were only two adjectives in Admiral Burke's lexicon, *good* and *bad*. He held that the difference between a bad officer and a good officer was about ten seconds. Ten seconds of decision making by a gunnery, torpedo, missile, or conning officer translated into three five-inch salvos, the firing of a torpedo spread by either a surface ship or a submarine, a missile firing, a battery-unmasking turn, or the performance of an evasive maneuver. Ten seconds can mean the enemy's destruction or yours.

The same comparison applies to commanding officers. Be *quickly* aggressive if you want to add surprise and confusion of the enemy to your attack plan. By Admiral Burke's standards you are a *good* CO if you take advantage of the time given you by a good gunnery, torpedo, missile, or conning officer by making a quick (but correct) decision. Fritter it away with indecision and you are a *bad* CO who will end up with holes in the ship or a forty-degree list. Speed of decision goes hand-in-hand with aggressiveness, and aggressiveness has always been one of the hallmarks of our Navy. Make it one of yours.

Ingenuity. Yankee ingenuity produced the fast-sailing schooners and clippers of the eighteenth and nineteenth centuries. Their design and speed were incorporated into the ships of our early navy. Further ingenuity put speed and endurance into our steam-powered naval vessels and eventually produced the nuclear-powered ship and submarine, with both speed and unlimited endurance. Industrial ingenuity gave our navy superior armor, excellent major-caliber guns and fire control systems, missiles, computers, solid-state electronics, and a host of other improvements. Bluejacket ingenuity kept them operational in peacetime with shortages of money and spare parts and in wartime in spite of damage and lack of repair facilities. The American naval person, officer or enlisted, is without peer in mechanical ingenuity. Fortunately, the same characteristic extends to strategy and tactics. Formations for air defense, combined anti-submarine search-and-attack procedures, amphibious landing techniques, and submarine and aircraft attack tactics are but a few of the ideas pioneered by our navy.

Our tradition of ingenuity is superb, and you can depend upon this characteristic of our officers and sailors to carry you through many difficult situations. You, as commanding officer, will also be called upon to exercise ingenuity. You will have to improvise tactics, communication plans, personnel reassignments, and emergency repairs of equipment and machinery to meet various contingencies of operations and battle. Ingenuity by a commanding officer can make a superb ship out of a commonplace vessel.

Initiative of Juniors. Our navy has always excelled in using the initiative of our junior officers and enlisted sailors. Fortunately, this process comes naturally to citizens of the United States, where family and cultural atmosphere generally foster initiative. It is a part of our way of life. By contrast, some other cultures discourage the initiative of juniors, and they suffered accordingly in wartime when seniors were killed or incapacitated. Their juniors were neither trained nor expected to take the initiative, and their ships rapidly lost their efficiency when damaged in battle. Our crews were able to take prompt and heroic measures after damage with little guidance.

Add to the natural bent of your officers and crew by encouraging them to display initiative in peace. Your efforts will pay for themselves some bleak day when your ship is heavily damaged or has internal communication problems. If you have prepared your crew, you will find the other end of the ship running just as well as if your orders had been received.

Decision Making. Now that you have decided on the elements of your personal combat philosophy, you should remember that "philosophy" never fired a shot. Only a decision starts the firing process.

The human brain is the finest computer ever made. Like a computer, it stores millions of bits of information. The results of your readings and study are all there, as are the distillation of your experience; your observations of the experiences of others; the Navy's traditions; your own personal characteristics; and, on a shorter time basis, the input from your senses—what you have most recently seen, heard, and otherwise observed. With all this information in your memory, and from your current observation, you will have to make your decision.

The proper way to make a decision is to take in all the facts that are available, meld them in your mind with the information already there, and then reach a *tentative* decision. In war, as in life, there is always additional information being developed and brought to your attention. Consider such information and revise your decision accordingly and continuously. Keep your mind open, however, until the moment arrives when a *final* decision is necessary. Then make it, announce it firmly and vigorously, and see that it is carried out instantly.

There are shortsighted persons who think that a commander should make a final decision early and stick to it. They feel that allowing change indicates poor decision-making ability. The exact opposite is true. This type of decision maker is, to speak charitably, a fool who will end up on a large rock because early on he chose a course heading for it and refused to change his direction.

An example from real life: a U.S. ship, steaming in wartime in an area of patchy fog, detected a radar contact approaching at high speed. A radio challenge produced no response. The decision-making process began. The CO decided *tentatively* to take the contact under fire, but he decided to wait until it cleared the fog patches before making a *final* decision. The contact did appear; it was a British destroyer with a defective radio.

Another, slower-paced example from the experience of Admiral Claude Ricketts, an outstanding decision maker, occurred with respect to a mast case. The day before a supposed culprit was to appear at captain's mast, then-Commander Ricketts was asked by his executive officer what punishment he was going to assign the man.

"I don't know," said Commander Ricketts. "I haven't made a final decision yet."

"But, Sir," said the executive officer, "we have all the facts, and they indicate he's guilty. Let's get on with it."

The next day a surprise witness appeared, testified that there had been a case of mistaken identity, and the case was dismissed.

As they walked away from the mast area, Ricketts said with his usual compassion to a considerably subdued XO, "Don't make a final decision until you have *all* the facts."

A good decision, with all facts included, is vital to success, but *speed* of decision is also important, particularly in time of war. With a *tentative* decision always in your mind, you can produce a *final* decision quickly if circumstances require it. Don't be afraid of making a quick decision. If you have done your homework, it will be a good one. If subsequent developments show that it wasn't, remember that even John Paul Jones made a few bad decisions. Also remember that probably no one else could have made a better decision in the same circumstances. You are as good a commanding officer as the navy system produces. It is true that the selection system produced a few failures in World War II and the two decades thereafter, but in more recent years the selection system has been tightened and improved to the point where only the very best officers are honored with command. If you are one of these, *humbly* remember that you have been judged to have all the attributes and experience needed to be a superb commanding officer. The rest is up to you.

Losing Your Ship. Now that you have decided that you will have a positive attitude toward your success in combat, it is difficult ever to consider the possibility of the loss of your ship. Nevertheless, thought must be given to it. *Navy Regulations,* as discussed in previous chapters, states positively and without equivocation that you will fight your ship to the end. There can never be a single thought about surrendering your ship, allowing boarding, or permitting capture or removal of your crew. The aftermath of the *Pueblo* incident reaffirmed this historical tradition of our navy.

Once your crew is off the ship, you have discharged your responsibilities according to *Navy Regulations*. You are then free to leave, and you are *expected* to do so. Don't be burdened by nineteenth-century stories of captains going down with their ships. Most who did so were badly wounded, and only a few took this final step. The modern Royal Navy and the United States Navy long ago discarded any remnants of this tradition. There is no current regulation or tradition that prevents you from leaving your ship after you have discharged your duties, if you are absolutely sure that it is about to sink. You should, of course, remain in the vicinity until it goes under to prevent any enemy from coming on the scene and boarding her. If you have commanded well and fought well, the Navy will want to use your experience and talents again.

Summary. Put the thought of losing your ship behind you, and remember only the positive combat philosophy you determine to make your own and to import to your officers and men. Hope that you do not have to demonstrate it, but decide that if you do, you will be bold, courageous, daring, tenacious, and aggressive, and that you will exercise the initiative with all the ingenuity you can muster. No one could do more.

The Captain's Role

A final thought. Never forget that you are the chief planner, tactician, and mariner or airman of your command. The reason young men and women join the Navy and aspire to command is not paperwork, administration, personnel management, or any of the other important—but somewhat mundane—things we do on a day-to-day basis.

They join to go to sea and operate ships, submarines, and aircraft in exciting and challenging ways. Let them see your enjoyment and professional skill in a profession that is at once historical, unique, important, and dynamic. Take advantage of the excellent tactical library in your ship, try new and different tactical approaches, drive your ship or aircraft with skill and enthusiasm, and you will truly live the words of John Paul Jones to his young crewmen:

"Sign on, young man, and sail with me. The stature of our homeland is but a measure of ourselves. Our job is to keep her free. To that end, I call on the young, the brave, the strong, the free. Sign on, young man, and sail with me."

Sail safely, Captain. Godspeed and open water to you.

Glossary of Terms Regarding Joint Operations

administrative control. Direction or exercise of authority over subordinate or other organizations in respect to administration and support, including organization of Service forces, control of resources and equipment, personnel management, unit logistics, individual and unit training, readiness, mobilization, demobilization, discipline, and other matters not included in the operational missions of the subordinate or other organizations. Also called *ADCON.* (Joint Pub. 1-02)

area of responsibility. 1. The geographical area associated with a combatant command within which a combatant commander has authority to plan and conduct operations. 2. In naval usage, a predefined area of enemy terrain for which supporting ships are responsible for covering by fire on known targets or targets of opportunity and by observation. (N.B. Generally used today to refer to the theater in which operations occur.) Also called *AOR.* (Joint Pub. 1-02)

armed forces. The military forces of a nation or a group of nations. (Joint Pub. 1-02)

assign. 1. To place units or personnel in an organization where such placement is relatively permanent, and/or where such organization controls and administers the units or personnel for the primary function, or greater portion of the functions, of the unit or personnel. 2. To detail individuals to specific duties or functions where such duties or functions are primary and/or relatively permanent. *See also* **attach.** (Joint Pub. 1-02)

attach. 1. The placement of units or personnel in an organization where such placement is relatively temporary. 2. The detailing of individuals to specific functions where such functions are secondary or relatively temporary, e.g., attached for quarters and rations; attached for flying duty. *See also* **assign.** (Joint Pub. 1-02)

boundary. A line which delineates surface areas for the purpose of facilitating coordination and deconfliction of operations between adjacent units, formations, or areas. (Joint Pub. 1-02)

campaign. A series of related military operations aimed at accomplishing a strategic or operational objective within a given time and space. *See also* **campaign plan.** (Joint Pub. 1-02)

campaign plan. A plan for a series of related military operations aimed at accomplishing a strategic or operational objective within a given time and space. *See also* **campaign.** (Joint Pub. 1-02)

chain of command. The succession of commanding officers from a superior to a subordinate through which command is exercised. Also called *command channel.* (Joint Pub. 1-02)

change of operational control. The date and time (Coordinated Universal Time) at which a force or unit is reassigned or attached from one commander to another where the gaining commander will exercise operational control over that force or unit. Also called *CHOP.* (Joint Pub. 1-02)

close support. That action of the supporting force against targets or objectives which are sufficiently near the supported force as to require detailed integration or coordination of the supporting action with the fire, movement, or other actions of the supported force. (Joint Pub. 1-02)

coalition. An ad hoc arrangement between two or more nations for common action. (Joint Pub. 1-02)

combatant command. A unified or specified command with a broad continuing mission under a single commander established and so designated by the President, through the Secretary of Defense and with the advice and assistance of the Chairman of the Joint Chiefs of Staff. Combatant commands typically have geographic or functional responsibilities. (Joint Pub. 1-02)

combatant command (command authority). Nontransferable command authority established by title 10 ("Armed Forces"), United States Code, section 164, exercised only by commanders of unified or specified combatant commands unless otherwise directed by the President or the Secretary of Defense. Combatant command (command authority) cannot be delegated and is the authority of a combatant commander to perform those functions of command over assigned forces involving organizing and employing commands and forces, assigning tasks, designating objectives, and giving authoritative direction over all aspects of military operations, joint training, and logistics necessary to accomplish the missions assigned to the command. Combatant command (command authority) should be exercised through the commanders of subordinate organizations. Normally this authority is exercised through subordinate joint force commanders and Service and/or functional component commanders. Combatant command (command authority) provides full authority to organize and employ commands and forces as the combatant commander considers necessary to accomplish assigned missions. Operational control is inherent in combatant command (command authority). Also called *COCOM. See also* **combatant command; combatant commander; operational control; tactical control.** (Joint Pub. 1-02)

combatant commander. A commander-in-chief of one of the unified or specified combatant commands established by the President. (Joint Pub. 1-02)

combined. Between two or more forces or agencies of two or more allies. (When all allies or services are not involved, the participating nations and services shall be identified; e.g., Combined Navies.) (Joint Pub. 1-02)

command. 1. The authority that a commander in the Military Service lawfully exercises over subordinates by virtue of rank or assignment. Command includes the authority and responsibility for effectively using available resources and for planning the employment of, organizing, directing, coordinating, and controlling military forces for the accomplishment of assigned missions. It also includes responsibility for health, welfare, morale, and discipline of assigned personnel. 2. An order given by a commander; that is, the will of the commander expressed for the purpose of bringing about a particular action. 3. A unit or units, an organization, or an area under the command of one individual. *See also* **combatant command; combatant command (command authority).** (Joint Pub. 1-02)

command and control. The exercise of authority and direction by a properly designated commander over assigned and attached forces in the accomplishment of the mission. Command and control functions are performed through an arrangement of personnel, equipment, communications, facilities, and procedures employed by a commander in planning, directing, coordinating, and controlling forces and operations in the accomplishment of the mission. Also called *C2*. (Joint Pub. 1-02)

command relationships. The interrelated responsibilities between commanders, as well as the authority of commanders in the chain of command. (Joint Pub. 1-02)

communications. A method or means of conveying information of any kind from one person or place to another. (Joint Pub. 1-02)

component. 1. One of the subordinate organizations that constitute a joint force. Normally a joint force is organized with a combination of Service and functional components. 2. In logistics, a part or combination of parts having a specific function that can be installed or replaced only as an entity. (Joint Pub. 1-02)

direct liaison authorized. Coordinate an action with a command or agency within or outside of the granting command. Direct liaison authorized is more applicable to planning than operations and always carries with it the requirement of keeping the commander granting direct liaison authorized informed. Direct liaison authorized is a coordination relationship, not an authority through which command may be exercised. Also called *DIRLAUTH*. (Joint Pub. 1-02)

direct support. A mission requiring a force to support another specific force and authorizing it to answer directly the supported force's request for assistance. (Joint Pub. 1-02)

doctrine. Fundamental principles by which the military forces or elements thereof guide their actions in support of national objectives. It is authoritative but requires judgment in application. (Joint Pub. 1-02)

general support. That support which is given to the supported force as a whole and not to any particular subdivision thereof. (Joint Pub. 1-02)

joint. Connotes activities, operations, organizations, etc., in which elements of two or more Military Departments participate. (Joint Pub. 1-02)

joint force. A general term applied to a force composed of significant elements, assigned or attached, of two or more Military Departments, operating under a single commander authorized to exercise operational control. (Joint Pub. 1-02)

joint force commander. A general term applied to a combatant commander, subunified commander, or joint task force commander authorized to exercise combatant command (command authority) or operational control over a joint force. Also called *JFC*. (Joint Pub. 1-02)

joint operations. A general term to describe military actions conducted by joint forces, or by Service forces in relationships (e.g., support, coordinating authority) which, of themselves, do not create joint forces. (Joint Pub. 1-02)

joint operations area. An area of land, sea, and airspace, defined by a geographic combatant commander or subordinate unified commander, in which a joint force commander (normally a joint task force commander) conducts military operations.

joint staff. 1. The staff of a commander of a unified or specified command, subordinate unified command, joint task force, or subordinate functional component (when a functional component command will employ forces from more than one Military Department), which includes members from the several Services comprising the force.

These members should be assigned in such a manner as to ensure that the commander understands the tactics, techniques, capabilities, needs, and limitations of the component parts of the force. Positions on the staff should be divided so that Service representation and influence generally reflect the Service composition of the force. 2. (capitalized as Joint Staff) The staff under the Chairman of the Joint Chiefs of Staff as provided for in the National Security Act of 1947, as amended by the Goldwater-Nichols Department of Defense Reorganization Act of 1986. The Joint Staff assists the Chairman and, subject to the authority, direction, and control of the Chairman, the other members of the Joint Chiefs of Staff and the Vice Chairman in carrying out their responsibilities. (Joint Pub. 1-02)

joint task force. A joint force that is constituted and so designated by the Secretary of Defense, a combatant commander, a subunified commander, or an existing joint task force commander. Also called *JTF*. (Joint Pub. 1-02)

multinational operations. A collective term to describe military actions conducted by forces of two or more nations, typically organized within the structure of a coalition or alliance. (Joint Pub. 1-02)

National Command Authorities. The President and the Secretary of Defense or their duly deputized alternates or successors. Also called *NCA*. (Joint Pub. 1-02)

operational authority. That authority exercised by a commander in the chain of command, defined further as combatant command (command authority), operational control, tactical control, or a support relationship. (Joint Pub. 1-02)

operational control. Transferable command authority that may be exercised by commanders at any echelon at or below the level of combatant command. Operational control is inherent in combatant command (command authority). Operational control may be delegated and is the authority to perform those functions of command over subordinate forces involving organizing and employing commands and forces, assigning tasks, designating objectives, and giving authoritative direction necessary to accomplish the mission. Operational control includes authoritative direction over all aspects of military operations and joint training necessary to accomplish missions assigned to the command. Operational control should be exercised through the commanders of subordinate organizations. Normally this authority is exercised through subordinate joint force commanders and Service and/or functional component commanders. Operational control normally provides full authority to organize commands and forces and to employ those forces as the commander in operational control considers necessary to accomplish assigned missions. Operational control does not, in and of itself, include authoritative direction for logistics or matters of administration, discipline, internal organization, or unit training. Also called *OPCON*. (Joint Pub. 1-02)

subordinate unified command. A command established by commanders of unified commands, when so authorized through the Chairman of the Joint Chiefs of Staff, to conduct operations on a continuing basis in accordance with the criteria set forth for unified commands. A subordinate unified command may be established on an area or functional basis. Commanders of subordinate unified commands have functions and responsibilities similar to those of the commanders of unified commands and exercise operational control of assigned commands and forces within the assigned joint operations area. Also called *subunified command*. (Joint Pub. 1-02)

supported commander. The commander having primary responsibility for all aspects of a task assigned by the Joint Strategic Capabilities Plan or other joint operation planning authority. In the context of joint operation planning, this term refers to the commander who prepares operation plans or operation orders in response to requirements of the Chairman of the Joint Chiefs of Staff. (Joint Pub. 1-02)

supporting commander. A commander who provides augmentation forces or other support to a supported commander or who develops a supporting plan. Includes the designated combatant commands and Defense agencies as appropriate. (Joint Pub. 1-02)

tactical control. Command authority over assigned or attached forces or commands, or military capability or forces made available for tasking, that is limited to the detailed and, usually, local direction and control of movements or maneuvers necessary to accomplish missions or tasks assigned. Tactical control is inherent in operational control. Tactical control may be delegated to, and exercised at any level at or below the level of combatant command. Also called *TACON*. (Joint Pub. 1-02)

transient forces. Forces which pass or stage through, or base temporarily within, the area of responsibility or joint operations area of another command but are not under its operational control. (Joint Pub. 1-02)

unified command. A command with a broad continuing mission under a single commander and composed of significant assigned components of two or more Military Departments, and which is established and so designated by the President, through the Secretary of Defense with the advice and assistance of the Chairman of the Joint Chiefs of Staff. Also called *unified combatant command.* (Joint Pub. 1-02)

There are currently nine unified combatant commands. All of them can be either supported or supporting commanders in a given operation, and all are warfighters. Five are geographic, which means they are in charge of a specified area of the world: US Atlantic Command (commonly referred to as ACOM, headquartered in Norfolk, Virginia), US Central Command (CENTCOM, Tampa, Florida), US Southern Command (SOUTHCOM, Miami, Florida), US European Command (EUCOM, Stuttgart, Germany), and US Pacific Command (PACOM, Pearl Harbor, Hawaii). There are four functional commands: US Space Command (SPACECOM, Colorado Springs, Colorado), US Special Operations Command (SOCOM, Tampa, Florida), US Transportation Command (TRANSCOM, Fort Scott, Illinois), and US Strategic Command (STRATCOM, Omaha, Nebraska). Of note, ACOM has both geographic responsibility (primarily for the Atlantic Ocean and the western approaches to Europe under the NATO SACLANT "hat") as well as significant functional responsibilities as the Joint Force trainer, provider, and integrator.

Unified Command Plan. The document, approved by the President, which sets forth basic guidance to all unified combatant commanders;

establishes their missions, responsibilities, and force structure; delineates the general geographical areas of responsibility for geographic combatant commanders; and specifies functional responsibilities for functional combatant commanders. Also called the *UCP*. (Joint Pub. 1-02) Essentially the "constitution" of the armed forces, this document sets out the fundamental structure of the warfighting organization of the Department of Defense.

Appendix 1

Sample Turnover Plan

USS FISKE (DDG XX) NOTICE 5060

Subj: CHANGE OF COMMAND TURNOVER PLAN
Ref: (a) USS FISKE NOTICE 5060
Encl: (1) Notional Turnover Schedule
       (2) Briefing Guidelines
       (3) Department Information Books

1. *Purpose.* To provide guidance for the preparation and execution of a smooth and thorough change of command turnover between Commander J. Barry and Commander J. P. Jones.

2. *Background.* Reference (a) discusses general duties, responsibilities and deadlines for the completion of key preparations for the change of command of USS FISKE (DDG XX). In order to ensure that the transfer for the responsibilities of command is conducted smoothly and thoroughly, this notice provides detailed guidance for the preparation of presentations and briefings for the Prospective Commanding Officer (PCO) by Department Heads and special assistants. A notional schedule is also provided for planning purposes at enclosure (1).

3. *Action.* Each individual assigned responsibilities herein will be prepared to thoroughly brief the PCO on the subjects listed in enclosure (2) as well as such other matters as the Commanding Officer may direct or the PCO may request. Although enclosure (1) is a notional schedule to which specific dates will be assigned later, it should be followed as a guideline for the amount of time each briefer will have with the PCO. Department Heads will also provide the PCO with briefing books containing at a minimum those

items listed in enclosure (3) and will ensure their subordinates are aware of and prepared for any briefing topic under their cognizance.

J. BARRY

(1) Notional Turnover Schedule

12 JUN:	0700 - NC1 Brief
	0730 - NAV Brief
	0800 - Sea and Anchor
	0800 - ESO
	1030 - Moor
	1030 - Keys with CO
	1230 - PCO/NAV Brief
	1330 - XO turnover
	1430 - Call on CDS-21 CSO
13 JUN:	0730 - PCO arrives
	0800 - PCO call on CDS-23
	0830 - Review relieving letter with XO/CO
	0845 - PCO Senior Watch Officer Brief
	0915 - PCO CSO/WEPS Brief
	0945 - PCO Tour CSO/WEPS Spaces
16 JUN:	- Admin Day
17 JUN:	- MEFEX Phase I
18 JUN:	- MEFEX Phase I
19 JUN:	1000 - Rehearsal
	MEFEX Phase I
20 JUN:	0830 - CO signs pertinent documents and logs
	0900 - PCO Meeting with CO sign relieving letter
	1000 - Change of Command/Reception
	1230 - CDR Barry Departs
	1300 - CO signs pertinent documents/release messages

(2) Briefing Guidelines

1. Each Department Head shall review the following with the Prospective Commanding Officer during the scheduled briefing times:

   a. Departmental Organization

   b. Personnel Status

     c. Material Status
     d. Certification and Qualification Status
     e. Overview of Equipment/Capabilities and Tag-Out Procedures
     f. SRA Package
     g. Inspection Preparations
     h. PQS Status
     i. CSMP/3-M Status
     j. Training (Teams, School Grads, Departmental/Divisional, etc.)
     k. Departmental Budget
     l. Status of Controlled Equipage

2. Each Department Head will conduct a tour of all assigned spaces with the PCO for familiarization purposes.

3. The Operations Officer shall be prepared to discuss/show PCO the following:

     a. Operations-General

          _____ Departmental Doctrines
          _____ Current Task Organization/Assignments
          _____ OPREP 3 Reporting Procedures/Guide for CDO's
          _____ Long Range Training Schedule
          _____ Operational Security/INFO Security/Personnel
          Security Clearances
          _____ Eight O'clock Reports
          _____ Training and Schools Program
          _____ OPSUM/SITREP Procedures
          _____ Top Secret/Secret Inventories

     b. Combat Information Center

          _____ AIC and ASAC Status
          _____ Naval Warfare Publications Library
          _____ TRAREP

     c. Electronic Warfare/Intelligence

          _____ INTEL Publications
          _____ INTEL Gathering Team/Camera/etc.

_____ SLQ-32 Installation
_____ SRBOC Certification
_____ SSES

d. Communications
_____ Message Processing Procedures
_____ "PERSONAL FOR" Procedures
_____ COMM Standing Orders
_____ Last COMM Assist Team Visit
_____ Routing/Releasing Procedures
_____ General Message Files (NAVOPS/ALNAVS/AL-
             PACFLTS/ALNAVSURFPACS)
_____ Secret Message/Procedures
_____ Watch-to-Watch Crypto Material Accountability
_____ TTY Repairman
_____ EA Folder pre-cut Tapes
_____ Antenna Maintenance
_____ Portable COMM gear

e. CMS
_____ Custodian/Alternate
_____ Couriers
_____ CMS Training
_____ CMS Required Reading
_____ Required Spot Checks
_____ CMS Assist Visit Results
_____ CMS Inspection Results
_____ Last Draw
_____ Next Draw
_____ Results of Inventory

f. First Division
_____ Weight Test Status
_____ Helmsman Training/Qualification
_____ Age of the HIGHLINE/TOW RIG
_____ Status of Mooring Lines
_____ Flammable Liquid Stowage

_____ UNREP Gear
_____ Paint Control and Inventory/Issue/Stowage Procedures
_____ Boats and Boat gear
_____ Coxswain Training
_____ Heavy Weather Bill
_____ Helo Operations/Helo Gear
_____ Respiratory Protection Program
_____ Lead Control Program
_____ LSE/HCO Training/Qualification
_____ Lifeboat Certification Status
_____ SAR Swimmer Status

g. Miscellaneous
_____ Short/Long Range Training Program
_____ Ship's Schedule
_____ Status of Inspections
_____ Status of SELEX's for competitive cycle/TRX's for mission readiness ratings

4. The Combat System Officer and Weapons Control Officer shall be prepared to discuss/show PCO the following:

a. Combat Systems—General
_____ Battle Orders
_____ Departmental Organization/Smooth Logs
_____ Physical Security Plan
_____ Ammunition Allowance/NCEA
_____ Eight O'clock Reports/Daily Combat Systems Report
_____ Explosive Safety Review Results
_____ Manning/School Status

b. Anti-submarine Warfare
_____ OBT ASW Exercises
_____ SQS-53B Operation/Material Status

_____ SQR-19 Operation/Material Status
_____ MMT Inventory
_____ ASW Watch Stations
_____ Noise/Source Levels
_____ SVTT Status
_____ XBT Inventory/Procedures

c. Electronic Material
_____ Personal Electronic Safety Program
_____ Combat Systems Control Procedures
_____ Communications
_____ LINK 11, 4A
_____ Surface Search Radar/IFF/TACAN
_____ 2M Certification
_____ General Purpose Electronic Test Equipment (GPETE)
_____ Antenna Photos and Fade Charts
_____ NEC Status
_____ TEMPEST Status
_____ CASREP Status

d. Fire Control
_____ FCS Operation/Material Status
_____ Computer Suite Operation/Material Status
_____ AN/SPY-1B Operation/Material Status
_____ Dry Air System
_____ M Cap

e. Ordnance/Missile
_____ Missile Loadout Status/Offload Preparations
_____ Pre-fire checks for guns
_____ Harpoon Operation/Material Status
_____ CIWS PACFIRE Procedures
_____ Dud Procedures/Misfire procedures
_____ Mag Sprinkler OPS/Procedures
_____ Missile Deluge System

_____ Small Arms Allowance/25mm Installation
_____ Ammunition Handling Equipment
_____ Small Arms Security/Inventory/Key Control
_____ Magazine Temperature Reports
_____ Explosive Safety Review Status
_____ Small Arms Qualifications
_____ Sensitive Ordnance Handling
_____ Conventional Ordnance Handling and Certification Program
_____ Weight Test Status
_____ Night Vision Devices

f. System Test Officer (STO)

_____ SERT Team
_____ System Testing (OCSOT)
_____ Departmental 3-M
_____ CSTT Organization and Training
_____ CSOSS Implementation/CSOOW
_____ Combat System Maintenance Manual
_____ Master Software Tape/Disk Control
_____ ACTS Training

g. ADP Security

_____ ADP Program
_____ SNAP II
_____ Security/Software Control

5. Supply Officer shall be prepared to discuss/show PCO the following:

_____ Latest Weekly Reports
_____ Line Items in SIM (Last Inventory)
_____ CASREP Processing Supply Input
_____ DLR Control/Remain in Place Procedures
_____ Last SMA and Disbursing Audits
_____ Financial Conditions of the general Mess, Discuss Mess Management

_____ Daily Meal Sampling Form and Procedures
_____ Ship's Store Financial Status/Operating Procedures
_____ Ship's Store Stock Turn
_____ Material Obligation validation Program
_____ Vending Machine Operation
_____ FSA Procedures/CO's Mess
_____ Laundry Procedures
_____ Maint/Other OPTAR Procedures and Status
_____ Ready Service Spares/MAMs Inventory
_____ HAZMAT/HAZWASTE Management
_____ Controlled Equipage
_____ Organizational Issue Material
_____ Plastics Management
_____ % DDS Participation
_____ Travel Claim Processing
_____ Disbursing Accountability/SALTS

6. The Navigator shall be prepared to discuss/show PCO the following:

_____ Most Recent CO Chart and Publication Letter
_____ Most Recent Notice to Mariners
_____ Chart and NAV Publication Update Procedures
_____ Most Recent Chart and Navigation Publication Inventory
_____ Equipment Inventory and Accounting (Watch-to-Watch/Inport)
_____ Boat Compasses
_____ Most Recent Swing Ship and Compass Card/Compass Log
_____ Standing Orders/Navigation Standards and Procedures
_____ Degaussing Folder—Location—Who has Control—Last Results
_____ Deck Logs
_____ Navigation Briefs/Procedures
_____ Standard Watch-to-Watch Procedures

_____ Night Order Book/Last Thirty days
_____ Harbor Chart on Bridge
_____ Tactical Data Folder
_____ Letter of Designation of Navigator/Assistant Navigator
_____ Sea Detail/UNREP Helmsman
_____ Navigation Light Certification/SUEZ Canal Certification
_____ Low Visibility (SUPPLY)
_____ Special Sea and Anchor Detail Checkoff List
_____ Clocks/Chronometers Check Procedures
_____ SATNAV/GPS
_____ MOVREP/OTSR
_____ LOGREQ Procedures

a. Admin Officer

_____ TEMADD Funding (TADTAR)
_____ Routing System
_____ Postal Program/Last Audit
_____ Registered Mail Handling
_____ DMSR Procedures
_____ Service record Access
_____ Service Record Entries
_____ ID Card Accountability
_____ Inspection Status (Admin/Medical/Postal)
_____ ADMIN Tickler

7. Engineer Officer shall be prepared to discuss/show PCO the following:

a. Engineering

_____ Logs and Records
_____ Casualty Control/EOSS/Restricted Maneuvering Doctrine
_____ Last OPPE Report—Status
_____ Engineering Standing Orders

_____ Tag-Out Procedures
_____ Welder Qualifications/Hot Work Bill
_____ Engineering Drills/Training/ECCTT
_____ Conditions of HP/LPAC Air Compressors
_____ Main Drainage Systems Procedures
_____ Oil Lab Inspection/Procedures/Records
_____ LOQM Program
_____ BW/FW Program
_____ Docking Plan—last Docking Report
_____ Gas Free Engineer Letter of Designation
_____ Fuel Consumption Curves
_____ NEURS Reports
_____ Fueling Bill
_____ Boiler Inspection Status
_____ Last Full Power Trials
_____ Heat Stress Program
_____ Site TV (Tape Security/Accountability)
_____ Hearing Conservation Program
_____ Shore Power Procedures
_____ 8 and 12 O'clock Reports/Light Off Orders
_____ Gage Cal Program
_____ Valve Maintenance Program
_____ EOOW's and EOOW Qualification
_____ Watch Bill
_____ Technical Publications/NSTM's/Tech Library
_____ Electrical Safety
_____ Cathodic Protection
_____ Degaussing
_____ Asbestos
_____ QA Program/Level One Material Control
_____ Auxillary Equipment Status/Problems
_____ IC Systems/WSN-5

b. Damage Control
_____ DCTT Organization/Procedures
_____ Repair Party Organization/Training

_____ Main Space Fire Doctrine
_____ CBR Suits/Equipment
_____ RADIACS
_____ OBA Training
_____ DC Plates/DC Book
_____ DC Organization/DC Drills Underway, Inport
_____ Inport Fire Parties
_____ OBA Allowance/Location
_____ DC WIFCOM
_____ DC PQS Program

OTHER BRIEFING GUIDELINES

1. In addition to discussions with the Department Heads, the PCO will be briefed by the following personnel concerned with major collateral or administrative duties as indicated below:

a. Executive Officer
_____ Personnel Status/LOTARP/Manning/TPU/ Berthing
_____ Upcoming Visits/Commitments
_____ Planning Board for Training
_____ Ombudsman
_____ Discipline/XOI/Mast/ADSEPS
_____ Liberty Policy (Briefs/Liberty Risks)
_____ Deployment Awards (NAM/CAPS)
_____ Evals/Fitreps
_____ Change of Command
_____ XO Memos

b. Senior Watch Officer
_____ Officer Assignments/Watch Qualifications
_____ Officer Watch Qualification Procedures (Tests/ Board)
_____ Inport Duty Sections
_____ CDO/ACDO Rotation

_____ Officer Training
_____ Surface Warfare Officer Qualification
_____ PQS Program

c. Master Chief Petty Officer of the Command
_____ CMEO Program
_____ Professional Development Board
_____ CPO Review Board
_____ Commanding Officer's Suggestion Box
_____ Petty Officer Indoctrination
_____ "I" Division
_____ Sailor of the Quarter/Month
_____ Enlisted Surface Warfare Specialty Qualification
_____ Navy Rights and Responsibilities

d. Senior Medical Department Representative
_____ Medical Organization
_____ Accountability/Controlled Medicinals
_____ Inspections/Food Service/Water/Sanitation/Hazardous Material
_____ Medical Department Training
_____ Sick Call Procedures
_____ Treatment of Potable Water
_____ Heat Stress/Hearing Conservation Programs
_____ Medical Records
_____ Dental/Shots
_____ Daily Reports to CO
_____ Medical Waste Handling
_____ Supply/AMAL
_____ Status of Inspections (Last conducted/Next due)

e. Command Career Counselor
_____ Retention Program/Status
_____ Guard III/Score/SRB Procedures
_____ Status of Retention Team
_____ Interview Procedures

_____ HARP Duty
_____ Submission of NAVPERS 1306/7

f. Chief Master at Arms
_____ Discipline/EMI
_____ Drugs, Alcohol, UA's
_____ Current Cases
_____ Liberty Cards/Liberty Risk Program
_____ Lucky Bag
_____ NIS Interface
_____ Urinalysis/Chain of Custody

g. 3-M Coordinator/SMMO
_____ PMS Accomplishment Rate last 13 weeks
_____ Ship's 3-M Program/Reports
_____ Last 3-M Inspection Results
_____ CO's Spotchecks
_____ CSMP
_____ 3-PQS
_____ IMAV Procedures in San Diego
_____ Job Sign-Off/QA

h. Safety Officer
_____ Overview of Program
_____ Reports
_____ Last NAVSAFECEN Inspection/Assist Visit
_____ Personal Injury Investigation
_____ Safety Committee/Council
_____ Safety Training
_____ Tag-Out Program

i. DAPA/Aftercare
_____ DAPA Instruction
_____ Program Overview
_____ Reports
_____ Current Status of Personnel

j. Legal Officer Brief
_____ Unit Punishment Log
_____ Mast Procedures
_____ Appeals
_____ Court Martial Procedures
_____ Case Pending
_____ Cruise Book

k. Public Affairs Officer
_____ Command Presentation
_____ Welcome Aboard Pamphlets
_____ Family Gram
_____ News Releases
_____ Tiger Cruise
_____ FHTNR Program

l. Physical Readiness/Athletic Officer
_____ PRT Program/Mandatory PT/Weight Control Program
_____ Ship's Athletic Teams

m. Welfare and Recreation Officer/Treasurer
_____ Status of Account/Upcoming Plans
_____ Cruise Book
_____ Inventory

n. Test Control/Educational Services Officer
_____ Off Duty Education
_____ Functional Skills
_____ Exam Procedures

o. SRA Coordinator SMMO 3-M Coordinator
_____ SRA Work Package

(3) Department Information Books

1. Each Department Head will provide the PCO, upon his arrival, with tabbed notebooks containing copies of the following documents (in order as shown):

ADMIN:

- Nav/Admin Department organization/key personnel and manning deficiencies
- Most recent muster report
- EDVR (Section 4)
- ODCR
- Prospective gains/losses list
- Wardroom social rosters
- Collateral Duties List
- List of Effective Instructions
- List of submitted/outstanding awards and Command NAMS/CAPS remaining
- List of personnel in a disciplinary status or awaiting ADSEP or SPCM
- Most recent correspondence TICKLER and list of required reports
- Sea and Anchor Detail checklist
- USS FISKEINST 3120.2 (USS FISKE'S DAILY ROUTINE)

A separate copy of the ship's SORM, the Commanding Officer's Standing Orders, and XO's memos will also be provided for the PCO's review along with a folder, containing a copy of all pertinent change of command notices, the guest and announcement list, a COC pamphlet, a sample announcement and a script.

SUPPLY:

- Supply Department organization, key personnel and manning deficiencies
- Most recent monthly report to CO
- 8 O'clock reports
- List of major SRA jobs

- Results of Controlled Equipment Inventory and all audits
- List of required Inspections (last conducted/next due)

The Supply Officer will also provide the PCO with a folder containing a pad of blank paper, pencils/pens, a Welcome Aboard pamphlet, a ship's phone book, and an officer roster/telephone number listing (and whatever other touches he deems appropriate).

OPERATIONS:

- OPS Department organization, key personnel and manning deficiencies
- Current Plan of the Week
- Current SOE
- Ship's long-range training plan and projected cycle schedule
- 8 O'clock reports
- Copy of OPS CASREPS
- List of major SRA jobs
- Daily boat report
- List of required inspections, certs, qual (last conducted/next due)
- List of required exercises and SELEXS (last conducted periodicity, M rating, due by, grade)
- Officer watch qualification matrix
- Current underway watchbill/CDO watchbill

COMBAT SYSTEMS:

- Combat Systems Department organization, key personnel and manning deficiencies
- 8 O'clock reports
- Copy of CS CASREPS
- Daily Combat Systems report
- List of major SRA jobs
- Current ammo load out/NCEA
- Last OCSOT results
- List of required inspections, certs, quals (last conducted/next due)
- CO's Battle Orders

ENGINEERING:

- Engineering Department organization, key personnel and manning deficiencies
- 8 O'clock reports
- Copy of Engineering CASREPS
- Daily Fuel and Water report and Draft report
- List of major SRA jobs
- List of required inspections, certs, quals (last conducted/next due)
- List of departures from specs
- Sample light-off orders
- Sample refueling/transfer of fuel checklist
- Sample ECC briefing form
- Fuel consumption data
- Copy of last full power report
- Copy of last OPPE with IOP Status

The Chief Engineer will also make the following documents available to the PCO: EDORM and the Main Space Fire Doctrine.

Appendix 2

Sample Change of Command Plan

USS FISKE (DDG XX) NOTICE 5061

Subj: CHANGE OF COMMAND ON 20 JUNE 1997

Encl: (1) Script

       (2) Seating Plan

       (3) Personnel Requirements

       (4) Remaining Actions

1. *Purpose.* To provide a sequence of events for each speaker for USS FISKE (DDG XX) Change of Command on 20 June 1997.

2. *Discussion.* Commander J. Barry, Commanding Officer, USS FISKE (DDG XX) will be relieved by Commander J. P. Jones on 20 June 1997.

3. *Information.*

   a. All participants should assemble on the flight deck no later than 0830.

   b. Uniforms:

      (1) Officer/CPO: Service Dress Whites (medals and ribbons). Officers will wear swords.

      (2) E-6 and below: Dress Whites (medals and ribbons).

      (3) Guests: Appropriate civilian attire.

   c. Guests will arrive via brow on the flightdeck and official guests will arrive via the midships brow. The ship's quarterdeck will be midships, but a ceremonial OOD with a Boatswain and side-boys will be stationed at both brows to pipe officials aboard. No one will be "bonged aboard."

                                         J. BARRY

(1) Script for
Commanding Officer, USS Fiske(DDG XX)
Change of Command
****

20 June 1997

****   Following participants muster in assigned areas at pier and onboard USS FISKE.

0600   - Reserved parking guards

0830   - Band (fantail)
        - Quarterdeck OOD with long glass, two POOW's, two MSGRS, Boatswain and sideboys
        - Fantail OOD, Two MSGRs, Boatswain and sideboys
        - Color guard (fantail)
        - Ushers and escorts (starboard amidships)
        - Main gate and road directors

0915   Ship's company fall in for ceremony.

0930   CO/PCO families/special guests assemble in the wardroom.

0930   Ship's company in place. Band commences music program. Program notebooks placed on lecterns.

        Commander Surface Forces Pacific departs for USS FISKE (with ship's force escort).

        CDO awaits arrival of Commander Surface Forces Pacific and informs CDR Barry when he arrives.

0945   Commander Surface Forces Pacific arrives.

        CDR Barry goes to the quarterdeck to escort CNSP to CO's cabin.

        Quarterdeck OOD calls "Attention to port" (not using the 1MC, which would affect personnel on the pier), band continues to play.

        - Eight sideboys and piped aboard

Official party will proceed to Commanding Officer's inport cabin escorted by CDR Barry.

0950   Escort families to flight deck (officer's escort).

0955   Mrs. Barry, the Commanding Officer's mother, and the Prospective Commanding Officer's mother are met by ship's company officers and escorted to their seats. Flowers presented during CO's remarks to CO's mother and spouse.

         Chaplain escorted to platform and seated.

         Following personnel take positions onboard USS FISKE.

         - XO USS FISKE at master of ceremony lectern.

         - CMC seated to the right of the master of ceremony lectern.

After guests   Music ceases.
are seated

0958XO   "Good morning, ladies and gentlemen. Welcome to United States Ship FISKE change of command. In just a few minutes, the Commander Surface Forces Pacific, Vice Admiral A. Burke, Commander Destroyer Squadron Twenty-One, CAPT Johnson, the Commanding Officer, USS FISKE, CDR J. Barry, and the Prospective Commanding Officer, USS FISKE, CDR J. P. Jones, will arrive. A gun salute will be rendered this morning to Admiral Burke. The ceremony will commence with the playing of the National Anthem, followed by the invocation offered by Chaplain East."

0958   Band strikes up appropriate music. (Playing time 2 minutes).

1000   Band ceases to play. (Band plays Attention).

XO	"Ship's company, Attention."

XO	"Will the guests please rise (for the arrival of the official party, honors to Commander Surface Forces Pacific, Vice Admiral Burke, parading of the colors followed by our National Anthem) and remain standing until the color guard has posted."

During arrival of official party, the following will salute during honors:

> - XO
> - Chaplain
> - FISKE fantail OOD
> - Honors bosun/sideboys
> - Formation leaders and guest in uniform
> - *Personnel in ranks will not salute*

(When CDR Jones is at entrance to the air lock XO announces)

XO	"CDR J. P. Jones, Prospective Commanding Officer, USS FISKE"
	(Bosun's pipe through sideboys)
	CDR Jones walks through ceremonial quarterdeck. After passing through sideboys, CDR Jones proceeds to and stands in front of designated chair.
	(When CDR Barry steps through air lock)
XO	"CDR J. Barry, Commanding Officer, USS FISKE"
	CDR Barry walks through ceremonial quarterdeck. After passing through sideboys, CDR Barry proceeds to and stands in front of designated chair.
	(When CAPT Johnson steps through the air lock)
XO	"CAPT Johnson, Destroyer Squadron Twenty-One, acting"

CAPT Johnson walks through ceremonial quarterdeck. After passing through sideboys, CAPT Johnson proceeds to and stands in front of designated chair.

(When Vice Admiral Burke steps through the air lock)

XO   "Vice Admiral Arleigh Burke, Commander Naval Surface Forces Pacific"

Admiral Burke walks through ceremonial quarterdeck. After passing through sideboys, Vice Admiral Burke proceeds to and stands in front of designated chair. Bosun's pipe ceases.

Ruffles and flourishes and gun salute for Vice Admiral Burke

XO   "Parade the colors." (The band playing in the background)

Note: Color guard on fantail starboard side. Parade to front of podium, wheel, face guest, dip flags for National Anthem.

XO	When colors are in place amidships: "Ladies and Gentlemen, our National Anthem."
Band	Plays National Anthem
XO	"Color guard, post." Color guard proceeds to portside of fantail. "Sideboys, post."
XO	"Chaplain East will now offer the invocation."
XO	"Will the guests please be seated."
Official Party	Take seats. [Platform guests remove gloves]
XO	"Ship's company, parade rest."

XO	"Ladies and Gentlemen, Commander J. Barry, United States Navy, Commanding Officer, USS FISKE."
CDR Barry	Introductory remarks/Introduces Vice Admiral Burke
CNSP	Remarks
XO	"Ship's company, attention."
CNSP	Award presentation to Commander Barry
XO	"Ship's company, parade rest."
XO	"Ladies and Gentlemen, Commander Barry, United States Navy, Commanding Officer, USS FISKE."
CDR Barry	Remarks. (Present flowers to CO's wife/mother during remarks)
CDR Barry	"I will now read my orders." Pause.
XO	"Ship's company, attention."

CDR Barry	From: Chief of Naval Personnel Washington, DC
	To: Commanding Officer, USS FISKE
	Subj: BUPERS Order 0417
	When directed by reporting senior, detach from duty as Commanding Officer, USS FISKE, and report to Harvard University, Cambridge, Massachusetts, to the John F. Kennedy School of Government as a Federal Executive Fellow.
	    (Signed)
	    C. Nimitz
	    Vice Admiral, US Navy, Chief of Naval Personnel

CDR Jones	Stands
CDR Barry	"Commander Jones, I am ready to be relieved."
XO	"Ladies and Gentlemen, Commander J. P. Jones, United States Navy."

CDR Jones	From: Chief of Naval Personnel Washington, DC To: CDR J. P. Jones Subj: BUPERS Order 2076 When directed by the Secretary of Defense, detach as his military assistant and after a period of leave and training and report to Commanding Officer, USS FISKE, as his relief. Upon relieving, report to the immediate superior in command, Commander Destroyer Squadron Twenty-One. (Signed) C. Nimitz Vice Admiral, US Navy, Chief of Naval Personnel
CDR Jones	Reads orders and turns to CDR Barry
CDR Jones	Salutes CDR Barry and states: "I relieve you, Sir."
CDR Barry	Returns salute and states: "I stand relieved."
CNSP	Stands
CDR Barry	Turns to CAPT Johnson, Acting CDS-21, salutes and states: "CAPT Johnson, I have been relieved."
CDS-21	Returns salute and states, "Very well."
CDR Jones	Turns to CAPT Johnson, salutes and states: "CAPT Johnson, I have assumed command of USS FISKE."
CDS-21	Returns salute and states, "Very well."
XO	"Ship's company, parade rest."
XO	"Ladies and Gentlemen, Commander J. P. Jones, United States Navy, Commanding Officer, USS FISKE."
CDR Jones	Remarks
XO	"Ship's company, attention."

XO	"Master Chief Smith, Command Master Chief, USS FISKE, representing nearly 300 crewmembers on DDG XX, will now present to CDR Barry the ship's commissioning pennant."
CMC Smith	Salutes and presents the pennant to CDR Barry
XO	"Will the guests please rise for the benediction."
Chaplain	Benediction
Band	Plays Navy Hymn softly in background.
XO	"Retire the colors."
Color guard	March from port to starboard wheel and order colors.
XO	"Ladies and Gentlemen, the change of command ceremony is concluded. All guests are cordially invited to the reception on the pier. Will the guests please allow a few moments for the departure of the official party and distinguished guests."
Escorts	Will proceed to front row as the XO announces the reception and escorts Mrs. Barry, the Commanding Officer's mother.
Sideboys	Fantail OOD, Boatswain and sideboys post for departing guests
Band	Plays Anchors Aweigh/patriotic medley.
Official party	Proceed fantail quarterdeck where sideboys and honors boatswain's mate are in position. Proceed in order through sideboys and off via the brow. - Vice Admiral Burke - CDR Barry - CDR Jones
XO	(Upon official party departure) "Ship's company, dismissed."

Upon completion of change of command program, ushers and escorts take post and expedite official party, spouses, families, and distinguished guests to the reception. Ushers will direct guests to the reception via the fantail brow.

(2) Seating Plan

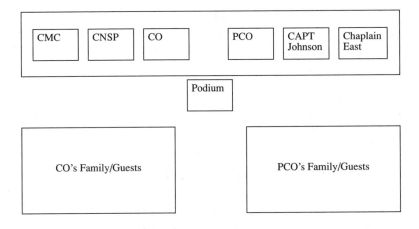

(3) Personnel Requirements

Quarterdeck

Midships	Flight Deck
OOD	OOD
(2) POOW's	(2) Messengers
(2) Messengers	(1) Boatswain with pipe
(1) Boatswain with pipe	(8) Sideboys
(8) Sideboys	

Ushers

(4) Chief Petty Officers on the flight deck

Escorts

(4) Division Officers on midships quarterdeck

CNSP Escort
> (1) LT with Vice Admiral Burke

Directors
> (1) CPO at the main gate
> (5) Personnel along the route giving directions

Parking Lot
> (5) Parking lot attendants

Pier
> (2) Gate guards
> (2) Brow directors

Communications

The main gate lookout, (1) gate guard, the OOD at each brow, the CDO, the change of command coordinator, and the CDO will have walkie-talkies coordinating and tracking VIPs

(4) Remaining Actions

1. Titivate ship—all hands.
2. Reserve a truck for 19–20 JUN 97—SUPPO.
3. Report to base MWR for change of command materials NLT 1200 19 JUN 97, and set up flight deck—FCCM Ball.
4. After RSVP's are received, reserve appropriate seating and make VIP cards—Admin Officer.
5. After RSVP's are received, determine who will receive flowers—Coordinator/XO.
6. Rehearse ceremony 1630 19 JUN 97 with CNSP's aide.
7. Write commissioning ceremony watchbill—FCCM Ball.
8. Determine and order required flowers. Coordinator and SUPPO.

Appendix 3

Sample Division in the Spotlight Program

USS FISKE (DDG XX) INSTRUCTION 5040.1B

Subj: DIVISION IN THE SPOTLIGHT PROGRAM

Ref: (a) FISKEINST 3502.1C
(b) FISKEINST 4790.3B
(c) OPNAVINST 3120.32 (series), Standard Organization and Regulations of the U.S. Navy
(d) COMNAVSURFPACINST 9000.1 (series), COMNAV SURFPAC Maintenance Manual

Encl: (1) Zone Inspection Material Checklist/Inspection Criteria
(2) Commanding Officer's Personnel Inspection
(3) Damage Control Readiness Assessment
(4) Valve Maintenance Checklist
(5) Repair Parts Petty Officer Assessment
(6) Hazardous Material Assessment
(7) Personnel and Automated Information Security
(8) Retention Program Spot-Check Inspection Form
(9) Manning Program Spot-Check Inspection Form
(10) Service Record Audit
(11) Disbursing Pay Record Audit
(12) Medical/Dental Division Review
(13) Safety Inspection Form
(14) Personnel Electrical/Electronic Equipment Report
(15) Electrical Safety Readiness Assessment

1. *Purpose.* To define the scope, responsibilities, and procedures for management of Divisional Programs.

2. *Responsibility for this Instruction.* The Executive Officer is responsible for this instruction.

3. *Background.* The goal of the Division in the Spotlight Program is to maintain FISKE in the highest state of material, manpower and administrative readiness by ensuring the crew "routinely does the routine," despite whatever else may be going on. This program helps divisions avoid the "peaks and valleys" of operational readiness between cyclical inspections. Designated program experts are tasked to assist the division meet/maintain program requirements on a quarterly basis. The following schedule applies:

Week	Division
1	MP
2	OC
3	CO
4	S1/S3/S4
5	NN/NX/NM
6	E
7	OI
8	CA
9	S2, S5
10	R
11	OT
12	CE
13	A
14	OD
15	CF
16	CM

During the course of one week, designated program managers will audit cognizant programs, provide training as required, and assist the division as necessary to ensure program requirements are met. In addition, the Personnel Officer and the Disbursing Officer will audit the division's service and pay records and brief each divisional member on the results. A copy of the audit form will be provided to each member. Each division will be audited/inspected as follows:

a. A zone inspection of all divisional spaces by the Commanding Officer. Spaces will be presented by the person in charge of the space (enclosure (1)). Both the Division Officer and the Division Chief will accompany the Commanding Officer. **The Division Officer or Leading Chief Petty Officer (LCPO) shall present the prior zone inspection ZIDLs to the Commanding Officer as the Commanding Officer enters the space. Previous zone inspection discrepancies should either be cleared by the Department Head (his initials on the ZIDL) or they should be reflected on the division's latest CSMP.**

b. A formal personnel inspection by the Commanding Officer. The inspection uniform will be designated in sufficient time to allow proper crew preparation (enclosure (2)).

   NOTE: The Barber Shop will grant head-of-line privileges to Division in the Spotlight personnel during inspection *week*.

c. A formal training program audit by the Commanding Officer and Training Officer (enclosure (8), section 2 of reference (a)).

d. A formal PQS program audit by the Commanding Officer and the PQS Coordinator (enclosure (2), section 3 of reference (a)).

e. A formal review of Divisional Damage Control program by the DCA (enclosure (3)).

f. A formal review of Divisional Valve Maintenance by the Auxiliaries Officer (enclosure (4)).

g. A Divisional Supply audit by the Supply Officer. This will include review of outstanding requisitions, inventory of RSSs/DLRs and the Repair Parts Petty Officer (RPPO) (enclosure (5)).

h. A formal review of Divisional HAZMAT compliance by Command HAZMAT Coordinator (enclosure (6)). HAZMAT refresher training will be conducted for the Division in the Spotlight, and a copy of the training muster sheet will be retained to the Command HAZMAT Coordinator.

    i. A formal review of Divisional Security by the Assistant Command Security Officer. This will include review of personnel security clearance and access compliance as well as an inventory of material held by division and an ADP security review (enclosure (7)).

    j. A formal review of Divisional Retention, Manning and NEC Management by the Command Career Counselor and Personnel Office (enclosures (8) and (9)).

    k. A formal Administrative Program audit to include Service and Pay record audits and a review of medical records by the SMDR (enclosures (10), (11), and (12)).

    l. A formal review of Divisional Safety Program by the *Command* Safety Officer. This will include review of *NAVOSH* compliance and related training as well as *electrical* safety compliance within the division (enclosures (13), and (14), (15)).

    m. A formal review of the divisional 3M/SNAP III programs will be conducted in accordance with the checklist in reference (b).

4. *Responsibilities*

    a. The Executive Officer will:

      (1) Ensure each division in FISKE is inspected in accordance with references (c) and (d) and this instruction. The Executive Officer will make a recommendation to the Commanding Officer to defer the program for one week when the pace of operations precludes conduct of Division in the Spotlight. Only the Commanding Officer may defer Division in the Spotlight, and it will be deferred only under the most challenging of circumstances.

      (2) Oversee Division in the Spotlight debriefs.

      (3) Ensure Division in the Spotlight deficiencies are documented and corrected.

      (4) Participate in zone inspections as necessary to assist the Commanding Officer.

      (5) Publish the zones, date and time of the zone inspection and of the debrief of the week's activities.

     (6) Assign inspecting officers and teams.
- b. The Chief Engineer shall:
    - (1) Review requests for assistance to correct discrepancies (via trouble log) and notify the appropriate Department Head if a job is beyond ship's force capability. The appropriate Department Head is then responsible for submission of an OPNAV 4790/2K and ensuring updated annotation on the respective ZIDL.
    - (2) Ensure damage control, quality assurance, electrical safety, and valve maintenance inspections are conducted on the division being inspected and have appropriate petty officers present at the debrief.
- c. The Safety Officer shall act immediately to correct any safety related discrepancies identified during the inspection and will have the Assistant Safety Officer conduct the safety inspection of the Division in the Spotlight.
- d. The Damage Control Assistant (DCA)/Repair Officer will review the trouble log, screening for assistance to correct discrepancies noted in zone inspections. He will report serious, long-standing, or damage control discrepancies to the Chief Engineer and Executive Officer.
- e. Department Heads will:
    - (1) Provide personnel for inspecting teams as specified below.
    - (2) Require Division Officers to prepare and report spaces and selected programs ready for inspection prior to the time published for zone inspection.
    - (3) Review inspection reports and ensure discrepancies noted within the department are corrected. Material deficiencies not considered correctable within thirty days will be recorded in the Current Ship's Maintenance Plan (CSMP) and monitored until corrected. Deficiencies requiring the assistance of another department to repair (typically engineering) will be reported via the trouble log system.
    - (4) Attend command debriefs.
    - (5) Ensure action is taken on all identified safety hazards within 24 hours.

(6) Ensure discrepancies which are placed on the CSMP are selected for inclusion in FISKE's next regularly scheduled availability.

(7) Assist the Commanding Officer, as requested, in the conduct of zone inspections.

f. The Division Officers shall:

(1) Report divisional readiness to their Department Head.

(2) Provide the previous inspection ZIDLs to the inspecting officer at the commencement of the zone inspection.

(3) Accompany the inspecting officer.

(4) Present the division for personnel inspection.

(5) Assign personnel to present division spaces to the inspecting officer along with a recorder. Further they will ensure all lockers, stowage cabinets and drawers are unlocked and opened for inspection.

(6) Review inspection reports and ensure correction of discrepancies.

(7) Submit the ZIDLs with a status report on correction of discrepancies to the Department Head.

(8) Ensure that when his organization is the Division in the Spotlight, divisional administrative records are available for review.

Note: All known discrepancies will be presented at commencement of the review.

(9) Forward ZIDLs from zone inspection, appropriately annotated, to the Department Head within 5 working days of the zone inspection.

(10) Maintain a separate ZIDL file for each space under his/her cognizance. Do not remove previous ZIDLs, as this file provides an auditable record of zone inspections.

(11) Attend Divisional Debrief.

g. Division Chief Petty Officers will accompany the inspection party. Additionally they will ensure the zone inspection material checklist in enclosure (1) is properly annotated, signed and presented to the inspecting officer at the commencement of space inspection.

    h. Workcenter supervisor/Petty Officer-in-Charge (POIC) of spaces scheduled for inspection will:
      (1) Ensure spaces are prepared for inspection as directed by the Division Officer.
      (2) Ensure responsible personnel are standing by to present their spaces.
      (3) Have an annotated copy of the previous ZIDL reflecting current status of all outstanding items.
      (4) Accompany the inspecting party.

5. *Procedures.* Program managers will make necessary arrangements to conduct program audits/reviews and training with applicable counterpart. The zone inspection, personnel inspection and debrief will be scheduled by the Executive Officer during the previous week's PBFT.
    a. On Thursday, all spaces owned by the Division in the Spotlight will be inspected by the Commanding Officer or by an officer designated by the Commanding Officer.
    b. The command debrief will be guided by the Executive Officer. Persons assigned to inspect designated programs will brief the Commanding Officer on their findings. Copies of their reports and ZIDLs will be provided to the Commanding Officer, Executive Officer, and the Division Officer.
    c. On Friday, a Commanding Officers Personnel Inspection shall be conducted. Uniforms shall be determined during PBFT the week prior to the inspection.
    d. The Executive Officer and cognizant division officers shall maintain a file of the inspection reports.

6. *Report of Corrective Action*
    a. Division Officers shall note corrective action taken on all ZIDLs and forward them to the Department Head within five days. These same ZIDLs will be presented to the Commanding Officer at the beginning of the next zone inspection.
    b. The cognizant Department Head will ensure all safety discrepancies are corrected immediately. Discrepancies which cannot be immediately corrected will be directly reported to the Commanding Officer and the Executive Officer and

placed in a configuration which does not threaten life or equipment.

J. Barry

Distribution: (FISKEINST 5216.1)

List I

(1) Zone Inspection Material Checklist

	SAT/UNSAT
Compartment Checkoff List.	_____
Compartment/space label plates, numbering and division assigned.	_____
Piping and ventilation duct markings and bulkhead penetrations.	_____
Valve condition, labeling and classification.	_____
Doors, hatches and scuttle classification, numbering and condition.	_____
Fire hose overboard discharge fitting, classification and numbering.	_____
Air test fitting caps.	_____
Sounding tube fittings, classification and numbering.	
General preservation.	_____
First aid, decontamination and traffic markings.	_____
T-wrenches/dogging wrenches.	
Loose or frayed wiring, lighting fixtures, shields, mounting covers, terminal box covers, receptacle covers with attached chain and sound-powered telephone covers.	_____
Rubber matting or dielectric sheet associated with electrical gear.	_____

Electrical cable bulkhead and deck penetrations.   _____

Insulation and lagging.   _____

Floor plates, deck tile, and grating.   _____

Equipment foundation and supports.   _____

Non-watertight doors.   _____

Sound shorts.   _____

Warning signs/labels properly posted.   _____

Posted safety precautions, warning signs and
operating instructions.   _____

Safety nets in trunks.   _____

Casualty power cables and risers.   _____

Turn off lights in space and inspect bulkheads for
holes that admit light into space from normal lighting
in adjacent compartment(s).   _____

Battle lanterns operational.   _____

Installed/portable firefighting equipment.   _____

Ventilation closures and controls operational
(including lights).   _____

Inspect for unauthorized flammable and
hazardous materials.   _____

Inspect for improperly stowed gear/missile hazards.   _____

Fire stations complete, properly stowed and labeled.   _____

Review previous Zone Inspection Discrepancy List.   _____

Check to ensure all personal electrical/electronic
equipment is safety checked.   _____

Check to ensure any danger/caution tags are
properly filled out and placed.   _____

Deck drains open/close   _____

(2) Commanding Officer's Personnel Inspection

DATE:	DIV:	OVERALL RESULTS: SAT UNSAT
NAME/RATE		DISCREPANCY

(3) Damage Control Readiness Assessment

DATE: _____

NOTE: This checklist is a guide to assist the inspector in identifying damage control discrepancies throughout the ship. Discrepancies are in the remarks section.

Overall _____ Division Grade: SAT   UNSAT

ADMINISTRATIVE CHECKS

	Total Spaces	Total Hits
1. CCOL–proper posting, grouping, numbering, fitting classification, fitting numbering, division responsibility assigned for maintenance and General Quarters.		
2. BULLSEYE—12 × 15, COMPT #, FRAME #s, Division responsibility, visible.		
3. CCOL marked "Duplicate" or "Partial" if req'd.		
4. DCPO responsibility placards complete.		
5. Fire station inventories and Bullseye posted.		
6. Damage control fittings numbered and classified as per CCOL.		
7. Doors, hatches, and scuttles labeled to include fitting number, with adjacent compartment name and number.		

FUNCTIONAL CHECKS

8. Piping and ductwork directional arrows, system and valve(s) labeled.		
9. Number of fittings in INOP log _____. Number active over 3 months _____.		
10. Door, hatch, and scuttle knife edges and moving parts free of paint and excessive wear.		

	Total Spaces	Total Hits
11. Do all classified DC fittings operate correctly.		
12. Dogging wrenches and/or T-wrenches available.		
13. Sounding tubes fitted with ball check valves, caps, and retaining chains.		
14. Compartment free of fire hazards		
15. Any stuffing tubes open, holes in BLKHD/DECK/OVHD.		
16. Portable extinguisher PMS within periodicity.		
17. Differential pressure indicator within limits.		
18. Photoluminescent paint/sticker attached properly without sections missing.		

19. OBA training was held for _____ of _____ divisional personnel.
20. EEBD and EGRESS training was held for _____ of _____ divisional personnel.
21. Gas masks assigned to personnel are in their General Quarters station.

Remarks:

_____

_____

_____

_____

_____

_____

_____

_____

_____

_____

Submitted by: _____ Approved by: _____
                  (Name/Rate)   (Name/Rank)

(4) Valve Maintainance Checklist

DATE: _____

From: Auxiliaries Officer
To: Commanding Officer
Via: Executive Officer
       ____ Department Head
       ____ Division Officer
Subj: Valve Maintenance Spot Check

COMPARTMENT NO: _____
COMPARTMENT NAME: _____
DIVISION REPRESENTATIVE: _____

1. HANDWHEEL
   A. Proper material.   _____
   B. Proper color code.   _____
   C. Free of cracks and breaks.   _____
   D. Secured tightly to valve.   _____
   E. Properly labeled per ship specifications.   _____
   F. Proper locking device installed per EOSS and
       physical security instruction.   _____
   G. Remote operator secured to valve and operates
       freely (where applicable).   _____
2. STEM
   A. Free of paint, dirt, rust, or other debris.   _____
       **Note: Metallized preservation such as wire
       aluminum (WSA) only on non-packing gland
       area of the stem, Sermetal-725 on the round
       and threaded areas above the packing gland area.**
   B. Lubricated (as specified for its service).   _____
   C. Free of bends, nicks, or burrs.   _____
   D. Bushing secured and free of excessive
       lubricant.   _____

3. PACKING GLAND

A. Gland retainer not cocked. _____

B. At least one packing ring thickness between bottom of retainer and bonnet. _____

C. All glands studs and nuts in place and secured. _____

D. No paint on studs or nuts. _____

E. No short studs (at least one thread length above the nut) per reference (D). _____

F. No long studs (no more than five thread lengths for limited clearances; never more than ten thread lengths) per reference (D). _____

G. Threads clean and free of rust or other debris. _____

H. Proper stud material (monel or brass in salt water system). _____

I. No dissimilar metals. Apply an antiseize compound to prevent seizing during assembly/ disassembly and to provide some corrosion protection. _____

J. Packing of correct number, size, and style. _____

K. When assembled valves are preserved with WSA or Seremental-725, both the packing gland, and fasteners (equal to or greater than $\frac{3}{8}''$ in diameter) should be preserved with the metallized system. _____

4. BONNET AND BODY

A. Properly preserved and free of encrustation of any kind. Metallized system or proper paint should be used where required. Stainless steel, bronze, monel, and other non-corrosive metals do not require paint. _____

B. Studs and nuts in place and secured. Must be of proper material (no dissimilar metals.) _____

C. No short studs. _____

D. No long studs. _____

E. No paint on threaded surfaces. _____

F. No body to bonnet leaks. _____

G. Proper gasket installed between body and
    bonnet.   _____
5. GENERAL
    A. Valve installed in proper flow direction.   _____
    B. Cycle the valve (only if operating conditions
        permit), following proper safety precautions
        (including required tag out and notification of
        on watch personnel).   _____

**Note: Record any uncorrected discrepancies in the appropiate
workcenter deficiency log.**

INSPECTED BY: DATE:
REMARKS/COMMENTS:

(5) Repair Parts Petty Officer Assessment

DATE: _____

MEMORANDUM

From: Supply Officer
To: Commanding Officer
Via: Executive Officer
       ____ Department Head
       ____ Division Officer
Subj: REPAIR PARTS PETTY OFFICER ASSESSMENT FOR
       _____ DIVISION

1. Grade: SAT/UNSAT
2. The following items were assessed:
    - Internal MOV program was aggressively maintained.
       YES   NO

- DLR/MTR records were maintained accurately.
  YES   NO

- DLR carcasses were turned in properly and in a timely manner.
  YES   NO

- Remain-in-Place certifications were used properly.
  YES   NO

- RPPO requisition log was maintained correctly.
  YES   NO

- RPPO was SNAP III Basic User and MDS Operator PQS qualified.
  YES   NO

Comments:

_____
_____
_____
_____
_____
_____

Copy to:
XO, DH
Divo. LCPO/LPO

(6) Hazardous Material Assessment

DATE: _____

MEMORANDUM

From: Supply Officer
To: Commanding Officer
         Executive Officer
         ____ Department Head
         ____ Division Officer
SUBJ: HAZARDOUS MATERIAL (HAZMAT) ASSESSMENT
         OF _____ DIVISION

1. OVERALL GRADE: SAT _____   UNSAT _____
2. The following HAZMAT program areas were examined:
   a. All HAZMAT users are Hazardous Material Handling Petty
      Officer PQS qualified.
      YES _____ NO _____
   b. All HAZMAT users are familiar with FISKE'S HAZMAT
      procedures for receiving material form HAZMATCENTRAL.
      YES _____ NO _____
   c. All HAZMAT users are familiar with the proper procedures
      and requirements for the turn-in of both RFI and used
      HAZMAT.
      YES _____ NO _____
   d. All Hazardous material under divisional control is properly
      marked, packaged and stored within an approved HAZMAT
      stowage locker.
      YES _____ NO _____
   e. All Hazardous material in the division's HAZMAT stowage
      locker was properly inventoried and accounted for.
      YES _____ NO _____
   f. All issues and receipts from the division's HAZMAT
      stowage locker was properly recorded and posted inside the
      HAZMAT locker door.
      YES _____ NO _____

g. All HAZMAT users knew where MATERIAL SAFETY DATA SHEETS (MSDS'S) were located.
YES _____ NO _____

h. All HAZMAT users are familiar with MSDS'S and knew how to find specific information in them.
YES _____ NO _____

i. All HAZMAT users are familiar with HAZMAT spill response procedures.
YES _____ NO _____

j. All HAZMAT users knew the points of contact for information pertaining to Hazardous Material use.
YES _____ NO _____

3. COMMENTS:

_____
_____
_____
_____
_____
_____

_____
Signature

Copy to:
XO
DH
DIVO
LCPO
LPO/WCS

(7) **Personnel Security**

DATE: ____

From: Operations Officer

To: Commanding Officer

        Executive Officer

        ____ Department Head

        ____ Division Officer

Subj: RESULT OF PERSONNEL SECURITY REVIEW CON-DUCTED FOR ____ DIVISION ON _____

                               (Date)

Ref: (a) OPNAVINST 5510 (series)

       (b) FISKEINST 5510.1 (Command Info & Personnel Security Program)

Total number in the division	—
Total number of Personnel in division checked	—
Total number of items on check sheet	17
Number of items checked / passed	__/__
Number of items not checked / not passed	__/__

Remarks: OVERALL SAT / UNSAT

_____

PERSONNEL-

_____

SECURITY-

_____

_____

_____

_____

_____

_____

_____

                             _____

                                  Signature

Personnel Security Review Check Sheet

CHECKLIST ITEMS

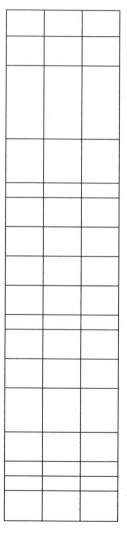

	YES	NO	N/A
1. Have division SECURITY REQUIREMENTS been reviewed?			
2. Have CLEARANCES been granted only to those with a "NEED TO KNOW"?			
3. Have supervisory personnel been BRIEFED and MADE AWARE of their RESPONSIBILITY TO CONTINUOUSLY EVALUATE SUBORDINATES FOR ACCESS OR ASSIGNMENT TO SENSITIVE DUTIES?			
4. Have spaces containing CLASSIFIED MATERIAL been IDENTIFIED? (I.E., LEVEL OF CLASSIFIED MATERIAL DETERMINED)			
5. Are PROPER ACCESS CONTROLS in effect?			
6. Do CLASSIFIED MATERIAL storage containers have "OPEN SAFE" instructions?			
7. Do storage containers have SAFE RECORD sheets and INVENTORY sheets?			
8. Have safe combinations been updated within the last year or after the last custodian detached?			
9. Is a security container information envelope (Form 700. 8-85) held by CDO/SM?			
10. Are all BURN BAGS accessible?			
11. Are BURN BAGS at least six feet or more away from trash cans?			
12. Are BURN BAGS properly numbered IAW FISKE policy?			
13. Have divisional personnel been briefed and made aware of the proper care and processing of classified material?			
14. Has an EMERGENCY ACTION PLAN (EAP) been implemented?			
15. EAP—Are personnel familiar with procedures?			
16. EAP—Is all classified material prioritized?			
17. EAP—Are required tools/materials readily available?			

(8) Retention Program Spot-Check Inspection Form

DATE: _____

USS FISKE (DDG XX)
RETENTION PROGRAM SPOT-CHECK FORM
FOR _____ DIVISION

From: Command Career Counselor
To: Commanding Officer
Via: Executive Officer
         _____ Department Head
         _____ Division Officer
Subj: RETENTION PROGRAM SPOT-CHECK INSPECTION

Overall Program Grade: SAT / UNSAT

	YES	NO
1. Are required counseling sessions being held (initial, 6 mos, etc.)?	_____	_____
2. Does the Division have an active awards program? Are Divisional personnel nominated for SOY/SOM/CAP or other recognition programs?	_____	_____
3. Are Divisional personnel receiving informational training covering available programs such as BOOST, ECP, etc.?	_____	_____
4. Is the Division Officer's notebook up-to-date and used effectively to manage advancement?	_____	_____
5. Are Divisional personnel completing advancement requirements prior to being TIR eligible for next paygrade?	_____	_____
6. Does the Division encourage off-duty education and allow time for an individual to participate?	_____	_____
7. Does the Division reward personnel who re-enlist?	_____	_____

Remarks/Comments:

_____

_____

_____
Signature

(9) Manning Program Spot-Check Inspection Form
USS FISKE (DDG XX)
MANNING PROGRAM SPOT-CHECK FORM
FOR _____ DIVISION

From: Administrative Officer
To: Commanding Officer
Via: Executive Officer
        ____ Department Head
        ____ Division Officer
Subj: MANNING PROGRAM SPOT-CHECK INSPECTION

1. Overall Program Grade: SAT / UNSAT

2. Are the Division Officer and the LCPO familiar with the Enlisted Distribution and Verification Report (EDVR) and the Activity Manning Document (AMD) and their location?   YES / NO

3. Do they effectively use the documents to verify manning levels, NEC losses/gains and PRDs to ensure qualified personnel are on board to maintain installed equipment carry out FISKE's assigned mission?   YES / NO

4. Have manning/NEC shortfalls been formally identified and corrective action initiated?   YES / NO

5. Remarks/Comments:

_____
_____
_____
_____
_____

                                        _____
                                                Signature

(10) Service Record Audit
USS FISKE (DDG XX)
DIVISION IN THE SPOTLIGHT
PERSONNEL SERVICE RECORD AUDIT

DATE: _____

FOR _____ DIVISION

Rate	Name	DOR	TIR	ADSD	EAOS	PRD	SDCD	P2	UPDATE	PNEC	GCAD	PEBD	LAST EVAL

OVERALL GRADE: SAT OR UNSAT
TOTAL RECORDS SCREENED:

PERSONNEL OFFICER

(11) Disbursing Pay Record Audit

USS FISKE (DDG XX)

DIVISION IN THE SPOTLIGHT

DISBURSING PAY RECORD AUDIT

FOR _____ DIVISION

DATE: _____

SERVICE MEMBER	CURRENT ENTITLED TO PAY GRADE	BAQ	ENTITLED TO VHA	CURRENT LEASE AGREEMENT	ENTITLED TO CSP	ENTITLED TO SDIP	EAOS EXPIRE W/IN 60 DAYS
SERVICE MEMBER	ENROLLED W-4	O/S TRAVEL	OVER	PAY ADJ	RETURNED FSA	SGLI	LEAVE BALANCE

* MBRS DOES NOT HAVE RENTAL AGREEMENT (i.e., depns staying w/ parents or friends) AND PROVIDED LEASE/RENT AGREEMENT NOTICED.

** SERVICE MEMBER'S RECORD ELECTED $100,000.00 INSURANCE.

TOTAL MEMBER: 1

OVERALL GRADE: SAT

VERY RESPECTFULLY,

(12) Medical/Dental Division Review
USS FISKE (DDG XX)
MEDICAL/DENTAL INSPECTION SPOT-CHECK
FORM FOR _____ DIVISION

DATE: ____

From: SMDR
To: Commanding Officer
        Executive Officer
        ____ Department Head
        ____ Division Officer
Subj: MEDICAL/DENTAL DIVISIONAL REVIEW

1. Overall Grade: SAT / UNSAT
2. Total records screened: _____
3. The following areas were assessed: # SAT # DUE # N/A
   a. Immunizations   ____   ____   ____
   b. Physicals   ____   ____   ____
   c. Audiograms (includes ear protection   ____   ____   ____
   d. Eye exams (includes special eyewear)   ____   ____   ____
   e. Dental exams (annual)   ____   ____   ____
   f. Nutritional counseling for personnel
      on command fitness program   ____   ____   ____
4. Personnel enrolled in Exceptional Family
   Member Program: ____

Remarks/Comments:

_____
Signature

(13) Safety Inspection Form

DATE: _____

From: Assistant Safety Officer
To: Commanding Officer
Via: Executive Officer
        _____ Safety Officer
        _____ Division Officer
Subj: _____ Division in the Spotlight Safety Inspection
Encl: (1) _____ Division Safety Inspection Form

1. Sir, division is responsible for _____ spaces. The following is a list of safety deficiencies which were identified and corrected:

2. _____ is _____ Division Safety Petty Officer, he is PQS qualified. When quotas are available, _____ will attend Forces Afloat Safety School.

Overall evaluation:

(14) Personnel Electrical/Electronic Equipment Report

DATE: _____

From: Electrical/Electronic (circle one) Safety Officer
To: Commanding Officer
Via: Executive Officer
        Department Head
        Division Officer
Subj: RESULTS OF ELECTRICAL/ELECTRONIC
        SAFETY INSPECTION CONDUCTED FOR
        _____ DIVISION ON _____ .
                                    (DATE)
OVERALL GRADE: SAT   UNSAT

1. Total number of Personal Electrical/Electronic Items on
   record for the Division.   _____
2. Number of items checked/passed.   _____
3. Number of items not checked/failed (detailed in remarks)   _____

Remarks:

_____

_____

_____

_____

_____

_____

_____

_____

_____

_____

                                        _____
                                        Signature

(15) Electrical Safety Readiness Assessment
                                               DATE: _____

From: Electrical Safety Officer
To: Commanding Officer
Via: Executive Officer
        _____ Department Head
        _____ Division Officer
Subj: ELECTRICAL SAFETY ASSESSMENT
COMPARTMENT NO: _____
NAME OF COMPT: _____   OVERALL GRADE:
DIVISION RESP: _____   SAT / UNSAT

NOTE: THIS CHECKLIST, BASED ON OPNAVINST 5100.19 (SERIES), APPENDIX B7-4, ASSISTS THE INSPECTOR IN IDENTIFYING ELECTRICAL SAFETY DISCREPANCIES THROUGHOUT THE SHIP. DISCREPANCIES ARE LISTED IN THE "REMARKS" SECTION.

A. LIGHTING FIXTURE/SYSTEMS   NR DISC
    1. Fixtures mounted, secured, and housing
        properly grounded.
    2. Fixture covers free of cracks, paint, and
        discoloration.   ____
    3. Lamps/bulbs in working condition?   ____
B. SWITCHES/BREAKERS/ABTs
    1. Properly mounted and secure.
    2. Switches covered with rubber boots.   ____
    3. Labels in place.   ____
    4. Enclosures free of dents, cracks, or holes.   ____
C. RECEPTACLES
    1. Receptacles properly mounted and secure.   ____
    2. Receptacles are 3-prong.   ____
    3. Receptacles free of cracks and paint.   ____
    4. Receptacle boxes free of dents.   ____
    5. Receptacles show evidence of overheating.   ____
D. ELECTRICAL DISTRIBUTION PANELS
    1. Free of overfusing (tamper seal intact).   ____
    2. Panels properly mounted and secure.   ____
    3. Panel locks, sliding-bolts, etc., complete and in
        working condition.   ____
    4. Panels labeled.   ____
    5. Panels free of dents, cracks, or holes?   ____
    6. Panel front accessible.   ____
    7. Ground indicators operational and free of ground.   ____
E. PORTABLE/MOBILE ELECTRICAL/ELECTRONIC
    EQUIPMENT
    1. Equipment safety check IAW PMS.   ____
    2. Equipment provided with 3-pronged plug.   ____

  3. If not 3-prong, is plug stamped or marked with "UL
     approved," double insulated?   _____
F. CABLES AND CABLEWAYS
  1. Space free of dead-ended cables.   _____
  2. Cables and cableways clean and not being used
     for stowage/hangers.   _____
G. MOTORS AND CONTROLLERS
  1. Motors properly grounded.   _____
  2. Controllers marked and labeled.   _____
  3. Controllers free of dents or holes.   _____
H. SWITCHBOARDS
  1. Approved matting installed adjacent to switchboards.   _____
  2. Matting cemented to the deck.   _____
     a. If not cemented, outline of matting stenciled on
        deck with "electrical grade matting required" inside
        of stencil using ¾″ letters or larger.   _____
  3. Matting surface free of cracks, punctures,
     perforations, and conductive particles.   _____
  4. Circuit diagram and CPR instruction posted.   _____
  5. Approved shorting probe available with end of
     handle filled with RTV.   _____
  6. Electrical rubber gloves available.   _____
  7. Airway tube available.   _____
  8. "Warning! High Voltage" signs posted.   _____
I. ELECTRICAL/ELECTRONIC WORKBENCHES
  1. Work surfaces insulated:
     a. Exposed front surfaces of cabinet and auxiliary
        table assemblies.   _____
     b. Knee surface under auxiliary table.   _____
     c. Drawer fronts and work surfaces.   _____
     d. Work surfaces with electrical grade matting.   _____
     e. Deck area—immediately in front of workbench and
        under auxiliary table with electrical grade matting.   _____
  2. Grounding straps with alligator clips provided.   _____
  3. Emergency electrical disconnects provided and
     labeled "electrical/electronic workbench emergency

electrical disconnect" source indicated (115V, 440V, 60HZ, etc.) and readily accessible.   ____

4. "Danger, Working on Energized Electrical/Electronic Equipment Is Prohibited on This Workbench" sign posted on workbenches not authorized for energized work.   ____

5. CPR instruction posted.   ____

_____

_____

_____

_____

Signature

Appendix 4

Sample Standing Orders

USS FISKE (DDG XX) INSTRUCTION 3121.1C

Subj: COMMANDING OFFICER'S STANDING ORDERS
Ref: (a) U.S. Navy Regulations, 1990
    (b) OPNAVINST 3120.1 (Series) SORM
    (c) Navigational Rules COMDTINST M16672.2C
    (d) ATP-1(C) Volume I, Allied Maritime Tactical
        Instructions and Procedures
    (e) ATP-1(C) Volume II, Allied Maritime Tactical
        Signal and Maneuvering Book
    (f) Watch Officer's Guide
Encl: (1) Standing Orders

1. *Purpose.* To promulgate my Standing Orders to the Officer of the Deck (OOD) while FISKE is underway or at anchor. Supplemental Night Orders will be issued daily when underway or as required. This instruction amplifies references (a) through (f), which contain information basic to OOD responsibilities.
2. *Discussion.*
   a. Reference (a) formalizes the time-honored tradition of the Commanding Officer's absolute responsibility for the safety of his or her ship and the ship's crew.
   b. As an OOD in FISKE, your responsibilities are clear: do not collide or ground. You will not go wrong if, in peacetime, you act to keep the ship safe, and in battle, you carry out the mission.
   c. I will never criticize an OOD who maneuvers FISKE into

open sea room because they are uncertain of navigation or are concerned about maneuvering safety.

3. *Responsibility.* As the Commanding Officer, I am completely and inescapably responsible for this ship, its equipment, and the lives of all personnel on board. I depend upon and trust you to assist me in this responsibility with forehandedness and action, and by informing me promptly and fully of any event or occurrence which bears upon the safety and operability of FISKE.

4. *Action.*

   a. These orders are permanent. If there is ever a conflict between these Standing Orders and my supplemental Night Orders, the Night Orders take precedence. However, bring the conflict to my immediate attention.

   b. The Navigator will maintain FISKE's Night Order Book and keep a copy of these Standing Orders in front of that book along with a "Record of Acknowledgment" sheet. Each Officer of the Deck, Junior Officer of the Deck, Tactical Action Officer, Combat Systems Coordinator, Combat Systems Officer of the Watch, CIC Watch Officer, CIC Watch Supervisor, Engineering Officer of the Watch, Quartermaster of the Watch, and Boatswain's Mate of the Watch will read and signify they understand these orders monthly, by signing the "Record of Acknowledgment" sheet. Supplemental Night Orders prepared by the Navigator for my signature will be reviewed by the Operations Officer (who will make appropriate operational entries as well as verify the correctness of the Navigator's entries) and the Executive Officer prior to my review.

   c. All officers or chief petty officers standing an operational underway watch between 2000 and 0800 shall initial the Night Orders prior to relieving the watch.

   d. Recommendations for changes or additions to this instruction may be made at any time. Forward them to the Senior Watch Officer or the Navigator.

   e. The Navigator is responsible for the proper maintenance of this instruction and will maintain the Night Order Book, consisting of a copy of this instruction and my supplemental Night Orders, as a permanent record.

J. Barry

Distribution (via LAN):
All Officers
All Chief Petty Officers
All First Class Petty Officers
All Quartermasters

LIST OF EFFECTIVE ORDERS

Order Number	Title
1.	Responsibility and Authority
2.	Required Reports
3.	Conduct of the Watch
4.	Relieving the Watch
5.	Restricted Maneuvering Doctrine
6.	Man Overboard Procedures
7.	Navigation
8.	Formation Steaming
9.	Planeguard Operations
10.	Communications
11.	Helicopter Operations
12.	Ship Anchored
13.	Towed Array Operations
14.	Embarked Staff

STANDING ORDER NUMBER ONE
RESPONSIBILITY AND AUTHORITY

1. *Command Responsibility.*
   a. I am completely and inescapably responsible for FISKE and all lives, equipment, and property onboard at all times. Your designation as an Officer of the Deck (OOD) means you have earned my trust and confidence in both your watch-standing abilities and your mature judgment.

b. Never hesitate to call me. I am always on duty. When reports are required, make certain I understand your report. I will never criticize an OOD for reporting any situation deemed important. If you have any doubt whether I understand your report, or if you would just feel better if I were on the Bridge, request my presence. In an emergency, concentrate on the safety of the ship and have the BMOW pass "Captain to the Bridge" on the 1MC. Should my immediate presence be required in CIC, modify the above word to, "Captain to Combat."

2. *Officer of the Deck (OOD).*

a. The Officer of the Deck is responsible for the conduct of the watch and for compliance with these Standing Orders. Underway, the OOD is the officer on watch charged with the safety of the ship. During the period of the watch, the Officer of the Deck has authority from me over all other officers and crewmen except the Executive Officer. When I am absent from the Bridge the Executive Officer and the Senior Watch Officer have the authority to relieve the Officer of the Deck when, in their judgment, such urgent action is considered necessary for the safety of the ship. The Officer of the Deck has the authority to take immediate action without waiting for my arrival on the Bridge when, in his or her judgment, that action is necessary to ensure the safety of the ship or crew. As OOD you have the responsibility of keeping me promptly and completely informed on the action you do take.

b. When in Condition III or a higher state of readiness, the Tactical Action Officer (TAO) will direct the employment of weapons systems subject to my negation. The OOD will follow direction from the TAO unless such direction or maneuvers will cause imminent danger to the ship. Call me in either case.

c. You are required to be rested, alert, and, at night, with your eyes adapted to darkness upon taking the watch. If you do not feel fit to take the watch, notify me of the circumstances. If you become ill while on watch, call a relief and notify me. You will remain on the Bridge and in charge until properly relieved. These principles apply to each member of your watch team.

d. The use of standard phraseology and repeat back is of utmost importance to clear understanding of orders. Use standard phraseology and repeat back and ensure that all members of the watch team do likewise. Standard phraseology is prescribed in reference (f).

e. Although "control" in the sense of positive speed or course orders may be passed to the TAO, USWE, ASUWC, or EWC under certain circumstances, CONN in the accepted sense, and the responsibility it entails, never leaves the Bridge. The relief of the watch and of the CONN shall be distinct and separate actions on the part of the relieving OOD. The officer relieving the CONN shall in every case inform the watch that he or she has the CONN so that no doubt will exist as to the control of the rudder and engines. Should I give a direct order to the Helm or Lee Helm at any time, it will be understood that I have assumed the CONN. The officer having the CONN will announce that I have assumed the CONN to preclude any misunderstanding. The relieving officer shall require the Helmsman to report the helm and engine status immediately after he assumes the CONN. The fact that the CONN has been taken by myself or the Executive Officer does not relieve the OOD from his or her responsibility to keep the whole situation in hand, to carry out the normal routine, and to state positively and forcefully opinions and recommendations for the safe operation of the ship.

f. Relationship with the Senior Watch Officer. Immediately notify the Senior Watch Officer if any of your assigned watchstanders are incapable of performing their duties. This order applies to all watchstations, including the OOD and other key watchstanders. The Senior Watch Officer has the authority to assume the Deck or Conn whenever such action is deemed necessary.

g. Relationship with the Navigator. The OOD shares responsibility for the safe navigation of FISKE with the Navigator.

The Navigator shall advise the OOD of safe courses and speeds to steer; however, I do not expect the OOD to blindly follow all recommendations provided. The OOD must evaluate each maneuvering recommendation against the actual situation.

(1) Provided the OOD evaluates the Navigator's maneuvering recommendation as sound, such advice is sufficient authority to change course. Report the change to me after it has been taken if insufficient time exists to obtain my concurrence in advance.

(2) Before assuming your watch, review the chart actually in use and observe FISKE's present position and predicted track. Satisfy yourself that the methods being used to fix our position are valid and sufficient. Bear in mind all available information must be considered.

(3) Never hesitate to call the Navigator at any time to check FISKE's position or projected track during your watch. The Navigator—like the Captain—is on watch 24 hours a day.

(4) The Navigator is authorized to summon me to the bridge by any means necessary (including the 1MC) when, in his or her opinion, the OOD is not taking sufficient action necessary to preserve FISKE's safety.

STANDING ORDER NUMBER TWO
REQUIRED REPORTS

1. The following is a list of reports you, as OOD, are required to make to me when they occur:

   a. General

   (1) Relief of the deck when I am on the Bridge.

   (2) In the event you are relieved by the Executive Officer or Senior Watch Officer or feel it is unsafe to follow the direction of the TAO.

   (3) All occurrences the OOD feels are worthy of note by me, especially those which bear on the safety and operability of FISKE.

    (4) Conflicting instructions from higher authority or orders from an embarked staff contrary to these standing orders or standard procedure.

    (5) Conflicting interpretations of tactical signals, maneuvers, or situations between yourself and the TAO or CICWO.

    (6) Any deviation from these Standing Orders or my Night Orders.

    (7) Anytime you decline to relieve the watch, whatever the reason.

b. Formal Reports

    (1) 12 O'clock Reports. The hour of 1200 with the following required reports. This report may be made by the Messenger if I am not on the Bridge and it will contain:

        (a) Muster Report.

        (b) Combat Systems 12 O'clock Report (Magazine Temps).

        (c) Fuel and Water Report.

        (d) Draft Report.

        (e) Boat Report.

        (f) Chronometer Report.

        (g) Position Report.

    (2) Position reports at 0800 and 2000 when underway. These reports may be made by the messenger if I am not on the Bridge. This report is also made to an embarked commander at 0800, 1200, and 2000.

c. Schedule

    (1) Commencement and completion of significant evolutions.

    (2) Inability to complete check-off lists or steps for:

        (a) Getting Underway.

        (b) Entering Port.

        (c) Helicopter Operations.

        (d) Underway Replenishment.

    (3) Expected arrival and departure times of VIP and Senior officers.

d. Emergencies
  (1) Whenever in doubt or when a possible emergency is developing.
  (2) When you take necessary action in an emergency to avoid collision, grounding, or other danger.
  (3) Planes and vessels in distress.
  (4) Any accidents or injuries to personnel.
  (5) Any potentially dangerous, unusual, or important sighting such as breakers, unlighted or derelict vessels or flotsam, discolored water, audible or visible emergency/distress signals, waterspouts, and any other occurrence you deem out of the ordinary.
e. Weather
  (1) Marked changes in the weather, specifically:
    (a) Sustained true wind of 20 knots or greater.
    (b) Wind speed changes of 10 knots or veer of 20 degrees in one hour.
    (c) Increase in seas of 2 feet in a two-hour period.
    (d) Barometric pressure at or below 29.5 inches *or* a change in barometric pressure of 0.04 inches in one hour *or* 0.10 inches in a four-hour period.
    (e) When temperature drops to 45 degrees Fahrenheit.
    (f) If visibility changes significantly or reduces to 5 miles or less.
f. Navigation
  (1) When any navigational sensor indicates FISKE is standing into danger.
  (2) When crossing the 50 fathom curve.
  (3) If fathometer depth and charted depth differ by more than 20%, or when the fathometer unexpectedly reads less than 100 feet.
  (4) When the ship's position is in doubt.
  (5) When fixes plot outside the drag circle at anchor, or when there is an indication of dragging.
  (6) When navigational sightings are not sighted within 15 minutes of expected time, 15 degrees of expected bear-

ing, or radar landfall is not made within 10% of expected range. Call the Navigator too.

(7) Unexpected deviation in the magnetic compass.

(8) When turning on lights during a period when FISKE is fully darkened or has lights dimmed.

(9) When encountering any unexpected buoys, navigation lights, or hazards to navigation.

(10) Whenever fixes deviate from the Navigator's track by 5 miles or 10% of the distance to the nearest unsafe water, whichever is less.

(11) Upon entering inland/international waters as determined by COLREGS Demarcation Line.

g. Contacts. Maintain a maneuvering board plot of all contacts that will have a CPA of 10,000 yards or less. Do not delay required action for want of information. Maintain a scope-head plot on all contacts within 20 nautical miles.

(1) Call me for any surface contact with a CPA less than 10,000 yards giving:

    (a) Present position (relative).

    (b) Target angle.

    (c) Bearing drift.

    (d) CPA.

    (e) Appropriate Rule(s) of the Road.

    (f) Maneuvering intentions.

(2) Contact Reports should be clear and succinct. Make the report as follows: "Captain, this is (name), OOD. I have a (type of vessel, if known), off my (port/stbd bow/beam/quarter) with a target angle of _____ . The vessel has (left/right) bearing drift and has a CPA off my (port/stbd bow/beam/quarter) at a range of _____ yards. This is a (meeting/crossing/overtaking) situation. I am the (stand on/give way vessel). My intentions are to _____ ."

(3) Any difference in contact data between Bridge and CIC.

(4) When a contact is identified as a naval vessel, inform me of the Commanding Officer's identity and relative se-

niority. Promptly request or grant permission to proceed on duty assigned, as appropriate, then advise me.

(5) When other naval vessels or auxiliaries are operating in the vicinity.

(6) Presence of a potentially hostile ship, submarine, or aircraft.

(7) Prior to calling away the SNOOPIE (Shipping, Naval or Otherwise Photographic Intelligence and Evaluation) Team to gather information on a vessel with intelligence value or significance.

h. Communications

(1) Tactical signals, including changes in formation, course, or speed of this or any other ship in company.

(2) Any changes in the EMCON condition in effect.

(3) Loss of communications on any maneuvering or warfare commander circuit for a period of 10 minutes.

i. Maneuvering

(1) Inform me of unplanned course and speed changes prior to their execution except as follows:

(a) When you are required to take immediate action to avoid risk of collision in accordance with the Navigation Rules.

(b) To avoid objects in the water ahead which may be hazardous to the sonar dome or screws.

(c) Course and speed adjustments required to maintain PIM or assigned station.

(d) Course and speed changes required to patrol an assigned screen sector.

(e) "Immediate Execute" signals from the OTC, which alter our course or speed. Inform me as soon thereafter as practical.

j. Formation Steaming

(1) Whenever a ship joins or departs the formation.

(2) All sonar contacts held by FISKE or by other units in our formation/exercise.

(3) Breakdown of ship(s) in company.

(4) When station limits are exceeded by 2 degrees in bearing or 5% of range.

(5) When unable to maintain station, when other ships in company are significantly out of station, or when other ships in company change course or speed unexpectedly.

(6) If any unit questions your movements or actions, or issues a reprimand.

(7) If unable to comply with a tactical signal.

k. Material

(1) Fresh water drops below 70% and every 10% change below that.

(2) Any degradation to steering system or inability to conduct daily equipment shifts or drills.

(3) All degradations of equipment which may affect FISKE's safety or could have an adverse impact on current or planned operations.

l. Environmental. Prior to using the main drain system, regardless of the ship's distance from land.

2. Do not assume that because I am on the Bridge I see and/or hear all contacts, signals, voice transmissions, etc. Make reports on the assumption that I have not. Do not be reticent about reporting any unusual circumstances or events, whether internal or external to FISKE, even if only a matter of interest. Keep me fully informed at all times. I will do the same for you in order to permit you to discharge your duties most effectively.

3. Minimize multiple reports to me on the same event. The most appropriate watchstander should make a report to me (e.g., the TAO should report a loss of the AN/SPY-1D and the OOD should call regarding HELO OPS). The same report from multiple watchstanders is an indication of poor internal coordination. Department Heads may, as appropriate, call me with amplifying information.

4. On occasion, I may direct that all reports be made to the Executive Officer. When I do so, the Executive Officer will decide if a report is critical enough to warrant my immediate attention. I will be very specific with watchstanders when I exercise this option.

STANDING ORDER NUMBER THREE
CONDUCT OF THE WATCH

1. *General.* As Officer of the Deck, you are in full charge of everyone standing watch in FISKE. As such, you are responsible for continuous improvement of your watch team. You are also responsible for the watchstanding standards of all crew members assigned to your watch section.

2. *Safety.*
   a. Whenever you consider it dangerous for personnel to go topside (e.g., the weatherdecks, mast, etc.), restrict such access or traffic by passing appropriate word over the 1MC. When it is imperative to visit such locations, take all required and prudent precautions such as:
      (1) Obtain my permission.
      (2) Get the best person for the job.
      (3) Ensure the "buddy system" is used.
      (4) Insist on life preservers and tended safety lines.
      (5) Alter course and/or speed if such action provides more favorable conditions.
      (6) Ensure competent supervision.
      (7) Ensure you are included in the specially tailored Safety Brief that must be conducted prior to beginning any such visit.
   b. Remember to give warnings over all 1MC circuits when you anticipate heavy rolls or heels.
   c. Always ensure the After Lookout is properly equipped and posted where best suited to prevailing weather conditions and upcoming operations. The After Lookout must always have binoculars, a life ring, light, and smoke float immediately available. Ensure he or she knows what is expected in the event of a man overboard.

3. *Required Permission.* Obtain my permission prior to:
   a. Sending sailors aloft.
   b. Sending sailors over the side.
   c. Setting special details.

    d. Allowing work on any energized circuits or equipment containing a component with more than 30 volts potential.

    e. Allowing anyone to enter a fuel tank, void, or sump.

    f. Transferring or handling live ammunition.

    g. Testing main engines.

    h. Turning shafts.

4. *Watch Administration.*

    a. The Executive Officer runs the ship. Carry out the daily routine as published in the Plan of the Day and keep the Executive Officer advised of any changes you feel are necessary.

    b. Control the proper use of the general announcing system and the General, Chemical, Collision, and Flight Crash alarms and the ship's whistle.

    c. Keep tactical publications and CMS handy and be prepared to use them.

    d. Render honors to passing ships as required by custom and regulations.

    e. Ensure the Executive Officer and Department Heads are promptly informed of changes to the tactical situation, operational schedule or the approach of heavy weather and any other circumstance which will require action on their part or a change in routine.

5. *CIC Relationship.* Insist CIC employ its full range of capabilities to keep you informed of the surface and air pictures. CIC is required to scopehead track and report to you all surface contacts within 20 miles. For contacts with a CPA < 10,000 yards, maneuvering board and DDRT will be used to provide course, speed, CPA, and time of CPA, until you authorize CIC to cease reporting. Ensure this information is provided to you promptly.

    a. Exchange information with CIC. Information between the Bridge and CIC must flow in both directions. Always keep CIC informed of your course and speed, prevailing weather conditions, and any changes that occur. Stay attuned to the requirement to provide CIC with visual information they may not have. Most importantly, always keep CIC apprised of your intentions in sufficient time to permit them to utilize the information.

   b. Instruct your CIC Watch Officer to contact you directly whenever he or she feels a danger exists or your actions are not understood. Make certain you convey your intentions clearly and directly to the CIC Watch Officer whenever necessary. Take advantage of opportunities to discuss possible courses of action with your CIC Watch Officer for mutual support and more effective watch section coordination. The general principles outlined below provide additional guidance:

      (1) When maneuvering to avoid other ships, or recommending a maneuver, always use sufficient rudder to ensure your intentions are clearly apparent to the other vessel.

      (2) Insist CIC keep track of the identity and position of other ships in company at all times when they are within radar range.

      (3) In situations where risk of collision exists (CPA < 10,000 yds), require CIC utilize both a record geographic plot (DRT) as well as the maneuvering board relative plot.

   c. If you and CIC ever disagree regarding an impending situation, notify me immediately.

6. *Relationship with the Engineering Officer of the Watch (EOOW).*

   a. The Engineering Officer of the Watch (EOOW) is responsible for the safe and proper operation of FISKE's propulsion, electrical, and auxiliary systems. I require him to operate the engineering plant in accordance with good engineering practices, and strict adherence to approved specific operating and casualty procedures (EOP and EOCC).

   b. The OOD shall normally limit his or her orders for control of the engineering plant to:

      (1) Orders to start or secure main engines after first obtaining my permission.

      (2) Speed changes by use of the throttle controls, engine

revolution indicators, IVCS Net 83, or the 21MC. In an emergency where none of the primary means of communication are available, the 1MC may be used.

c. The EOOW is required to report any changes, conditions, or casualties to machinery or equipment which may limit ship's operation.

d. The EOOW is required to request permission from the OOD for the following:

    (1) Start Main Engines and Gas Turbine Generators (except as noted in the Restricted Maneuvering Doctrine).

    (2) Pump bilges.

    (3) Place any vital machinery or equipment out of commission for preventive maintenance.

    (4) Refueling boats.

e. The OOD shall inform the EOOW of the following:

    (1) Anticipated upcoming speed and/or power requirements (as early as practicable).

    (2) Anticipated and actual times of:

        (a) Setting or entering Restricted Maneuvering Conditions.

        (b) Arriving at or departing from all pollution discharge restriction zones.

    (3) Whenever FISKE enters or passes through areas containing debris or vegetation which might clog sea chests/suctions or cooling water systems.

    (4) Any other operations affecting the engineering plant.

    (5) Abnormal stack smoke emission.

    (6) Unexpected liquid discharge overboard.

    (7) Whenever FISKE is within 12 miles of land or within 2,000 yards directly astern of another vessel (distilling plant operations).

STANDING ORDER NUMBER FOUR
RELIEVING THE WATCH

1. *Prior to Relieving the Watch.* The Officer of the Deck (underway) shall:

a. Ensure you are physically fit, appropriately clothed, equipped, and (for night watches) have adequate night vision to stand an alert watch.

   (1) You will avail yourself of sufficient rest before relieving the watch. You will not relieve when feeling sick or overly tired, or if you judge yourself unable to fulfill your responsibilities as a watchstander. Any watchstander who has not had a total of five hours of sleep in the previous 24 hours must notify his or her immediate supervisor who will specifically evaluate the relief's ability to stand a proper watch. The OOD must report this "lack of sleep" condition to the Senior Watch Officer. In the event the watch is not relieved under these circumstances, I shall be immediately notified.

   (2) If you become ill, you shall call a relief and notify the Senior Watch Officer and myself.

   (3) Upon watch relief, both the on-coming and off-going watchstanders shall satisfy themselves that the relieving watchstander is fit to relieve the watch. If not, that watch shall not be relieved.

   (4) Any changes to assignments on any underway watch bill must be submitted to the Senior Watch Officer, recommended by the Executive Officer, and specifically approved by me before that change goes into effect.

b. Ensure you have a thorough knowledge and clear understanding of FISKE's material and operational status and any changes expected during your watch. To this end, you shall:

   (1) Visit CIC and get briefed by the CICWO or TAO. Inspect radar and EW displays and status boards.

   (2) Read and be familiar with the schedule of events in the Plan of the Day, PRE-EX messages, and any special instructions. Read and initial my Night Order Book and seek verbal amplification from myself, the Executive Officer, the Operations Officer and/or the Navigator if you have any doubts or confusion regarding FISKE's status, upcoming evolutions, or any other aspect of your watch.

   (3) Study the navigation chart. Note our present position, planned track, all possible navigation hazards, and available navigation aids.

c. Ensure a complete exchange of information with the previous Officer of the Deck, including as a minimum data with regard to:

   (1) The Night Orders. Review and carry out my Night Orders. Check the data contained in the Night Orders against the navigation plot, OPORDER, and any special orders. If there is any discrepancy or doubt concerning FISKE's position, situation, or the intent of the Night Orders, do not relieve the watch. Call me immediately.

   (2) The accuracy of the ship's position. Make yourself aware of all navigation aids in use or expected. Check the chart and bearing book for completeness, accuracy, and neatness. If any questions concerning FISKE's position exist, notify the OOD and call the Navigator prior to relieving.

   (3) Set and Drift experienced or expected.

   (4) OPORDERS, Plans, and SOEs in effect including events scheduled during your watch.

   (5) Tactical formation and organization, including FISKE's station and any unexpected signals.

   (6) Gyrocompass in use and all compass errors.

   (7) Status of communications circuits and stations responsible for guarding those circuits.

   (8) The surface radar picture, the location, identity, and voice calls of the guide, OTC, OCE, Screen Commander, other ships in company, and all surface contacts.

   (9) Status of all contacts, to include relative position, course and speed, CPA and time of CPA, and whether or not I have been notified.

   (10) Existing and forecasted weather.

   (11) Our course, speed, and propulsion plant status, to include major equipment out of commission and the resultant impact on FISKE's mobility.

(12) Steering pumps and units in use.

(13) Material condition set, condition of readiness, and EMCON status.

(14) Status of weapons systems and navigational equipment.

(15) Any major equipment out of commission and the estimated time of repair (ETR).

(16) Any special work or evolution, such as weapons handling in progress, scheduled that may occur during your watch. In the case of planned evolutions, ascertain the status of their preparations.

(17) Lighting measures in effect. Ensure proper navigation lights are displayed. When, in your opinion, running lights are essential to safety USE THEM, even during darkened ship.

(18) Status of your watch section (relief, qualification, appearance, night adaptation, and rest). Neither the OOD nor the BMOW shall be relieved until all watch reliefs are on deck.

(19) All FISKE guard ship assignments.

(20) Any unexecuted orders, either external or internal.

(21) My location.

d. Ensure an inventory of Bridge publications and CRYPTO materials is made by the JOOD and initialed in the Bridge inventory folder.

2. *Pattern of Relieving.*

a. Promptness in reporting to relieve a watch is required as a matter of simple courtesy. The actual time required to relieve will vary and be circumstance dependent, and reliefs should plan to be on deck and complete their relieving process to conform with the times listed in sub-paragraph (g), below. However, officers must never allow themselves to feel pressured to relieve by a certain time. Never accept a watch until you are comfortable with the situation and have all information you require.

b. Whenever an oncoming watch officer feels he or she cannot relieve the watch, notify me.

c. Oncoming OODs will not normally be relieved until all signals have been executed.

d. The watch shall not be relieved during complex maneuvers which require the undivided attention of the OOD. At such times, the oncoming watch team should remain in the after portion of the Bridge or on the wings until the specific maneuver(s) is/are completed.

e. Relieving watch officers will be on the Bridge 15 minutes prior to actually relieving, in order to be thoroughly prepared to relieve and if not able to be there shall contact the Senior Watch Officer as far in advance as possible to arrange for a relief.

f. The actual change of the OOD watch shall be made with meticulous care and formality as the relieving OOD is completely responsible for FISKE once he or she has relieved. The OOD will not be relieved until the rest of the watch is relieved and settled, normally on the hour.

g. Watches will be relieved in accordance with the following schedule:

   (1) JOOD—1/2 hour before the hour
   (2) CICWO/TAO—15 minutes before the hour
   (3) OOD—on the hour

h. Be particularly alert during the change of the watch. Keep the noise level down. Remember, watches in ships around you are probably being changed at the same time. Additionally, any knowledgeable "adversary" will probably time his attacks to coincide with customary watch rotation times.

3. *Upon Relief.* The off-going Officer of the Deck (Underway) shall:

a. Review the Deck Log for accuracy and completeness, then sign it. Initial all corrections in the margin.

b. Debrief the BMOW and specific watchstanders, if appropriate, concerning the watch team's performance. "Continuous

Improvement" must always be your guiding goal in these debriefs.

4. *Declining to Relieve.*
   a. An officer may decline to relieve the deck when he or she:
      (1) Considers FISKE to be in peril.
      (2) Finds we are appreciably out of station.
      (3) Does not feel physically capable of relieving the watch.
      (4) Is not satisfied with the completeness of the tactical picture being turned over.
   b. Any officer who declines to relieve the deck, shall immediately notify me of this fact and state his or her reasons.

5. *Relieving the OOD Underway.*
   a. I may assume the Deck or Conn at any time. Normally, I will make the announcement, "This is the Captain. I have the Conn." However, should I ever give a direct order to the Helm or Lee Helm without such previous announcement, or should the Helmsmen or Lee Helmsman respond as though I had issued them a direct order, the Conning Officer shall immediately announce, "The Captain has the Conn." I will continue to exercise the Conn until it has been properly and positively turned over to another Conning Officer or OOD.
   b. There must never be any misunderstanding as to the identity of the Conning Officer. In case of doubt, it is the OOD's responsibility to immediately clarify who has the Conn. The question, "Captain, do you have the Conn?" is proper in this situation. Upon all such occasions, the OOD shall continue to perform those functions of which he or she has not been relieved. Specifically, the OOD shall continue to forcefully express recommendations regarding the safe and proper operation of FISKE.
   c. The Executive Officer, when on the Bridge at sea, may relieve the OOD in any situation when I am not on the Bridge when such action is necessary for FISKE's safety.
   d. The Executive Officer, when in CIC at sea, may also relieve the TAO or CIC Watch Officer in any situation when I am not in CIC when such action is necessary for FISKE's safety.

e. The Senior Watch Officer has the authority to assume the Deck or Conn whenever such action is deemed necessary and I am not on the Bridge.

STANDING ORDER NUMBER FIVE
RESTRICTED MANEUVERING POLICY

1. *Purpose.* This instruction provides guidance to operate FISKE during "Restricted Maneuvering Conditions."

2. *Background.* EOCC consists of technically correct, logically sequenced procedures for responding to and controlling commonly occurring casualties. When properly followed, these procedures place the plant in a safe, stable condition while the cause is determined. However, these procedures do not consider the impact that controlling or immediate actions might have during operations in close proximity to danger. Therefore, this order specifies FISKE policy and procedures to be followed whenever ship safety takes precedence over propulsion plant protection.

3. *Restricted Maneuvering Doctrine.* "Restricted Maneuvering Conditions" exist whenever FISKE is:

   a. Operating in restricted waters.

   b. Steaming in close formation at reduced standard distance or interval.

   c. Engaged in replenishment at sea operations alongside another vessel (UNREP).

   d. Whenever "Restricted Maneuvering Casualty Control Procedures are now in effect" is passed over the 1MC.

4. *Maximum Reliability Lineup.* This is a specific propulsion and electrical plant configuration which provides FISKE maximum plant reliability. Maximum Reliability Lineup will be directed by me, the Executive Officer, or the Officer of the Deck, prior to entering a restricted maneuvering condition. Maximum Plant Reliability will be automatically set by the Engineering Officer of the Watch (EOOW) when:

   a. General Quarters is sounded.

   b. The Underway Replenishment Detail is set.

c. The Sea Detail is stationed for returning to port. In the foregoing circumstances, the EOOW will notify the OOD the
plant is being configured for Maximum Reliability. When
the Sea Detail is set for getting underway, the OOD may
grant the EOOW permission to bring the plant to Maximum
Reliability configuration once the Sea Detail is stationed, the
OOD is on the Bridge, communications are established with
the fantail (to ensure vicinity around screws are clear), and
communications are established between the OOD and
EOOW.

FISKE will never knowingly enter a Restricted Maneuvering Condition without first establishing the Maximum
Reliability Lineup configuration. "Manned and Ready" reports from Central Control Station (CCS) and After Steering
during the above details will *not* be made until all provisions
of Maximum Reliability Lineup have been satisfied. I will be
personally advised of any inability to achieve "Maximum
Reliability Lineup."

Whenever a "Maximum Reliability Lineup" is ordered,
the engineering plant will be configured as follows:
a. Main Propulsion
   - Full Power Mode.
   - GTM 16th stage bleed air valves CLOSED.
   - Oil Distribution (OD) Boxed manned.
b. Electrical Plant
   - Two Generators aligned to a ring bus; a third GTG will
     be "on" with its generator breaker open.
   - 14th stage bleed air valves CLOSED.
   - 60HZ Switchboards manned.
c. Steering Gear
   - After Steering manned by a qualified after steersman,
     engineman, electrician, and safety officer (normally
     AUXO).
   - Computer assisted manual mode of control.

Once established, no changes to the "Maximum Reliability Lineup" plant configurations are authorized unless ex-

pressly approved by me, the Executive Officer, or the OOD. No preventive or corrective maintenance or testing will be accomplished that might cause loss of electrical power or ship control. When "Maximum Reliability Lineup" is no longer required, "Secure from Restricted Maneuvering Casualty Control Procedures" will be passed over the 1MC.

5. *Restricted Maneuvering Casualty Control Procedures.* Restricted Maneuvering Casualty Control Procedures are only authorized when the following word is passed over the 1MC: "Restricted Maneuvering Casualty Control Procedures are now in effect."

Passing of this word must be logged in both the Deck and Engineering Logs. Central Control Station will repeat back "Restricted Maneuvering Casualty Control Procedures are in Effect" to the Bridge via NET 83.

I will limit the time FISKE operates under "Restricted Maneuvering Casualty Control Procedures" to only those times I feel engineering casualties would compound the potential for immediate danger due to maneuvering restrictions.

A verbal order to the EOOW from me, the Executive Officer, or OOD, in that hierarchy, takes precedence over any other means of transmitting propulsion orders from the Bridge to CCS, the SCU, or OD Box Operator (e.g., a verbal order from me over the 1MC takes precedence over orders received via the EOT).

The Restricted Maneuvering Casualty Control Procedures specified below are to be followed by all Bridge and Engineering watchstanders whenever FISKE is restricted in her ability to maneuver. Generally, these provisions do not differ from standard EOCC, except that:

EOCC casualty procedures will NOT be peremptorily taken if such actions will take shaft control or electrical power away without expressed permission from me, the Executive Officer, or OOD except as specifically outlined below.

All ship control stations will always be in communication and aware of ordered course and speed. All throttle control station Manual or Programmed Control Levers will precisely match ordered speed. After Steering personnel will always maintain a clear picture of the maneuvering situation.

a. *GTM CASUALTY.* Carry out EOCC procedures except:
  (1) Do not stop the last GTM on the affected shaft.
  (2) Do not transfer thrust control.
  (3) Do not move program control levers to idle.

Until so directed by me, the Executive Officer, or the OOD. For a post-shutdown fire, the PACC operator shall motor the affected GTM using high-pressure air.

b. *LOSS OF LUBE/FUEL/CRP OIL SYSTEM PRESSURE/MAJOR OIL LEAK.* Carry out EOCC procedures except:
  (1) Do not stop the last GTM on the affected shaft.
  (2) Do not transfer thrust control.
  (3) Do not order the affected shaft slowed, stopped, or locked.
  (4) Do not stop the affected lube/fuel/CRP oil service pumps unless a major leak in that system has been identified as the cause of the casualty.

Until so directed by me, the Executive Officer, or the OOD.

c. *REDUCTION GEAR/SHAFTING CASUALTY.* The EOOW shall report the casualty to the OOD and recommend slowing the ship or stopping the affected shaft. The OOD will acknowledge the report and direct the EOOW to postpone EOCC actions if the ship's safety is in jeopardy. Once the ship is clear of hazards and safe to maneuver, the OOD shall order full EOCC procedures.

d. *LOSS OF CONTROLLABLE REVERSIBLE PITCH PROPELLER (CRP) CONTROL.* Carry out EOCC procedures except:
  (1) Do not transfer thrust control to PACC.

The EOOW shall order the affected system OD Box operator to take local pitch control. Conning orders shall be passed by the Lee Helm via Net 83 to the OD Box operator who will acknowledge and answer desired pitch commands. If pitch is not controllable at the OD Box, the manual control valves will be placed in the "off" position, and treated as a loss of CRP hydraulic pressure.

e. *CLASS BRAVO FIRE IN A MAINSPACE*. Carry out EOCC and Main Space Fire Doctrine procedures except:

(1) Propulsion shafts *originating in an unaffected* space will not be slowed or stopped.

(2) A propulsion shaft *originating in the space containing the fire* will be trailed vice locked until so directed by me, the Executive Officer, or the OOD.

(3) Do not stop the lube oil service pump on the affected shaft, unless lube oil leak is the source of the fire.

If the fire becomes uncontrollable, full EOCC and Main Space Fire Doctrine procedures commence except the transfer of thrust control on the unaffected shaft, which will remain with the Helm.

f. *INADVERTENT SPACE HALON RELEASE*. The affected space shall be immediately evacuated and online equipment will remain in operation. Ventilation will commence and the space will be manned by watchstanders in Oxygen Breathing Apparatus (OBA) until the Gas Free Engineer certifies the space "safe for personnel."

6. *Battle Override*. Battle Override will be employed only with my permission except that the EOOW shall apply Battle Override to the last GTM on the last shaft during use of Restricted Maneuvering Casualty Control Procedures.

7. *Restricted Maneuvering Doctrine at General Quarters*. When GQ is sounded, configure the plant for Maximum Plant Reliability in accordance with the guidance contained on this Standing Order. When at General Quarters and the need to ensure propulsion and electrical continuity prudent, the Executive Officer, OOD, or I will order the setting of "Restricted Maneuvering Casualty Control Procedures." In this instance, the provisions of this order will be followed, except that OD Boxes will not be manned unless a casualty affecting CRP Control is experienced.

STANDING ORDER NUMBER SIX
MAN OVERBOARD PROCEDURES

1. *General.* Historical data compiled by the Naval Safety Center indicates that any person falling over the side only has a 70% chance of survival. I will probably not be on the Bridge when a person falls over the side. Both I and the person in the water are completely dependent upon the judgment and initial responses of the OOD. Accordingly, should a shipmate fall over the side, prompt and correct action on the part of the entire watch team will make the difference between life and death.

   a. During a shipboard recovery, initially maneuver to "try to run over" the individual.

   b. When you get close, fall off upwind and position him forward of the bridgewing, ideally beneath the J-Bar Davit.

2. *Procedures.* A basic, safe man overboard recovery will entail these fundamental steps:

   a. MANEUVER FISKE

      (1) Swing the stern away from the side the person fell over, using full rudder.

      (2) Normally, use a tight direct full-circle recovery (Anderson Turn), Williamson Turn, or Racetrack Turn or based on sighting, visibility, maneuvering limitations, speed, and anticipated recovery method. At very slow speeds and when the AN/SQR-19B Towed Array is deployed, it is best to use the RHIB.

   b. PASS THE WORD—TWICE—On all circuits

      (1) Three basic segments.

         (a) The words "Man overboard."

         (b) The "side."

         (c) Type "recovery" planned (ship, boat, or helo [if a helo is airborne in the area]).

   c. NOTIFY OTHER SHIPS

      (1) Sound SIX short blasts on ship's whistle.

      (2) Break OSCAR by day and two pulsating lights (red over red) by night.

 (3) Deploy smoke floats and a life ring.

 (4) Radio/telephone transmission.

d. MARK POSITION

 (1) All Lookouts (port, starboard) will deploy a smoke float. Additionally, the aft lookout will deploy a life ring with strobe light.

 (2) Keep the person in sight. Everyone topside who can see the person must point to the individual. During reduced visibility and at night, ensure people topside remain quiet—we may hear the person in the water before he or she can actually be seen.

 (3) On the Bridge, use the ARPA trackball to position the cursor close aboard astern to mark the approximate position of the person. Then depress the "TRUE MARKS" button to "freeze" a geographic point at the spot marked. This point will be helpful in verifying CIC's bearing and range to the individual.

 (4) Shift the DRT plot scale in CIC to the 200 yards per inch scale.

e. ESTABLISH COMMUNICATION WITH RECOVERY DECK STATIONS (Foc'sle or Boat Deck)

 (1) Monitor progress, readiness, and status of rescue detail.

 (2) Keep all stations informed of your intentions on IVCS nets and/or 1MC.

f. RIG/POSITION LIFESAVING EQUIPMENT

 (1) Search lights.

 (2) Heaving lines.

 (3) Swimmer's gear.

 (4) Debarkation nets.

 (5) J-bar davits/rescue collar.

g. POSITION PERSON IN WATER. Downwind forward of the weather break with all way off.

3. The above guidance is general in nature and will vary with the particular circumstances of each "man overboard" emergency. Before you label the situation as a classic maneuver, consider

who else is out there. For instance, is there a ship astern? Is a helo airborne and nearby? If our ability to maneuver is limited (proximity of other ships, TACTAS deployed, etc.) do not maneuver into a collision or a cascading casualty.

4. Preplanning, training, and practice are the only ways to recover a man overboard safely. You must always be ready for a man overboard emergency.

STANDING ORDER NUMBER SEVEN
NAVIGATION

1. *Requirements.* Keep yourself continually advised of FISKE's position, course, speed, and intended track. Personally supervise the navigation plot maintained by your QMOW and ensure an accurate, up-to-date DR plot is always maintained.

   a. Dependent upon EMCON in effect, you are directed to make free use of CIC, radar, sonar, fathometer, Global Positioning System (GPS), lookouts' visual bearings, and other means available to establish and/or verify FISKE's position. Do not blindly depend upon one NAV AID; use all sensors available. However, if even one sensor or means of navigating indicates FISKE is standing into danger, believe it, take appropriate precautionary action, and inform me.

   b. Positive knowledge of our position is never more imperative than when making landfall or in waters whose depth is 50 fathoms or less. In addition to charts in CIC and on the Bridge, separate charts will be prepared for me and the Conning Officer indicating the track, courses, and speeds FISKE is to follow.

   c. If you are ever in doubt of FISKE's position, or believe it could be substantially different than plotted, slow or stop the ship to remain in known good water. Immediately call me and the Navigator to the Bridge.

   d. Ensure FISKE's navigational position is fixed at least as often as indicated in the following matrix:

Area	Distance from Nearest Land	Fix Frequency
Restricted Waters	Less than 2 nautical miles	2 minutes
Piloting Waters	2–10 nautical miles	3–15 minutes as conditions warant
Coastal Waters	10–30 nautical miles	15 minutes
Enroute Navigation (open ocean)	Over 30 nautical miles	30 minutes

(1) A good rule of thumb for fix intervals is "if hazard to navigation falls within a circle whose radius is that of two DR intervals," then either the fix interval or ship's speed requires adjusting.

(2) The Bridge and CIC will each maintain an independent plot which will be compared after each fix. Set and Drift will be computed after every fix and shall be applied to subsequent DR positions to determine an EP in the event that planned fixes are not obtained.

(3) A DR position will be plotted on the Bridge and in CIC at least:
 (a) Every hour on the hour.
 (b) At the time of every course change.
 (c) At the time of every speed change.
 (d) For the time at which a fix was obtained.
 (e) For the time at which a running fix was obtained.
 (f) For the time at which a single LOP was obtained.

(4) Before entering restricted waters, the Navigation Detail will be set in sufficient time to avoid danger.

(5) All other navigational information available, e.g., GPS, soundings, DR track, visual navigational aids, shall be compared to the fix taken to ensure proper correlation. Should the various data not match with the fix taken, steps shall immediately be taken to determine the source of the error. Never place blind reliance on any single source of information. Should the position be in doubt, the OOD will first ensure that he or she is not standing

into danger (immediately take all way off the ship if necessary), then notify the Navigator and me.

(6) The Navigator is responsible for ensuring that both the Bridge and CIC are using the same track. I will sign all charts (Bridge and CIC) used in conjunction with entering/leaving port after satisfying myself with the information presented.

(7) Record all Navigational Sightings. Ensure positive identification of all navigational lights using a stopwatch. Call me and the Navigator promptly if an aid is not sighted within 15 minutes after the predicted time of sighting.

(8) Approach to Land or Shoal Water. Approach land no closer than 12 NM and enter water no shallower than 50 fathoms without my permission. Never take the ship into less than 10 fathoms of water unless I am on the Bridge or I otherwise direct such action.

2. *Sounds.* The following general procedures are in effect for the use of the fathometer, subject to modification by me. Depth readings will be taken and recorded:

a. Whenever a fix is taken.

b. When in water over 100 fathoms: at least hourly.

c. When in water over 100 feet but less than 100 fathoms: at least every 15 minutes.

d. When in water less than 100 feet: at least every 3 minutes.

e. Continuously during Sea and Anchor Detail and other times when maneuvering in restricted waters.

f. Use the fathometer at all times and compare the indicated depth with the chart, except as otherwise dictated by the EMCON conditions or other operational considerations.

g. *Shoaling.* The fathometer is normally the best indicator of shoaling water. Ensure its reading is compared with charted depth whenever a fix is obtained. The scale in use (i.e., fathoms or feet) must be proper for the anticipated charted depth. If FISKE is ever in a shoaling situation (fathometer depth is dangerously decreasing continuously), your first reaction should be to take all way off, verify position and fathometer accuracy, and call the Navigator and me.

3. *Navigational Running Lights.* Display required navigational running lights and shapes. Navigational running lights will be checked one-half hour prior to sunset and burned between the hours of sunset and sunrise or during reduced visibility unless otherwise ordered. Require the Boatswain's Mate of the Watch to report "All navigation lights are bright lights" hourly while navigation lights are burning. Remember that DIM lights do not comply with Navigation Rules and will not be used without my approval.

4. *Relationship with Navigator.*

   a. The Officer of the Deck shares responsibility with the Navigator for the safe navigation of the ship. In this regard OODs are not to blindly steer recommended courses, but are to make their own evaluations on each recommended action based on their knowledge of the tactical situation. Before relieving, you will have reviewed the chart actually in use, observed the present and predicted position of the ship during your watch, and satisfied yourself on the validity of the methods being employed to fix the ship's position. Do not hesitate to call the Navigator at any time to check the ship's position or its projected track during your watch.

   b. The Navigator shall advise the Officer of the Deck of a safe course to be steered, and the OOD shall regard such advice as sufficient authority to change course if timeliness requires such a course change, but the change will be reported to me immediately thereafter.

5. *Rules of the Road.*

   a. You are expected to know and comply with the Rules of the Road. This requires study and frequent review.

   b. You are expected to take all appropriate measures to avoid embarrassment to other vessels. If required to maneuver in accordance with the Rules of the Road, do so early. It is normally most appropriate to change course rather than speed, since this meticulously shows the other ship your actions.

Whether you change course or speed, make the change large enough that it is readily observable on the other ship. *TAKE ACTION EARLY.* The least desirable of many correct solutions, taken early, is preferable to the best solution taken too late.

c. Small craft operators are often ignorant of the Rules of the Road. Never assume that a small craft or sailboat will act lawfully, or even intelligently, in any given situation. Always anticipate the unexpected and leave yourself a way out. Do not hesitate to use the VHF Bridge to Bridge radio or whistle signals to alert the other vessel to the danger of the situation.

6. *General.*

a. The OOD will ensure the ARPA's plot is maintained in a condition appropriate to the existing conditions. At a minimum, auto tracking will be initiated on all surface tracks within 20 NM. While the OOD may adjust the ARPA as deemed best, it will normally be kept in "true" to assist me in rapidly assimilating the surface picture. The ARPA is an outstanding safety tool and I expect it to be used by Bridge watchstanders.

b. Maneuvering boards will be used on the Bridge and in CIC for surface tracks with CPAs < 10,000 yards. The DDRT will also be used for surface tracks with CPAs < 10,000 yards. The OOD will compare Bridge and CIC results, comparing these also with the ARPA.

c. When in piloting waters, ensure the gyro error is determined at least once each watch and posted on the bridge. It should be determined daily in the open sea.

d. Determine surface radar and/or repeater range and bearing errors and ensure they are posted on the Bridge.

e. Report to me and the Navigator radar landfall and the sighting of all land, shoals, rocks, lighthouses, beacons, discolored water, aids to navigation, and the like.

STANDING ORDER NUMBER EIGHT
FORMATION STEAMING

I will never criticize an OOD who maneuvers FISKE out of a station, sector, or screen and into open sea room because he or she is uncertain of navigation or maneuvering safety.

1. Anticipate maneuvers and events. Think ahead and formulate a plan. When joining a formation, have its disposition plotted well in advance and keep current positions of each ship. Report to me whenever a ship is joining or leaving the formation.

2. Be vigilant. You are your own best lookout. Use mechanical and electronic sensors and navigation aids, but do not become solely dependent on them. LOOK where you are going, step onto the open bridge wing on the side toward which you are about to turn. Learn to recognize aspects and determine approximate ranges with binoculars, particularly at night.

3. You are required to maintain an accurate up-to-date formation diagram including all ships with which we are in company.

4. Whenever you take emergency action, keep other ships in formation informed using radio circuits and visual signals.

5. See that the ship is skillfully steered and kept on course and that the assigned station is maintained within plus or minus 2 degrees and plus or minus 5% of range; report to me if these limits are ever exceeded.

6. Except in cases of patrolling an area station or conforming to a signaled zig-zag, course changes of 5 degrees or more, or speed changes of 2 knots or more required to maintain station are not minor changes and you must inform me.

7. No change in course should be made unless an officer on watch has been stationed on the side to which the ship is turning and has checked astern in that direction. Never turn toward a ship abaft your beam—even with what appears to be safe maneuvering space—if it can be avoided.

8. Upon receipt of an IMMEDIATE EXECUTE signal, I expect you to take the required action (put over rudder, increase

speed, etc.) before or as you inform me of the signal. In this case do not delay action to make the required report. A change in speed of not less than 4 knots or a change in course of not less than 20 degrees, or both, generally is considered appropriate. Review your solutions for possible course and/or speed adjustments. Advise me when any ship(s) is seriously off station.

9. Notify me immediately if:
   a. You are unable to maintain station or if other ships in company are significantly out of their assigned station.
   b. You suddenly find you need an unexpected speed or course change to maintain station, or you do not understand the movements of the Guide or any other ship in the formation.

10. You are not authorized to cross ahead of another combatant or vessel closer than 3,000 yards, pass abeam less than 2,000 yards or astern less than 1,000 yards unless in an emergency, without first discussing such a course of action with me. The above-mentioned areas are to be construed as stay out zones. Always have in the back of your mind a clear area into which the ship may be safely headed to avoid danger. Constantly run over in your mind emergency procedures, "What do I do if . . . ," so that if the situation arises, the action is second nature. These ranges are doubled if the vessel in proximity is an aircraft carrier or large-deck amphib.

11. When range permits, utilize the stadimeter to maintain station. Practice estimating visual ranges to specific ships so as to permit accurate ranging when in EMCON.

12. The fact that the ship is in formation does not relieve you from responsibility for avoiding contacts and ensuring safe navigation. Make timely recommendations or raise questions concerning contemplated OTC actions with regard to contacts or navigational hazards. Do not hesitate to maneuver independently if necessary to avoid contacts, or ships in formation having difficulty, or to give a wide berth to a navigation hazard. Keep me informed.

13. Always keep other ships in mind and try to assist them if in any difficulty. For example, when at the head of a column and

contacts or hazards are spotted, or avoiding maneuvers are necessary, inform ships astern.

14. Signals received by radio or via the signal bridge will be simultaneously broken by the Bridge and CIC. Once broken, CIC will pass their interpretation of the signal to the Bridge, which will either concur or nonconcur with CIC's interpretation. The OOD will ensure concurrence between CIC and the Bridge before acting on a signal. Advise me if concurrence is not reached promptly.

15. Use the ARPA's auto track capability to monitor the movements of all units in the formation. Compare ARPA information to the SRC's presentation for units in proximity to FISKE.

16. Ensure a Bridge ASTAB is configured for "Surface Friend" and that the call sign ASTAB indicates Link PUs for easy cross reference. Remember for Link participants, the course/speed indication on the "Surface Friend" ASTAB is the course/speed that unit is reporting itself on over Link 11, so it, along with ARPA information, is a good corroborative source of a friend's course/speed.

STANDING ORDER NUMBER NINE
PLANEGUARD OPERATIONS

I will never criticize an OOD who maneuvers FISKE out of planeguard station and into open sea room because he or she is uncertain of the carrier's aspect, movement, or intentions.

1. *CV Operations.* Operations in close proximity to an aircraft carrier landing and launching aircraft require extraordinary vigilance and adherence to prudent seamanship to ensure the safety of the ship. When assigned as a planeguard, FISKE must be ready to recover a downed aviator or man overboard at a moment's notice. Nothing must be permitted to delay execution of this critical mission. Prior preparation is required, as well as frequent rehearsal of planned emergency actions.

2. When operating with CVs, stay out of a moving envelope 6,000 yards ahead, 4,000 yards abeam, and 2,000 yards astern unless directed to a station within this envelope by competent authority and I am on the bridge. Never turn toward a CV during maneuvers. If in doubt about a carrier's aspect or course during maneuvers, turn away to open range and call me immediately.

3. *Preparations.* The Officer of the Deck is fully responsible for making the ship ready to rapidly recover a downed aviator, and taking and maintaining assigned stations. In preparing for planeguard operations the following guidelines, though not all-inclusive, should be considered:

   a. Upon notification of impending planeguard operations, or 2 hours prior to the start of land/launch operations, inform me of your intentions and begin timely preparations.

   b. Review the standard operating procedures for the specific carrier involved and note specific actions required by you or your watch team.

   c. Muster the lifeboat crew and ensure they are instructed on specific procedures and your intentions with regard to type of pickup, maneuvering, etc. Personally instruct the Petty Officer in charge and Boat Officer on their duties. Ensure portable radios are ready and tested and sound-powered phones have been connected and checked. At night, provide and test necessary lighting.

   d. Research the appropriate lighting measure. Unless otherwise directed by a specific carrier's SOP, lighting measure GREEN will normally be set during actual flight operations. This includes side lights set on dim, aircraft warning lights, a blue stern light, and no masthead lights. Ensure normal running lights are displayed on bright except when actually conducting flight operations, and especially when the carrier is reversing course or otherwise maneuvering. Follow the motions of the carrier in this regard by observing shifts between white and blue stern lights, but do not hesitate to turn normal running lights on bright if the carrier begins to maneuver unexpectedly or you otherwise are uncertain as to the carrier's intentions or your position. In such circumstances, inform me immediately.

e. Be forehanded in bringing up required communication circuits such as CCA, land launch, departure, marshall, the primary maneuvering circuit, and the designated Bridge-to-Bridge channel. Obtain radio checks as operations and the situation permit, but do not fill the airwaves with repeated call ups.

f. Know the station you are to be assigned, or query the carrier early enough to enable you to proceed to station so as to be in position at the appointed time or 30 minutes prior to sunset. Anticipate carrier maneuvers up or downwind to ensure you are not grossly out of position and end up in a long tail chase.

4. *Stationing.* Normally carriers will assign a station 170 degrees relative, 1,000–2,000 yards astern. 170 degrees relative at 2,000 yards is typical.

a. Station limits in bearing remain 2 degrees. If in 170 degrees relative position, simply position yourself in line with angled deck line up lights and you should be well within limits.

b. Since the carrier can be expected to make frequent speed changes, station limits in range will normally be extended from 200 yards short to 500 yards long in range. Make speed changes boldly to remain within limits set by me. Remember, the carrier's reported and actual speed may be several knots different. Do not stop adjusting speed until the measured range rate is zero.

c. I expect you to stay on station. Continue to aggressively drive the ship towards the exact point station. Do not be an incrementalist. Maneuver boldly. Change course by 5 or 10 degrees or more, and speed by 5 or more knots until you see the relative motion required to get you to station. Watch bearing drift and range rate carefully. Keep checking and rechecking. Do not assume a specific course and speed for the carrier until you have verified her actual course over several minutes and can control your closing and opening rate at will.

d. The best estimate of the carrier's course and speed is the data reported over Link 11 tempered by your own observations and judgment. Ensure the carrier's PU is present on a surface contact ASTAB. Also ensure an ARPA track is initiated on the carrier. Note tactical signals and flashing light messages and obtain the best possible data from the DRT or maneuvering board, but do not rely on these aids alone. Watch the carrier's aspect, bearing drift, and range closely to obtain course and speed.

e. Ensure you anticipate carrier movements and react in a timely manner. If the carrier turns toward your side, turn away. If the carrier turns away from you, you can usually safely parallel the carrier's movements. Be alert for the unexpected.

5. *Maneuvering*. Expect the carrier to do the unexpected. Never assume it will turn or slow until you actually see a change in aspect, bearing drift, or range. Anticipate the carrier's next turn, especially during cyclic operations.

a. The objective is to remain astern, or off the quarter of a maneuvering carrier. Do not allow yourself to get ahead of the carrier's beam; take action to preclude the carrier turning inside of you when it reverses course. Remember, the carrier may turn greater than 180 degrees, or even 360 degrees, to reduce angle of heel or find a better wind.

b. If you are on the carrier's starboard quarter (e.g., 170 degrees relative, 2,000 yards) and the carrier turns to port away from you, simply maintain your original course and follow around outside the carrier's wake. Increase speed markedly if necessary to close the turning point, and/or turn outboard to prevent the carrier from closing your projected course when coming all the way around. Do not turn too early or slow. Watch the carrier's wake and follow around. At night, use the 3-minute rule to calculate time to turn and start a stop watch when the carrier signals its rudder is over or when the turn is detected first by Bridge personnel.

c. If you are on the carrier's starboard quarter (e.g., 170 degrees relative, 2,000 yards) and the carrier turns to starboard towards you, immediately put on left standard rudder and come 40 degrees left of original course. Cross through the carrier's wake and then come back right, following the carrier through the turn just outside the carrier's wake as above. Remember, the OOD on the carrier will be looking for your starboard running light so he or she knows you have turned towards the carrier's wake and will be well clear. Show your sidelight smartly.

d. If the carrier increases speed, as determined by an opening range or tactical signal, increase speed markedly so you will not get left behind. It is always easier to slow than regain lost ground. However, do not close inside your inner station limits without my permission.

e. If the carrier slows, as detected by a decreasing range or tactical signal, decrease speed slowly as we will tend to slow more quickly than the much larger carrier. If range decreases noticeably, slow 5 or 10 knots to regain control of your range rate. If you reach the inner edge of your station, slow to 5 knots or bare steerage way until range begins to open again, then quickly resume ordered course. Do not hesitate to stop, sheer out, or back down to preclude closing dangerously close. Keep me fully informed.

f. Ensure regular running lights are displayed on bright whenever the carrier and/or we are maneuvering.

g. Do not hesitate to use the radio to resolve a developing emergency situation. If you take such action, immediately inform me and:

(1) Use plain language and ships' names vice tactical signals and call signs; e.g., "AMERICA this is FISKE, my rudder is right. My speed is 12. I do not understand your intentions."

(2) Always give your course, speed, and intentions.

(3) Use any circuit on which you have good communications with the carrier's bridge. Usually this will be the tactical circuit in use or designated Bridge-to-Bridge channel.

(4) Use the whistle to signal your actions.

h. Do not hesitate to take action to resolve an emergency situation. Inform me immediately, but do not let this reporting requirement detract from your primary responsibility for ship safety. If circumstances warrant, simply direct the Boatswain's Mate to pass "Captain to the Bridge" on the 1MC or sound the collision alarm.

i. If the situation warrants, or the carrier's maneuvers are unclear, turn away smartly, increase speed, and place the carrier astern to open your range. In all situations you should have an escape course in mind to use if the situation becomes unclear.

6. *Man Overboard.* In the event of an aircraft crash or man overboard, the objective is to recover the person as quickly as possible.

   a. If a helo is assigned planeguard, it will normally be the primary recovery vehicle. However, be alert, especially at night, to assume this role if the helo becomes disoriented or two or more people are positioned in the water a good ways apart from each other.

   b. Close the area to within about 500 yards and stand by to assist. Remain well clear of the area upwind of the man if a helo is making the recovery.

   c. Primary concern is to mark the area with a light/ring buoy and/or smoke afloat. If need be, order the carrier or helo to drop a marker.

   d. Rehearse in your mind the myriad of specific procedures to take in various scenarios. Discuss the merits of a shipboard or boat recovery with me and get my concurrence with your intentions.

   e. Use the best radio circuit to coordinate initial operations.

Usually this will be the CCA, departure, or Land Launch in use. Emergency/SAR forces will not shift frequencies. Instead, forces involved in continuing operations should shift to an alternate frequency. Use plain language and any other means to facilitate a timely rescue.

f. At night, immediately break out lights and begin preparations for a lengthy search.

g. Ensure the best possible location of the crash or person in the water is plotted on the DRT and logged in the deck log.

STANDING ORDER NUMBER TEN
COMMUNICATIONS

1. *General.*

   a. Ensure the ship is maintaining a proper communications guard on those tactical circuits specified in the approved communications plan.

   b. In consonance with the TAO/CICWO, direct whether the Bridge or CIC will guard specific circuits. The primary maneuvering circuit in use will always be guarded on the Bridge. Answer all transmissions promptly, in proper order, but only when required.

   c. Do not permit changes in equipment or circuits unless the tactical situation permits and the TAO or Operation Officer has approved the modification. All changes in equipment or circuits will be coordinated through the CIC Watch Supervisor who directs the Radio Watch Supervisor in the performance of his or her duties.

   d. Be alert to access applicable SAS channels on the Bridge when necessary for specific operations (Helo land/launch, Carrier Marshal, ASW C&R, etc.).

   e. Ensure call signs, authentication aids, and other communications software are ready for instant use.

   f. Ensure that you are fully aware of all recognition signals, voice radio and visual codes and call signs, both administrative and tactical, that are in effect and in use in the particular area, formation, or operation in which this ship is engaged.

Guard Channel 16 on Bridge-to-Bridge, or other channel specified for the area.

g. Require the assignment of a qualified radio telephone talker to the Bridge whenever the volume of traffic on the Bridge-to-Bridge radio is too great to permit monitoring by the normal steaming watch.

h. Keep a correct up-to-date tactical signal log on the Bridge so as to permit reconstruction. Scraps of paper, grease pencil notes, etc., are not acceptable.

i. Be alert to the possibility that some ships in formation may not have received a signal, especially in immediate execute situations. On turning, always look carefully to both sides and watch ships in company to ensure they move in a safe direction.

j. Use your signalmen. They are experts at tactical signals.

k. Require the timely change of daily codes and verify their successful insertion as EMCON permits.

2. *Record Message Traffic.* During Condition IV steaming, and such other times as message traffic shall be routed to the OOD, the OOD shall screen such message traffic and have routed to me:

a. All messages addressed action to the ship, by name, of immediate precedence or higher.

b. Weather messages which indicate a deterioration in conditions.

c. Any other such messages he or she deems are appropriate for me to see immediately.

3. *Visual and Radio Signals.* The following guidelines are set forth to ensure prompt and correct action on all signals transmitted and received:

a. Time permitting, have CIC break and interpret signals before they are hoisted and/or transmitted to ensure that there is not part of the signal that is confusing or incorrect.

b. Ensure that the Signal Bridge reports visual signals to the Bridge and CIC concurrently.

c. CIC will break and interpret *all* incoming tactical signals and have the Signal Bridge do the same on visual signals before execution of the signal in order to compare their decoding to that of the Bridge.

d. Control of the primary maneuvering circuit will remain on the Bridge. CIC will normally cover this circuit at all times.

4. *Radiotelephone Procedures.* Insist upon professional, seamanlike procedures over all radio telephone circuits. Sharp, short responses should be routine.

   a. Do not pass long, rambling administrative messages over R/T circuits.

   b. Do not conduct repeated radio checks—assume our equipment is faulty and get it fixed/changed.

   c. Keep transmissions short. The best transmission on an R/T circuit is "Roger, Out." Use it frequently.

   d. Do not get involved in repeated relays for other units.

   e. If given a reprimand, the only proper response is "Roger, Out." Then inform me.

5. *Operation of Bridge-to-Bridge Radio.* Operation of the Bridge-to-Bridge radio must conform to the United States Public Laws cited in USCG Manual CG-439.

   a. No person shall operate the Bridge-to-Bridge radio except myself and the OOD, unless I direct otherwise.

   b. A log required by USCG Manual CG-439 shall be maintained on the Bridge near the transceiver.

   c. Specific attention is directed to USCG Manual CG-439 and OPNAVINST 2400.24A for proper procedures and limitations on the use of the high power mode of the transmitter.

   d. When underway in, or entering U.S. territorial waters, Channel 13 must be guarded by the OOD, JOOD, or other officer under the control of the OOD.

   e. References are to be maintained by the Navigator in the charthouse.

6. *Exchanging Calls with Unidentified Contacts.*

   a. I do not desire to routinely discuss maneuvering intentions with other vessels on Bridge-to-Bridge radio, during open ocean steaming unless the OOD is concerned about the intentions of another vessel. This in no way restricts the OOD from answering calls of other vessels, subject to the EMCON constraints under which we may be operating.

b. Flashing light can be used to alert other ships, particularly "give-way" vessels if a constant bearing, or near constant bearing, decreasing range short CPA time (less than 10 minutes) exists. Bridge-to-Bridge radio shall be used at night and during daylight if there is no response by another ship to our flashing light. Make appropriate entries in the VHF Bridge-to-Bridge log.

c. Advise me if the ship is challenged by any ship not part of our task organization. Unless otherwise directed, do not delay in answering a challenge.

STANDING ORDER NUMBER ELEVEN
HELICOPTER OPERATIONS

1. *General.* Helicopter operations shall be conducted in accordance with FISKEINST 3710.1 series, (AVIATION STANDARD OPERATING PROCEDURES).

   a. Anticipate the setting of Flight Quarters well in advance to permit thorough preparations and safety checks. Be aware of alert conditions established. Advise me when ready to launch, recover, or hover an aircraft and I will give "Green Deck."

   b. Ensure proper communications are established among the Bridge, CIC, Helo Control Station, the crash detail, and the helo.

   c. Verify the helo pilot is in possession of the latest navigational data.

   d. Position the ship for desired wind conditions prior to engaging rotors. Do not request a green deck unless you are within the NWP-42 wind and roll/pitch envelopes for the type helo you are receiving. If you cannot obtain satisfactory winds and roll/pitch, ensure you apprise me.

   e. Control the following specific actions from the Bridge, after obtaining my permission:

    (1) Green Deck: Helo operations authorized.

    (2) Amber Deck: Engaging and Disengaging rotors authorized.

    (3) Red Deck: Helo operations not authorized.

2. *Emergencies.* In the case of an emergency involving a helicopter under our control, set emergency Flight Quarters, close the helicopter's position at maximum speed (including coming to Full Power), determine the helicopter's problem, determine if we are the best platform to recover the helicopter and, if not, immediately contact the platform which may be, and notify our immediate Operational Commander. In the case of an emergency recovery the OOD may give a green deck. Should a helicopter not under our control declare an emergency and FISKE's TAO or OOD determines we are in a position to provide an emergency recovery, immediately contact the helicopter's controlling unit and offer FISKE's assistance. If appropriate to the circumstances (i.e., we are in the best position to provide assistance), simultaneously with offering our assistance to the helicopter's control unit, close the helicopter's position at maximum speed and set emergency Flight Quarters. In the case of such a recovery, the OOD may give a green deck.

3. *Wind and Sea Considerations.* NWP 42, Shipboard Helicopter Operating Procedures, provides guidance, operational procedures, and training requirements for the shipboard employment of helicopters. The Officer of the Deck shall be thoroughly familiar with all the requirements of this publication. In addition he or she shall:

    a. Ensure the helicopter check-off list located in the Bridge OOD folder is completed prior to helicopter operations.

    b. Maneuver the ship only during a "Red Deck" condition to obtain optimum wind, pitch, and roll conditions. The OOD must be cognizant of the tactical situation and maneuver the ship for minimum disruption of the formation or speed of advance while obtaining true wind from forward of the beam for all launch or recovery operations.

STANDING ORDER NUMBER TWELVE
SHIP ANCHORED

1. *General.* As Officer of the Deck while the ship is anchored, your primary attentions should be directed towards the safety of the ship and its personnel.

2. *Navigation.* When at anchor, have visual anchor bearings and radar ranges taken and logged and the ship's position plotted at least every 15 minutes. Report to the CDO immediately if the fix plots outside the drag circle as specified by the Navigator, or if you have any indication that the ship is dragging anchor. If two fixes plot outside the drag circle, or you feel the ship is actually dragging anchor, take immediate action to station the sea anchor detail, veer chain, bring main engines on line on one or both shafts or radio for tug assist. Do not delay action to enhance the readiness and safety of the ship while you are further assessing the situation.

   a. Station an anchor watch who is qualified to determine how the anchor is tending, strain of the anchor chain, and if the anchor is dragging. Establish continuous sound powered phone communications between the foc'sle and the Bridge and require frequent reports on the anchor.

   b. Ensure the QMOW is qualified and instructed as to the specified visual bearings and radar ranges specified by the Navigator to record and plot.

   c. As OOD, personally take a fix at least every 2 hours to verify the position of the ship yourself.

   d. At night, show proper anchor lights, aircraft warning lights, and standing deck lights as directed.

3. *Weather.* Be alert for changes in the weather, make reports to the CDO regarding changes in weather as specified in these Standing Orders. Be specifically alert for unusual wind shift, approach of a thunderstorm or squall line, and increasing waves or swells. In event of reduced visibility or fog, sound appropriate signals on the bell and gong as required by the Navigation Rules. Ensure the ship is brightly lighted.

4. *Approaching Ships/Contacts.* Inform the CDO of all ships that

enter, leave, or pass nearby the vicinity of the anchorage. Report if a ship is anchoring or weighing anchor, appears to be dragging, or otherwise could become a hazard to the ship.

   a. Record the range and bearing of ships anchored nearby and report any significant changes or unusual activity.

   b. Allow no small craft, water taxis, or barges to approach the ship without your permission. Use radio loud hailer, the 1MC, or other means to warn them away, if situations require, launch the RHIB to direct other boats to keep clear. Keep the CDO informed.

5. *Propulsion Status.* Whenever the ship is at anchor, propulsion plant readiness will be such as to permit reducing the strain on the anchor and getting underway on at least one shaft within 10 minutes. The steering system will be aligned for starting on the Bridge.

6. *Boats.* As OOD, you control the dispatch of and are responsible for the safety of the ship's boats. You may exercise your authority through the Quarterdeck Watch, but the responsibility remains with the Officer of the Deck.

   a. Be especially alert to deteriorating weather. Make recommendations to the CDO concerning implementation of heavy weather precautions or cessation of boating if circumstances dictate.

   b. Ensure boats are manned by fully qualified crews, are operated in a seamanlike manner, maintain positive communications with the ship, and are refueled regularly.

   c. Hoist boats aboard during the night or when no longer required.

7. *Communications.* Maintain guard on the Bridge on all required inport circuits specified by SOPA.

   a. Ensure you have voice communications with any ship's boat before you permit it to cast off.

   b. Maintain a listening watch on the specified Bridge-to-Bridge channel for the port in which anchored.

   c. Have the harbor operations or administrative net ready for use.

    d. If established, maintain positive communications with ship's beach guard and be prepared to provide assistance as required.

    e. If stationed, ensure the visual signaling watch is alert and carrying out their duties. If a signal watch is not posted, assume their duties yourself.

8. *Security.* Take all necessary precautions to protect the ship and its boats from theft, terrorist attack, intrusion, or other untoward event.

    a. Station an anchor watch and other such lookouts as may be required to warn you of the approach of boats or swimmers.

    b. Station sentries as necessary to warn off boats or provide topside security. Arm them as required by the situation.

    c. At night, ensure the water adjacent to the ship, the waterline, itself, and any ladders, boats' booms, or other fixtures/lines over the side are well illuminated.

9. *Watches.* In addition to a normal Quarterdeck watch and specified inport engineering security watches, the following watches will be established as a minimum while at anchor:

    a. Bridge:

       (1) QMOW/OS qualified as Anchor Watch.

    b. Topside:

       (1) Anchor Watch/Phone Talker.

       (2) Sentries as required.

    c. CIC:

       (1) 2 qualified OSs.

    d. Other:

       (1) Qualified Duty Boat Crew.

       (2) Boat Officer in foreign ports, when appropriate.

10. *Emergency Actions.* In the event you suspect the ship is dragging anchor, or another ship is approaching or dragging anchor dangerously close, consider the following actions:

    a. Establish communications with CCS.

    b. Light off steering on the Bridge.

    c. Veer additional anchor chain.

    d. Station the Special Sea and Anchor Detail.

    e. Direct CCS to light off at least one engine and order ahead turns to ease the strain on the anchor, move away from shoal water, or permit weighing anchor and proceeding to sea.

    f. Radio for tugs or other assistance.

    g. Inform nearby ships.

11. Do not delay taking any or all of the above actions while you assess the situation further. It is better to start an engine and station the sea detail needlessly based on early/false indications of dragging, than to jeopardize the safety of the ship while "confirming" the ship is dragging anchor. Act on the first indication that something is wrong.

12. *Reports.* Make the following reports to the CDO:

    a. If any fix plots outside the drag circle of the Bridge as specified by the Navigator.

    b. Inability to obtain a fix or confusion with navigational aids. Any doubt whatsoever.

    c. Veering of chain, starting of steering units or main engines, stationing the sea detail, or any other emergency actions you take or recommend.

    d. Evidence of the ship dragging anchor. A bumping or grinding of the anchor chain. Heavy strain on the anchor, or a "walking" anchor.

    e. Changes in the weather.

    f. Reduced visibility.

    g. Cessation of boating.

    h. Ships entering, departing, or nearing the anchorage, or those out of position or appearing to drag anchor.

    i. Approach of small craft, burn boats, etc.

    j. Any change in propulsion status or readiness.

    k. Disposition of boats and any difficulties encountered.

    l. Noteworthy communications from other ships or harbor authorities.

    m. Security precautions taken or recommended.

    n. The presence or absence of the CO and XO.

STANDING ORDER NUMBER THIRTEEN
TOWED ARRAY OPERATIONS

1. *General.* While the towed array is deployed, there are important speed and maneuvering considerations which apply.

2. *Maneuvering Restrictions.*

	LAUNCH (2)	RECOVERY (2)	ARRAY IMMINENT (on deck or within 200 ft of skin)	TOWING
SPEED	5–15 KTS	10–15 KTS	Maintain Speed	Steerage Way to 30 KTS
SEA STATE	5 or Less	5 or Less	5	6 (note (1))
RUDDER RESTRICTION	5° Rudder max	5° Rudder max	Maintain CSE	None
COURSE CHANGE RESTRICTION	180° max	180°max	Maintain CSE	180° max

(1) For Sea States of 6 or above, if array is already streamed, full scope is recommended. Maintain forward motion and avoid following seas.

(2) *Avoid Following Seas* when launching and recovering the array.

3. *Emergency Situations*

   a. Man Overboard. The recommended recovery of a man overboard with TACTAS deployed is a race track turn. Launch the RHIB at the earliest acceptable opportunity (i.e., when you have a good lee). Also, take the winds into account. If the course you are on will establish a lee for launching the RHIB, then slow, maintain course, launch the RHIB. Once RHIB is in the water, increase speed and complete a race track turn to take a position near the person in the water. Use your best judgment in establishing a lee for launching the RHIB, and maintaining a visual on the person in the water. Maintain speed above that which would ground the array. I will make the decision to ground the array should it ever become necessary.

   b. Propulsion System Failure

      (1) Immediately begin emergency recovery of the array. Pass the following over the 1MC twice: "Engineering

Casualty. Commence emergency retrieval of the towed array. SONARMEN man TACTAS room."

(2) If propulsion is not restored prior to losing all way through the water, order the EOOW to lock the shafts. Continue to recover the array. When the array is on deck, unlock the shafts and start main engines to get underway.

STANDING ORDER NUMBER FOURTEEN
EMBARKED STAFF

1. If a staff is embarked in FISKE, one of our primary missions is to support that staff in the execution of their responsibilities. You are directed to take such action as will enhance our performance as flagship.

2. When a staff watch is posted, establish a cooperative, supportive environment, providing all possible assistance.

3. When a staff watch is not posted, the TAO (if posted) or CICWO will assume duties as the Staff Watch Officer. Ensure all provisions of the Embarked Commander's Standing Orders are carried out and all reports made as required.

4. As flagship, one of our primary functions is to provide rapid, reliable communications. Ensure the staff communications plan is in effect and that circuit restoration priorities are posted, completely understood, and enforced. Do not permit routinely shifting frequencies or equipment on important circuits without the prior knowledge and approval of the Operations Officer and/or the Staff Watch Officer.

   a. Supervise the Signalmen in the performance of their duties as staff watchstanders. Specifically, ensure the Embarked Commander's call sign and seniority are used in replies to standard call ups and exchanges, whenever appropriate.

   b. Be alert to answer all radio circuits for the staff if they are otherwise occupied. Know their proper call sign(s) and ensure you immediately inform them of the message received.

   c. Never assume it is not necessary to make formal or routine reports to the staff simply because they are onboard, or in the space when a report is received or an incident occurs. Remember, other units are trying to keep the big picture and rely on information they copy on the nets. You can assist the staff in the accomplishment of their mission by making a judicious, timely report or request. The CIC watch must establish suitable divisions of labor with staff personnel for guarding circuits, controlling aircraft, plotting contacts of interest, etc.

5. Maintain the best possible connectivity on all circuits (including the link picture) for the staff as conditions permit.

6. Cooperation is critical to a smooth-running ship and staff team. However, you are expressly charged to bring all cases of conflicting instructions or interpretation to my personal attention immediately when such instructions affect the safety of FISKE. If you are ever confronted by a situation where the Embarked Commander or a member of his staff has directed or requested you to act contrary to these Standing Orders or any other orders or regulations in effect, you are directed to request my immediate presence to resolve the uncertainty.

Appendix 5

The *Belknap-Kennedy* Collision

The Chief of Naval Operations memorandum issued after the completion of the administrative and judicial processes incident to the Belknap-Kennedy collision.

2 October 1976

MEMORANDUM FOR ALL FLAG OFFICERS AND OFFICERS IN COMMAND

Subj: BELKNAP/KENNEDY Collision

Encl: (1) Summary of Circumstances of Collision and Related Administrative and Judicial Processes

1.   On 22 November 1975, USS BELKNAP (CG 26) was severely damaged in a collision at sea with USS JOHN F. KENNEDY (CV 67) which cost the lives of eight Navy personnel and injured forty-eight others. A formal investigation held the Commanding Officer and the Officer of the Deck of BELKNAP accountable for the tragic incident. The Commanding Officer was subsequently referred to trial by general court-martial which resulted in disposition tantamount to acquittal on all charges and specifications. The Officer of the Deck was also tried by general court-martial and, although convicted of three separate charges, was sentenced to no punishment. There has been some outspoken criticism of the outcome of the BELKNAP courts-martial. Much of that criticism reflects concern that the principle of commend responsibility may have been imperiled as a result of the BELKNAP cases. I want to here address that concern, and to as-

sure each of you that resolution of the BELKNAP cases will not in any way jeopardize the concepts of command responsibility, authority and accountability.

2. There has always been a fundamental principle of maritime law and life which has been consistently observed over the centuries by seafarers of all nations: The responsibility of the master, captain or commanding officer on board his ship is absolute. That principle is as valid in this technical era of nuclear propulsion and advanced weapons systems as it was when our Navy was founded two hundred years ago. This responsibility, and its corollaries of authority and accountability, have been the foundation of safe navigation at sea and the cornerstone of naval efficiency and effectiveness throughout our history. The essence of this concept is reflected in Article 0702.1 of Navy Regulations, 1973, which provides in pertinent part that: "'The responsibility of the commanding officer for his command is absolute, except when, and to the extent, relieved therefrom by competent authority, or as provided otherwise in these regulations."

3. To understand fully this essential principle, it must first be recognized that it is not a test for measuring the *criminal* responsibility of a commanding officer. Under our system of criminal justice, in both civilian and military forums, in order that a man's life, liberty and property may he placed at hazard, it is not enough to show simply that he was the commanding officer of a Navy ship involved in a collision and that he failed to execute to perfection his awesome and wide ranging command responsibilities. Rather, it must he established by legally admissible evidence and beyond a reasonable doubt that he personally violated carefully delineated and specifically charged provisions of the criminal code enacted by the Congress to govern the armed forces—the Uniform Code of Military Justice— before a commanding officer can be found criminally responsible for his conduct. Military courts-martial are federal courts and the rules of evidence and procedure applicable therein are essentially the same as those which pertain in any other federal criminal court and the rights of an accused, whether seaman or commanding officer, are closely analogous to those enjoyed by any federal criminal court defendant. The determination of criminal responsibility is therefore properly the

province of our system of military justice. The acquittal of a commanding officer by a duly constituted court-martial absolves him of *criminal* responsibility for the offenses charged. It does *not,* however, absolve him of his responsibility as a commanding officer as delineated in U.S. Navy Regulations.

4. When the results of the BELKNAP cases were reported in the press, many assumed that the Commanding Officer and the Officer of the Deck of BELKNAP had been absolved of all responsibility for the collision by the military judges that presided over their respective courts-martial and that the principle of command responsibility had thereby been imperiled. Soon thereafter I began to receive letters from concerned members of both the retired and active naval community. Much of this reaction was critical of the results of the two courts-martial and revealed a serious misunderstanding of the role of military justice in the naval service.

5. The responsibility of a commanding officer for his command is established by long tradition and is clearly stated in U.S. Navy Regulations. In the case of the BELKNAP-KENNEDY incident, the JAG MANUAL investigating officer determined that both the Commanding Officer and the Officer of the Deck of BELKNAP were personally responsible for the collision. CINCUSNAVEUR, the convening authority of the investigation, approved that finding on review, as did I, when I took action on the investigative report as CNO. BELKNAP's Commanding Officer and Officer of the Deck were thereby held to be accountable for that tragic accident.

6. Responsibility having been officially and unequivocally established, it then remained to determine what sanctions, if any, were to be taken against the two officers concerned. It goes without saying that documented professional shortcomings are appropriately noted in reports of fitness and that errors in judgment thus detailed are taken into account before the individual concerned is considered for assignment or promotion or entrusted with command. However, in this instance, it was determined that further official action was warranted. Accordingly, CINCUSNAVEUR issued a letter of reprimand to the Commanding Officer and recommended that the Officer of the Deck be tried by general court-martial. CINCLANTFLT subsequently re-

ferred criminal charges against both the Commanding Officer and the Officer of the Deck to trial by general court-martial. As previously noted, the trial of the Commanding Officer resulted in disposition equivalent to acquittal and the trial of the Officer of the Deck resulted in his conviction. (Enclosure (1) is a summary of these administrative and judicial processes as well as a brief description of the circumstances of the collision itself.)

7. The imposition of the punitive letter of reprimand as nonjudicial punishment constituted a formal sanction against the Commanding Officer. The subsequent judicial resolution of his general court-martial in a manner tantamount to acquittal could not and did not vitiate the established fact of his accountability. It simply determined that the evidence of record was not legally sufficient to find him guilty of the criminal charges for which he had not previously been punished. In the case of the Officer of the Deck of BELKNAP, the court determined that the evidence of record was legally sufficient to find him guilty beyond reasonable doubt of all but one of the criminal offenses charged.

8. In summary, the Commander's responsibility for his command is absolute and he must and will be held accountable for its safety, well-being and efficiency. That is the very foundation of our maritime heritage, the cornerstone of naval efficiency and effectiveness and the key to victory in combat. This is the essence of the special trust and confidence placed in an officer's patriotism, valor, fidelity and abilities. Every day in command tests the strength of character, judgment and professional abilities of those in command. In some cases, Commanders will be called upon to answer for their conduct in a court of law. In all cases, they will be professionally judged by seagoing officers—a far more stringent accountability in the eyes of those who follow the sea. We in the Navy would have it no other way, for the richest reward of command is the personal satisfaction of having measured up to this responsibility and accountability. The loss of life, personal injuries, and material damages sustained in the collision of USS BELKNAP and USS JOHN F. KENNEDY serve as a tragic reminder of the necessity and immutability of the principle of command responsibility. The Commanding Officer and the Officer of the

Deck of BELKNAP have been held accountable for that terrible loss of men and equipment. The concept of command responsibility has not been eroded.

9. The JAG MANUAL investigating officer's report of the collision included a number of lessons learned and specific recommendations designed to ensure that corrective action is taken. I have directed that those recommendations be implemented expeditiously and some of you are now personally involved in that task.

J. L. HOLLOWAY III

Summary of Circumstances Relating to the Belknap-Kennedy Collision and the Administrative and Judicial Processes Emanating Therefrom

The following is a brief description of the circumstances of the collision and of the administrative and judicial processes which should help you understand why the principle of command responsibility in the Navy has not been eroded by the BELKNAP cases.

Collision

On the evening of 22 November 1975, elements of Task Group 60.1, including USS JOHN F. KENNEDY (CV 67) and USS BELKNAP (CG 96), were operating in the Ionian Sea. At 2130 BELKNAP and KENNEDY were in a line of bearing formation on course 200°, speed 10 kts, with the screen operating independently. BELKNAP was maintaining a station on a relative bearing of 200°, 4000 yards from KENNEDY. At approximately 2145 KENNEDY began preparations for the last recovery of aircraft, scheduled for 2200, and was displaying flight deck lighting for aircraft operations. KENNEDY transmitted her intentions to turn into the wind with a "CORPEN J PORT 025-12" signal. The signal was acknowledged in BELKNAP and KENNEDY's execute signal followed very closely thereafter. The OOD in BELKNAP planned to slow, allow KENNEDY to complete her turn in front, and then bring BELKNAP around to port to the new course and maneuver into station. The CO of BELKNAP was not on the bridge at the time this maneuver was commenced and it is not clear whether he was apprised of the signal before the OOD executed his plan of action. The OOD and CO had discussed two previous CORPEN J STARBOARD maneuvers and the CO had concurred in the OOD's intention to "slow and follow the carrier around" in both prior instances. However, a course of action in the event of a possible CORPEN J PORT maneuver had not been discussed.

At about 2148 BELKNAP began to slow and ease to port as KENNEDY increased speed and came left toward the new course of 025T. Shortly thereafter the OOD in BELKNAP began to evidence first doubts as to the target angle of KENNEDY. CIC, realizing that the CPA would be close, recommended that BELKNAP come right. That recommendation, however, was not acknowledged by the bridge. The OOD, becoming less and less sure of KENNEDY's target angle, summoned the CO to the bridge at 2156. Immediately prior to the CO's arrival, the OOD ordered left full rudder causing BELKNAP's head to swing left and prompting KENNEDY to signal "Interrogative your intentions" followed by "come right full rudder now." CO, BELKNAP, now on the bridge, recognized that his ship was in extremis, and ordered right full rudder, all engines back emergency. KENNEDY had also applied right full rudder and all engines back full and BELKNAP passed down KENNEDY's port side close aboard on an approximately opposing course (see attached diagram). However, KENNEDY's flight deck extension collided with BELKNAP's bridge, sheared off a large portion of BELKNAP's superstructure and knocked over the macks. Fire fed by aviation fuel from KENNEDY engulfed BELKNAP. A total of eight crewmen were killed and forty-eight injured in the two ships as a direct result of the collision. Damages exceeded $100,000,000.00.

JAG Manual Investigation

RADM Donald D. Engen, USN, was appointed by CINCUSNAVEUR to conduct a formal one officer investigation of the collision and to "fix individual responsibilities for the incident." The commanding officers and officers of the deck of both BELKNAP and KENNEDY were designated as parties to the investigation. The investigation was begun on 23 November 1975 and was completed on 31 December. The investigating officer determined that BELKNAP's Commanding Officer and Officer of the Deck were responsible for the collision and the ensuing personnel casualties and material damages.

The investigating officer recommended, among other things, that the Commanding Officer of BELKNAP be awarded a punitive letter of reprimand for his failure to ensure the safety, well-being, and efficiency of his command, as evidenced by his "failure to be present on the bridge . . . during the initial maneuvers in a new station in close proximity . . . to KENNEDY and his failure to assure the proper training of . . . bridge team members." The convening authority, CINCUSNAVEUR, also determined that the Commanding Officer was responsible for the collision and approved the investigating officer's recommendation that a punitive letter of reprimand be issued. A punitive letter of reprimand was awarded to the Commanding Officer by CINCUSNAVEUR on 2 January 1976 for failing to secure a clear description of the Officer of the Deck's plan for the maneuver prior to its execution, for failure to assure himself that the Officer of the Deck understood the maneuvering requirements which should have been anticipated, and for failing to ensure that only adequately trained and competent personnel were permitted to assume positions of responsibility on BELKNAP's bridge team.

The investigating officer recommended that BELKNAP's Officer of the Deck be referred for trial by general court-martial for his failure to keep himself informed of the tactical situation, his failure to take appropriate action to avoid collision in accordance with the International Rules of the Road and accepted Navy doctrine, and his failure to make required reports to the Commanding Officer. CINCUSNAVEUR approved that recommendation and forwarded a charge sheet to COMNAVSURFLANT alleging violations of Article 92, UCMJ (disobedience of OPNAV Instructions and BELKNAP Standing Orders), Article 108, UCMJ (suffering the two ships to be damaged through neglect), Article 110, UCMJ (suffering the two ships to be hazarded through neglect) and Article 110, UCMJ (manslaughter).

Court-Martial of *Belknap*'s Commanding Officer

Notwithstanding the prior imposition of a punitive letter of reprimand on the Commanding Officer of BELKNAP as non-judicial punishment by CINCUSNAVEUR, COMNAVSURFLANT caused an Article 32, UCMJ, pretrial investigation to be conducted to inquire into the Commanding Officer's role in the collision. The pretrial investigating officer recommended that the Commanding Officer be tried by general court-martial on two specifications of violation of Navy Regulations and three specifications of dereliction of duty, all in violation of Article 92, UCMJ; one specification of suffering damage to BELKNAP and KENNEDY through neglect, in violation of Article 108, UCMJ; and one specification of suffering the two ships to be hazarded through neglect, in violation of Article 110, UCMJ.

COMNAVSURFLANT concurred in that recommendation and forwarded the sworn charges to CINCLANTFLT for consideration. On 12 March 1976, CINCLANTFLT referred the charges to trial by general court-martial.

At his request. the accused, Commanding Officer, USS BELKNAP, was tried by military judge alone. During the course of the trial that ensued, the two specifications alleging violation of Article 0702, U.S. Navy Regulations, were dismissed by the military judge on the ground that Article 0702 constitutes a guideline for performance and not an order to be enforced with criminal sanctions. Two specifications alleging that the Commanding Officer was derelict in his duty by failing to ascertain the specific maneuvers contemplated by the Officer of the Deck and by failing to ensure that only adequately trained personnel were permitted to assume responsible positions on the bridge watch were dismissed by the military judge on the ground that the Commanding Officer had previously been punished for those offenses by virtue of the punitive letter of reprimand imposed upon him by CINCUSNAVEUR. One specification alleging that the Commanding Officer was derelict in his duty in that he failed personally to supervise the Officer of the Deck during BELKNAP's maneuvering in close proximity to KENNEDY was dismissed by the military judge on the ground that it involved the same misconduct alleged under the charge of suffering the hazarding of the two vessels through neglect, and was therefore an undue multiplication of the charges.

As a result, the Commanding Officer was arraigned on one specification alleging that through neglect he suffered the two ships to be damaged by failing to personally supervise and instruct his OOD and JOOD and by failing to post a fully qualified bridge watch section, in violation of Article 108, UCMJ, and one specification of negligently suffering the two ships to be hazarded, also by his failure to provide personal supervision and training to his OOD and JOOD and by his failure to post a fully qualified bridge watch section. The Commanding Officer entered pleas of Not Guilty to these remaining charges and specifications. On 12 May 1976, following two days of testimony from eighteen Government witnesses, the military judge granted a defense motion for findings of Not Guilty as to both charges and their specifications on the ground that testimony of the witnesses failed to establish that the bridge watch was improperly qualified or that the Commanding Officer was negligent in not personally supervising and instructing his OOD and JOOD, and, therefore, that the evidence of record failed to establish a prima facie case that the Commanding Officer was criminally negligent as alleged.

Court-Martial of *Belknap*'s Officer of the Deck

Pursuant to the recommendations of the JAG MANUAL investigating officer, of CINCUSNAVEUR and of COMNAVSURFLANT, CINCLANTFLT referred the charges against the Officer of the Deck of BELKNAP to trial by general court-martial on one specification of failure to obey OPNAV Instruction 3120.32 by failing to keep fully informed of the tactical situation and to take appropriate action to avoid the collision, failing to issue necessary orders to the BELKNAP's helm and main engine control to avoid danger, and failing to make required reports to the Commanding Officer, and one specification of failure to obey BELKNAP Standing Orders to notify the Commanding Officer of a major course change order by the Officer in Tactical Command, both in violation of Article 92, UCMJ; one specification of suffering damage to the two ships through neglect, in violation of Article 108, UCMJ; and one specification of suffering the two ships to be hazarded through neglect, in violation of Article 110, UCMJ. At his request, the Officer of the Deck was also tried by military judge alone and entered pleas of Not Guilty to the offenses charged. The military judge found the accused Not Guilty of the specification alleging failure to obey BELKNAP's Standing Orders but found him Guilty of the remaining charges and specifications. Subsequent to presentation of matters in mitigation and extenuation, the military judge elected not to impose punishment on the accused on the ground that, under the circumstances, the conviction by general court-martial itself constituted an adequate and appropriate punishment.

Trial by Military Judge Alone

An additional misunderstanding of military justice which came to light in the aftermath of the BELKNAP courts-martial involves the concept of trial by military judge alone. As you are undoubtedly aware, every accused in a non-capital case tried by general court-martial or by a special court-martial presided over by a military judge has the unqualified right to request trial by judge alone. The military judge's ruling on such a request is final. This provision for trial by military judge alone is modeled after Rule 23(a) of the Federal Rules of Criminal Procedure. Unlike the Federal Rule, however, Article 16 of the UCMJ makes the accused's right to waive trial by court members independent of the consent of the Government. The Senate Report on the proposed legislation which ultimately became the Military Justice Act of 1968, makes it clear that this difference was generated by Congressional concern over the spectre of unlawful command influence. Consequently, the election of the accused in the BELKNAP cases to exercise their right to trial by military judge alone and the granting of that request by the military judges in those two cases, was entirely proper under the law.

In any event, it would be well to remember that the concept of an independent judiciary is as essential to the administration of military justice as is the concept of command responsibility to fleet operations. Moreover, these two concepts are as compatible as they are essential. Strict adherence to one does no violence to the other.

Appendix 6

A Commodore's Advice

Dear Commander Jones,

I was delighted to receive your letter of introduction last evening and hope you are finding the long command pipeline both useful and enjoyable. As the days draw you close to assumption of command you will undoubtedly have many questions and I trust you will feel free to communicate with my staff. We are committed to ensuring that you receive the support that you and your ship require. I am confident that the DESRON 23 Little Beavers tradition will flourish as we form a new column in our squadron history. You will be a big part of that formation.

General Thoughts

Forget your last assignment. Focus now on your ship.

Not everything will go well—manage your schedule within your capabilities and scheme of priorities.

If you can't get everything done perfectly (and you can't), then accept the inevitable up front rather than giving your crew and chain of command the impression that life overwhelmed you.

Your crew will (amazingly, perhaps) accept as important what seems important to you—by your statements and questions, by what you appear to pay attention to, and by what you react to. If it's not important to you, then it will become increasingly less important to them. Think hard about what you'll shrug off as uninteresting.

Your first six months will be the most uncomfortable, your last three the most dangerous.

When bad things happen, waste no time wondering whether you ought to tell your boss—tell him what happened, how awful it was, and what you're doing to make things right. Don't force him to find out from somebody else. Understand from the beginning that there is no such thing as a ship in which nothing bad ever happens—if you try to give that wishful impression, nobody will trust you. Without trust from above, you'll never make a move on your own.

Avoid the "one-man band" syndrome. If you do your homework and engage your staff (i.e., PBFT, ITT, etc.) in planning for upcoming events, you and they will know what to expect and can prepare for what will be required. Examples include DIVTACs, UNREPs, boat ops, and similar evolutions. From my perspective, the absence of micromanagement and reactive direction by the commanding officer indicates effective leadership, thorough training, and thoughtful planning.

Read the most recent edition of *Command at Sea,* from USNI.

Savor the small victories—the large ones are rare.

The first report is undependable.

Ask to see Ref. A.

Sarcasm and subtlety are often lost on the easily confused.

Your crew expects you to be confident, professional, and a little mysterious and distant. You have no peers on your ship—get to know the other COs in your homeport and share your experiences and concerns with them.

Pay especially close attention to navigation, classified material, and public funds. Mind the weather. Know where your barrel is pointing before releasing the battery. Know where your helicopters and boats are. Know where your next load of fuel is coming from and when you'll get it. Let your OOD/CDO know how to contact you in a hurry.

The more mature your ombudsman, the better.

Make going to sea an enjoyable experience by thinking hard about it beforehand—what can we do underway that we can't do inport? Not just drills or exercises, but unusual surprises like swim call, nighttime machine gun practice, topside movies, anything else you've done well on other ships.

Demand accuracy, currency, and formality in daily reports—if you don't feel that they tell you what you want to know when you want to know it, then change the system immediately. It can be useful to ask pointed questions based on daily reports from time to time, and especially to compare the supply department eight o'clock reports to those submitted by the line department heads.

Beware of radar-based overconfidence in fog.

Zone inspections have great potential as teaching evolutions and will reflect your interest in your ship's material condition and general readiness. Wear coveralls and make them dirty. Use a flashlight. Brief the inspection party beforehand and afterwards. Track corrective action.

People will judge your ship by its appearance inport and when you go alongside the carrier underway. Many believe there is no reason for a ship's sides ever to show streaks inport. Also keep an eye on the section of pier adjacent to your ship—it should be well policed and free of vehicles.

Most COs normally arrive on the ship each inport day around 0800 and depart around 1700. Most make it a point to attend church services on board. Consider visiting the ship briefly each weekend and spending the night on board before getting underway each time. It is amazing how many interesting things you can find to do on those evenings before getting underway—observing MLOC, reviewing op orders, walking around the spaces to get a feel for the crew's state of mind and the ship's general readiness for sea, and getting settled in yourself.

You will be invited to many formal functions while in command—changes of command, retirement ceremonies, COs' breakfasts, waterfront all-officers meetings, etc. It would be a good idea not to gaff them off until you have a good sense of their relative importance in your homeport. It's hard to know how your absence (which will somehow be noted) will be interpreted.

Exercise a little reticence at your first couple of COs' meetings with your squadron or group commander: it's a good way to avoid developing a reputation for "knowing it all" in the eyes of your fellow COs who have been in the job a little longer.

Take pains to ensure that your CASREP list correlates well with your SORTS status. Your chain of command will let you know otherwise.

Work closely with NCIS but remember that their priorities may be different from yours.

If you carry a unit commander, make it a wonderful experience for him.

Demand absolute adherence to EOSS, especially involving movement of fuel (inport, in particular), activation of educators, operation and testing of steering gear, and rigging shore power.

Make well known to the wardroom your expectations regarding attendance at social functions, personal behavior ashore, wardroom standards, and officer/enlisted relations. The earlier you establish your policies, the fewer will be your outrages. Don't tolerate poor food or service in the wardroom or in the general mess, particularly on holidays.

Demonstrate to your crew physical fitness, self-control, sobriety, a grasp of the big picture, commitment to their welfare, delight in their efforts, and a restrained sense of humor.

Ride in your boats. Often. In port and at sea. At night.

Exercise your rescue swimmers during man overboard drills.

Take pains to develop a strong, mutually trustful and friendly relationship with your chiefs. It will pay off in ways that you may never realize, and at times when you may very much need their support. On the other hand, if you have a bad guy in the mess, be merciless in doing the right thing.

Take a conservative dark business suit along with you whenever your ship leaves homeport. Keep a full seabag on the ship, regardless of the season and your schedule.

You've got to play the cards you're dealt as far as personnel are concerned. If an officer is weak, make him stronger. If you're becoming convinced that he just won't cut it, make your feelings known to him and to your chain of command early. Give the individual a fair shot at coming up to speed, but don't let him hurt your ship. Document the problem thoroughly and accurately and don't just pass the problem on to another command.

Look at holiday-period duty rosters with an eagle eye—where principle is involved, be deaf to expediency.

Insist that your Integrated Training Team thoroughly plan and conduct frequent general quarters exercises to maintain crew qualification at battle stations. Don't allow a comfortable condition III mentality to excuse your crew from rigorous and necessary combat training.

Use your judgment regarding the use of tugs and pilots—nobody else's matters very much.

Be very curious regarding the binnacle list. Take the time to visit every sick-in-quarters sailor every day. Ask questions of your corpsman and get a feel for how he is regarded by your crew. If he's not what you expect, obtain help from your squadron doctor.

Insist that your XO do messing, berthing, and sanitary inspections daily and independently from the IDC. Take a look yourself from time to time. Unannounced.

Climb the mast from time to time and crawl around in your bilges. Look behind and under things.

Keep your own files and ticklers on special items—such as investigations, congressional inquiries, etc. Don't expect your XO to be as perfect as you were, but ensure your standards are known and satisfied.

Make it your air department, not "the air detachment." Get an up-chit, go through aviation physiology and water survival training, and fly in your aircraft.

Think hard about message release authority. Are you trying to prove something by your policy? Demand absolutely professional and unemotional record traffic and voice transmissions from your ship.

Stay ahead of the exhaustion curve by taking naps in anticipation of all-nighters or whenever you feel it to be a good idea. Let the XO know if you need him on the bridge.

The XO stuff you learned in your last sea tour is still important, but you've got to try hard to let him take care of most of the detail stuff. Start out by seeing all correspondence, then reduce your personal routing as appropriate.

Let everyone around you see how much you enjoy your job. Keep your whining to yourself—they don't need to hear it.

When referring to your ship to outsiders, use "we" for good news and "I" for bad news.

Maintain your composure.

Relieving

Send a modest but comprehensive letter to your commodore just before commencing SOSMRC. He wants to know about your family as well as where you've been. Call the chief staff officer about a week later to ensure he got the letter and provide any other information he may need. This is also the time to send the letter of introduction your predecessor has been dreading but awaiting.

Depending on squadron SOP, you may want to report to the squadron a week before you arrive at the ship itself. You'll want to go through all the relevant principal's message files, meet the staff, and make calls around the naval station. You will find it useful to meet with the commanding officers at RSG, SIMA, FISC, ATG, NAVSTA, TPU, NCIS, the Brig, Base Ops, and any others that come to mind. Most of them have not met all the waterfront COs and will be delighted that you have taken the time to call on them. Some will be mildly insulted if you do not, some don't care—but you should do it anyway. Visit the harbor master and pilot station. Take the time to tour the channel and harbor with one of the pilots—particularly if the homeport is new to you. Local knowledge is priceless and is usually available only from pilots.

If you visit another homeport during your tour, have your ops officer call ahead of time to see about your paying a call on the group commander in that port, as well as the NAVSTA commander—you could save yourself a little embarrassment for having failed to do so. During your initial week with the squadron staff you should also call on your group commander.

The ship should send a copy of the relieving schedule about a month before you arrive. If anything seems missing, let the CO know that you will want to witness that evolution, or see that document, or talk to that person. Don't wait until turnover week to identify something that's important to you if you can help it—enough will come up all on its own to fill the time.

Don't feel any great responsibility to protect your predecessor. If an item is important (and you'll know) and it's not the way it's supposed to be, then identify it as such. The chances are that your commodore already knows or expects that a problem exists—he expects you to be fair but critical of the ship whose command you have assumed.

As you inspect the ship, ask questions of your guides. You'll be amazed at how much your new crew will tell you that your predecessor may either not know or has forgotten. Issue no judgments until you have relieved, but ask questions and take notes. The word will spread quickly around the ship that you are interested, that you ask tough questions, that you are serious—or not. Try to visit every space in the ship before you relieve. Ask to see a recent underwater hull inspection. If one's not available, make every effort to schedule one prior to the first time you get the ship underway.

Three old rules for the new CO at the change of command ceremony: show up, stand up, wrap up. If your remarks go on for more than thirty seconds, you've overstepped the bounds of good manners and everyone present will know it. Remember, it's a great day for you but *the* great day for the CO you're relieving.

Schedule a call on your commodore for the week following the change of command. Go prepared with an agenda of initial impressions, a plan of action, and a list of goals, and be prepared for some heartfelt advice.

Never mention your predecessor's name again. Now it's your ship, warts and all, and your charge to make it as perfect as possible.

Potential post-relieving surprises: an inspection/assessment/assist visit in the week following the change of command, dings on screw blades, SWOs not qualified as OODU, deck and engineering standard practices in direct variance with CO's Standing Orders, OODs unwilling to "bother" the CO with "routine" contacts well inside minimum reporting distances, OODs unwilling to maneuver the ship without specific direction from the CO, all-enlisted inport duty sections (including "CDO"), and a long list of unofficial and unwritten "command policies." Some surprises take quite a bit of time and effort to unearth.

General Standards

3-M: Do all the maintenance requirements, do them perfectly. Apply a quality culture to maintenance and safety, insist on complete khaki involvement and attention to detail. Do several spot checks yourself every week. Pay particular attention to senior petty officer migration away from PMS, the electrical safety program (and the qualifications of the responsible officer), the tag-out program, calibration, and safety.

Ask tough questions about the EDC1 workcenter PMS matrix (work-center versus assigned fittings), and ensure your XO understands his responsibility for maintenance.

Combat Systems: Participate in oral exams for watchstanders, de-mand a realistic reading program, and institute a system of reinforc-ing formal training through professional watchstanding standards all the time. Go through PMS spot checks on combat systems–related equipment, test equipment, repair parts, MAMs, etc. Make DTEs a standard daily practice during routine ops. Demand superb perfor-mance from your systems all the time—take the time to ask the ques-tion that, as XO, you might have left for the CSO to figure out. Con-sider that the captain's principal responsibility is to connect doctrine, systems, and people to success in battle.

Run your hand over everything topside—if you feel salt or rust, get it cleaned or fixed.

Spot-check service records, medical records, training records, travel claims, classified material accountability records, and anything else you can think of.

Propulsion: Your watchwords are safety and reliability. Visit every main space every day you're on the ship. Take notes. Look deeply into the lube oil management program, firefighting, and training. Have your squadron staff engineers inspect your spaces and equip-ment quarterly, even if it does irritate your engineer. Give orals your-self to EOOWs, EPPCOs, sounding and security watchstanders, and duty engineers. If a "qualified" watchstander fails a drill set, rescind his qualification. Be prepared to give the PEB senior examiner a de-tailed tour of all your spaces (including all firepump rooms) yourself. Assign your XO to help you out during the course of the inspection in terms of keeping an eye on the bridge, etc. Expect your commodore or CSO to ride for the OPPE. Become very familiar with your type com-mander's maintenance manual and the PEB instruction.

Logistics: Read SURFSUP. Press hard on accountability, inventory control, COSAL, financial management, supply department training, and all the other stuff you learned as an XO. Get close to the LMA in-spectors at RSG and have them visit your ship about nine months before your LMA. Remember that some problems take an awful lot of manpower (and OPTAR) to fix.

Cruise Missile Cert: Imbed yourself in the targeting process. You know a lot more about the subject than your best-trained TAOs. Be there for exercises and training sessions.

These remarks represent a few of my thoughts and experiences concerning destroyer command. I have not addressed combat operations or the issues covered during your pipeline training, but I have considered a number of matters that COs seem to deal with regularly. My intention has been to give you a few things to think about. In any event, the most important piece of advice I can give is this: give the ship everything you've got—time, energy, thought, and care—and you will find real success and deep satisfaction in command.

Kevin Green
Captain, U.S. Navy
Commander, Destroyer Squadron Twenty-Three

Appendix 7

Suggested Reading List

You should try and find the time to do a little reading during your command tour. Encourage the officers in your wardroom—and indeed the entire crew—to be readers. It is a rewarding and professionally enriching experience. Here are some suggested titles relating to the profession of arms, the art and science of taking ships to sea, and national security issues:

Title	Author
Admiral Arleigh Burke: A Biography	E. B. Potter
All Quiet on the Western Front	Erich Remarque
The American Way of War	Russell Weigley
The Art of War ✓	Sun Tzu
Assignment Pentagon	Perry Smith
The Bedford Incident	Mark Rascovich
Bull Halsey: A Biography	E. B. Potter
The Caine Mutiny ✓	Herman Wouk
Command of the Seas: A Personal Story	John F. Lehman
The Cruel Sea	Nicholas Monsarrat
Democracy in America	Alexis de Toqueville
Division Officers Guide ✓	James Stavridis
Dreadnought	Robert Massie
The Face of Battle	John Keegan
First to Fight: Inside View of the USMC	Victor Krulak
Fleet Tactics ✓	Wayne Hughes
Flight of the Intruder ✓	Stephen Coontz
The Geopolitics of Superpowers	Colin Gray
Goodbye to All That	Robert Graves

Guide to Naval Writing ✓	Robert Shenk
The Guns of August	Barbara Tuchman
Hunt for Red October	Tom Clancy
The Influence of Seapower upon History	Alfred T. Mahan
In Love and War	James and Sybil Stockdale
John Paul Jones	Samuel E. Morison
The Killer Angels ✓	Michael Shaara
Knight's Modern Seamanship	John Noel
Makers of Modern Strategy	Peter Paret
The Mask of Command	John Keegan
Master and Commander	Patrick O'Brian
Master of Seapower (biography of Ernest King)	Thomas Buell
Military Strategy	Joseph Wiley
Miracle at Midway	Gordon Prange
Mister Roberts	Thomas Heggen
Naval Shiphandling ✓	Russell Crenshaw
Nelson, The Biography	David Walder
One Hundred Days: Falklands Campaign	Sandy Woodward
On War	Karl Von Clausewitz
On Watch	Elmo Zumwalt
The Perfect Storm	Sebastian Junger
Post Captain	Patrick O'Brian
The Price of Admiralty	John Keegan
The Quiet Warrior (biography of Spruance)	Thomas Buell ✓
Red Badge of Courage	Stephen Crane
The Right Stuff	Tom Wolfe
The Rise and Fall of British Naval Mastery	Paul Kennedy
The Rise of American Naval Forces, 1776–1918	Harold and Margaret Sprout
Run Silent, Run Deep	Edward Beach
Sailing Alone Around the World	Joshua Slocum
The Sand Pebbles	Richard McKenna
Sea Power: A Navy History	E. B. Potter

Seapower and Strategy	Colin Gray and Roger Barnett
The Ship	C. S. Forester
The Soldier and the State	Samuel Huntington
Some Principles of Maritime Strategy	Julian Corbett
Thirteen Days: Cuban Missile Crisis	Robert Kennedy
Two-Ocean War	Samuel E. Morison
The U.S. Navy: A Two Hundred Year History	Edward Beach
Vietnam: A History	Stanley Karnow
War and Remembrance	Herman Wouk
Watch Officer's Guide ✓	James Stavridis
Winds of War	Herman Wouk
With the Old Breed	E. B. Sledge

Index

acceptance trial, 29

accident prevention education: Naval Safety Center and, 181–82; responsibility, 179; routine inspections, 181; safety investigations, 182; safety officer and, 179, 181

accountability: food service, 173; *SORN* on, 38; taking command, 5–7

"Action with the Enemy," 305

Admiral Arleigh Burke Fleet Trophy, 232

admiralty claims/reports, independent operations and, 281

advancement, 116–17

AER (Alteration Equivalent to a Repair), 169

Afloat Training Group (ATG): CART II and, 205; check rides and, 188; ECERT and, 205; LOA and, 205

aggressiveness, combat and, 309–10

air department, officers of, 93–94

air wing commander, 94

alcohol, wardroom-to-wardroom calls and, 274–75

allied tactical publications, AXP series, 219–20

Allowance Parts List (APL), 167–68

Alteration and Improvement Program, 169–71

Alteration Equivalent to a Repair (AER), 169

ambassadors, U.S., 271, 293

Amphibious Readiness Group activities, 296

Anderson turn, man overboard and, 263, 264, 265

Arizona Memorial Trophy, 232

Article 32 hearings, 124–25

ASWEX (ASW Hunter-Killer Exercise), 221

asylum, 266–67, 288

attempted boarding/capture, 268

Aubrey, Jack (O'Brien character), 4–5

authority: amplifying, from organizational position, 78; basic officer's, 77; general officer's, 77; limits on, 79; organizational, 78–79; *SORN* on, 38, 78–79

automation, shipboard training/administration and, 235

availability(ies), 143, 148–51; arrival conference, 150; management meetings, 150–51; organization chart of, 151; planning, CSMP and, 149–50

awards: inspection, 231–32; safety and, 199

Battenberg Cup, 232

battle: organization for, 42; XO preparation for, 69

battle bill, 42–43

Battle Efficiency Competition, 232

Belknap, USS: *John F. Kennedy* collision and, 6–7, 433–42

boarding officer's call, 270–71

Board of Inspection and Survey (INSURV), 146, 227–29; acceptance trial and, 29; safety and, 181

boards and committees, ship, 51

boldness, command philosophy and, 21–22

Bucher, Loyd, 268

builder's trials, 29

Bureau of Naval Personnel (BUPERS): officer distribution system and, 82–83; precommissioning crew and, 26, 27–28

Burke, Arleigh: aggressiveness of, 310; command philosophy of, 17, 22; on discipline, 121; Fleet Trophy, 232; on maintenance and logistics, 135, 176; tenacity of, 308

Caine Mutiny, The (Wouk), 6, 79

calls: captain's formal, 303–4; liberty, 302–3; SOPA responsibilities and, 274–75

cannibalizations, supply, 164